HALF A CENTURY OF
FURTHER EDUCATION IN ENGLAND

Half a Century of Further Education in England

by

Peter Ronald Shuker

The Memoir Club

First published in 2010 by
The Memoir Club
Arya House
Langley Park
Durham
DH7 9XE
Tel: 0191 373 5660
Email: memoirclub@msn.com

British Library Cataloguing in
Publication Data.
A catalogue record for this book
is available from the
British Library

ISBN: 978-1-84104-519-1

Typeset by TW Typesetting, Plymouth, Devon
Printed by J F Print, Sparkford, Somerset

To my dear wife Veronica for her constant support and encouragement and to Helen and Edward for the happiness and enthusiasm they have brought to our lives.

Contents

List of Illustrations ix

Foreword xiii

Introduction xv

Chapter 1 The Early Days 1

Chapter 2 Into the World of Work 9

Chapter 3 A New Career 23

Chapter 4 Huddersfield College of Education (Technical) 41

Chapter 5 Cleveland Technical College 1973–77 75

Chapter 6 Leeds College of Building 1977–82 99

Chapter 7 My First Years as a Principal 122

Chapter 8 Darlington College of Technology 143

Chapter 9 Widening Horizons 176

Chapter 10 Opportunities in Europe 189

Chapter 11 1992 Preparing for Incorporation 206

Chapter 12 1993 Into Incorporation 223

Chapter 13 Adjusting to Change 240

Chapter 14 Rising to the Challenges 259

Chapter 15 More Target Setting 279

Chapter 16 Inspection and Developments 299

Chapter 17 College Centenary Year 319

Chapter 18 Darlington College at Catterick 339

Chapter 19 Into the 21st Century 365

Chapter 20 Final Year 380

Chapter 21 Post Retirement 399

Index 422

List of Illustrations

Referee in 1960s 40

Between pages 94–95

1. My parents' wedding October 1936
2. Middlesbrough Dr Barnardos Home evacuated to Ripley Castle 1943
3. Hugh Bell School play 1952, 'The Admirable Crichton'. Playing Lord Loam with his three daughters
4. Mons Officer Cadet School, June 1959
5. After the Officer Commissioning Parade with mother, October 1959
6. Holiday Fellowship Marske Centre 1962
7. Huddersfield Technical Teacher Training College 1962
8. Huddersfield TTC 1993. Alex MacLennan addresses the students at the end of year concert
9. Eppleton Cricket Club 2nd IX 1965
10. Huddersfield College of Education (Technical) 1965
11. Wedding 1972
12. Presentation of Territorial Decoration 1978
13. Darlington College of Technology 1990
14. Margaret Bell performs the official opening ceremony of the Open Access Computing Centre with chairman Geoff Nichol 1994
15. Kostroma visit with Kevin Frame in discussion with Rector
16. Visit to Poznan University of Technology with Gary Groom 2000

Between pages 206–207

17. Shuker family gathering for Christine's 21st birthday 1960
18. Stainsby Old Boys Cricket team 1962
19. Holly Bank Resident Tutors visit to Windermere 1971
20. Visit to Taj Mahal with Colin Browning and Rabi Das Gupta 1974
21. Lord Mayor's visit to Leeds College of Building 1980

22. Jack Place

23. Darlington College Enterprise Centre 1990 – Student trying out the new facilities

24. Construction in Schools Project 1991 – Presentation of £50,000 cheque being signed by the local manager of the NatWest Bank, with project chairman, Bob Carnell

25. Humber Bridge visit by Brno Technical University Students with Bridge Master Malcolm Stockwell – July 1991

26. Retiring chairman Lewis Gordon receives a clock, made by the construction department, from new chairman, Geoff Nichol 1992

27. With Roger Ward and college principals for an EU briefing in Dusseldorf, December 1994

28. Hotel and catering students celebrating another successful Tate Vin evening

29. Firthmoor Presentations by Frank Robson, Mayor of Darlington

30. Prime Minister John Major presenting the crystal Charter Mark December 1995

31. With Pat Gale and the Charter Mark at the Darlington College stand

32. Visit of HRH Prince Andrew, with the Lord Lieutenant, students and Angus Byrne

Managed IP Presentation Service (MIPPS) 286

Between pages 318–319

33. NILTA visit to Winnipeg and Minneapolis 1998

34. Mother's 90th birthday with family members 1998

35. Dinner in the College Restaurant December 1998

36. Darlington College Executive 1999

37. Alan Milburn MP at the College Charter Mark stand 1999

38. Darlington College at Catterick opens for business September 1999

39. Darlington College at Catterick official opening by HRH The Prince of Wales June 2000

40. Darlington College at Catterick. HRH Prince Charles meets the customers when he officially opened the Child Care Centre

41. FE+ Partnership Principals 2000

42. Retirement event 2001

43. Retirement event with Alan Wells and Jaz, Basic Skills Agency
44. Receiving music score from Bryan Robinson
45. With Veronica and The Newcastle Pipe and Drums Band
46. Retirement Dinner at Headlam Hall Hotel organised by the Corporation Board
47. The family after the OBE Investiture 2002.
48. Presentation of the Peter Shuker Award

Education is not about college
It entails a wider range of knowledge
Supplying a market of skills shortage

Education is great
It creates and decides upon ones fate
Never leave it too late

Education makes it a priority
To provide you with opportunities

Sylvia Chidi

Foreword

Peter, in his autobiographical account of his career in further education, has captured the massive changes within the FE world during this time. From a period in the early part of the 20th Century, when engineering and construction dominated FE, to the present day when FE offers a comprehensive range of courses and modes of attendance. People reading this book will be surprised how the sector has responded to the demands placed on the service and the manner in which it has responded.

During the period under review the colleges have grown from relatively small institutions controlled by the Local Education Authorities (LEAs) to frequently extremely large organisations operating as autonomous institutions. The author explains the difficulties faced by the colleges and the adjustments they have had to make in this process.

Peter explains his belief and dream, during the whole of his time in FE, in student centred learning even during his time as a tutor in FE teacher training.

The amount and range of his commitments on committees outside of his college was impressive as is his commitment to developing contacts with European institutions. He also showed the way to developing good relations with schools and universities in the region as well as strong links to other colleges in the area.

Without a doubt the topic Peter will be best remembered for is the outstanding work he did over many years in the development of Computer Aided Learning (CAL) sometimes referred to as ICL (Information and Communications Learning) and more latterly as e-learning., all to move towards putting the student at the centre of the learning process His work in the founding of NILTA and then his leadership as chair of this organisation for many years helped to guide and push the development of this work. Peter sums up the need for further development of this work in the article he wrote for the Army Quests magazine when he said 'Education is on the threshold of a revolution . . . the new distance learning will not be dependant on the postal service Learning materials will be available 24 hours a day in service.'

His lasting legacy is the development of the Catterick College using entirely the e-learning approach to study showing what is possible to achieve.

★   ★   ★

Malcolm W. Himsworth
Former HMI in Further and Higher Education, first as a business and computer studies HMI with national responsibility for computing in business and management studies and latterly as Staff Inspector for Computing and IT. In between these roles he served as the Regional Staff Inspector (RSI) for the Midlands.

Introduction

Further education has often been referred to as 'the Cinderella of English education' as it sits uncomfortably between compulsory education and higher education. It owes its formal origins to the Technical Instruction Act of 1889 that gave local authorities the power to levy a one-penny rate towards the support of technical or manual instruction. A year later the Local Taxation (Customs and Excise) Act allowed the use of further funds, 'Assigned Revenue', for this purpose. The Exchequer paid local authorities Assigned Revenue as compensation for publicans deprived of business under other legislation, hence the name 'Whisky Money'. Together these Acts led to a considerable expansion of technical education all over the country. The first colleges were founded in the late nineteenth century mainly in industrial centres where there was an urgent need to train young people for the engineering and construction industries.

The First World War not only broadened the experiences of men and women, it raised their awareness of the value of education and training. Many recognised the need to improve their levels of basic and technical skills to meet the changing requirements of industry and commerce. Nationally there was a realisation that elementary and technical education in the United Kingdom compared poorly with that of other nations, notably Germany. The 'Fisher' Education Act of 1918, passed by the wartime National Government, promised radical reforms throughout the state educational system. Of particular importance were proposals to:

- allow local education authorities to raise the school-leaving age to fifteen;
- set up of day continuation schools for all children up to the age of sixteen initially;
- make full-time attendance compulsory to the end of the term containing a child's fourteenth birthday.

Unfortunately, because of the worsening economic situation after the First World War, a series of massive cuts in government spending on education (known as the 'Geddes Axe') led to the scheme for the new schools and the raising the leaving age to fifteen being shelved.

The passing of the 1944 Education Act – bringing free and compulsory secondary education for all until their fifteenth birthday, the proposals for day release, and the definition of the Further Education sector – was to have lasting impact on the work of the further education sector. The Act defined Further Education as a service distinct from Primary and Secondary, and placed a duty on local education authorities to make 'adequate facilities' available.

The definition of Further Education encompassed:

(a) Full-time and part-time education for persons over compulsory school age; and
(b) Leisure time occupation, such as organised cultural training and recreational activities as are suited to their requirements for any persons over compulsory school age who are able and willing to profit . . .

The heavy emphasis on courses to meet the needs of the engineering industries continued. Nevertheless, there were significant changes in the work of colleges to reflect a national shift in attitude towards the qualifications being provided. Employers needed workers who were both qualified and more mobile. As a consequence industrialists and the engineering professional bodies sought a nationally recognised system of qualifications. The result was the inauguration of the scheme of National Certificates and Diplomas. Awards were made at two levels: Ordinary (ONC/D), and after a further two years of study, Higher (HNC/D). A Joint Committee of the Board of Education and the recognised professional bodies regulated the awards. Three years of part-time study led to the award of a certificate and of full-time study to a diploma. The Joint Committee appointed external examiners to moderate examinations that were set and marked by colleges.

The move to national vocational qualifications did not rest entirely with the National Certificates and Diplomas. Other awarding bodies, notably the City and Guilds of London Institute (CGLI), and the Royal Society of Arts (RSA) had established qualifications with nationally recognised standards and worth.

The period from the late 1940s through to the 1970s was one of significant change, not only in industry but also in the social and educational structure of the country. The period started with the challenge of the 1944 Act in economic post-war austerity and ended with the freedom of 'Flower Power' and growth in individualism following the student unrest of the 1960s. The sparkle of optimism of the 1950s and 1960s fed the new Further Education system with the opportunity to grow and diversify to meet its emerging role.

The first two chapters deal with my life prior to commencing a career in further education. This period covers the dark days of the Second World War and the challenges facing the population of overcoming the economic and cultural difficulties that followed.

CHAPTER 1

The Early Days

I WAS BORN ON 21 JULY 1937 at Coniston Grove, Middlesbrough. My
parents, Ronald Shuker and Muriel Hutchinson, married the
previous October. Father was an inspector for an insurance company
and, prior to her marriage, my mother was a nurse with a Dr
Barnardo's home. The matron of the home was Maude Hutchinson,
an older sister of my mother. My father's job provided a company car
to enable him to visit his many customers. At that time very few
people had a car of their own and, as a family, we were fortunate to
be able to travel to local places of interest on roads which carried very
little traffic.

I had my first birthday party at Coniston Grove and within a few
weeks the family removed from Middlesbrough to Sunderland. We
lived for a short while in temporary accommodation in the village of
Grindon, eventually moving to our permanent address on The
Broadway, Grindon. This was an imposing semi-detached Tudor-
style house with gardens to front and rear and a drive with a
good-sized garage. The front garden was surrounded by a high fence,
which gave privacy from passing vehicles and pedestrians. My sister,
Christine, was born in June 1939. Later that year the Second World
War commenced and it was to last until 1945, by which time I was
eight years old.

Grindon was then a small village about two miles from the centre
of Sunderland and during the war the Sunderland docks were targets
for enemy aeroplanes. In the earliest years of the war we were
regularly disturbed by air raid sirens that required people to evacuate
from their homes to local shelters. We had an Anderson shelter built
in the rear garden of our home and this was shared with our
neighbours. This shelter was named after John Anderson, the then
Home Secretary, who was responsible for Air Raid Precautions. The
shelters were made from straight and curved galvanised corrugated
steel panels, which were bolted together. Six curved panels, bolted at
the top, formed the body of the shelter, and the straight panels

1

formed the ends, with a door located in one end. The shelter was partially buried in the ground and was then provided with a concrete floor. I recall many cold miserable evening in that shelter waiting for the all clear to sound.

Eventually, for the last two years of the war, we had a steel Morrison shelter built under the dining room table and this proved to be much more comfortable as the number of air raids increased. My Aunt Maud and the girls from Dr Barnardo's home had been evacuated to the village of Ripley in North Yorkshire, where her girls were accommodated in Ripley Castle. Maud had no idea or experience of the war so that when she came to visit, my father had to explain to her the actions needed when there was an air raid. On her first evening with us, the sirens started at one o'clock in the morning and my sister and I made our way sleepily downstairs to the shelter. Much to our amusement Maud, speedily passing us on the stairs, was in the shelter before us.

My father had the misfortune to suffer a detached retina in his eye, which required several operations; some of these were performed at Sunderland Eye Infirmary and others at Moorfields Hospital in London. None of the operations were completely successful, which left my father with impaired vision in one eye. This disability meant that he was not conscripted by the armed forces to serve in the war. Instead, he volunteered to serve in the special constabulary which required him to be on duty in the local neighbourhood for several nights each week.

At the age of four, I started my primary education at Aros House School in Chester Road. On some days my mother would take me to school on a local bus from Grindon. At other times I would have the luxury of being taken to school in father's car. Christine also attended Aros House School. At the age of five, I was diagnosed with tonsillitis and was required to have an operation to remove my tonsils. At that time it was common for children to have that operation and our family doctor advised that Christine should have a tonsillectomy at the same time! So, that at the tender age of three years old, Christine had to accompany me to the hospital where we had our operations.

In 1944, I left Aros House and continued my education at Tunstall Preparatory School for Boys. This was a school where young boys

2

were prepared to enter for the Common Entrance examination at the age of thirteen. The curriculum was very traditional. The pupils studied mathematics, English, sciences, French, Latin, English history and geography. The day started with an assembly presided over by the headmaster, Mr Cheshire, a man of imposing stature, ruddy face and a quick temper. The assembly commenced with a rousing hymn with all the boys singing at the top of their voices. 'Morning has broken, like the first morning, blackbird has spoken, like the first bird . . .', which was one of Mr Cheshire's favourite hymns. After classes we had a light tea followed by a period of prep, which ended at six o'clock. It was a long day and we were expected to carry our gas masks at all times.

The most popular activity for many of the boys was the sports afternoons on Tuesdays and Thursdays when we would march from the school to the playing fields at Ashbrooke, which was used by Sunderland Cricket Club during the summer and Sunderland Hockey Club during the winter. Durham County also played some of their minor counties matches on this ground and the adjacent tennis courts were used for County Championships. One summer the West Indies cricket team played a County Durham Cricket Team at Ashbrooke and Mr Cheshire gave permission for boys to attend the match. It was a wonderful experience for all of us and I particularly remember seeing bowlers Ramadin and Valentine displaying their wonderful skills of slow bowling. The facilities at the Ashbrooke club were excellent. In the winter we played soccer and used the changing rooms to shower and change back into our winter school uniform of grey blazers, short trousers and caps. In the summer, we changed into cricket whites in school and wore our summer uniform of red blazers and caps on the walk to the ground.

It was towards the end of my first year at Tunstall that my mother experienced a lengthy period of illness, which confined her to bed for several weeks. I recall returning from school one evening and finding mother in great distress. She had had an appointment with a specialist who had informed her that her condition had deteriorated and that she might only have one year to live. At that time my mother was thirty-six years old and was determined that the opinion of the specialist was mistaken. Not only did she make a full recovery but continued to enjoy a full life until her death at ninety years old.

I developed a number of friendships during those years at Grindon. Robin Greenshields lived on a farm just outside the Grindon village and during the summer holidays I often helped Robin and his father on their milk rounds. The milk float was drawn by an ageing horse which was docile most of the time but one morning, when I was trying to be friendly to the beast, it bit me on the chest and that was the end of my first part-time job! Despite this setback, Robin and I continued as good friends and spent many happy hours exploring the local bluebell woods, fields and sand quarries.

I had little concept of money in those days, as pocket money was almost irrelevant. The war had required the Government to impose restrictions on the availability of clothes, food and luxury goods. Rationing was imposed upon the population so that items that are readily available today were either not available at all or restricted by the number of coupons that were allocated. Sweets were not available and the only edible goodie for children in the local shop was liquorice root. Part of our rear garden was used to grow vegetables and father also had a small allotment that enabled him to provide fresh vegetables throughout the year. He was particularly successful in growing spinach, my least favourite vegetable!

Television was not yet available; most sporting events were cancelled as professional sportsmen were conscripted into the armed forces, and the blackout imposed every evening meant that there was an effective curfew on all outside evening activities. Therefore, people had to make their own entertainment and in my family both of my parents had skills with musical instruments. Father played the violin and mother accompanied him on the piano. On a number of Saturday evenings during the year my parents invited their friends to an evening of entertainment, which included a supper. During the winter months we would have evenings of organised activities, which included various card games, board games, quizzes and party games such as charades. On Sundays my parents attended St Gabriel's Church and Christine and I attended the Sunday school.

Another aspect of the war was the restrictions necessarily imposed on travel. Road signs were removed to thwart infiltrating spies of the enemy who had managed to enter the country. Holidays were limited to visits to relatives. We exchanged visits with my mother's sister's family in Leeds.

With the ending of the war in 1945 there was little immediate change as the country slowly returned to normal. Although I had enjoyed a secure and relatively affluent childhood, I was aware of the poverty that existed in many parts of Sunderland. Evidence of that poverty could be observed by the ragged clothing worn by children, many of whom did not even have footwear.

In April 1946 my brother Richard was born and there was a family gathering to celebrate the occasion of his christening. Mother, who was born in North Yorkshire, was the youngest in a family of ten surviving children; eight girls and two boys. Her oldest brother Clarence and one of her brothers-in-law were killed during the war, but the rest survived. My father, who had been born in Middlesbrough, was the youngest of three. All together I had nineteen cousins, most of whom resided in at the Teesside area, stretching from Redcar in the East to Darlington in the West.

1947 was a memorable year and one that was to change my life completely and have long term repercussions. The year started spectacularly as from 22 January to 17 March snow fell every day somewhere in the UK, with the weather so cold that the country was snowbound. The temperature seldom rose more than a degree or two above freezing. Snow accumulated to hedge height in the local roads, making them impassable for days. February 1947 was the coldest February on record.

The good news was that we had two family holidays in the summer, one at Blenheim Palace and the second in Snowdonia. My Aunt Maud had retired from Dr Barnardo's and had been engaged as a Lady-in-Waiting to the Duchess of Marlborough and she had been provided with a large apartment in Blenheim Palace. Maud had invited our family and my Aunt Nora's family from Leeds to stay with her for a summer holiday. We travelled by road in father's ageing Vauxhall Ten car whilst our cousins and their parents travelled by train to Woodstock station. My Uncle Billy worked on the railways and he had a pass for his family to travel anywhere in the country by rail. At that time Blenheim Palace was not open to the public and we had a wonderful holiday with glorious weather. The palace rose garden was sheltered by a ring of high bushes and in the centre was a large fountain filled to a good height with water so that the four older children had a grand time paddling in the very warm weather.

A film company had hired the Palace for some of its action scenes and we were able to watch the shooting of the film *Saraband for Dead Lovers* starring Stewart Granger, Joan Greenwood and Flora Robson. For years I treasured the autograph of Stewart Granger before it got lost in one of my many moves.

Our second holiday was very different to the grandeur of Blenheim Palace. Before their marriage my parents had taken holidays with the Holiday Fellowship, an organisation that arranged walking holidays using centres throughout the United Kingdom. My father had selected Bryn Corach in Conway, North Wales, as a suitable centre for a family holiday. I am not sure how he persuaded the organisation to accept our booking as Conway was not a family centre and all three children were under the stipulated age of fourteen. Nevertheless, we travelled from Sunderland to North Wales in the Vauxhall and had an interesting holiday. During the week there was an excursion to Snowdon and those who were willing to take on the mountain climbed to the summit. My mother, accompanied by Christine and Richard in a pram, ventured part way but I was determined not to fail and, with my father, arrived breathless but triumphant at the peak.

In parallel with the summer activity, my father had announced that we were moving home from Sunderland to Middlesbrough. We sadly left our Tudor-style house for a three-storey town house in Park Road North, adjacent to Albert Park.

Christine and I were informed that we were to attend Ayresome Street Junior School, which was close to Ayresome Park, the home of Middlesbrough Football Club. Our parents took us to visit the school before the start of the autumn term. This visit was a cultural shock to me. In comparison with the facilities that I had enjoyed at Tunstall School, our new school was a dump! It was an early Victorian building surrounded by concrete play areas and outside toilets. The meeting with the head teacher, Mr Herring, was courteous but unsatisfactory from my point of view. I would have to enter the final year before the Eleven Plus examinations, which meant that I had only about six months to prepare for a challenge that the other school children had been preparing for at least two years. Mr Herring was adamant that my prep school education was so different that I had very little chance of passing the Eleven Plus and in any case his 'A stream' class was already full of his existing pupils. I was therefore placed in the 'B stream' class comprising pupils who were not expected to progress to the grammar school (for boys) or the high school (for girls). Ayresome School was about half a mile from home and so I walked from Park Road North. I had to cross the main Linthorpe Road into Parliament Road with Forbes bakery on the right hand corner and Linthorpe Cemetery on the left hand side. As the school was on the left side of Parliament Road, the walk alongside the cemetery was a bit frightening in the winter mornings and evenings, but the wall of the bakery was hot enough to warm cold hands!

My class teacher was Mrs Pickering, who was very kind and sympathetic but also shared the head teacher's views of my chances. I was introduced to the kind of questions that would be included in the Eleven Plus papers and found the educational experience during the year of little value compared with the steady progress that I had made in Sunderland. The outcome of the Eleven Plus was as expected. I did not secure sufficient marks for a grammar school place but did well enough to be offered a place at Hugh Bell School, which was a secondary selective school.

With only one year at the school, I did not make many friends as most of them lived in the maze of terraced houses in the immediate vicinity of the school. One boy that I did get to know was Terry Simpson who was to join me at Hugh Bell School in September 1948.

Secondary education

At the end of the five years of secondary education at Hugh Bell, my teachers had expectations for me to achieve good passes in the GCE O-level examinations. Instead of the five passes that had been predicted by my tutors the actual outcome was only two passes, in mathematics and in geography. On reflection, my motivation at school had not been stimulated by the staff who were a mixture of aging has-beens and a number of those who had left the armed forces after the war and taken a crash course in teaching. Corporal punishment was seen as the major motivator, with most of the pupils in my class rarely escaping a day without at least one stroke of the cane. All of the staff used the cane, although I had the impression that the head teacher, Mr Harmer, was not an enthusiastic user or promoter. He had joined the school as head at the same time that I joined in 1948. His predecessor had a reputation for liberal use of the cane and most of the staff members were of a similar disposition. The most enthusiastic user was Mr William 'Buller' Madden, who taught mathematics and rejoiced in mental arithmetic tests where each wrong answer resulted in a stroke of the cane. During his lessons it was not uncommon for every pupil to be struck at least once. Fortunately for me, I was pretty good at maths and often escaped the worst excesses of this bully.

History with Mr 'Dan' Fawley was extremely dull, with the aging teacher mainly reading aloud from a textbook. In those days we had to use pen and ink to take notes in class and Mr Fawley gave one stroke of the cane for each blot on the page. Among the more liberal staff who rarely resorted to physical punishment were Mr 'Baggy' Jones, who taught English; Mr Mick Proctor, who took Physical Education (PT in those days); and, in my latter days, Mr Gwynne Morris, who taught music. Mr 'Jock' McBretty, who taught geography, fell somewhere between the extremes and I tended to enjoy most of his lessons. I sometimes reflect that my Hugh Bell days were eased by the sports afternoons where we escaped to North Ormesby playing fields for soccer in the winter and cricket in the summer. I was already playing with Middlesbrough juniors at cricket and enjoyed my school cricket. I was team captain in my last year when we won the Middlesbrough Schools league and defeated the town team in the final match of the season.

Despite all the deficiencies of the school, there was a close bond between many of the pupils and I still retain regular contact with four of them.

CHAPTER 2

Into the World of Work

I NOW HAD TO CONSIDER MY options for employment. At that time the local industries of iron and steel and chemical engineering were desperately keen to recruit younger people to replace the loss of so many men that did not return after the Second World War. I applied to three engineering companies for a technical apprenticeship and I was invited to take the tests of two those companies. I attended interviews at both companies and Dorman Long (Bridge and Constructional) Ltd offered me a five-year technical apprenticeship in their structural engineering drawing offices at Britannia Works in Middlesbrough.

I commenced employment in September 1953. In addition to the normal working week of forty hours, apprentices were expected to follow a course of study at Constantine College leading to the award of a Higher National Certificate in structural engineering after five years of study. In those days most employers did not grant any time off for the studies, even when they were closely related to the job that we were doing, so when I was enrolled at Constantine College, I discovered that I was required to attend three hour-long classes on three evenings per week. This left me with little time for social and sporting activities, although I was keen to continue playing soccer and basketball during the winter and cricket and tennis during the summer. I had joined Middlesbrough CC as a junior to play cricket and began to be selected for the third and second elevens. I also played for the company's cricket team in the interdepartmental competition with the Dorman Cup going to the winning team. During my six years with the company we won the cup several times and I managed to put together some useful scores in opening the batting.

Constantine College was officially opened by the Prince of Wales on 2 July 1930. This was over thirty years after other towns in the region had established a further education college. For example, Darlington and Hartlepool opened their colleges in 1897. In the 1950s most of the students attended on an evening basis but some employers did allow a day or half a day per week with the balance of study in the evenings. Lectures tended to be very formal, with teachers either dictating from books or writing reams of notes on the chalkboards. One had to develop rapid writing skills as no allowance was made for a drop in attention. Structural engineering was strongly underpinned by a sound knowledge of mathematics. Each year of the course consisted of mathematics, engineering science and materials and technology. Fortunately, I was good at maths and managed to progress satisfactorily each year. It was not uncommon for a student to fail mathematics or science and this meant a complete resit the following year as no credit was carried forward for subjects passed. This meant that several of my friends at Dorman Long who failed a subject dropped their ambition to achieve the HNC and settled for an Ordinary National Certificate within the five years of their apprentice-ship. I worked diligently to keep pace with the relentless homework that was given in each subject every week and I often met up with my friend Charles (Charlie) Morris at weekends to share problems and find solutions. The Crowther Report in 1959 identified the high wasteage rates in HNC engineering courses with only nine per cent of students completing the qualification in five years. Interestingly, out of the initial cohort of eighteen apprentices at Dorman Long who started with me in 1953, fourteen succeeded in achieving the HNC in five years. During the Higher National studies, I had the benefit of three excellent tutors: Bill Grieg taught mathematics, John Henderson taught principles of structures and Laurie Taylor covered surveying. In the final year, the company decided that it would allow successful trainees to study for half a day and two evenings instead of three evenings and this was appreciated. I was pleased to obtain high marks in achieving the Higher National qualification.

With a number of my school friends, including Max Richman and Steve Richardson, we had established an Old Boys' Association for Hugh Bell School. At an early meeting of the association, I was elected secretary, Max was elected treasurer and Stephen was elected chairman. Shortly after I finished school, the Education Authority decided to close Hugh Bell School and relocated it on the fringe of the town and called the new campus Stainsby. The new headmaster, Mr Murray, was keen to co-operate with the Old Boys' Association and allowed us to use the premises for events to raise money to support social and sporting activities. By 1955 there was a well-established soccer team and a basketball team operating in a local league. Stainsby School had an enthusiastic groundsman in John Hutton, who was keen on cricket. It took him several years to prepare a suitable cricket square so that it was 1956 before it was possible to play our first friendly match, which was against the school staff. By 1958, we had assembled a strong team that enabled us to enter the Middlesbrough Midweek League. There were four divisions in the League and we had to commence in the D division. In our first season the team gained promotion and I topped the batting averages for all four divisions.

My soccer playing days came to an abrupt end in 1955 when I suffered a twisted knee playing tennis. In the late summer of 1955 I saw an advertisement in the *Evening Gazette*, inviting people to attend coaching classes to become referees. I decided to attend and quite enjoyed the experience and, after four or five sessions, I passed the tests to become a Class Three referee, which allowed me to officiate at the lowest levels of local football. I had a motorcycle in those days and could travel around the Teesside area relatively easily. Some of the grounds had changing rooms but many did not and in those cases players and officials had to change at the side of the ground. I would often travel to games in my referee kit under my riding gear. I must have had a reasonably good first season and impressed club officials and referee assessors who had to put in reports to the local Referees' Association as I was promoted to Class Two, which allowed me to apply to a wider range of leagues to be included in their lists. At the end of the 1957–58 season I was promoted to Class One status and at the age of twenty-one, I was one of the youngest referees with that grading, which opened up all possibilities for promotion. One of the unexpected benefits of being a member of the Referees' Association was the annual draw of tickets to attend the FA Cup Final that were allocated to each local organisation. In 1956, in only my second year, I drew one of the winning tickets and travelled to London to see Manchester City beat Birmingham 3–1 at Wembley Stadium before a full house of 100,000. The match was renowned for Manchester City's German goalkeeper, Bert Trautmann, breaking his neck with only fifteen minutes of the game remaining. Yet he managed to continue and made two more good saves.

My first year at Dorman Long was divided into a variety of experiences in different sections of the company. I spent three months in the general office on the ground floor. Another three months were spent in the printing department and the rest of the year I was allocated to work in Walter Gill's section in the main drawing office. This first year of experience enabled me to meet many new people to explore most of the working areas of this large company, which employed 30,000 people in its various activities in Middlesbrough. There were 120 people engaged at the drawing office and it was essential that a young apprentice had a sense of humour as some of the older employees were in the practice of playing a practical joke. I recall being sent to get 'a long stand' and also for 'a big weight'.

I was nineteen when my parents moved from Middlesbrough to Sunderland as my father took up a new post with the Friends Provident. I had lived at home until then and although I had a 350 cc motorcycle, I did not fancy commuting daily from Sunderland. I therefore made some enquires and eventually secured digs with the Martin Family, Ernie and Doris together with their three young daughters. There were two other young men staying with the Martins and we all got on very well. I spent weekends at Sunderland from Friday night to Monday morning and four nights in Middlesbrough. I registered with football leagues in the Sunderland area and soon had a full diary of fixtures.

For some strange reason I had the unusual pleasure of being invited to be best man for three people in a relatively short period of time. The first was my cousin, Brian Carter from Leeds, who married Olwyn in 1956. Then another cousin, Leslie Gledhill, who had been married before and had been divorced, asked me to do the honours at his wedding to Christine in 1956 in Middlesbrough. The following year, my old school friend and colleague from Dorman Long, Charlie Morris, asked me to be his best man at his marriage to Janet, also in Middlesbrough.

National Service

In 1958 National Service was still compulsory in the UK for all males over the age of eighteen and I had been deferred for three years because of my traineeship. Most of the twenty- and thirty year-olds in the office had served either in the Army, Navy or Air Force and I had known that I would have to serve unless I could find a further activity that would defer the call-up decision. As I was very fit at the time, it was unlikely that I would be rejected on medical grounds. My friend Charles Morris and I applied for a BSc course in Civil Engineering at Sunderland. I was almost a year older than Charles and that gave him the advantage of receiving an offer from the university before his twenty-first birthday. On 21 July 1958 I celebrated my twenty-first birthday and, as was usually the case, my work area had been 'decorated' with a variety of memorabilia and gifts from my colleagues. This day coincided with the end of my traineeship and I had been awarded a permanent contract with the company. I received my National Service 'joining instructions' a week after my twenty-first birthday. In the Joining Instructions I was invited to indicate a preference for the type of service I wished to undertake. My first choice was the Royal Air Force with a second choice of the Army, serving with the Royal Engineers. I had selected the latter as it was likely to provide the closest match to by civilian experience. I was unsuccessful on both counts. My 'calling-up' papers directed me to report to the Royal Army Ordnance Corps Training Battalion at Deepcut Barracks in Hampshire on 20 January 1959. National servicemen received pay at the rate of four shillings per day in those days; equivalent to £1.40 per week and in my joining instructions was a postal order for four shillings!

The first phase of National Service was Basic Training which lasted seven weeks. During that time recruits were subjected to severe physical and mental stresses to ensure that each one had reached a minimum level of physical fitness and a sufficient range of military skills to cope with an attachment to a regular army unit within the UK or abroad. Although I had regarded myself as very fit, having played a range of competitive sports, the harsh regime was quite a shock. Those recruits who were very unfit suffered considerable pain and exhaustion. Civilian clothing had to be sent home and no leave was allowed during basic training so that the only contact with family and friends was by telephone or letter. Also, recruits were not allowed out of the barracks during this period and the only place for recreation was the NAAFI – a large building offering food, drink and indoor games such as snooker and table tennis.

The accommodation was primitive with twenty recruits to each dormitory-style hut or brick building. There was no central heating and the only source of heat was a stove in the centre of the sleeping area that burned 'coke'– a fuel derived from coal. In the winter it was essential to keep the stove alight, as the process of relighting was complex. A typical day of basic training involved reveille at 0600 and everyone had to be on parade by 0630. With limited facilities for washing and shaving, the half-hour from getting out of bed to be a smart, clean recruit was short. Anyone who was late on parade was put on report and given additional duties. The 0630 parade involved a roll call and personal inspection of each recruit, followed by thirty minutes of drill-marching, both with and without a rifle. Again, anyone on parade improperly dressed or who made a mistake in the drill movement was likely to receive additional duties. Breakfast followed in a large canteen and the young men usually made the most of the hot substantial meal. The weather during January and February was harsh with bitterly cold mornings and I developed a severe shaving rash due to shaving in tepid water. A visit to the medical officer (MO) resulted in an 'excused shaving' note for a week. This was a blessing for me but the training staff members were not amused and I was made to suffer in other ways.

At 0800, the day's training programme commenced. Each day, Monday to Saturday, comprised a combination of military training and physical exercise. The military training comprised weapon handling and firing, map reading and practical orienteering, history of the Army and endless drill sessions. Wednesday afternoons were reserved for sports activities and everyone had to participate. Good sportsmen had an advantage and as I was a Class 1 football referee, I was assured of slightly better treatment for three hours every week! I was also invited to referee matches on a Saturday afternoon involving regular army teams, which enabled me to miss some of the training routine of the other recruits. Sundays provided a little free time, although a morning church parade was compulsory. Recruits had to be smartly dressed in their best uniform and were inspected and marched from the barracks to the church. The rest of the day was usually taken up in letter writing, cleaning uniforms and boots for the following week and doing the extra duties that had been imposed during the previous week.

From about week four of Basic Training, recruits had a number of interviews with Personnel Selection Officers (PSO). The object was to match each person's abilities to the most appropriate activity for rest of their national service. Most people were selected to serve in a regular army unit in the UK or abroad. The routine tended to be much more relaxed than that experienced in basic training and many people spent a relatively happy time during the following year and forty-five weeks. My interviews with the PSO changed my preference for a posting to Cyprus or Germany into further training to become a commissioned officer. This involved a further period of training at the Deepcut Barracks but in slightly better accommodation, shared with others who had been selected for potential officer training. This training was designed to assist trainees to pass the War Office Selection Board (WOSB) course and progress to full officer training at Mons Barracks near Aldershot.

Those months in the OR's 1 Platoon, awaiting WOSB were quite pleasant. A young officer, Captain John Jackson, who came from Middlesbrough, was responsible for our training programme and he encouraged rather than dictated our progress. The physical demands increased with regular route marches over many miles of rough terrain and weekly runs over the regular army assault courses. The academic programme became more important as a considerable depth of military knowledge was essential to satisfy WOSB. Weekends were generally free to visit home or to develop some sort of social life.

Eventually my turn came to attend the four-day WOSB programme at Barton Stacey. The potential officers came from all over the country and from many regiments. The time consisted of individual and group tasks, some practical, some written. At day three, we were all lined up and an officer presented each person with a slip of paper. There were two possible messages: 'selected for Officer Training' or 'RTU' – return to unit, meaning unsuccessful. The waiting was agonising but mine was positive – quite a relief because I had been convinced that I had not performed to my best standard.

I had to return to Deepcut Barracks to wait my turn to move to Mons. This took much longer than I had expected and it was July 1959, some six months after joining the Army, that I commenced officer training and became an Officer Cadet. Officer training was designed to last four months if all elements were completed satisfactorily on time. However, it quickly became clear that more than half the original entrants would not complete and be 'RTU'd'. The officer training was intended to give every cadet skills in infantry training and leadership rather than specialist technical skills. Much time was spent in field exercises developing tactical skills and the ability to use many different weapons. Personal behaviour was monitored very carefully. Our company commander was Captain Chris Piggin from one of the Midlands' infantry regiments. He seemed rather stuck up to many of us but he was fair. Dress code was very strict as officers were expected to set high standards for their subordinates. Uniforms had to be immaculate and more time was spent in cleaning shoes and boots, pressing uniforms and shirts, and personal hygiene than during the rigours of basic training. Civilian clothing had to be smart; suits were worn during the week with appropriate headwear and sports jacket and flannels at weekends. The accommodation was in 'spider huts' with rooms for four people. I shared a room with Dick Scantleberry from Newcastle, Keith Haggerty from Sunderland and Johnny Fernando, an officer on secondment from the Malaysian Army. Dick had managed to avoid conscription until he was twenty-five and he and Keith were not the fittest cadets; I wondered if they would survive the four months. As it happens they did, although Dick had to settle for a commission in the Pioneer Corps.

Some of the cadets came from military families and had fathers who were senior officers. Others had attended cadet training at a public school. They had the advantage over those of us who had no previous military connections, but they were more anxious about success and letting down the family tradition. As my officer training ran throughout the summer of 1959, we had no time off for holidays. The summer was particularly hot and dry and made the physical side of training more arduous. Any failure to complete a task meant a return to unit and some of the route marches and assault courses were very challenging. Perhaps it was the threat of failure that created a keen spirit of teamwork. On one very hot day in early August we were on a route march in full combat dress with large backpack and rifles. After seven miles one of our RAOC colleagues, Mike Major, was really suffering. We were allowed a short rest with about two miles to go and Mike was near to exhaustion. It was agreed that we had to get him back and two men took his knapsack and rifle and two others carried or dragged Mike back to camp. The last I heard of him was that he had taken a regular commission and was Major Mike Major; no doubt he made at least colonel!

The ultimate object was to arrive at the final hurdle – battle camp. This was an exercise on the Brecon Beacon Mountains in South Wales that lasted for two weeks. It was a war game using live ammunition with regular army soldiers acting as the enemy. Although this was a simulated activity and every effort was made to avoid a serious accident, the stress levels were high and mistakes were made. Each day at roll call, one or two cadets were RTU'd, devastated to have failed at the final hurdle. Each cadet took their turn over the two weeks to be the platoon commander and to lead an attack based upon a complex briefing from the senior officers. When it came to my turn, I was faced with two options and really did not know which was the most likely to achieve the target. Luckily I made the right decision that gave the outcome that I had hoped and so my battle camp ended successfully. After battle camp the cadets returned to Mons to prepare for the Passing Out Parade – a really prestigious event to mark the commissioning of the cadets, presided over by a senior general and with a military band to lead the parade and the March Past on the parade ground. For our last two weeks we spent most of the time practising for the Passing Out Parade under the direction of RSM 'Noddy' Lynch, an Irish Guardsman with a no-nonsense reputation. He claimed to be able to spot a specific regimental cap badge at a great distance. Family and friends were invited and I was proud to have my parents present on a memorable occasion in October with the band of the Royal Marines leading us onto the parade ground.

Near the end of officer training, cadets were interviewed for potential postings on commissioning. I again hoped for an overseas experience but was disappointed to be allocated to the Army School of Civil Defence at Haverigg camp, near Millom in Cumberland. I held the lowest officer rank of second lieutenant (2/Lt) and on my arrival at Millom I was quite pleased to discover that of the twenty-five officers, nineteen were second lieutenants, of which seventeen were national servicemen. The medical officer (MO) was also a national service officer with the rank of captain. The camp was over thirty miles away from the nearest town of Barrow and its remote location meant that the officers had to make the most of the local amenities, especially the officers' mess.

The remit of the camp was to train soldiers in the skills of civil defence, which comprised rescue techniques and first aid to support the civilian population in the event of a nuclear, biological and chemical war. During the winter, most of the trainees were national servicemen in their last four weeks of service. It was not surprising that they were more interested in counting the days to demobilisation than in learning to tie knots or place a splint on a broken leg. The summer time was devoted to training for the Territorial Army who came for two weeks at a time and occupied a large field and lived in tents rather than the permanent camp buildings.

Of course, along with the young officers, I had to go for civil defence training and first aid training. The civil defence training was received at a military unit in Mytchett, near Camberley in Surrey; the first aid and rescue training was held at Taymouth Castle, Perthshire in Scotland. I went to Mytchett in November for two weeks and to Taymouth Castle for four weeks in January/February 1960.

Lecturing on principles of first aid in a lecture theatre to groups of three hundred National servicemen in their final month of national service was a baptism of fire, which I survived without the heavy hands of the RSM who lurked in the background hoping that the novice officers would be intimidated by the experience. In the summer I was part of a team that trained hundreds of TA soldiers during their annual camp. In those days nuclear, biological and chemical (NBC) warfare was anticipated and our task was to ensure that every community in the UK had fully trained people to respond in the event of an NBC attack.

I quite enjoyed my fifteen months at Millom. The main work of instructing trainees was interesting and I grew to use the powers of authority over soldiers in a sensitive rather than aggressive manner. I led a small team of NCO instructors, many of whom had many years of military service behind them, and they were loyal to, and tolerant, of the rookie officer.

I graduated from teaching national service soldiers to TA senior ranks during the summer camps. These groups included warrant officers, sergeants and staff sergeants who tended to be at least twice my age. However, I seemed to establish a good rapport with them and they responded enthusiastically and enjoyed the end of camp exercises. After the TA season, I was allowed to be part of the team training regular army units and again I was allocated senior ranks and eventually was trusted with groups of officers. One of the national service officers in our team was Richard Fothergill who had been commissioned into the Royal Army Service Corps. Richard was university educated and perhaps too sensitive to be engaged in military activities as he rarely dressed as smartly as was expected of the training team. He also talked politics which was a taboo subject and he was reported to the adjutant for discussing his views of China with some of his students. This resulted in an uncomfortable interview with the commanding officer and Richard was removed from all training activities until he finished his service.

In addition to the training duties, I had to take my turn of orderly officer duties, which involved taking muster parades in the morning, inspecting the training and living accommodation and being on call for emergencies throughout the period of duty. After working hours dress for the orderly officer was No 1 dress, a most uncomfortable tight fitting uniform with stiff white collar. Outside of the Officers' Mess a Sam Browne belt had to be worn with the uniform. (Sam Browne was a British army officer serving in India in the nineteenth century. In those days officers always carried a sword into battle. It hung from a little metal clip on the waist belt, called a 'frog'.) Prior to commencing duty, the orderly officer had to report to the camp adjutant, a relatively elderly bachelor major from the Royal Artillery. He liked to play a little game of chance with his innocent victims that involved throwing dice to determine the times of visiting the guardroom during the night. If you were lucky you would draw a time before midnight, but the worst scenario was three visits throughout the night, leaving the individual feeling weary during the next day.

The Army tradition of Wednesday sports afternoons enabled me to maintain my interest in football refereeing and cricket and I developed skills in a new sport of squash. In those days squash was just becoming popular and was not widely available outside of military centres. With the camp being at the south end of the Lake

District, there were opportunities to visit the Dudden Valley, the Cumbria Coast up to Whitehaven and occasionally, Scar Fell Pike. On several Wednesday afternoons I organised and led trips with some of the national servicemen who opted for a different activity on sports afternoons.

I had upgraded my motorcycle to a 500 cc BSA, which enabled me to travel home when on leave much more quickly than by rail. The rail journey from Sunderland involved changes at Newcastle and Carnforth and on the return journey it was not uncommon to spend a night on the station at Carnforth when the local evening train did not run. We had to make our own entertainment and the local pub was the King William, but most of us took advantage of the lower prices in the Officers' Mess bar when we needed a drink. The commander held frequent dining-in nights where the regular officers came in their colourful mess kit dress whilst the subalterns had to wear No 1 dress, which was not at all popular.

We were a close-knit community and when one of our team announced that he was going to get married in Croydon, everyone was keen to attend. I was asked to be best man and I accepted. The wedding was to take place in July 1960 and most of the officers had decided to travel to Croydon the day before. My parents happened to be taking a Holiday Fellowship holiday at Bourton-on-the-Water and I decided to motorcycle from Haverigg to Bourton to have a few days with them and then to travel onto Croydon on the morning of the wedding. I set off very early and made good progress until reaching High Wycombe where I had a breakdown. It took a considerable amount of time to identify the fault and make it good and I was covered in grime. When I eventually arrived at the bridegroom's home, the wedding party had left and a relative helped me to clean up and get into my No 1 uniform. We raced to the church but the ceremony had already started and another officer had taken my role. It was most embarrassing, particularly during the reception when I was referred to as the 'worst man'.

During my last two months, the camp commandant Colonel Batten, another aging Royal Artillery officer and the President of the Officers' Mess, Major Gerry Evea, asked me to do an audit of the Officers' Mess inventory and accounts, including the bar. I am not sure why I was selected for the task but it took a considerable amount

INTO THE WORLD OF WORK

of my time, in addition to my normal duties, and I finished about a week before my demob date. These skills proved to be of great value in the later years in my professional career.

It was a full life but there were compensations. We were paid at regular officer rates and had our own personal accommodation with a small team of 'batmen' to keep our rooms clean and tidy, polish our boots and Sam Browne belts, blanco our working dress gaiters, belts and back packs and run our errands. Officers were expected to wear uniform whenever they were on duty including travelling on trains. However, we were issued with first class warrants for rail travel, which was appreciated on busy trains. As my time to leave the army approached, I was asked to consider applying to extend my commission or apply for a regular commission. Perhaps if I had been stationed in an ordnance depot in the South or abroad I may have been tempted; however, Haverigg camp had not been particularly inspiring, so I was not too unhappy when the time came for my dining-out dinner and I bade farewell to those who were remaining.

Back to civilian life

I was discharged from National Service on 21 January 1961 and returned to my former employer in Middlesbrough. With hindsight, my two years of National Service changed my life in a very positive way. The Army gave me a range of skills that had enhanced my life and almost certainly enabled me to be more confident in decision-making.

By the summer of 1961 my life was almost back to normal. Instead of going into digs again, I decided to rent a flat and secured an apartment in Southfield Road. I had picked up my refereeing commitments and rejoined Middlesbrough Cricket Club and played with Stainsby Old Boys in the Teesside Mid Week League. I took advantage of the agreement that the Referees' Association had with Middlesbrough Football Club and trained once or twice a week at Ayresome Park under the watchful eye of coach Jimmy Gordon. It was through the Referees' Association that I won a second ticket to the Cup Final and enjoyed a splendid day in London on 6 May, travelling to Wembley on a bus full of sailors. Tottenham beat Leicester 2–0. I had visited Constantine College to consider picking up my professional studies. I had been considering targeting the examinations of the Institute of Structural Engineers but eventually decided to take a course leading to the Higher National Certificate in Civil Engineering, which would also give me some credits towards the professional qualification. The Army had not let me go lightly as all national servicemen were automatically placed on the reservist list. I had been urged to join the Territorial Army as it was pointed out that the cost of training an officer was high and they needed the skills of NS commissioned officers. After about six months of pressure, I agreed to join the Army Emergency Reserve (AER) with a commitment of two weekends and two weeks of annual camp as the minimum requirement. My headquarters was in Deepcut, Surrey, but I was attached to a northeast unit commanded by Major Arthur Blythin, a primary school head teacher. Captain Alan Emmerson was second in command and the rest of the officers were lieutenants. Bill Henderson became a good friend. He lived in Sunderland and was a Conservative Party agent. I will refer to the activities of the unit and other military experiences later.

I had not appreciated how much the national service experience had influenced my thinking and ambitions. Despite working at Dorman Long on several major projects including the Forth Road Bridge and the Auckland Harbour Bridge, I was frustrated by the lack of action and poor prospects for promotion. It was about this time that I spotted an advertisement in the local press for potential technical teachers. Three centres were mentioned: London, Bolton and Huddersfield and I sent for further details for the Huddersfield option. I received details from Huddersfield Technical Teacher Training College and decided to apply. I was invited for interview and sat before a panel chaired by Denis Carroll, the Head of Engineering. It was a strange experience, as the members of the panel seemed to do their best to convince me that I had a better future in industry. However, I persisted and I was offered a place for September 1962. When I returned to work and informed the chief draughtsman, Mr Heseltine, of my intentions, he was most upset and I was glad to get out of his office. Most of my friends were more supportive and wished me well and I started to plan the next stage of my career.

CHAPTER 3

A New Career

M Y PARENTS HAD INTRODUCED THE family to Holiday Fellowship holidays during the 1950s and I decided that I would apply for a post with HF for the summer to get away from Dorman's several weeks earlier than was originally expected by the company. I was offered a ten week appointment as secretary at Cliff House at Marske-by-the-Sea. This post involved the responsibility for all of the walks and the collection and banking of monies. I had given up motorcycling and now had a car, which enabled me to carry all of my gear from Sunderland to Marske. I met the manageress, Dylis Powell, a delightful Welsh lady with a wicked sense of humour and we were to get on very well together over the next ten weeks. My predecessor had waited to hand over the books and the office with all the directions and maps that I would need. He gave me a list of all the contacts for transport and refreshment stops together with a list of prices for the season. Marske was a family centre and could accommodate about sixty guests, but he explained that so far there had been very few guests to justify hiring transport and that he had persuaded guests to use their own cars for the excursions. I was more fortunate and the numbers built up rapidly and for most of the weeks we were at capacity.

The walking programme repeated itself every fortnight as many people chose to come for two weeks and did not want to repeat any of the walks. Saturday was the changeover and Dylis was quite happy to allow me to play cricket at Middlesbrough whilst she and the appointed host/hostess welcomed the new guests. After dinner on a Saturday I would outline the programme for the week and there was usually country dancing in the evening. HF was a teetotal organisation and also did not allow television in the house. Therefore, the host and hostess were responsible for organising the evening entertainment. On Sunday morning, after a short family service, I offered to take the guests for a walk along the beach to Redcar. This helped to loosen up the muscles of those parents who did little

23

exercise, whilst the children chose to run around and enjoy the seaside. Monday was the first serious walk and I offered at least two categories of difficulty. 'A' party, under my direction, would be a fairly good walk of about ten miles over undulating countryside. The 'B' party under the guidance of the host would be about half the distance and was usually suitable for pushchairs where very young children were involved. The Tuesday and Thursday walks were always the most challenging and involved a coach journey from the house into North Yorkshire. The 'A' party walk would be in the region of fourteen miles with a fair amount of climbing and the 'B' party walk would be around eight miles. If I had a third leader, I would offer a 'C' party for those who wished to venture out but could not manage a full day of walking. Wednesday was an off day and guests would normally make their own arrangements. Occasionally, I would offer an outing by coach if there were many guests without their own transport. However, I tried to keep Wednesday evening free to play cricket in the Mid-week League. Friday excursions tended to be similar to Monday's with walks directly from the house and not too tiring as some of the guests faced long journeys on Saturday. I thoroughly enjoyed my ten weeks at Marske and it proved to be the forerunner of a further nine consecutive HF working holidays.

Technical teacher training

Prior to the Second World War there was no provision for the training of teachers in post-school education. However, after the war, the government decided to open three centres specifically for technical teacher training. The centres in London and Bolton opened in 1946 and in Huddersfield a year later. Alex McLennan was appointed director of the Huddersfield Centre after serving with the Royal Air Force and then one year at Bolton College. Initially, there were no purpose-built facilities and teaching took place in rooms over the Cooperative shop in the town. Large houses were purchased in the Edgerton district of Huddersfield to serve as residential accommodation and to provide a catering facility. It was not until 1960 that a plot of land in Holly Bank Road was purchased to accommodate purpose-built teaching accommodation and in September 1962 the eight-storey hall of residence opened.

When I arrived as a student at Holly Bank in 1962 I was allocated Room 103 on the first floor which was very convenient for the refectory. The building had a central hub with a lift shaft housing two lifts and on each floor of the residence there were two wings on either side of the hub containing ten single study bedrooms. At the end of each corridor there were bathrooms, toilets and a utility room with facilities for laundry and light refreshments. For its time, this was quite palatial accommodation and appreciated by the new intake of students. The average age of the student intake was thirty-three and twenty-five was the minimum age for entry for technical teachers; at twenty-five I was one of the youngest students. Minimum entry qualifications were a Full Technological Certificate for craft teachers and a Higher National Certificate for technician teachers. For those who were not training to teach technical subjects entry was possible at twenty-one but an appropriate first degree was required.

On the same residential wing that I was allocated to were nine other students and I developed good relationships with five of them. Jim Moore was from Derby, Colin Salisbury from Nottingham, Dave Enderby from the Birmingham area, Denis Howard from Kings Lynn and Wilf Duffet from Sunderland. The other four were friendly but tended to leave on Friday afternoons and appear again on Monday, whereas our little gang enjoyed the social aspects of the weekends.

The first week of the course was a procession of introductions to the teaching staff, starting with Director Alexander McLennan, affectionately known as 'Mac'. He addressed all of the students in the main hall and we were harangued for a significant part of the morning. Mac had been brought up in Glasgow and still had a very strong accent. He was not averse to slipping (quite deliberately) a few swear words into his presentation to shock the complacent in an attempt to toughen them up for the real world of teaching in FE. This was to be the first of many lectures from the Director during our year at Holly Bank. Other staff that addressed us during the first week included Fred Topping who covered Education Principles, William Herbert (Bill) Green who made History of Education a most interesting subject and Frank Barr who dealt with the sociology side of education. Students were allocated a 'general method' group and a 'special method' group, the latter relating to their industrial experience. A general method group would include students from a variety of disciplines and in my group Barbara Taylor was our tutor. For special method, I was included in a mechanical engineering group with Walter Corns as our tutor. It was made very clear that the course did not include technical subject matter as it was assumed that every student was well versed in his or her specialist areas. The students were predominantly male and that was also reflected in the staff with only three female tutors: Margaret Rooker, who was the Principal Librarian; Dorothy Comley, a rare female electrical engineer; and Margaret Cottier, a charming lady covering education who took some sessions with my group on elocution. The only activity I recall regarding Margaret Comley was how to use a chalkboard and to hold a piece of chalk correctly! We had to practice on one of the many boards that had been set up in the garages of the hostel.

This was my first experience of full-time education since leaving school at sixteen, and with my savings and the government grant that covered fees, accommodation and all meals I had sufficient resources to fully participate in all social and sporting activities. Jack Hall was the tutor with responsibility for proving advice to the Students' Union (SU) and he addressed all the students to explain the established practices. There was an election for SU officers and I found myself elected as sports secretary with a place on the SU Council. There were so many sporting, cultural and social activities that it was a bit overwhelming, but it was an interesting experience and I joined the Rambling Club and the Football Club.

In addition to the academic studies, each student had to complete twelve weeks of teaching practice, usually in two separate sessions. My first four weeks of teaching practice in late October and November were at Shipley College and a building student accompanied me. We were surprised to see how small the College was, with only four full-time staff. I met Philip Stanford-Bewley, who was a head of department and I was to meet up with him many years later in Darlington. The College did not offer any subjects in my specialism and I had to wonder why I had been sent there. Eventually I negotiated a programme that I thought I could manage and, as we only had to do a few hours a week, I survived and satisfied the tutor that observed my lessons. There were only a few weeks left of the autumn term before we departed for the Christmas holiday, with the prospect of a further eight weeks of teaching practice starting in January at York College of Arts and Technology.

In the case of Shipley, I was able to travel daily from Huddersfield but for York I went into lodgings in the house owned by Ron Evans and his wife. Ron was a tutor at Huddersfield and had been appointed at the same time as Mac. The home of Mr and Mrs Evans was about a mile from the College and I had a first floor room looking onto the main road. The weather during January and February was appalling with sub zero temperatures that froze the River Ouse for many weeks. I travelled from home to York on a Monday morning and by the evening the car was so cold it would not start and remained stationary until the Friday evening when one of the college staff would give me a tow start. The window in my bedroom would not close completely and my towel would be stiff with ice each morning.

I was attached to the Engineering Department at York and again had to negotiate a timetable, as the College did not offer structural or civil engineering subjects. After a week of observing full-time teachers, I commenced my programme which consisted of mainly maths, science and engineering drawing classes, with a challenging group of agricultural mechanics students on a Friday afternoon. Agricultural mechanic was a polite name for blacksmiths who lived in remote villages in North Yorkshire. They were willing lads but struggled with the very basic arithmetic that I had been asked to cover. York was and still is one of my favourite cities, but that eight weeks was more about surviving the weather than enjoying the experience. My refereeing came to a halt for most of that period as matches throughout the country were postponed. I had several visits from tutors, including Ron Evans, and happily received good reports from all of them.

I had enjoyed working at York College and had made several friends amongst the staff but I was quite pleased to return to Holly Bank in March for the remainder of the course. At the beginning of the course I had joined the Rambling Club and was elected its secretary. Margaret Rooker helped to co-ordinate and encourage and we quickly identified students with local knowledge and experience of the Yorkshire area. There was a programme of walks both mid-week and at weekends for those who did not go home. Margaret knew the area well and the enthusiastic regular walkers appreciated her expertise and knowledge. With my experience of Holiday Fellowship, I also organised walks and planned one of the weekends in the Lake District for the summer term. I did not want to miss too much of the cricket season and it was by good fortune that when I called in at Acklam Park, Middlesbrough Cricket Club's ground, a friend told me that a former captain of the second team was now working in Huddersfield and gave me the contact. Peter Lorraine was teaching at the Catholic secondary school and he was delighted to see me and arranged for me to have a net practice at Fartown, the ground of Huddersfield Cricket Club. It must have gone well as I played for the second XI from the start of the season for six league matches of which we won 5 and drew 1. I also drove up to Middlesbrough on four occasions, three to play cricket for Stainsby Old Boys in the Mid-week League and also to attend a money-raising social for the cricket team – we attracted 350 people and were able to purchase a new set of equipment. In April I did my first AER annual camp at Whitburn Camp and traded in my Triumph Mayflower car for a Ford Anglia.

Mac had stressed to all the students that they would get as much out of the course as the effort they put in and this was undoubtedly true. Huddersfield was the only one of the training colleges that did not have end of year examinations and we were encouraged to work hard throughout the year on our coursework and projects. I did a joint project with Ernie East, an engineer who was about fifty and was freewheeling through the course. I finished up doing most of the work and typed up the report on my portable typewriter. Walter Corns was a likeable tutor with a passion for programmed learning and he encouraged me to write a linear programme for The Muldivo Mentor, a mechanical calculator. I quite enjoyed the experience and produced a piece of work that I could use with students. Many of the student teachers took the view that teaching practice was the only useful element of the course but I did not share that opinion. I was fascinated by all aspects of learning and found the psychology and sociology very interesting and indeed relevant for the profession that I had chosen. The obvious statement that teaching does not necessarily mean that the students learn is easily forgotten. All teachers should have a good understanding of how their students learn and what motivates them to learn. I was invited to participate in some research with Stocksbridge College where the principal,

Raynor Hewitt, was working on a project with Holly Bank. I had an enjoyable two days at the college meeting students and staff and then compiling a report.

After the spring bank holiday, we were encouraged to start applying for posts. In those days there were two grades of assistant lecturer; Grade A being the entry point and Grade B slightly better remunerated but with a similar teaching commitment. One or two of my colleagues thought that their experience and qualifications justified them to apply for a lecturer's post, but most, including me, aimed at an assistant lectureship. I was delighted to get two interview invitations from my first three applications; one at Carlisle College and one at Newcastle College. The interview for Newcastle came first and I travelled north on 3 May to meet Mr Norman Parker who was the Head of the Building and Civil Engineering Department and Joe Vallance, head of the civil engineering section. They gave the candidates some background information and a briefing for the interview. Principal Jack Innes chaired this accompanied by Norman Parker and it lasted for about forty minutes. As was usual, the candidates were taken in alphabetical order and so I was last to go in. Eventually, I was invited to return to the interview room and was offered an assistant lecturer Grade B post to commence on 1 September 1962.

As the end of the course approached Mac informed the assembled throng of students 'you have all passed' and gave us a pep talk and wished us well. It was time for the end of year celebrations and I participated in one of the sketches at the concert. Our playlet, Jack's Return Home, was a skit on the teaching staff with a Roman theme and seemed to be enjoyed by the good-natured audience. The following day was the garden party and in the evening a dinner/dance in the hall of residence. The Rambling Club had an evening out at Kirkburton and the final grades were distributed on 27 June, the last day of the course. So ended a most enjoyable year, which I believe gave me a flying start into further education teaching.

Summer 1963

I had decided to spend part of the summer with Holiday Fellowship and again I was allocated to Marske-by-the-Sea for four weeks commencing on 29 June. I had hardly time to pack away all the

29

materials I had developed at Huddersfield before I was packing for the four weeks of HF. I had been looking forward to meting Dylis again but I was disappointed to find that she had been allocated to another centre and the new manageress had only recently retired from life as an army captain and was new to the HF customs. To make matters worse, the host for my first week had little experience and he had not brought any ideas or materials to motivate the guests in the evenings. The Sunday morning committee was dire and I finished up having to provide most of the ideas with some help from the guests. The manageress sat silently throughout the proceedings without comment. It soon became apparent that she had upset most of the staff, comprised mainly of students doing paid work in their vacation. Normally staff members were encouraged to participate in the evening activities but this did not appeal to the manageress. By Thursday of my first week, things seemed to be getting out of hand and I was inundated with complaints. I had a fairly stormy meeting with the manageress and the host; the latter agreed to leave rather than complete his second week. Two of the staff went home at the end of the week and I had a private conversation with head office. The situation started to improve as the manageress began to keep a lower profile and I coped until a new host arrived.

The walks were a relief from the tensions in the house and I enjoyed the Cleveland countryside and the company of the guests. Being a family centre, there were always a sizeable crowd of young children and I often felt like the pied piper of Hamelin leading my party of up to sixty people with the children always at the front with me. I managed to fit in some cricket on Wednesdays and Saturdays and also visited the Yorkshire Show at Harrogate. I wrote a lengthy letter to the HF headquarters regarding the unsuitability of the manageress and two days after leaving I received a phone call from HF agreeing with me as they had received many complaints from guests. They said they would replace the manageress and would I act as host for the following week as they had been let down. So I squeezed in another week and rather enjoyed the different role. However, as I was due to start my annual camp on the same day that I was due to finish my hosting job, it meant some quick negotiations and I departed from Marske early morning to travel to Sunderland for my army equipment.

With my AER colleague Bill Henderson I drove to Ashchurch Camp in Gloucestershire. The camp was an RAOC Depot on the outskirts of Tewksbury. At the briefing on Sunday morning I was given the duties of a platoon commander and pay officer. The programme was military training involving drill, weapons handling, map reading exercises and two days on the firing range. We also had a day in the vehicle park and I had the interesting experience of driving a tank. The middle Saturday was a free day and I took the opportunity to visit Broadway, Bourton-on-the-Water, Stow, and Cheltenham, where I saw some cricket being played. Training ended one week before I was due to start my teaching post at Newcastle. It had been an interesting summer with little time to think of my new duties.

Newcastle College

The 1950s and 1960s was a time when the manufacturing infrastructure began to suffer from the decline in heavy industry, the change from steam to other motive power on the railways and the savaging of the railway system following the Beeching review. Towards the end of this period there were major changes in the organisation of further education following the Crowther and Robbins reports and the emergence of degree courses in the Polytechnics outside the traditional university system.

In 1963, Newcastle College consisted primarily of engineering and construction courses and it was housed in the old Rutherford School buildings in Bath Lane near the centre of the city. There was also Newcastle College of Commerce. However, a new college was being constructed on the Rye Hill site and was due to be opened in 1964. During the first week Jack Innes invited all new staff to a sherry evening to meet other key members of staff and this was a very worthwhile exercise, which I tried to follow in later years. The civil engineering section was quite small; Joe Vallance led a team of three people that including David Mills, a maths graduate who was also a new starter, 'Jock' Anderson, who taught mainly science and had been at the College for many years and me. Planning a further education programme is rather different than for secondary or higher education. In those days the vast majority of students were part time and advanced planning of workloads for staff was fraught with problems, as enrolment did not commence until the first Monday in September, with classes often starting a week later. An assistant lecturer's workload was twenty-four hours per week and Norman Parker had given me a provisional programme. On the Thursday of enrolment week, I was called to Norman's office and told that in addition to the twenty-four hours, I would have an additional two evening classes per week, taking my total to thirty hours per week. In telling me that I would receive overtime for these additional hours I believed that Norman thought he was doing me a favour but I was on the verge of panic as the evening classes were building surveying and all my experience was in civil engineering surveying! About half my contact hours were with full time Ordinary National Diploma students and one group of G* students and the other half were part time students on ONC or HNC programmes. There was little overlap except for two parallel maths classes and the two surveying classes. In addition to maths, science and surveying, I also had a couple of engineering drawing classes. It was during one of my drawing classes, in the first term that Jack Innes slipped into the room and stayed for some time observing my performance. In some respects I was pleased that he had found the time to visit one of my classes and I later learned that he had been a tutor at the teacher training college in Bolton early in his career.

I soon found out the reality of first year teaching, as I needed at least two hours of preparation for every taught hour. Allowing for the slight overlap, I spent about fifty hours per week in preparation and marking, thirty hours of class contact and ten hours of travelling between Sunderland and Newcastle. The surveying classes required a substantial element of practical work and, as all of the students were in employment, the only opportunity in the first term was on Saturday mornings when we gathered in the College car park, or at a local park, to practice the basics. Because of the winter weather, I limited the early practical sessions in anticipation of completing that part of the syllabus in the summer term. It was during the autumn term on 22 November 1963 that President John Kennedy was assassinated, which caused repercussions around the world. The full-time students were a likeable group of lads who were keen to learn and I enjoyed taking them on a visit to the Newcastle bridges

32

to illustrate the different methods of construction as part of their technology lessons. I also took the group for maths and engineering science. One morning I arrived at the College to take my group of thirty students for engineering science and was informed that Jock was indisposed and could I take his group of students with mine for the morning. The combined group totalled sixty students and the plans that I had made for experiments in the science laboratory had to be shelved for a more theoretical session.

My teaching commitments left little time for other activities, although at the end of my second week I had an AER weekend at Deepcut, which meant catching the Friday night sleeper to London and arriving back into Newcastle at 0140 on Monday morning. At the beginning of November, I resumed refereeing on Saturdays in the Sunderland and South Shields leagues and occasionally found myself officiating morning and afternoon because of the shortage of referees at that time. I was selected to officiate in two Durham FA cup matches, one at Stockton and one at West Auckland. I was also selected by the South Shields league to referee one of the semi-finals of the Boldon Aged Miners Cup. I must have satisfied all parties, as I was soon appointed to referee the final.

During the spring term, I had a further AER training weekend at the York Study Centre based at the White Swan Hotel and Major Arthur Blythin called a meeting at his home to prepare for the weekend. This was rather different from the usual military training and very enjoyable. The only downside was that the York Minister clock chimed on the hour throughout the night and that disturbed our sleep. After the coldest Easter on record, I was considering my cricket activities when one of the building staff, Jack Hamilton, approached me with an offer of an opportunity to play for his club, Eppleton, that played in the Durham Senior League. I took up his offer and turned up to the nets at the ground near Houghton-le-Spring. I found the culture very different from Middlesbrough, but the players were very friendly and made me welcome and so I joined the club and played in the Second team for two seasons. I also intended to play with Stainsby OB in the Mid-Week League, thereby keeping my links with Middlesbrough and Teesside. My first home game for Eppleton was against Gateshead Fell and I scored forty before being stumped, a very rare mode of dismissal for me. In June,

I was invited to join the Doghouse Cricket Club for a short Lake District tour. The Doghouse team was organised by Bernard Gent, the sports reporter on the *Evening Gazette* newspaper. The team comprised players from several local teams. The tour started in Barnard Castle before moving onto Penrith. We won both matches where I accumulated forty-five runs without being dismissed. The final match at Kendal was rained off.

The day after the cricket tour, there was a staff visit to the new college. We had been preparing for the move for most of the year, listing and ordering all the equipment and facilities that we would need. The new college name was the Charles Trevelyan College and we were impressed by its size and spaciousness compared with the Bath Lane site. The term ended with the national certificate examinations and thankfully all of my first year students progressed successfully and most of the second year students achieved good results. It had been a challenging year but I had enjoyed the experience.

The weekend before the College closed for the summer I attended my first Former Students' Reunion at Holly Bank and had a great time with many of my former colleagues. Mac kept the costs low by claiming it was 'an educational weekend' and there was a lecture on the Saturday morning to justify his claims. However, for the rest for the weekend we all let our hair down and enjoyed the fun. I had been offered a Holiday Fellowship appointment at the Scarborough Centre and had agreed to do three weeks prior to my AER Camp. To get into some sort of trim, I called into the HF Centre at Marske and led a walk over Roseberry Topping to Great Ayton and Guisborough. I was not familiar with the walks in the Scarborough area, so before each walk, I did a reconnaissance to try to ensure I did not get lost. At Marske, the walks at a distance from the House started with a coach journey; however, at Scarborough, trains and local buses were mainly used. Many of the guests were regulars who were more interested in the social aspects rather than the walks and I had fewer walkers than I had anticipated. On my birthday, we had quite a long walk to Deepdale, Lockton and the Hole of Horcum. In the evening we had a barbecue on the beach.

I had only one week after Scarborough to prepare for the AER annual camp that required my unit to assemble at RAOC Donnington prior to an exercise in South Wales. I was appointed as

Reconnaissance Officer and I was expected to set off for South Wales the following afternoon. In an army Jeep I travelled to Haverfordwest and secured overnight accommodation from the local TA personnel. I carried out a reconnaissance of Templeton, checking on such issues as rations, approach roads and access, before returning to Donnington. The next two days involved preparation before the unit moved in convoy to Sennybridge for an overnight stay before moving to Templeton via the narrow streets of Carmarthen. A tented camp was set up and for the next week we participated in a variety of exercises at the end of which, we had a night out in Shrewsbury before the return journey to Donnington and dispersal. I had a week to myself before the start of the next academic year.

Charles Trevelyan College 1964–65

The College year was planned to start on 7 September, but the staff had the opportunity to visit the site on 4 September and to identify classrooms, laboratories, staff rooms and other amenities. The civil engineering section was based on the fifth floor and all the team shared a workroom. On the day that the students started, I had to have three teeth removed at the dentist. This had resulted from an accident in Stainsby School gymnasium playing basketball, which damaged my front teeth – not the best way to start the year. My timetable included a similar range of subjects and I was pleased to have several classes with students from my first year. A new challenge was a maths class for building higher national certificate students. The level of mathematics required a lot of revision and preparation and I soon found that many of the students were going to struggle to reach the required level. I tried to guide them to concentrate on the parts of the syllabus where the maths could be related to their industrial experience and where they could see the relevance to help them with preparing for more senior positions. One of the main difficulties was the gap in the students' knowledge. Maths is a highly structured subject where conceptual understanding underpins the ability to progress forward. If the basic concepts are not fully understood then students often turn to rote learning.

Frank Stevenson was a senior member of the Building department and he also lived in Sunderland. He approached me with a proposal

35

for a car sharing arrangement with two other staff members from Wearside and I was pleased to agree. This made a saving in petrol costs and train fares and I got to know more people in the department. All went well until on one winter's morning we had just started to cross the Tyne Bridge. I was sitting in the rear nearside passenger seat when I noticed a tyre flying past the window. I shouted to my colleagues and one of them said he hoped it was not a serious accident, when our driver shouted, 'It's mine'. Luckily he managed to gently slow the car and bring it to a stop with all the weight on the three remaining tyres. We had assumed that the wheel had fallen into the river as it had been moving at speed but, again, luck was on our side. The tyre lay on the footpath near the parapet and the missing wheel nuts were all recovered. Apparently, the driver had the car serviced the previous day and obviously the mechanic had not properly tightened the nuts.

The weekend before teaching started, I had helped to organise a Stainsby OB trip to the Lake District and a group of twelve of us stayed at the King's Arms Hotel in Keswick. We had a great weekend and it helped to get me fit for a new year. My new timetable showed Tuesdays, Thursdays and Fridays were full days of class teaching and there were two evening classes. I had classes on Monday afternoon and evening and a clear day on Wednesday for departmental duties. In October there was a General Election and Harold Wilson became Prime Minister. At the same time it was the Olympic Games in Tokyo and there were several gold medals for British athletes including Lynne Davies, Ann Packer and Mary Peters.

Whilst the weather was still fine I took the surveying students for practical work at Leazes Park on Saturday mornings before dashing off to referee a match in the afternoon. On one occasion I played football for the staff team and then refereed a Jarrow League Cup tie. I had been promoted on to the Northern Intermediate League, initially as a linesman. This league was for up to eighteen year-olds on the books of the Football League clubs. My first match was Middlesbrough versus Leeds played on the Hutton Road ground and three weeks later I was at Ayresome Park for Middlesbrough's game with Sunderland, which Sunderland won 6–1, much to the disappointment of the few thousand fans that turned up. There had been some heavy snowfalls over the Christmas holiday period and some football matches had been postponed resulting in a backlog of fixtures towards the end of the season. In January Winston Churchill died and many of us watched the spectacular state funeral. In February I was honoured with a line appointment at Roker Park when Sunderland Youth played England Youth in a 3–3 exciting draw.

The term started with a similar timetable and I started to press my second year full-time students even harder as their results would influence their future. Several in the group were keen to progress to university or onto higher national diploma courses. Others hoped to gain employment with one of the local civil engineering companies. One of my new classes was an hour per week session on mechanical calculators and the College had a set of Muldivo Mentor calculators for the students to use in class and in their end of year examinations. Fortunately for me it had been that model of calculator that I had used at Huddersfield for the linear programmed learning exercise. I dug out the paperwork and with some minor tuning had sufficient copies produced for use with the students and, much to my delight, they enjoyed working through the text. It provided individual support and they could progress at their own pace. By the early part of the spring term the students were coping well with past examination papers and in due course they all passed with excellent results. This was a useful lesson for me. I understood the need to encourage students to learn and take ownership of their learning and I had produced a lot of material for the students to underpin the knowledge that I had tried to impart during the lessons. The structured material of the programmed learning text had been very successful too and although the time taken to produce the material to a satisfactory standard had taken many hours, the material could be used again with other groups to make the production cost effective.

It was early in the spring term that I saw an advertisement in the *Times Educational Supplement* for staff posts at Holly Bank, now called Huddersfield College of Education (Technical). One of the posts was for a lectureship in the teaching of mathematics and I decided that it was worth applying even though my experience was fairly modest for such a post. I approached Norman Parker to see if he would be willing to support my application and I was surprised how supportive he was. He told me that, like the principal, he had also been a teacher-training tutor at Bolton and had loved the job.

I was invited for an interview on 21 April 1965 and travelled down on the previous day and booked into a guesthouse in Halifax Road. Another candidate for the maths post, John Crosby, was also staying there and we were able to exchange experiences. He was an electrical engineer and had worked for Marconi before training at Garnett College, London, and then teaching at Colchester College. The following morning we walked to the college and awaited the interview. John went in first and came out looking a bit red faced. As there were only two candidates for the post I did not have long to wait and entered the room to be met by the chairman of governors, Alderman Benny Gray and Director Alexander MacClennan. After a brief introduction by the chairman, Mac took over and gave me quite a grilling for more than thirty minutes. I then joined John to await the outcome. Eventually Mac emerged with a big grin to announce that, 'You have both got the job'. It was a moment to savour, as we were both expecting the other to succeed and our grins must have matched Mac's. On my return to Newcastle the next day I reported my news to Norman Parker, who shook my hand and expressed his pleasure at my success. I had a similar meeting with Jack Innes and I could not have had more encouragement from them. My parents were less enthusiastic, particularly my mother. I think they had adjusted to my return home, especially as my sister was now working in New Zealand and my brother was planning to go to university in Manchester.

I was still refereeing in at least one match per week and I had been invited to join the local HF group on Sunday walks. I traded my Ford Anglia car for an MG Magnette. I refereed the Wearside Apprentices League Cup Final and the deciding match for the championship of the South Shields League. This led to the start of the cricket season and straight into a series of games with Eppleton and Stainsby OB. I started quite well with Eppleton, averaging about thirty. I had been elected captain of Stainsby who were now in the A division and facing sterner competition and we lost our first five games before getting our act together. I was invited to tour with the Doghouse CC in Scotland in June with matches in Selkirk and Edinburgh.

My students in all of my classes seemed to be making good progress and the usual examination preparation sessions were encouraging. I had collected a packet of past examination papers and it did not take a genius to identify the 'banker' questions and to brief the students accordingly. The national certificate rules in those days were quite severe. A student had to pass all subjects in one sitting. A failure in one subject meant a complete retake the following year and unsurprisingly, students retaking a subject they had already passed were not very motivated. It was, therefore, my target to ensure that all students that had worked well throughout the year did succeed. The end of term arrived and I was presented with a book token as a leaving gift. I had been very happy at Newcastle and had made many good friends who had helped me to settle quickly into teaching. I was sorry to leave those first year students who would have a new tutor in September, but I was excited about the prospect of returning to Yorkshire.

A week after the end of term, I was driving to Donnington for the start of the AER Annual training. The first weekend was the usual setting up procedures with the medical officer ensuring that our inoculations were all up to date. I was appointed Motor Transport Officer (MTO) and had to sort out the vehicles we would need for the coming two weeks. Bob Manders, an officer I had known and admired for several years had been promoted to colonel and he did the initial briefing prior to the annual shoot and the visit from General Sheffield. The day before the exercise was due to start, I was roped in to play cricket for Donnington at Chilwell and enjoyed a day out. The exercise started at 0020 when we departed from Donnington for Wem, in the heart of North Shropshire. We set up camp and spent two days on manoeuvres before returning to Donnington on my birthday for a champagne party in the evening. Driving from Donnington I went straight to Marske to commence five weeks of Holiday Fellowship work.

When I commenced my teaching career public sector post-sixteen provision covered further and higher education outside of the university sector. In 1963 the Robbins Report on Higher Education proposed the establishment of new universities, polytechnics and colleges of higher education. The Council for National Academic Awards (CNAA) enabled colleges other than universities to offer degree courses. These courses were designed and examined by the colleges but approved, validated, moderated and overseen by the CNAA. The implementation of the Robbins Report led to the polarisation of public sector post school provision into further and higher education sectors although some FE colleges did manage to retain some of their HE work.

Referee in 1960s

CHAPTER 4

Huddersfield College of Education (Technical)

1965 to 1972

I TRAVELLED TO HUDDERSFIELD ON 31 August for a meeting with Frank Barr, who was emerging as Mac's unofficial deputy. I arranged accommodation at the Northfield Hotel in Halifax Road and then returned home to Sunderland for a few days, during which I ran the line at an FA Cup Preliminary Round at Whitley Bay who defeated Annfield Plain 11–0. My first official day as a lecturer in mathematics was 6 September and I was one of eight new starters. There were four who had been appointed to cover mathematics. In addition to John Crosby and I there was Mike McAllister, who had been a teacher trainer in Nigeria and had a physics background, and Derek Bush, whose background was computing. The other new staff members were Bob Dixon, Arthur Bunting, Les Hutchinson and Philip Machin. John Davies was principal lecturer and headed the maths team with Jim Jordan as his deputy.

Mac's strategy in appointing four maths staff was based upon a belief that the level of mathematics in further education colleges was not taught well by specialist mathematicians. He believed that specialist technical teachers could cover the mathematics in the technical syllabus and be able to relate the maths to the technology. I was allocated to building students, John covered engineering and Mike, Derek and Jim covered the rest. I was the youngest member of staff at that time, aged twenty-eight, and John was a year older. During August, Frank Barr had sent timetables to staff for the first term and I was surprised to see the initials PS against General Education. I wrote to Frank, indicating that I did not think that I had the necessary experience to cover the subject and he quickly responded by assuring me that PS was Peter Saunders and that timetables for new staff members had not been settled.

At our interview, John and I had been asked if we would be willing to be resident tutors and we had expressed an interest. Although the Holly Bank hostel had only opened in 1962 and could accommodate 180 resident students, the College had retained its five hostels in Edgerton district in anticipation of a further growth in numbers. Bill Green occupied the fifth floor flat in Holly Bank and Mac, who had a new house in the College grounds, also regarded himself as a resident tutor. Mac was keen to have a tutor in each of the Edgerton hostels and by the first week in October I had moved into Woodlands and John had moved into Buckden Mount. I had selected a large ground floor room, with a rear view over the gardens, as my study/bedroom. It was a comfortable room although the furniture was rather dated and I resolved to purchase some more appropriate furniture despite Mac's insistence that only college furniture could be accommodated. Over the next two or three years, other staff were appointed that also had residential duties.

All of the new staff took part in an induction conference and this lasted for all of September. Frank Barr gave an introductory talk and this was followed by a conducted tour of the new facilities. There were two or three sessions with Mac and he had lost none of his fire and enthusiasm since I was a student three years earlier. Peter Saunders also gave two presentations and Margaret Rooker gave an introduction to the library and all of its services. Fred Topping gave us an insight into the extra mural courses that he was managing and Les Hill with John Flinn gave an overview of science and engineering courses. Walter Corns weighed in with programmed learning and Bill Green entertained and amused us with his version of the history of education programme. Jack Hall described the workings of the Students' Union and John Davies gave an overview of the mathematics programme, which was of particular interest to four of us. As we approached the end of the month, Jim Pratt gave us a talk on the buildings and the history of the College and Frank returned to describe the research work. By the time that Mac brought the induction to an end, I think that all the new staff members were itching to get started. At the weekends I had fitted in my sporting interests. The Northern Intermediate League had indicated that I would be appointed to referee several matches as well as my normal line appointments and I was promoted onto the line of the Northern League that included the reserve teams of the Football League clubs, together with teams from towns within the northern region such as Consett, Ashington and Gateshead. My first game of the season was an FA Cup Preliminary Round tie at Whitley Bay followed by Sunderland Reserves versus Hartlepool Reserves at Roker Park.

At that time a lecturer at Holly Bank would be expected to have a timetable that included fifteen hours per week with direct contact with students together with other duties allocated by the team leader. On 27 September, the pre-service students started their course and I had been allocated to the general building group as their course tutor. The group was made up of people who had qualified to at least HNC level and had management or supervisory experience. At that time the course was divided into several sections and I was involved with special method for mathematics with various groups and general method with building students. On the first morning Mac gave his introductory pep talk that I remembered from an earlier experience. John Davies had convened a meeting of his new team and had set out his views on how we should tackle the tasks set by the director. Even at this very early stage, there were signs of disagreement within the team, with Mike and Derek proposing a different strategy whilst Jim tried to take the sensible view of a more cautious approach with weekly reviews of our progress. This seemed to me to be the right approach and it was eventually agreed upon. My first lesson was special method maths with a group of general studies students, most of whom were graduates. This session seemed to go quite well and, as one would have expected, the students were very motivated. Most of the students could see the value of the session but some did have reservations about teaching maths. On Wednesday afternoons students were encouraged to participate in various activities arranged by the Students' Union. As there were no classes, Mac convened a meeting of staff where I had my first experience of his complete domination of the staff and he spoke for at least ninety per cent of the time. There were few contributions from the senior staff members and the new boys just sat in amazement! Apparently, Mac had decided to make a few last minute changes to the programme and he made it quite clear that the changes were not open for discussion. The new staff had been encouraged to observe some of their more experienced colleagues and during the second week I sat in on a special method construction session with Bernard Alloway,

43

who had a group of carpentry and joinery students. It was an interesting experience and I noted the relaxed relationship between tutor and students that had been quickly established by a seasoned member of staff.

The move into Woodlands hostel was a big advantage, as I did not have the restrictions associated with living in a guesthouse and travelling to my parent's home every weekend. I had a responsibility for the resident students, most of whom were much older than me and all were married. John Crosby and I not only had the accommodation but also all of the meals were provided. These were mainly taken in the Holly Bank restaurant, although breakfast was available at Oakley House. This arrangement meant that we developed close relationships with Bill Green and the catering and housekeeping staff as we all had an evening meal together. Philip Barnes was the catering manager with Paul Grundy as his deputy and Myra Simpson was the housekeeper. They had a small team of staff, most of whom lived locally, although Myra and Paul Grundy had accommodation in Holly Bank. I had re-established links with Margaret Rooker with respect to the Rambling Club and on the first Sunday in October we led the first walk of the year to Laddow Rocks and Holme Moss. I had also refereed a college football match to help the Soccer Society to get started in between officiating at league games in Middlesbrough, Sheffield and Ashington. The College had well-established international links and we had a young German tutor, Jurgan Schroeder, in residence and he joined our second walk to Bolton Castle, where several of us were adventurous (stupid) enough to jump the Strid. Jim Pratt had organised the Film Society for several years but he saw the opportunity with so many new staff of passing it on. I must have been an easy target and soon found that, instead of giving Jim a bit of assistance, I was left with most of the weekly running responsibilities.

The Maths Club had been formed by Jim Jordan and the new team did take an interest in supporting him. However, Derek and Mike were independent thinkers and were keen on looking at the influence of computers on teaching and learning. I had little knowledge of this area and was keen to learn, so when Mike arranged for a visit to Blackburn College in November, I jumped at the opportunity to join him. Mike's brother was head of maths and computing at Blackburn

College and he had laid on several demonstrations using the College's equipment. I had my first experience of writing a computer program and seeing it work after two or three attempts. This was the start of an interesting month as I hosted a meeting of the Maths Club at Woodlands on the same day that Ian Smith declared UDI in Rhodesia. The following day Mac held another staff meeting, which lasted for three hours and followed a similar format to the previous meeting.

I had my first special method maths meetings with the Brickwork Group and it quickly became apparent that their maths knowledge was not of a satisfactory standard. This was a situation I was to find in many building and engineering groups and, with some reluctance, found myself running remedial numeracy classes in the evening. In the middle of the month, I attended a three-day conference organised by ICL at Huddersfield College of Technology (later Huddersfield Polytechnic and then University of Huddersfield). We were intro- duced to the latest hardware and software products and I became fascinated by the potential educational applications. It was also in November that I accompanied the building staff and students to the Building Exhibition at Olympia and thoroughly enjoyed the day. The first session of teaching practice was now approaching, but I had to ensure that my general building group completed visits to an infant, junior and secondary school. The first visit was to Reinwood Infant and Nursery School, soon to be followed by a visit to Birkby Junior School. Together with my students, I found these visits inspirational with so much pupil involvement in their own learning. The last visit was to King James' Grammar School at Almondbury and here we observed a much more traditional setting with the pupils attentive but passive during the lessons. My students then departed for four weeks of teaching practice to complete their first term and I was allocated to students attending Sheffield colleges. The planned first visits started badly. As I set off by car, heavy snow caused me to return to Huddersfield where I caught a train to Sheffield. However, the train was also seriously delayed and I eventually arrived at the Richmond College with only half an hour of the student's lesson remaining. Later, there were further visits to Richmond College and to Granville College as well as a visit to Newhill Secondary School.

There were a number of social activities at the end of term starting with an afternoon and evening visit from Bolton College of

Education (Technical) staff. Of course, part of the day was educational with an exchange of ideas and practices, but most people were looking forward to the food and drinks associated with the social side. I recall that prior to the arrival of the Bolton staff members Mac had called a staff meeting and spoke non-stop for two hours. We held a carol service followed by refreshments in the Senior Common Room. Two staff members were leaving for new appointments, Jack Hall and Les Hill, and they were given a warm send off.

I returned home for Christmas and was reunited with my sister Christine who had returned from four years in New Zealand. We had a wonderful Christmas party and a few days later we drove to Newcastle for dinner followed by a visit to the Flora Robson Playhouse to see a pantomime. I had a string of refereeing appointments over the vacation with games at Newcastle, Sunderland, Middlesbrough and Huddersfield. In January, despite the snow, I officiated at eight matches, mostly as referee.

The spring term was more purposeful than the previous term, at least from the students' point of view. They had survived teaching practice and the experience had made a big impression on them. My general building group had enjoyed most of their contact with students although those who had taken craft students for theory lessons had found it a challenge. Only one member of the group had received negative reports from visiting tutors and he had been given a number of difficult carpentry and joinery groups that, I suspect, the regular teachers were glad to pass to him. After seeking advice from more experienced colleagues, it was decided to find a more sympathetic establishment for his second session. The teaching practice experience helped to focus the students on their project work and I enjoyed all of my sessions with such motivated students. I continued with the remedial maths groups and it was pleasing to see some remarkable progress in many of the students.

In February the four new members of the maths team enrolled on a six weeks' evening computing course at Leeds University. To be honest, most of the lectures were incomprehensible to me as mainframe computer programming was the dominant theme, but I did get some benefit through talking to other people on the course and from some of the recommended literature.

I was allocated some new teaching practice commitments and

travelled over to Hull College, which necessitated an overnight stay. I also fitted in two army weekends, one at Blackfell Camp where I was appointed adjutant and a study weekend at the Black Swan Hotel in York. My additional refereeing duties together with some heavy snowfalls had limited my activities with the Rambling Club, but I did lead a group to Malham Tarn and Gordale Scar just before the Easter break. I also had a spate of four successive Northern Intermediate League games at Middlesbrough and I felt that I was in danger of becoming too familiar with the home players.

With all the travelling I had decided to upgrade my car and purchased a Vauxhall VX 4/90, which was quite a sporty model with a good all round performance. It was about this time that I started to consider the cricket season and made contact with Peter Lorraine who had been helpful in getting me into the Huddersfield team during my year as a student. Peter was most helpful and invited me to the first evening of nets at Fartown, where I met many of my friends from two years ago. I was selected to play for the second IX for the first game of the season at Honley and soon established a regular place. In parallel with this I also played for Stainsby OB in the Teesside Midweek League and, with the football season not finishing until mid May, I had fixtures at Ashington and finally refereed the Bradford Park Avenue versus Sheffield Wednesday match.

The students completed their second period of teaching practice that lasted for eight weeks and I spent a significant amount of time travelling to colleges to see as many of my tutorial group as possible. This involved many Yorkshire colleges and a trip to Sunderland. In the final term the students concentrated on their coursework and applications for teaching posts. Several of my group hoped to secure a post in secondary education at a school in their home town but most of them were willing to move to wherever there was a suitable post. It was at this time that the students appreciated the uniqueness of the Huddersfield 'continuous assessment' system compared with the traditional final examination system at Garnett and Bolton. I believed Mac was quite right to insist that students should work consistently throughout the year rather than leave their best effort to the last term in preparation for exams. As the end of term approached there was a Staff Association outing to the Ace of Clubs in Leeds where we had a dinner and enjoyed a cabaret. Just before the students departed there was a spate of job offers to members of my group and the celebrations began in earnest. Eventually, the entire group did gain employment as teachers. Immediately after the pre-service students departed former students started arriving for the reunion and I was pleased to see a fair number of old friends from my year as well as those who I had met at previous reunions. Philip Barnes' team, led by master cook Jerry, prepared an excellent meal. Mac gave his usual after dinner speech on Saturday and many of the staff joined in the evening dancing and festivities. The following week Geoff Sparrow, Paul Grundy and I drove down to Nottingham to see England play the West Indies in the Trent Bridge Test Match.

Her Majesty's Inspectors (HMI) Building Annual Summer School was due to begin on 5 July until 8 July and I had been invited to attend. The summer school was made up predominantly of heads of building departments and HMI construction staff members were there in force. Jim Pratt had organised the event with support from Howard Wainwright, the Staff HMI and Jack Place, the principal of Leeds College of Building. The programme included lectures, visits and tutorial work. I got roped into a number of sessions and established useful links with several of the heads as well as meeting the HMI for the first time.

Summer 1966

The day after the Summer School, I drove to Blackdown Barracks for the start of my Annual AER Camp. On the Sunday all of the troops had to have their medical checks together with assessment and issue of equipment ready for overseas travel. The following morning the unit travelled to Gatwick airport where we boarded an RAF VC 111 to Gutersloh Military Airport in Germany and then by road to Bielefeld. On this occasion, I did not have a unit to command as the group was divided up for individual training. I was based at the Bielefeld Officers' Mess, a converted large private dwelling near the centre of the town. The regular RAOC officers made me very welcome, but it soon became apparent that my programme had not been a high priority. On the Monday morning, I met with the commanding officer (CO) and he went over the possibilities and invited me to choose from his list. It did include participating in a military exercise at a location about 250 miles away, but most of the options were local visits. I started with a tour of the Bielefeld facilities, a pleasant lunch in Catterick Barracks and a visit to a printing company. That evening I packed the necessary equipment for the field exercise and the next morning I was driven to the site north of Hamburg, arriving in the early evening. It had been raining for days and it was quite clear that most of the military personnel were not enjoying the training with vehicles up to their axles in mud. After a fitful night's sleep in a tent, I observed the manoeuvres during the morning. I was approached by the CO who informed me that he was going to terminate the exercise and that I was free to return to Bielefeld that afternoon rather than stay for another two days as planned. My driver could not believe his good luck when I gave him the news – he had not been looking forward to another night under canvas. The next three days were of little value as nothing had been planned to cover the eventuality of my early return from the exercise. I tried to make myself useful with some administrative duties and spent some time exploring the town. The following three days were more worthwhile with a visit to Sennelager to see the Bomb Disposal Unit and the Corps Ammunition Company. The next day was a trip to Osnabrück to visit the Corps Vehicle Company and the 652 Training Company. The third visit was on my birthday and I had a tour of 85 Supply Company. In the evening I was given a Champagne birthday party. That was a happy end to Annual Training as my flight to the UK was the next morning and I returned to Huddersfield the following day. My fellow residents of Holly Bank had not forgotten my birthday and they had booked a table at Shibden Mill, where we had a great evening.

I had a week to recover before commencing my Holiday Fellowship contract in North Wales. I took a few days off to visit the family in Sunderland before driving to Colwyn Bay where I was welcomed by the host and hostess, Ken and Mary Rothery. As Colwyn Bay was a larger centre than Marske it justified two secretaries. I spent part of Sunday sorting out the administration procedures and studying maps of the week's walks. The Monday walk commenced with a coach ride to Trefrew, where we visited the woollen mill and did a lake walk. The route became a bit tricky in the Llanrwst area and we got a little lost, but in true HF style we arrived at the coach on time for the return journey to Colwyn Bay. Tuesday's walk left from the house and explored Old Conway and through Fairy Glen. Some of the official paths were closed and we had to make detours. Wednesday being the off day, I decided to recce the route for the long walk planned for Thursday. This was just as well as I had a large party. A coach took us to Betws-y-Coed and we visited the Swallow Falls before continuing on to Penmancho and the Lledr Valley. It was a long day and with little margin for error. On Friday we walked to the Little Orme and onto Shell Bay where we caught a bus to Llandudno and most of the party climbed the Great Orme. I used the weekend to recce the walks for the second week, the highlight being the Thursday walk in Snowdonia and an opportunity to climb Snowdon on the Llanberis track. The Tuesday walk also involved a climb of Conway Mountain. It was a very wet week, not unusual for Wales but disappointing for the guests. Friday involved a train journey to Llanfairfechan and Aber. I did five weeks at Colwyn Bay and I had enjoyed the company and the walks so that I felt invigorated for my second year at Holly Bank.

Holly Bank 1966–7

The first three weeks in September were devoted to general administration with the finalisation of programmes for the year and the allocation of student groups. The usual round of meetings was held to sort out the detail. For me it was within the maths group and the building group. I had taken on the responsibility for the Students' Union following the departure of Jack Hall at the end of last term so that there were a lot of issues to be resolved involving finance and checking that tutors who had assisted in start-up clubs were willing to continue.

The pre-service students arrived on 26 September; Mac held a staff meeting in the morning in which he changed a few of the strategic decisions that had been made during the last three weeks. Some staff called it fine tuning, others, rather cynically, referred to a lack of cooperation at the top. In the afternoon I welcomed my group of residents at Woodlands. Unlike my first year, when I had taken over the hostel duties well into the first term and habits had become established, I had the opportunity of agreeing house rules that were acceptable to all parties from day one. Also, during the last year, along with my new starter colleagues, I had not had any contact with students until the staff induction had been completed. Now, on day two, I met my general building group and started on their induction. The following day, after Mac's lecture, I met with my education group for general method. In the evening there was a resident tutors' meeting followed by a wine and cheese welcoming party. For the next two days the students were assembled in the morning for lectures in the hall. On Thursday it was Fred Topping followed by Jim Jordon and on the Friday, Brian Grant followed by Ron Evans, with their lectures followed up with tutorial group discussions.

I do not think that the students could have any complaints about a full start to the year. As many of the students were married with families there was a mass exodus on Friday afternoons as they made their way home. Some of those who lived much further away did remain in the hostels over the weekend but I found that the numbers in Woodlands rarely exceeded four. During the first week, I had an opportunity of talking to the student body about the Students' Union and the value of participating in the various clubs and activities. They were encouraged to sign up on the sheets that had been placed in the main hall as some of the clubs had planned their first meetings during week two. Indeed, the Film Society showed its first film, *Come September*, on Monday evening as Jim Pratt had booked films for the whole of the first term. There were fewer lectures and more tutorials in week two. John Blackshaw gave a science tutorial and I spent most of my time with the general building group. That weekend Margaret Rooker and I had organised a Rambling Club walk to Malham, and by using our cars with one of the student's vehicles it ensured all those who wished to participate could do so. Here the group visited the Tarn and Cove, before moving onto Gordale Scar. Frank Barr gave the first of his lectures on adolescence and I started to prepare my students for teaching practice, which had been arranged to start earlier than last year.

Several of the staff members had joined Huddersfield Squash club, which was conveniently situated in Edgerton. John Crosby, Paul Grundy and I played regularly and John Blackshaw and Mike McAllister joined us occasionally. We found that a hectic game of squash got rid of the frustrations of the day. Bill Green was in the habit of frequenting the local pub, The Cavalry Arms, and he enjoyed having an audience to regale with his train stories.

The resident tutor group had expanded to include Kate Gosling, who had a flat on the second floor of Holly Bank and her responsibilities covered the ladies residing on that floor. Harry Fletcher had moved into Oakley House and Brian Coombs into Oakwood. With the exception of Harry, who tended to keep to himself, the rest of us developed an excellent team spirit and enjoyed regular convivial outings ('convivs'), which included evening local outings or more adventurous weekend trips. During October, the government reorganised the Army Emergency Reserve and I was appointed as officer commanding a Stores Company.

In mid-October teaching practice began and I had been asked to cover northeast colleges, which happily coincided with some of my refereeing appointments in that region. It also enabled me to have some time with my parents in Sunderland. My first trip involved a full day in Middlesbrough with the morning at Kirby College and the afternoon at Longlands College. Being given a specific geographical area meant that I had to visit students of all disciplines rather than just students in my own group. This certainly added variety but it meant that I had to assess lessons where I was not familiar with the subject matter and therefore could not comment on accuracy or validity.

That weekend, the Rambling Club made a trip to the Lake District and we travelled to Wast Water and climbed Scafell Pike. It was quite misty and I was surprised to meet Mike McAllister appearing suddenly out of the gloom. The following week, before heading off for more teaching practice observations, there was a meeting of the Maths Research Group involving the six members of the team. After the meeting we went into the main hall and entrance to view the stands for the Commonwealth Education Conference, which was to be held at the College. Then it was back to Middlesbrough for a day and half at Longlands College before travelling to Redcar to visit Cleveland Technical College. Here I met Principal Laurie Robinson, who had been a student on the first Huddersfield course in 1947. Robbie, as he was affectionately known by his friends, was appointed by Leeds University as an external assessor for Huddersfield. I stayed in the Park Hotel in Redcar for two nights followed by two full days at the College.

I had an appointment for a Northern Intermediate League Cup match, Newcastle versus Hull City, on Saturday, so spent the weekend with my parents before a further three days of TP in Middlesbrough. It was back to Huddersfield to file reports and catch up with any developments before an Army weekend at Whitburn Camp on the north east coast. Whitburn was used to enable troops to meet the annual shooting requirements as it had a firing range that faced out to sea. The problem was the probability of a gale force wind blowing straight into the faces of the firers and scores were usually well below expectations. That weekend was no exception; indeed, it was so awful that after ninety minutes it was agreed that conditions were too bad to continue. As compensation, and to recover from the chilling conditions, the officers retired to the Seaburn Hotel for dinner rather than eat in the ramshackle Officers' Mess. The soldiers also left camp to frequent the local bars. There was no respite as on Monday morning I drove to Redcar for three more days of TP before returning to college to write up all the reports.

It was back to Middlesbrough to referee the Middlesbrough versus Sheffield United NIL game and I accepted an invitation to stay on to watch the Middlesbrough league game with Grimsby in the afternoon. The following week I made my first visit to Darlington College of Technology, where three students had been placed. As was customary I reported to reception and asked them to inform the principal that I was present in the College and that I would be seeing student teachers in the building department. I was asked to wait before being ushered into Principal Cyril Beynon's office where I was a captive for over an hour before I managed to escape to get on with the job. I later learned that Cyril was an 'occupational hazard' for Huddersfield tutors. On my return to Huddersfield I attended the first meeting of the 'Aims of Courses' study group and in my naivety, was elected secretary to the group. Teaching practice finished by the end of November and I was given a group of HNC engineers for tutorials and I quite enjoyed working with the group.

The Maths Board of Studies was concentrating on modern maths and although I could not see much relevance for FE students, I became as fascinated with the subject as the other members of the group. Jim Pratt had approached me with a view to take some sessions with a group of teachers in Stoke-on-Trent who were following teacher-training modules. Jim had been taking the group for general method and he wanted me to cover maths teaching. Always eager to please, I accepted the offer and travelled by car to Stoke for the afternoon class and was pleasantly surprised at the enthusiasm of these practicing teachers to consider the approaches I was promoting. The journey took about two hours, which meant, with the class, a round trip of six hours. On the penultimate weekend of the term I took the Rambling Club group to Bolton Abbey for the walk along the River Wharfe, via the Strid to Barden Mill. In the evening there was a Film Society meeting. On the last Thursday, I took my final meeting with the HNC engineers. There was a carol service followed by a Christmas lunch and a concert and social in the evening. The students departed on the following morning and our residents group had its own celebration with a meal at the Blue Ball at Norland and a few drinks at the Griffin in Huddersfield.

During the first month of the spring term, I spent some time with the students in my tutorial group reviewing their teaching practice experiences and relating the reports from tutors and host colleagues to their own perceptions. One student, who had had a torrid time at a South Yorkshire college, was on the verge of withdrawing from the course. Although he was in my general building group, the College had given him mainly carpentry and joinery classes. One of these classes had been on a Friday afternoon and the student teacher had lost control, which led to the unruly students throwing him out of the ground floor window. I think his pride suffered more than the bruises. I had travelled to the College at the request of the head of department and the student teacher had been withdrawn from the class. It was clear that he was a long way from being a competent teacher but the second year craft students were renowned for bad behaviour and it was agreed that he should not have been given the group, especially on a Friday afternoon. The College was not keen to take him back for the second period and, after discussions it was decided to place him in a secondary school with a reputation for supporting student teachers. Fortunately for me, this was the only problem in the whole group. The rest of the students had returned brimming with confidence and looking forward to their next teaching experiences.

On the first weekend of the new term I had an Army camp at Blackfell in north Durham and we spent most of the time trying to keep warm in bitter winter weather. The following weekend, the Rambling Club had a nine mile walk in the Hebden Bridge area. I had a full diary of refereeing commitments on Saturdays with most of the fixtures being in the North East. I did some more sessions with the in-service course students at Stoke-on-Trent and despite the travelling time, enjoyed working with the enthusiastic group. The Maths Team continued to meet and McAllister and Bush had declared almost open war on John Davies. Jim Jordan tried to mediate but the new boys had no respect for the leader. John Crosby and I distanced ourselves from the unseemly behaviour and refused to take sides, even though both of us regularly offered our services to baby-sit for Mike and Derek.

Being associated with the building team had its advantages for me. The team had expanded and now consisted of Jim Pratt as leader, Ian Duthie (painting & decorating), George Goldsmith (carpentry & joinery), Bill Squires (brickwork) and Norman Walsh (plumbing). Bernard Alloway was also nominally in the Building group but he had widened his horizons to more general education work. Jack Brown and Jack Hall, who had been key members in the group before I arrived, had left for head of department posts and would eventually become college principals. Jim Pratt had strong links with the colleges in the region and with the Institute of Building and as a result of these connections, he had organised a visit to Holland for five days in early April. The trip was billed as educational but wives were invited and a social programme was to run in parallel with the industrial visits. I was invited to join the group and accepted. Other than Jim, I was the only member of staff who participated, which I found surprising at the time. I drove to Hull with the chairman of the local branch of the Institute of Building as my passenger. We boarded the ferry and travelled overnight to Rotterdam. The boat would be our home for three nights whilst we travelled to various parts of the country. As some of the industrial visits were of little interest to me, I joined the ladies on two of their trips, which were very enjoyable.

I had always had a keen interest in classical music as my father played the violin and my mother played the piano. John Crosby was also keen on the classics and we took advantage of the concerts in the Huddersfield Town Hall. About the time of the Holland visit, there was a concert by the Warsaw Philharmonic Orchestra and it was truly a night to remember. A few weeks later, Margaret Rooker organised a trip for staff members to Manchester's Free Trade Hall to listen to the Halle Orchestra playing Beethoven. That was quickly followed by a Staff Association visit to the Bradford Alhambra to see *Brasilia*. I was keen to have regular access to my own music and I had found a specialist music shop in Huddersfield that stocked good quality equipment. This was in the days before the compacts and people bought individual units of hifi equipment. The owner of the Radio Craft shop had agreed to assemble a unit for me comprising amplifier, tuner and turntable with independent speakers. I collected it in late June and installed it in the bay window of my room in Woodlands. In that large room the sound quality was amazing and when I played some of my collection of LP records I heard sounds that were not noticeable when played on my previous inferior equipment. In the flat all that was lacking was some comfortable furniture to sit and relax. One Saturday in July Paul Grundy and I had driven into town to do some shopping and I decided to have a look in one of the specialist furniture shops. I was casually dressed at the time and was admiring an expensive black leather suite with Paul egging me on to sit on it. A rather pompous assistant came over and, in a rather sarcastic manner, demanded to know if we were interested in buying the suite. Without a second though I said, 'of course' and finished up with the settee and an armchair. With the new furniture installed facing the window with the speakers equidistant, I could relax, look into the garden and listen to the music flowing around me. The next week the resident tutors organised a weekend in the Lake District, where we were based in Kendal (thanks to George Chambers letting us use his second home) and we managed to explore most of the lakes.

During the spring term the students did their second teaching practice and once more I found myself on the northeast run with regular trips to Middlesbrough, Redcar and Darlington. At that time, some colleges had many annexes and Darlington was no exception. The building students were in cramped and ancient conditions in a run down part of the town and, at the other end of the spectrum, some of the business studies students were housed in Blackwell Grange, a magnificent stately building from the outside but decidedly dilapidated within. At least I could avoid Principal Beynan when I was visiting the students in the annexes! The trips to the north helped to reduce the travelling to football matches at weekends, as I could stay overnight with my parents in Sunderland. After Easter the football season was coming to a close with cup finals and league championships to be decided. I officiated at St James' Park in The Northern Intermediate League Cup Final between Newcastle and Sheffield United and also in the Durham FA Amateur Cup Final between Billingham and Hanstels at Bishop Auckland. On the last day of the season, I was asked to referee the South Shields League match that would determine the championship between Boldon Colliery Welfare and Reyrolles, with Reyrolles carrying off the honours.

One day during the summer term I made a call at the gent's toilets in the teaching block and found Mac was already there. We made some pleasant conversation, then, out of the blue, he suddenly said that I would be promoted to senior lecturer at the end of term. I could only mumble my thanks and he was gone. My trips to Stoke came to an end and many of my pre-service group of general building students had gained teaching appointments.

Summer 1967

The cricket season that had started slowly in April was now in full flow and I was well established with the Huddersfield second XI. I opened the batting with my old friend Peter Lorraine and we were reasonable successful. On my occasional outings with the First XI I usually had to bat in the middle of the order and as the matches were limited to forty overs a side, I either did not get an innings or had to hit out trying to reach a distant target.

My Annual Camp started at Browndown on the south coast near Portsmouth, and I travelled on the Saturday to spend the weekend preparing for training on Salisbury Plain. I had responsibility for the vehicles and my team worked all day Sunday to try to ensure that the various motors would stand up for a couple of weeks as the allocated vehicles were often discarded by the regular army. On Monday we travelled in convoy to a training area near Tidworth and occupied a defensive position. The following day was the annual range course where we all had to fire our designated weapons and achieve the required standard. Officers had to fire the pistol as well as participating in the rifle shooting. I usually managed a decent score with the rifle but to master the pistol required far more practice than was available. The weather was good but there were swarms of insects that inflicted bites on everyone and made the day uncomfortable. We moved to a new location and some units had a night exercise. I had my first experience in a helicopter when I flew over the area to do a reconnaissance for the following day's movements. That evening I led my unit in a night move and returned without any problems other than a burst radiator in one of the Bedford vehicles. In the morning I had to dash into Tidworth to hunt out a replacement radiator, quite a task as the model was ancient and we had to make three calls before tracking down the part. That night we moved back to Browndon arriving at 0430. There was no time to rest. Camp had to be re-established and the troops had to be fed. It was my luck that it was my day to be orderly officer and so I had to keep going for a third day with very little sleep. To compensate the next day was an 'off day' and some of us went into Winchester for a taste of civilisation.

Next day there was a thorough check on all of the vehicles, which identified another problem radiator that needed replacing. I did the personal interviews for my team members, as I had to do an annual report of each soldier. For the senior ranks this was a critical time as an adverse report could affect their bounty payment and future within the AER. This, of course, was the same for officers, as we had to be assessed by the CO. The following morning I drove to Bordon to find a replacement radiator and was back by midday. On the Wednesday of the second week, I had a visit from the REME commanding officer and inspector. Their task was to assess my performance with my new unit and we seemed to pass with flying colours. The downside was all the paperwork that had to be completed on every vehicle in the unit before they could be handed back to the regular army. On the following day there was a real treat for the unit. An experimental army hovercraft was undergoing trials in the Solent and as we had been working with some of their team we were invited to have a trip. As it could only take about four passengers at a time, it had to make several trips so that all those who wished to have a trip could do so. That evening I took my troop into Gosport for a social evening.

On returning to Huddersfield, the summer school was in full swing and I had a day with one of the building sandwich groups. I had agreed to do a four weeks engagement with Holiday Fellowship and they had assigned me to the Aberystwyth Centre on the coast of West Wales. On 29 July I drove to Aberystwyth in pouring rain. I did not know this part of Wales at all and I had little time to familiarise myself with the excursions and the Welsh language. The Holiday Fellowship used the Hall of Residence building of the University of Wales during the summer. This was situated on the promenade with seaside views. On the Monday we travelled by coach to Llanddeiniol, where we began a cliff path walk in heavy rain. It was a fairly gentle walk and the guests suffered the conditions bravely. The next day we took a coach to Devil's Bridge and our walk took us to Mynach, Myherin, and Dyffryn Castle. The paths were flooded in places but the rain had stopped. On the first Wednesday, I set out to do a recce for the Thursday walk to ensure that I did not lead the guests astray. On the Thursday a coach took the party to Cader Idris where we walked to the dramatic Llyn Cau down to Dolgellau. Cader Idris marks the southernmost limit of Snowdonia's mountains and it provides haunting views over the surrounding countryside.

Friday was very popular as we walked to the railway station to catch the NGT train to Devil's Bridge. The fairly gentle walk took us to the Mynach Falls and Parsons Bridge before returning on the Aberffrwd train. I had to spend most of Saturday sorting out the paper work and doing some homework for the second week. There was a changeover of guests, with about half staying on for their second week. On Sunday morning, after a short service in the common room, I took the keen walkers on a stroll up Constitution Hill to help them work up an appetite for lunch. I then jumped into the car to do a recce for Monday's walk in the Pont-Rhyd-y-Groes area. I was pleased that I had, as there were several junctions that did not appear in the HF guide notes. A coach took us southeast to Aber Magr. Then we walked to Banafan and Maen Arthur Wood before arriving at Pont-Rhyd-y-Groes, where the coach was waiting for the return journey. The weather had been steadily improving and the paths were not too muddy. The Tuesday walk was more challenging. We started with a coach journey to Pont-y-Hygaled and then climbed the 2469 ft. high Plinlimmon. Plinlimmon's lack of grandeur is redeemed by its profusion of historic associations and the respect it deserves as the source of five rivers, including the Seven and the Wye. The descent took us to Dyffryn Castle, where we met our transport. On my return to the Hall of Residence, I found a letter from the Army informing me of my promotion to captain, a pleasant surprise. Again I took advantage of the off day on Wednesday to carry out a recce for the following day. In the evening, the host had organised a treasure hunt followed by a barbecue on the beach. The Thursday walk started with a coach journey to Cwm Einion, also known as Artists' Valley. The walk took us by a reservoir and eventually to the Llyfnant Valley. The Friday walk required a train journey to Aberffrwd Woods where we did the precipice walk. The next two weeks repeated the walks of the first two weeks and I was able to relax a little more with the confidence of knowing the routes. The last Saturday was also the end of the HF season at Aberystwyth and I had received a request to transport all of the HF books, maps and assorted papers to the Towyn Centre that was open throughout the year. I was quite happy to do this, as Dylis Powell, who was the manageress at Marske for my first stint as an HF secretary, was the manageress at Towyn. So I had an enjoyable short visit before the long drive back to Huddersfield.

After two nights in Woodlands, I drove to Sunderland to visit my parents for two nights before taking a walking break in the Lake District where I met up with Paul Grundy and booked into a Keswick Guest House. The following day we climbed Great Gable and Green Gable. We drove to Seathwaite and on to Watendlath with a drink at King and Queens Hotel. In the evening we had a fine dinner at Ladore Swiss Hotel. The following day we drove to St Bees beach, then to Wastdale Head before returning to Huddersfield via Kendal.

My promotion to senior lecturer took effect from 1 September although the pre-service students did not arrive until 25 September. This gave ample time for staff meetings and personal preparation for my allocated classes. I visited Harrogate for Yorkshire versus Gloucestershire cricket match, after which Yorkshire became the League champions.

Although term started on 25 September many of the resident students arrived the day before, which gave me an opportunity to welcome the Woodlands residents and give them a briefing. This was the 21st Pre-Service course (PS21 and Frank Barr gave the welcome address in the main hall in the absence of the director. Margaret Rooker followed with her introduction to the library and then I did my Students' Union talk. As usual, Mac had made some changes to the programme and introduced a 'Unit System' in which all activities were expressed in units of study. The Maths Board of Studies had a hilarious meeting fitting last year's curriculum into the new structure. It was quite common for many resident students to stay on the first weekend as they assumed that they would have to work weekends. However, I knew that they would have little homework from the first week so I organised a Rambling Club outing to Laddow Rocks and had a large following. During the third week of term, I had a number of maths lectures to present to three building groups on consecutive days. The carpentry and joinery group was very large but they seemed to be interested in the topic and I agreed to take some smaller groups for tutorials. Also during that week, I started individual tutorials with my General Building Group and, in my role as SU coordinator I was involved in assisting with the Staff Dance for students.

The 16 October was a memorable day as I gave a student-centred learning presentation to the building students in the morning, Mac invited me to take over from Bill Green as the senior resident tutor in Holly Bank and in the evening, I was elected secretary of the College Club. Bill Green's announcement that he was going to get married was received with amazement by the resident tutors. Bill had often talked about 'his Enid' but we had not met the lady and thought it was one of his tales.

During my chat to Mac he suggested that I should look to update my qualifications and indicated that he would allow me some study time if I could find a suitable course. When I suggested an education qualification he advised that it would be too easy and I should consider finding a course in my technical specialism. At that time very few universities offered part-time degree courses, but after talking to several universities I was offered a place at Bradford University on a course leading to an MSc in Highways and Traffic Engineering from October the following year. The course tutor assured me that my existing qualifications and experience were an adequate preparation but suggested that it would be useful to pick up a qualification involving Principles of Electricity. I found a suitable

ONC module at Bradford College and in November dutifully enrolled on the evening course. Although I had missed a few sessions, I was able to do the necessary reading to make up the lost time.

The Staff Association started its programme with a visit to Watney's Brewery in Manchester on a Wednesday afternoon and the following weekend the Rambling Club visited Malham Cove and Tarn before going on to Gordale Scar. During the later part of October I commenced individual tutorials with my general building group to prepare them for their first teaching practice. Most of the students had been allocated colleges within travelling distance of either Holly Bank or their home but some would be in colleges where they would have to stay in local accommodation. Teaching practice commenced during the first week in November and it was customary not to visit during this early induction. However, all my students had a contact telephone number if they needed any support. It was during this quiet week for me that Philip Barnes and I travelled to Blackpool to visit the Club Trade Fair that was held in the Wintergardens. The visit was tied in with my new responsibilities as club secretary and there was a need to look at up-to-date equipment for the new bar area. The following week, Harry Fletcher hosted a Liberal Studies Week at Oakwood House. Liberal studies was the new thing in FE at that time, when it was assumed that all FE technical students needed to have their minds broadened and not just concentrate on their vocational studies. I had an input to the proceedings to students on ONC courses and in the evening enjoyed my 'liberal studies' at Huddersfield Town Hall with a Berlin Straatpeller concert. Teaching practice supervision then started with a vengeance, but I had to find time to go to Huddersfield Magistrates' Court to secure a licence for the College bar. The bulk of my TP work was at Doncaster and Cleveland Colleges. During my first visit to Redcar I had lunch with Principal Laurie Robinson.

The week the students returned from TP I transferred from Woodlands to the fifth floor flat in Holly Bank hostel with the help of my colleagues, including Paul Grundy. My new settee proved tricky but we managed to squeeze it into the lift end-on. The student debriefing after TP was always interesting and all of my students claimed to have enjoyed the experience and wished to be placed in the same institution for the second period.

Mac invited me to attend a meeting of the Academic Board Executive Committee to answer questions relating to the Students' Union and residential issues. There had been unrest within the College and some, if not all of it, was due to an influx of young graduates from Essex and Sussex Universities. The College regulations allowed graduates at twenty-one years old to be admitted on the assumption that they would not be teaching vocational courses that required industrial experience. This cohort had expanded quite rapidly with the introduction of Liberal Studies into the FE curriculum and the lifestyle of these youngsters was quite foreign to the bulk of the older traditional Holly Bank students. Conflicts had arisen and the Students' Union Committee was experiencing some difficulties. The president was at odds with the new brigade that was far more accomplished at the politics of SU life and some of the social events that had taken place had become drunken brawls. A week after my meeting with the Academic Board the SU president resigned and I had to move quickly to avoid a major conflict. Eventually, it was agreed that one of the more responsible of the graduate entries, John Taylor, would take over as president for the rest of the year and an uneasy truce was agreed. The move proved successful, as there were no further serious disputes. (I was to meet John Taylor in the distant future when we were both college principals). The resident tutors and Holly Bank senior staff administrators enjoyed a Christmas lunch at the Roma Italian Restaurant and on the last day of term there was a children's party in the hall. I set off for Sunderland for a family Christmas.

Derek Bush's enthusiasm for computing rubbed off on the other members of the maths team and we all enrolled at an evening course at Leeds University during the spring term. The course lasted six weeks and was rather disappointing with many of the sessions being taken by tutors with poor presentational skills. However, our enthusiasm was not dampened and I developed an interest in teaching machines and Computer Aided Administration (CAA). This interest developed into Computer Aided Learning (CAL) at a later stage. Meanwhile, I continued with my evening course at Bradford being the oldest member of the group (it made a change from being the youngest!)

During the 1960s further education expanded rapidly throughout the country and new buildings were replacing the pre-war structures and the many annexes and temporary buildings that had been placed around the colleges. This growth had been reflected in the expansion of teacher training and colleges were generally keen to take our students on teaching practice so that they could monitor them to see if they were worth appointing. I stressed this important point particularly to those students who had been placed in colleges close to their homes. Although most of my students were willing to apply for posts nationally, many expressed the hope that they could secure a post locally. Interestingly, about thirty per cent of pre-service students accepted a secondary appointment in or near their home town. Some had decided that the teaching of technical subjects in a school was their preferred choice; however, I was of the opinion that failure to obtain an appointment locally in FE meant that many students had to opt for secondary education rather than moving away from their home base.

Various government White Papers had proposed that teacher training should become compulsory in the further education sector but it was not adopted by Parliament. However, many people in the sector wished to see a rapid expansion of teacher trained lecturers and Huddersfield was in the forefront of expanding the provision, thanks to the vision of Alex MacLennan. In-service programmes were expanded from sandwich courses to include day release courses. Although Mac had proposed the development of day release courses, he did not receive support from Bolton or Garnett Colleges and his own staff members were not enthusiastic about a move they thought would 'dilute the quality of teacher education'. One of the first day release centres was in Durham where Principal George Garland had established a good relationship with Holly Bank. The programme involved day release at Durham and short periods of block attendance at Huddersfield, usually during traditional vacation time. In-service students were not limited to the staff of New College, Durham. Indeed, enrolment was open to all FE teachers in the northeast region where there were a large number of untrained teachers. With my connections with the northeast, it was not surprising that I soon found myself included in the team that made regular trips up the A1 road. In due course a small cadre of permanent staff was established at Durham, initially led by Peter Franklin and then by David Downing who still had his home in Sunderland. Because of the resistance of the other teacher training colleges to day release, colleges from outside of the Northern Region approached Huddersfield. Under normal circumstances developments outside of traditional catchment areas would have been resisted by the Department of Education and Science; however, both civil servants and HMI supported the expansion and we witnessed centres springing up across the Pennines and even as far south as Hertfordshire. This led to a further expansion in the staff at Holly Bank to cope with the additional workload together with a network of staff development officers who were employed in the host colleges.

Because of my residential duties and a fairly full programme of pre-service students, I was only involved with the Durham in-service students. However, other opportunities did arise. Jim Pratt had strong contacts with City and Guilds with respect to construction industry examinations. At that time the main qualifications were the Craft and Advanced Craft Certificates in the various building crafts and the Full Technological Certificate (FTC) in Building for potential supervisors. There was a gap in the qualifications for technicians that were not met by the National Certificate programme that tended to be too academic for many students and therefore had poor success rates for students progressing from craft courses. City and Guilds decided to develop the Construction Technicians Certificate and established a group based at Holly Bank to oversee the development of the syllabuses and the style of examination. Jim invited me to join the team that also included Norman Philips, the head of construction from Carlisle College. We were primarily involved with Part II, which was aimed at older students who had successfully progressed from Part I. It was agreed that the coursework and end of year examinations would be linked to a building project that would be sent to colleges at the start of the academic year. Norman Philips had an architectural background and he agreed to put forward ideas for the project and to produce the drawings based upon a real life situation. This was a major innovation, moving away from locally set coursework and traditional examinations. It proved a great success with teachers in the colleges and the students certainly preferred the system. City and Guilds maintained its direct involvement, with people such as Robin Bullough and Roger Fox attending the meetings in Huddersfield. Robin and Roger would eventually hold high offices in C&G in later years. During the first phase, I was involved as an assistant examiner and enjoyed the experience.

Jim then persuaded me to take on another C&G challenge, as the Chief Examiner for Mathematics in the FTC Construction course. This was new territory and I had to prepare an examination paper that related to the syllabus and then present it to the Moderating Committee at City and Guilds headquarters in London. The other members of the Moderating Panel were all principals of building colleges or heads of department and my predecessor as chief examiner had been a head of department with quite a reputation. I was very nervous having to present my efforts to this distinguished panel. I had first to sit through the moderation of two other papers that were given a severe mauling by the members before it was my turn. I briefly explained my thinking in preparing a paper that differed significantly from previous papers. I had expected some critical comment but, on the contrary, first the chairman and then individual members congratulated me on the best paper they had moderated for years. There was hardly a change made to any of the questions and I felt very relieved by the pat on the back. Having prepared the paper and passed the scrutiny of the committee, I had to recruit a team of markers as the number of candidates exceeded two thousand and included a number from overseas centres. I had prepared a detailed marking scheme for the moderating panel so that when I called a meeting of the assistant examiners, I could share the paper and the approved marking scheme with them. The team agreed a division of the candidates and I informed C&G of our proposals. It was the responsibility of the institute to allocate specific college entries to the examiners and I had to take responsibility for the overseas candidates. The completed papers arrived in early summer and we had a deadline to complete the marking and I had to submit an Examiner's Report on the results. The standards varied greatly with a number of candidates achieving one hundred per cent, but too many were at the other extreme with zero per cent or just a little more. This raised the issue of why had candidates been entered for the examination when they were obviously not ready. I was advised that some of the candidates would be external, meaning that they had not followed a teaching programme in a college. The results confirmed my own experience of construction students who were generally quite good with the technology subjects but struggled with the academic requirements of the maths and science papers.

From Easter onwards I played cricket for Huddersfield and enjoyed the company of the team members. The Rambling Club continued to have a loyal group of walkers and I found myself more and more involved with the Film Society. Squash was my main means of keeping fit between classroom-based inertia and on the one occasion that there was sufficient interest from the students to run a squash competition. The pre-service year finished with the usual round of festivities and I was pleased that many of my students had gained employment or were awaiting interviews. The Former Students' Reunion immediately followed the departure of the students and it was great to see all my old friends again. Now that I was in Holly Bank, I was closer to the action, but the downside was the noise that continued throughout most of the night. The Annual Heads of Construction course followed and I enjoyed meeting up with heads that I had seen during teaching practice visits. I did a short stint of Holiday Fellowship work at Marske where I was able to take things in my stride, as I knew all the walks well. My annual training with the AER was a military training fortnight at Deepcut and not very inspiring.

Huddersfield 1968–1970

The next two years followed a similar pattern to the previous year. I continued my professional commitments to the pre-service course students and the Durham in-service students. Jim Pratt was becoming increasingly involved with administrative duties allocated by Mac and Eric Tuxworth took over the running of the Construction Group. Eric's experience as a head of department at Keighley College was of great value to the team and indeed to the College. He had a much more business-like approach than Jim and the team responded positively to his encouragement. It was probably the case that there had been a certain amount of complacency in the team but Eric sorted that out without hurting too many feelings. In October I started at Bradford University on the Master of Science programme in Traffic Engineering and Highway Planning. Weekly attendance was on a Wednesday afternoon and evening and I soon settled into a range of new subject areas. In addition to the main technology areas, we had to study computer programming and statistics so that the course members could be prepared for the research work in years three and four. In the first year we did programming in Algol but in the second year it changed to Fortran. With my interest in mathematics, I did enjoy the computing and the statistics and although the technology was of little value to me professionally, I found it interesting. Mike McAllister was also involved at Bradford in the evenings and we regularly met up between my afternoon and evening sessions to use the facilities of the nearby Turkish baths. This was a new experience starting with the steam room then a cold plunge bath and massage followed by tea and scones whilst cooling off in our towelling robes.

I also retained my residential and Student Union responsibilities and continued to help organise the Rambling Club and the Film Society. During the winter weekends, there was nearly always a refereeing commitment and occasionally a convivial weekend with the resident staff. In the summer, I continued to play cricket for Huddersfield and recorded two centuries during this period. My highest score was 158 not out and the other century was in a record breaking opening partnership with Peter Lorraine, who also scored a century. Considering that each innings was limited to forty overs, the opportunity to reach a three figure score was limited. In 1968 my Holiday Fellowship Centre was at Bourton-on-the-Water and in 1968 at Freshwater Bay on the Isle of Wight. I particularly enjoyed the Freshwater Bay Centre, as I had not visited that part of the country before. The walks were relatively easy but the variety of scenery made up for it. Also in 1969, after the Holiday Fellowship stint, I had two weeks' holiday in Greece. This was the first holiday that I had taken abroad on my own. Indeed, it was my first holiday for many years. The first week was based in Athens and I booked excursions nearly every day. The second week was a seaside resort where I could relax and chat to local people. It was the time when the Army colonels ran Greece and nobody was prepared to talk about politics for fear of arrest.

In 1970 I completed the attendance stage of my MSc course and passed the coursework and examinations. The next stage was to produce a research dissertation and the target was to complete it within two years, although an extra year was permitted. After much discussion with my tutor, I decided to investigate *The Influence of Motorway Gradients on Vehicular Speed*. I made contact with the West Yorkshire Constabulary to seek permission to monitor vehicles on gradients on the M1 Motorway. They were very obliging and whenever I requested a specific time for the research fieldwork, I was escorted along the motorway to the designated gradient, at speeds far higher that the official limit. The main problem was the quality and reliability of the equipment that I had borrowed from the university. When it was set up it was supposed to record the speed of each vehicle that passed the determined point and then print out the results on a graph. However, it often broke down and I had to try to record each vehicle and its speed manually. A further problem was that the meter could not distinguish between the types of vehicle and I also had to record the type as well as the speed of each passing vehicle. I had to return to the motorway more times than I had intended because of equipment problems. Some of my fellow students on the course worked in offices where they had access to secretarial support, but that was not available to me, so I had to use my portable typewriter to produce the 267 pages of the research document. As three copies were required, I had to use carbon paper so that the third copy (mine) was not as clear as the original. However, the university accepted the dissertation and the visiting assessor did not give me too much hassle before agreeing the university grade.

In the summer of 1970, I returned to Marske-by-the-Sea for my stint with Holiday Fellowship. I took the walks in the first week in my stride, as I knew them well. In the evenings, the host had arranged a lively programme and many of the domestic staff joined in. I met the assistant cook, Veronica Woodward who was a student teacher at Worcester College. We got on very well together and I was sorry that she was leaving at the end of my first week. Her parents had driven up from her home in Retford to collect her and we had a chat on the Saturday morning before they departed. The manageress at Marske was Mrs Goulding, known as Mrs G, and we had quickly developed a good relationship. It was during my second week that she informed me that Veronica was going to return at the weekend and I was delighted. We renewed our friendship over the next couple of weeks before we parted for our respective colleges. We continued to see each other occasionally as the distance between Worcester and Huddersfield was considerable. Myra Simpson was always very obliging when Veronica visited Holly Bank and provided a study bedroom for her, a suitable distance away from my flat!

Huddersfield 1971–72

In 1971, I had two Spring AER camps at Deepcut and Whitburn and my Annual Camp was in May at Penhale in Devon. It was something of a busman's holiday as I was programmed to give instructor training on methods of instruction to officers and NCOs and there was plenty of free time between the sessions. I found time to visit Mrs Goulding who was manageress at the Lynmouth HF Centre and to have an evening at Bodmin where there was military parade with bands marching through the streets.

I had as many matches with Huddersfield first team as with the second team but both teams were struggling to find winning form. My best score for the First XI was thirty-seven out of a total of ninety-six all out. I managed to play a few games with the more successful Stainsby OB and scored a couple of forties. The Construction Technicians Certificate team held its meeting in Carlisle with Norman Phillips as our host.

Veronica had been appointed to a teaching post at Firth Moor School in Sheffield to start in September. So I had agreed with Veronica that we should have a holiday abroad together and I had booked rooms at the small town of Bol on the Island of Brac off the Yugoslavian coast for two weeks. We had a leisurely day after the long journey and the following day we visited the beautiful Zlatni Rat beach. We had a tour around the islands with a picnic lunch of lamb, salads and plenty of local wine. Our other trips included two visits to Hvar and a day in Dubrovnik. The other days were spent exploring the island or relaxing at Zlatni Rat beach. On our return to Gatwick my brother, Richard, who had looked after my car, met us. We drove to South Littleton and stayed the night with Veronica's friend Vera before I took Veronica back to her home in Retford.

Veronica and I had decided to try to take a Holiday Fellowship engagement in 1971 at the same centre and eventually it was agreed that we would be appointed to the Colwyn Bay Centre in North Wales. We set off only three days after our return from holiday. The walks were quite challenging and there was a climb in Snowdonia every week and with Veronica being kept very busy in the kitchen we only saw each other in the evenings. On one occasion, I took her to the Maenon Abbey Hotel for dinner. We had a lovely romantic meal in the candle-lit dining room. My brother Richard had booked at Colwyn Bay for our last two weeks at the centre and he joined in all of the walks and the social activities. We drove back together, arriving at Huddersfield in time for me to play for Huddersfield seconds against Holmfirth, who beat us by nine wickets. That was my last game of the season and I had to start preparing for a new term.

Veronica and I became engaged in September. She had secured lodgings in Sheffield with a Mrs Callas and it seemed that every time I visited she found a job for me to do. The new term started with the usual routine of induction talks and Students' Union activities. I did some work with the in-service groups that normally attended on day release but were required to attend for several short blocks at Holly Bank during vacation times. There was a welcome dance for the pre-service students and I took the Rambling Club to Malham Tarn and Gordale Scar. The following week I had arranged for the Film Club to start with *A Classroom of Your Own* that seemed to be popular with the students. During the term, I had three AER weekends at Holly Bank for instructor training courses, which were proving very popular and there was interest from some of the regular army instructors. I had a short meeting with Mac regarding a variety of residential and SU issues. This was followed by a full staff meeting, which inevitably resulted in a flurry of meetings within the various groups. Just before the pre-service students departed for teaching practice, the resident group had an evening out at the Wakefield Theatre Club where Val Doonigan was the star performer. Most of my TP commitments were in the West Yorkshire area and included Bradford, Wakefield, Keighley and Sheffield. I also had a single visit to Darlington. The term ended with an International Evening in Holly Bank and a staff dinner.

Veronica and I had agreed to get married in July 1972 and she began to seek a teaching appointment in Huddersfield. We started to look for a house, which would be my first having enjoyed Holly Bank hospitality for the last seven years. We eventually decided to purchase a new house in Highburton, on the Sheffield side of Huddersfield. Planning for the wedding and all the other related issues had to go on in parallel with our normal college/school activity. I also had to meet the deadline to submit my MSc dissertation, which was progressing slowly as my typing skills were not very good. Veronica joined in some of the resident group activities on the occasional weekend she stayed at Holly Bank. There was a weekend in London and one in the Lake District where we stayed at The Old England Hotel overlooking Lake Windermere.

I completed my MSc and had the pleasure of receiving the award from Prime Minister Harold Wilson, who was the Chancellor of Bradford University. My parents came down from Sunderland and Veronica took a day off from school at the expense of being docked a day's pay! Plans for our marriage at Retford were made for 29 July and it was a beautiful sunny day with so many family and friends attending. After the ceremony at St Joseph's Church, we travelled down the A1 to Sutton on Trent for the reception and enjoyed a fine meal. As was usual in those days Veronica and I withdrew from the celebrations, did a quick change and departed for our honeymoon in Yugoslavia. I had to drive to Manchester airport and the M62 Motorway had just opened that week. We were the only people on the road and I began to wonder if it really was open but we made excellent progress arriving in good time for our flight to Dubrovnik.

On our return to Huddersfield, we found that our new house was not quite ready for occupation so I had to ask Myra to let us have my flat at Holly Bank for a couple of nights. New houses in those days had few of the extras associated with the current practices. The garden was a wilderness, the walls needed painting and there were no appliances in the kitchen. With a couple of weeks to go to the start of the academic year, we set about sorting out the house. We had ordered furniture from Philip Barnes' brother but it had not arrived and we were allowed to borrow some furniture as a temporary measure. Veronica started a major house cleaning and I started the painting while Veronica's father started on the garden. We could see the Emley Moor transmitter from our windows, and radio and TV reception were excellent, a length of trailing wire acting as an effective aerial. Veronica started at Rawthorpe Secondary School and I started my term as a non-resident. It was probably all the sudden changes to my lifestyle that prompted a couple of applications for a new job. Both applications were for head of building department posts and I was pleasantly surprised to receive an invitation to attend an interview at Cleveland Technical College in Redcar. I knew the College from my numerous visits on teaching practice supervision and I was on good terms with Principal Robinson and the current post-holder Wesley Gale. It seemed that my main opposition was the current senior lecturer, Norman Greenwood, but the panel of governors offered me the post with effect from 1 January 1973, and I accepted.

I had to submit my notice to Mac who was very supportive and wished me well. I had a couple of months to prepare for the move and it seemed obvious that we were unlikely to sell the Highburton house and find a suitable property in Cleveland for the start of my appointment. As it happened we had no difficulty selling as a local couple called with a cash deposit as soon as the advertisement appeared in the local press. Veronica and I had to travel up to Redcar at weekends to look at property and eventually we made an offer for a house in Skelton-in-Cleveland, some eight miles from the College but we would not be able to move in until well into the new year. I booked a room at the Park Hotel on the sea front at Redcar for four nights per week, travelling on Mondays and Fridays. I was sorry to leave my pre-service students who were an excellent group. Over the last couple of years, I had been assigned to a number of sessions at the Durham in-service Centre, mainly with construction and engineering students on maths special method. When the students heard that I was coming to the northeast, they offered all sorts of advice, most of which I took with a big pinch of salt. Veronica had to give notice to the school and to look for teaching opportunities in Cleveland. Fortunately, she was quickly offered a post at Bydales Comprehensive School in Marske-by-the-Sea.

This change in career was not simply because of a change in personal circumstances. Several other factors contributed to disrupting the pleasant time at Holly Bank. At the corporate level, the government had indicated a preference for independent teacher training institutions to merge with either a university or a polytechnic

73

and discussions had been taking place for over a year between Huddersfield Polytechnic and Holly Bank. I had been a member of the Academic Board and was increasingly aware that the merger would take place and that my view was that Holly Bank would lose out. Also, a number of my close colleagues had moved onto new posts. John Crosby had moved to Scotland to work for the Scottish Vocational Examinations Council (SCOTVEC), Mike McAllister had taken up a post of head of department in Ipswich and Derek Bush had moved to Enfield College with the hope of becoming head of computing when the College merged with the local polytechnic. Amongst the other resident tutors, Dave Downing had been transferred full time to the Durham Outreach Centre, Brian Coombs had set up a private commercial college in Newcastle and Kate Gosling had become an HMI in schools. So in a very short period the maths team that was appointed in 1965 had moved on, leaving John Davies and Jim Jordon to carry on the work.

CHAPTER 5

Cleveland Technical College
1973–77

THE TRANSFER FROM TUTOR TO MANAGER was fairly straightforward with some help and support from Principal Lawrence Robinson (known locally as Robbo by the staff and Robbie to his friends). Norman Greenwood could not have been more accommodating. Of the other senior managers, Reg Richardson, formerly head of engineering, had recently been appointed vice-principal as the revised Burnham Regulations stipulated that colleges must have such a person. Clearly, the principal did not share that view and Reg became what was known at that time as a 'parked VP' with no senior responsibilities. He arranged tea breaks in his office for the heads and spent quite a bit of time playing the organ in the College hall. Andy White had been appointed to the head of engineering post at the same time as George Chambers and me. George was the first head of general studies. John Greenwood was head of science and George Cooper was head of business studies. Arthur Taylor was the registrar, completing the senior management team.

My experience at Huddersfield with Principal Robinson had always been very convivial. He had a good sense of humour and enjoyed a good night out. I was soon to find out that he had a completely different persona at Cleveland Technical College. He was feared by most staff and disliked by some of the other members. He had a reputation of being an autocrat and a bully and I soon discovered a level of arrogance that I had not perceived before. However, he did not interfere in the running of the departments and he expected the heads to get on with the job. He occasionally dropped in to see me in my cupboard-sized office where he relaxed a little without the presence of other staff. His secretary, Ann Wood, was nicknamed the 'other VP' and she certainly seemed to have more inside knowledge than any of the managers. We did not have management meetings as such. Instead, on Friday's, at about midday,

Robbo would knock on the door and state that he would see us in the pub. Dutifully, the heads and VP would make their way to the local public house where we were treated to the first pint. A general chat ensued over the next couple of hours, punctuated with someone getting 'the next round in'.

One of the first skills an FE manager had to gain was to master the Burnham Further Education Report. This set out the conditions of service and salaries of all staff members engaged as academic staff. The support staff members were employed under local authority terms and conditions. The report included a formula for calculating the size of colleges and departments and the salaries of principals and heads were linked to the size of the College and the departments. The size was based upon student enrolments and the type and level of course being taken. For example, students on practical courses such as engineering and construction attracted more points than students on classroom-based courses such as business studies or mathematics. Similarly, a higher weighting was allowed for more advanced work. At that time full-time students would be timetabled for thirty hours per week of class contact with tutors. At the end of each year the points were calculated and if a college or department had expanded into a higher bracket, it would be automatically upgraded and the post holder's salary increased accordingly. Fortunately for the post holders the reverse did not apply. If a college or department experienced contraction and fell into a lower category, the current postholder's salary would be protected as long as they stayed in that post. Cleveland College in 1973 was in Group 2 and my department was Grade 2. This meant that my new salary was very little more than my Huddersfield senior lecturer salary, which had been calculated under the Pelham system.

The Burnham system was far from perfect and was susceptible to sharp practice by senior post holders. Also, the report was advisory and could be ignored by local authorities. However, this rarely happened but the various ranges in the report allowed the authorities to adopt the least favourable interpretation. It was common knowledge in the FE Sector who were the 'generous' and who were the 'mean' authorities. At the time of my appointment, the College was part of Yorkshire North Riding LEA but as a result of a major review of local authorities, the government had determined that Redcar would become part of the new Cleveland LEA. Both the original and the new authorities chose a median position in interpreting Burnham. The most generous local authority was Inner London Education Authority (ILEA).

Although I was head of the building department, the bulk of the work was in the building crafts, with a modest amount of technician ONC and G course programmes. The craft teachers respected Norman Greenwood as he had been a joiner by trade. However, as 'a techy' I had to work hard to gain acceptance. One advantage that I did have was that two relatively new staff members, Jim Boland and Trevor Kitchen had been students of mine at Huddersfield and gave me a warm welcome. Arthur Barclay, who taught plumbing and Norbert Welsh, who taught painting and decorating, were long established staff and they gave me their full support, as did Sid Bell, who taught plastering. Some of the others, including Fred Hartley (carpentry and joinery), Fred Gettings (brickwork) were sceptical of my position for some time. Alan Marshall and Russell Grimshaw who were on the lecturer Grade 2 scale were generally supportive.

The principal agreed that I should attend the Heads of Department courses at the Staff College at Coombe Lodge, Blagdon (near Bristol) and I did enjoy the four one-week sessions held over two years. I carried forward my involvement with City and Guilds FTC examinations and maintained an interest in the Construction Technicians course. Heads of department were expected to undertake a certain amount of teaching and I did six hours per week of maths teaching on the ONC and G courses. Wesley Gale, my predecessor, did some part-time teaching and I was able to have confidential chats with him about the various personalities in the department. One feature of the College was the lack of staff turnover as most staff, once appointed, stayed in post for the rest of their teaching careers. Whilst this gave stability it also meant that innovation was not welcomed and I had numerous attempts of trying to improve the quality of the educational experience of the students with opposition from some of the staff.

I had been surprised to observe that all craftwork was completed in workshops and that there was no history of undertaking projects in the community. I spoke to Norman Greenwood about this issue and he supported my view that some of the students' practical activities should reflect industrial practices and conditions. However, he did express his doubts that the staff would collaborate. I raised the issue at a departmental meeting and it was met by complete silence. The prospect of working outdoors during the winter months was something that they thought they had left behind years ago and that the warm workshops were much more inviting. After a tussle, I broke down the resistance and the department took on several small tasks within the local community before we ventured into two major projects. The first project was to construct a full-sized bungalow on the tennis courts. (The courts had not been used for years and the principal supported my request despite objections from some of the other heads.) I was keen to incorporate the latest innovations in building practice and, in consultation with John Greenwood's science teachers, it was agreed to install solar panels to heat the hot water supply of the bungalow. This gave the construction students useful experience and the science students were able to monitor the effectiveness of the panels in heating the water. Again, I experienced some scepticism, but even those staff members were impressed by the quantity of hot water achieved so far north. The bungalow attracted a lot of attention in the locality and when it was completed, the *Evening Gazette* sent a reporter to cover the story.

The other project involved work on a swimming pool that was to be constructed for pupils at the local Special Educational Needs School in Kirkleatham. The head teacher was a friend of the Principal and also a member of Redcar Rotary Club that was raising money for the project. Sid Bell carried out the bulk of the work with his link course students. They tiled the pool and plastered some of the walls. Towards the end of my time at Cleveland College, we obtained an agreement to build a large construction workshop on the tennis courts that would accommodate full-sized projects. The local authority provided the funds for the structural framework and the department's staff and students built the external and internal structures.

Just before Veronica and I arrived at Redcar, the government had implemented ROSLA (Raising of the School Leaving Age) requiring pupils to remain at school until the age of sixteen. Previously, a high proportion of youngsters left school at fifteen to mainly enter employment or to attend local colleges. When I arrived at the College, the department had well established link courses for the

1. My parents' wedding October 1936

2. Middlesbrough Dr Barnardos Home evacuated to Ripley Castle 1943. Mother on right in nurses uniform, father back left, Peter left on second row, Christine sitting on knee of girl in front row

3. *Hugh Bell School play 1952, 'The Admirable Crichton'. Playing Lord Loam with his three daughters*

4. *Mons Officer Cadet School, June 1959. Second row, fourth from the right*

5. *After the Officer Commissioning Parade with mother, October 1959*

6. *Holiday Fellowship Marske Centre 1962. Middle of the front seated row with Dylis Powell on my right*

7. *Huddersfield Technical Teacher Training College 1962. Group of first floor resident students in Holly Bank*

8. *Huddersfield TTC 1993. Alex MacLennon addresses the students at the end of year concert*

9. *Eppleton Cricket Club 2nd IX 1965. (2nd from left on back row)*

10. *Huddersfield College of Education (Technical) 1965. With my first group of General Building students*

11. *Wedding 1972*

12. *Presentation of Territorial Decoration 1978*

13. *Darlington College of Technology 1990. Presentation of the National Examining Board for Supervisory Management Award by secretary Lionel Baxter with Michael Fallon MP*

14. *Margaret Bell performs the official opening ceremony of the Open Access Computing Centre with chairman Geoff Nichol 1994*

15. *Kostroma visit with Kevin Frame in discussion with Rector*

16. *Visit to Poznan University of Technology with Gary Groom 2000*

fifteen year olds, with the collaboration of the local schools. Many of those who became employed attended a college on a part-time basis. ROSLA meant that schools had to provide facilities and staff to cope with the additional year group whilst colleges had to reflect on the impact of losing courses such as the popular pre-apprenticeship opportunities. Veronica had gained a teaching post at Bydales School in Marske-by-the Sea and her classroom was based in the newly constructed ROSLA building that overlooked the sea.

I had been involved with the Annual Heads of Construction Conference at Huddersfield for several years and I attended my first conference as a head in June 1973. I was co-opted onto the planning group where I was to remain for the next fifteen years.

Vocational courses in colleges had to be approved by the regional council for further and higher education. These bodies comprised all of the local educational authorities in the region and they had the responsibility for ensuring that adequate provision was available throughout the region. When Cleveland Technical College was within North Yorkshire LEA, it was part of the Yorkshire and Humberside Council for Further Education and, if the College had the support of the LEA, it was almost certain to have gained regional approval. However, Cleveland LEA was part of the Northern Council for Further Education (NCFE) and traditionally County Durham and Newcastle LEAs had a controlling grip on course approvals that inevitably favoured Newcastle College and New College Durham. As a head of department, I was invited to join the Construction Committee of NCFE, which was a useful forum for meeting other heads. However, the committee chairman was the principal of Sunderland College, an unpleasant person, whose every sentence was liberally punctuated with expletives.

My new situation also brought me into contact with some of the national organisations that dealt with further education. The National Association of Teachers in Further and Higher Education (NATFHE) represented teachers and managers on the Burnham committee nationally and negotiated individual cases locally with LEAs. I had joined NATFHE as a lecturer at Newcastle and had continued my membership during my years at Huddersfield, despite the fact that NATFHE did not have a major negotiating position in teacher education. At that time managers as well as teachers were members of NATFHE that reflected the role of the LEA as the employer. Principals and other senior managers were enthusiastic members and many were elected to local or national posts with the union. Indeed, during my last two years at Redcar I was chairman of the College NATFHE branch and had to arbitrate between staff grievances against the principal – an interesting experience!

Veronica and I moved into our new home in Leyland Road, Skelton in the spring and we soon made local friends, which included Mavis and Guy Stephenson who had a farm on the west of the village. Guy farmed the field at the back of our house and we saw him regularly during the sowing and harvesting seasons. Mavis was the chairman of Skelton WI and recruited Veronica, who soon became secretary. Veronica commenced her teaching duties at Bydales School at Marske, which was conveniently on my route to the College. I was able to resume my membership of Middlesbrough Cricket Club and started playing in April 1973. I also found it easier to fit in games for Stainsby Old Boys during the week.

In 1973, the new academic year commenced on 1 September and staff members were expected to report for duty on the first Monday of the month. Teaching usually started in the third week, allowing time for enrolment and timetabling of classes. Being my first full year at Cleveland College, I had to adjust to this hectic process of trying to ensure a smooth start for the students, whilst handling so many variables. The uncertainty associated with the enrolment process with a probability that our best guesses would be wrong meant that it was essential to have a pool of good part-time teachers available to cover unexpected growth. The other challenge was matching rooms, workshops and laboratories to student groups to ensure appropriate learning accommodation. During the 1960s further education had experienced a rapid expansion in students and also a major investment in additional accommodation. The 1970s signalled a slowing down in the resources made available by national government to LEAs and the term 'within existing resources' became the norm when bidding for expansion.

Enrolment started during the first week and the inefficiency of the system was very apparent. There were a few peak times when the enrolment teams were kept very busy handling eager youngsters, but more often staff outnumbered students. The Building Department had a regular contract with the Construction Industry Training Board (CITB) for brickwork and carpentry and joinery students. In addition, Wimpey, a large local construction company, recruited sufficient trainees to form at least one group in each of these trades. The company had its own training centre in Middlesbrough and recruited across the Cleveland area. Therefore, the number of students allocated to Cleveland College reflected their home address and on some occasions there were two or more groups. The CITB provided a solid core of work for the department and many local employers took advantage of the CITB training schemes. The advantage to the College was that the courses covered two years and led to the Craft Certificate and many students chose to proceed for a further year to complete their Advanced Craft Certificate. Relationships with the local CITB officer had to be good and I did enjoy working with Barry Chapman who was always willing to find a compromise if a problem arose. The CITB also supported a Building Employers Group in Redcar and I was invited to join the group and give regular reports on college progress. Arthur Whatley was the director of the group and I established a good rapport with him.

Cleveland local education authority had slight variations in its implementation of the Burnham report as compared with Newcastle when I was teaching there. An assistant lecturer's contract was twenty-two hours of class contact per week compared with twenty-four in Newcastle. Unlike present day practice, as all full-time students were timetabled for thirty hours per week, the classrooms and workshops were heavily utilised and staff establishment was based upon the teaching load. The CITB courses often required up to thirty-five hours per week of staff time. Like all colleges, Cleveland had to rely heavily on part-time teachers to cover a proportion of the classes and I had little difficulty in filling vacancies as at that time the hourly rate for teaching was much higher than rates for local craftsmen in the building industry.

During that year, Huddersfield College of Education (Technical) approached the principal to request him to second me to act as an advisor for a project in India. They also asked if he had suitable staff in mechanical engineering and in electrical engineering to participate in the project. Robbie came to see me with Ken Brown, Huddersfield's international tutor, to outline the proposal and I expressed an interest, subject to considering Veronica's views. Robbie had approached Andy White but he was not interested and he had suggested that Colin Browning, his senior lecturer, might be willing to go. The outcome was that Colin and I were offered a contract with a planned start date for summer 1974. We had briefings in London by TETOC (Technical Education and Training in Overseas Countries), which was part of the British Council. Huddersfield had several contracts with TETOC for projects in India and Colin and I were to be attached to the Technical Teacher Training Institute (TTTI) in Bhopal. We were advised on clothing, injections, travel and local customs. Mike McAllister, my former colleague from Huddersfield, was already associated with Bhopal and he provided a first-hand account of Bhopal TTTI. Our task was to advise the departments of civil engineering and mechanical engineering on teaching methodology. The Institute was housed in the local polytechnic but a new building was under construction for the Institute and it was expected to be ready for occupation by the time we arrived. It was agreed that we would travel in August and return in November, spending a total of twelve weeks in India.

The Indian consultancy dates clashed with my AER annual training so I notified headquarters and they offered me two weeks in Cyprus in June. Principal Robinson was sympathetic to my request to take two weeks' leave, so I accepted the offer and flew with a group of AER soldiers on an RAF VC10 to Akrotiri, the British-based airport on the island. I had not been aware of the political situation in Cyprus with President Makarios being out of favour with the Greek generals that had taken control of Greece in late 1973. The EOKA terrorists in Cyprus had been banned by Makarios and on our arrival there was tension in the British Army base in Dhekelia. Our first week of military training passed without incident and the soldiers enjoyed the good weather and local nightlife. Towards the end of the second week a six-hour map reading exercise was planned in the local countryside with clear guidelines to stay within areas controlled by the British Army. We were divided into three teams of six: I led one group, the platoon sergeant led the second and a corporal led the third. My group returned with almost an hour to spare and the corporal brought his team in within the time limit. However, there was no sign of the third group after six hours. When a further hour elapsed the regular officers in charge of the exercise became worried and sent out a detachment of regular soldiers to investigate. The missing team was discovered well outside the proscribed area and had ventured into known EOKA territory and it was only by good fortune that they had not been captured.

Leaving my post in Redcar so soon after joining the staff meant that I had to hand over responsibilities for the department to Norman Greenwood, but I was confident that he would do a good job. Veronica and Colin's wife, Tara, took us to Teesside Airport where we caught a flight to Heathrow. We had excess baggage owing to all the materials that we needed to support our three months' consultancy The flight lasted eighteen hours, arriving in Bombay where we experienced overpowering temperatures and a high humidity. We were met at the terminal by British Council officials and taken in one of their cars to the Agrawal Hotel in the city. This was to be our base for several days, partly to allow time for us to acclimatise, but also to receive local briefings from the British Council advisors. The hotel was comfortable and the food was excellent. We were given a tour of the city and introduced to various British nationals who lived in Bombay. Our main contact was the science adviser, Julian Schneider, who was extremely helpful. We were due to fly to Bhopal after four days in Bombay, but a strike by India Air delayed our departure for a day whilst a booking was made on the railways. We had no experience of Indian trains but I had read about them and was feeling a bit apprehensive. Julian assured us that we were booked into a first class sleeping compartment with air conditioning. (We learned later that there was first class without air conditioning.) The eighteen-hour journey was reasonably comfortable with a most polite attendant to look after our needs. The train travelled at a modest pace, stopping regularly at overcrowded and noisy stations. There were only slits at the windows to allow us to see the passing countryside so we did not see very much of the rural parts that we passed through during the journey.

Arriving at about six o'clock in the morning we were greeted by a welcoming party from the Institute, and to my amazement, it included Mike McAllister, who had just called in on his way to another assignment. We travelled into Bhopal and were shown to our accommodation on the first floor of a modern two-storey house, where Mike had already booked in for two nights. This was the accommodation for official visitors and it was to a good standard, with air conditioning. We were given time to bathe, shave and change our clothing before travelling to the Institute, which to our surprise, was still based in the polytechnic.

History of Bhopal

Bhopal, the capital of Madhya Pradesh, was built on the site of the eleventh century City of Bhopal, founded by the Parmara King Bhoj (1000–1055). The city was originally known as Bhojpal, named after Bhoj and the dam that he is said to have constructed to form the lakes surrounding Bhopal. The present city of Bhopal was founded by one of Emperor Aurangzeb's Afghan soldiers Dost Mohammed Khan, who took advantage of the chaos that followed Aurangzeb's death in 1707 and managed to establish his small kingdom in Bhopal. Although the kingdom was small, it survived several wars and became a princely state in British India in 1818.

Bhopal reached its height of culture, arts and public works under the enlightened rule of the Begums, a nineteenth century dynasty of Muslim women. Although not officially recognised as a Begum, Mamola Bai (1744–95) ruled for fifty years from 'behind the curtain' (purdah) on behalf of her late husband's ineffective sons.

The accepted rule of the Begums dates from the accession of the eighteen year-old Qudsia Begum (1819–37), who seized control after the assassination of her husband. Although she was illiterate, she was brave and refused to follow the purdah tradition. She declared that her two year-old daughter Sikander would follow her as the ruler of Bhopal, and none of the male family members dared challenge her decision. She was legendary for the care that she took of her subjects, eating her meals only after receiving the news every night that all her subjects had taken meals. She also invested in public works, building the Jama Masjid of Bhopal and a beautiful palace, the Gohar Mahal, Qudsia. She carefully prepared her daughter Sikandar to rule, laying the foundations for what would become Bhopal's golden age.

In 1844, Sikander Begum (1844–68) rose to power. Her name, which means 'Alexander the Great' in Arabic, proved prophetic in its description of her physical power and courage. Sikander was trained in the martial arts, fought in many battles, and never observed the purdah. During the Indian rebellion of 1857, she sided with the British and crushed those who revolted against them. However, Sikander was also an enlightened modernist and a reformer, presiding over administrative, social and educational reform that made Bhopal a haven for scholarship and culture and a centre for building, arts and crafts.

Her successor, Shah Jahan Begum (1868–1901), proved a marked contrast to her powerful mother but she still left a considerable mark in architecture, music, poetry and the arts. In fact, like her Mughal namesake emperor Shah Jahan, she bore a particular passion for architecture, and invested heavily in a series of elaborate public works that beautified the city. Sultan Jahan Begum, daughter of Shah Jahan Begum, succeeded her in 1901, ruling until the succession of her son (and the end of the Begums) in 1926. She further advanced the emancipation of women and established a modern municipal system. She had her own palace Sardar Manzil, but she preferred the quiet and serene environment at the outskirts of the city. She developed her own walled mini-city, named Ahmedabad after her late husband. Sultan Jahan combined Muslim piety with ardent reform and became an international figure as first president of the All India Conference on Education and first chancellor of the Muslim University of Aligarh. The peaceful rule of Begums led to the rise of a unique mixed culture in Bhopal. The Hindus were given important administrative positions in the state. This led to communal peace and a cosmopolitan culture took its roots. Even the Pathans, famous for their roughness and soldier-like nature, acquired a taste of culture and indulged in poetry, arts and literature.

Today, Bhopal remains a city of considerable beauty. The two lakes of Bhopal still dominate the city; bordered along their shores is the old city with its marketplaces, magnificent mosques and palaces, and the new city with its verdant parks and gardens, broad avenues and streamlined modern buildings. Bhopal is located in the central part of India, just north of the upper limit of the Vindhya mountain ranges. Bhopal is a hilly (elevation 498m) but hot area, located on the Malwa plateau, higher than the north Indian plains and the land rises towards the Vindhya Range to the south.

The population consisted of fifty-six per cent Hindus and thirty-eight per cent Muslims, with the rest of the population including Christians, Sikhs, Jains, and, Buddhists. The chief languages are Hindi, Urdu and English, but there were a substantial number of Marathi speakers as well. Bhopal is divided into two parts: the Old City and the New Bhopal. The Old City (often referred to in Bhopal as just 'City') is the city built and developed by the Begums of Bhopal. The Cantt, the airport and Bairagarh are where the army and the air force have a strong presence.

Bhopal Technical Teacher Training Institute (TTTI)

India's four regional Technical Teachers' Training Institutes were established in the mid sixties, first at Calcutta and Madras and then at Bhopal and Chandigarh (Eastern, Southern, Western and Northern regions of India) by the Ministry of Education & Culture (now renamed as Ministry of Human Resource Development), Govt. of India, for quality improvement of technical education in general and technician education in particular.

The collaboration with the TTTIs and the UK began in 1971–72 and was to last until 1984. It involved faculty development through long-term projects in areas like: curriculum development, teacher training, educational management, laboratory instruction, educational evaluation, and instructional material development. Huddersfield College of Education (Technical) was the primary UK partner institution during this period and its staff had been involved in all of the TTTIs. At the time of our visit in 1974, the TTTI was based in the polytechnic buildings that were quite unsuitable for training further education teachers. The buildings and facilities were primitive and there was no air-conditioning, making working conditions difficult during the long hot season. The power supply was unreliable and meant that presentations that required electricity to support up-to-date technology were often disrupted. A new building was being constructed at Shimla Hills but it was significantly behind schedule. On our first visit to the site I was dismayed to see that so little progress had been made. It was encased in bamboo scaffolding poles and only the basic structure was in place. It was apparent that we would not be occupying the building during our three months in Bhopal.

On that first morning Colin and I were introduced to Director Saran, who gave us a welcome to the Institute and outlined a short history before sharing his plans and aspirations for the future. At that time there were three faculties: civil engineering, mechanical engineering and electrical engineering. I was to support the civil engineering faculty and Colin would work with the mechanical engineering team. A specialist in electrical engineering had not yet been recruited and Saran expressed the hope that someone would arrive from the UK during our secondment. There was an education tutor from Middlesex Polytechnic already at the TTTI with a secondment for one year and he had brought his wife and family with him. We were introduced to the heads of the respective faculties and then they introduced the other members of the teams. We were soon made to feel very welcome and any thoughts that I had that our presence would be resented quickly disappeared. One or two of the TTTI staff had visited Huddersfield but that did not include the civil engineering staff members who all hoped to have an opportunity to visit the UK. English was the official language of the Institute and all lessons had to be delivered in English. This proved to be quite challenging for some of the students who normally conversed in their own language and would be teaching in that language when they returned to their institutions.

The Institute had a very small budget for teaching and learning materials and it was fortunate that Colin and I had brought vast supplies of pens, acetate sheets, duplicating paper and foolscap paper. The quality of the Indian paper was poor and reflected negatively on the teaching team when they were making their presentations. They were therefore delighted when we handed over most of the resources to them and only retained sufficient for our own purposes. I worked closely with the head of civil engineering who was very intelligent and quick to respond to my suggestions. He had suffered serious illness and still had problems with his eyesight but he led his team in a most professional manner.

There was a short period to prepare for the arrival of the students at the commencement of the academic year in September. I ran several workshops with small groups of staff and enjoyed their obvious enthusiasm to embrace what were new ideas to them. Having said that, I also learned much from working with them and so came to respect and admire their commitment and dedication. By the time the students arrived from various parts of India we had planned the whole year and prepared materials for the first term. Lesson plans had been produced and handouts and visual aids were pooled so that any member of the team could have access to them.

The students were all employed in colleges or polytechnics and were of a similar age range to those in-service students I had met at Huddersfield and the out-reach centres. Most of them were married with children and had made the sacrifice to leave them for a year with just two short breaks for vacations. The new TTTI building would have purpose-built residential accommodation but our students had to accept local accommodation that was of a lower standard. Their enthusiasm was encouraging and I did not see any evidence of the cynicism often observed amongst UK in-service students. Although my role was to advise and assist the staff, it took little persuasion to take some of the teaching sessions when pressed by the Bhopal staff, who all turned up to 'see how it should be done'. However, after the first two weeks, I made it clear that they must cover all classes and I would sit in with sessions at their invitation.

Director Saran was a dictator and expected his staff to work for six days per week. With the weather very hot and humid during the middle hours of the day, I thought it would be sensible to have an early start at say, 7 a.m. and take a break between 11 a.m. and 2 p.m., finishing at 6 p.m. However, the staff seemed quite happy to start at 9 a.m. and work until 5 p.m. with an hour for lunch. It seemed to me that they believed that what was good in the UK was right for Bhopal. On Saturday afternoon, Saran would appear at 4.30 p.m. to ensure that none of the staff left early. He was proud of his three 'English Consultants' and on several occasions we were expected to travel at weekends to one of the neighbouring polytechnics where we were shown off by Saran.

Mike McAllister had warned us to be very careful about eating and drinking and he had advised us to restrict ourselves to bananas and Coca Cola when away from our flat. At the flat we had been allocated a houseboy who was responsible for cooking and keeping the flat tidy. He also arranged for our laundry to be cleaned. He was a willing lad who proudly told us he was a Christian. We briefed him about his cooking, explaining that all water had to be boiled for five minutes before use to kill off the bacteria. He was told to bottle the water and place it in the refrigerator so that we had cool water when we came home. Unfortunately, we did not tell him to let the water cool before placing it in the refrigerator! On returning to the flat on the first evening we found that the refrigerator was struggling to cope as our boy had put the boiling water into the bottles and straight into the refrigerator. Meat was very suspect from the local market so we had decided to be vegetarians during our stay. We also were provided with a car and a Muslim driver who was available to us throughout our visit. He took us into the TTTI each day and brought us back in the evenings. He also took us on Saran's trips to the polytechnics.

We were invited to meals at the home of Saran and other senior staff members and we just had to risk the food rather than upset our hosts. The women of the house prepared the meals but we rarely met them, as in some families wives were not seen by visitors. A buffet banquet was the usual format so that people could converse and eat. The food was generally of a high standard and very tasty. I had developed my taste for Indian curry in the Army and therefore enjoyed the spicy dishes. Only once was I taken ill during one of these evenings and desperately needed to go to the toilet. I was directed by my host and to my horror on opening the door found the 'hole in the floor' loo, used by most Indians who learn to squat from an early age. Somehow I managed to cope but I was glad to get back to the flat later that evening with its familiar WC!

Colin and I had been introduced to Rabi Das Gupta by Mike McAllister Rabi was the deputy director for education for the State of Madhya Pradesh and he lived in Bhopal. This was a most fortuitous introduction as he would become a very good friend and a 'Mr Fix it' for the rest of our stay in Bhopal. We were invited to Rabi's home for dinner and met his wife and son. She was a lecturer at the university and did not share the view that a wife should not be seen. Rabi enquired if we had visited much of the country and when we said that there had not been any opportunities because of the six-day working week, he offered to arrange some visits for us. He proposed that we could visit local sites using our driver on Sundays and he would be pleased to go with us. For the more distant places, he proposed that we travelled by rail overnight on Saturday, toured on Sunday then a late train back on Sunday evening. This sounded too good to be true, but the following Saturday, Rabi provided a conducted tour of Bhopal to visit the temples, mosques and museums. Over the weeks we had many visits, including the Bhopal lakes, and spent a most enjoyable day at Jabulpur, Rabi's hometown. His wife and young son accompanied us on the visit that included a boat trip along the river to the Marble Rocks.

The most ambitious trip was to Agra. Rabi proposed that we travel on the overnight sleeper to Agra and that he would arrange for us to visit the Taj Mahal. He was acquainted with the Imam of the Taj Mahal and agreed to send a telegram to inform him of our visit. The train journey passed quietly and we arrived at Agra station about 5.30 a.m. It was a short walk to the Taj Mahal and we arrived at the home of the Imam about 6 a.m. Rabi's knock on the door was not immediately answered, but eventually a sleepy-eyed cleric opened the door in his night attire and was very surprised to see us. Apparently, the telegram had not arrived (not unusual in India at that time), but we were ushered into the Imam's home whilst he left us to dress. He proved to be a charming man and a delightful host. He lived adjacent to the Taj Mahal, so we had our first sighting at dawn as the sun rose to reveal the spectacular vision. Majesty and magnificence, unrivalled, the Taj Mahal is the only one of its kind across the world – the monumental labour of love of a great ruler for his beloved queen. The construction of this marble masterpiece is credited to the Mughal emperor Shah Jahan who erected this mausoleum in memory of his wife, Arjumand Bano Begum, popularly known as Mumtaz Mahal, who died in 1630. Her last wish to her husband was 'to build a tomb in her memory such as the world had never seen before'. From 1631, it took twenty-two years in the making. An estimated twenty thousand people worked to complete the mausoleum on the banks of the Yamuna. The central dome is 187 feet high at the centre. Red sandstone was brought from Fatehpur Sikri, jasper from Punjab, jade and crystal from China, turquoise from Tibet, lapis lazuli and sapphire from Sri Lanka, coal and cornelian from Arabia and diamonds from Panna. In all twenty-eight kinds of rare, semi precious and precious stones were used for inlay work in the Taj Mahal. The chief building material, the white marble, was brought from the quarries of Makrana and the districts of Nagaur and Rajasthan.

Our host gave us a comprehensive tour of the buildings and we certainly saw far more than a normal tourist would have seen. The next stop was Agra Fort where he recited the history of Agra and the

Mogul Empire. He recommended that we should visit the abandoned city of Fatehpur Sikri and then return to Agra to see the sun setting on the Taj Mahal before boarding the train. He took us to a government approved jeweller's shop in Agra where he instructed the proprietor that his guests had to be treated well and given a good price for any products that we may purchase. He then left, having spent most of the morning guiding us around the amazing sites. Colin and I were impressed by the quality of the craftsmanship and the reasonable prices of the items in the shop. I was particularly attracted to a necklace, the only drawback was that the main stone was a ruby surrounded by diamonds and I knew that Veronica would prefer a sapphire. I mention this to the jeweller, who said that he could reset the necklace with a sapphire within two hours and I accepted his suggestion.

We then set off to Fatehpur Sikri, which was a royal city that is perfectly preserved. Akbar embarked on the construction of a new capital here when a prophecy of the birth of a male royal heir, by the Sufi Saint Salim Chisti of Sikri, came true. Imposing gateways and palaces were built in red sandstone within this fortified city only to be abandoned a few years later. Among its many architectural gems are the places for his queens − Jodha Bai, Mariyam and his Turkish sultana, built in varying styles, each perfect in itself. The Diwan-e-Khas is a tall vaulted room with an intricately carved central pillar and capital supporting a platform that once held the emperor's throne. Narrow galleries link this to the corners of the room where it is believed his ministers sat. The airy Panch Mahal is a five-storied structure, which rises in pyramidal fashion and was probably used by the ladies of the court. Set like a jewel in a courtyard of pink sandstone is the finest building, the marble tomb of Salim Chisti, enclosed by finely carved, lacy marble screens. The Buland Darwaza is an imposing gateway fifty-four metres high.

On returning to Agra, I called into the jeweller's shop and was presented with the necklace, now with a sapphire instead of a ruby − it looked spectacular and I hoped that Veronica would be similarly impressed. The light was fading so we dashed to the Taj Mahal to see the sunset and we were not disappointed. The colours of the structure were completely different to the early morning tones and even more breathtaking. It was a dash to the station to catch the overnight train to Bhopal, arriving in sufficient time to shower and shave before the start of another day at the TTTI.

With the long working week in hot, humid conditions and sight seeing Sundays this hectic life style required a lot of stamina. The British Council officers must have been sensitive to the situation as after six weeks in Bhopal, we were invited to take a short break in Bombay at the Agrawal Hotel. The Air India strike was over, so we flew to Bombay instead of the dreary train journey. Those days of relaxation with air conditioning and good food helped to recharge the batteries and equip us for the last five weeks of our secondment. Julian offered to take us to lunch in the Taj Mahal Hotel, the finest and most expensive in the city. However, he did warn us that the British Council hospitality fund could only afford sandwiches. We were delighted to accept the invitation just to sample to opulence of the surroundings and to note that the majority of the guests were Indians.

British Council had promised to arrange a trip to Goa, the seaside resort on the south west coast, but Saran was not keen to release us for any more time. It was a bit of a disappointment as we had probably done as much as we could to bring the TTTI teams up to speed with their programmes. Indeed, in some respects, we gained as much professionally from our Indian colleagues as they did from us. The rest of our time continued at a similar pace. We visited Gwalier Fort, which is situated at Gopachal, nearly one hundred metres above the town of Gwalier. The walls, which encircle the fort, are solid and nearly ten metres high. In places the cliff overhangs and elsewhere it has been clipped to make it steep and hence unscalable. It earned the reputation of being North and Central India's most impregnable fort. Babur described the fort as, 'The pearl amongst fortresses in India'. We also visited Indore, which is the largest city in Madhya Pradesh state. Rabi, knowing of my passion for cricket, arranged a visit to a monument in the form of a huge cricket bat called Vijay Balla, made out of concrete with names of the players of the Indian team who won the 1971 series against Gary Sobers' West Indies team.

As the consultancy was coming to an end we were entertained to several parties and on departure from Bhopal airport we were garlanded and presented with several gifts. It had been an enjoyable experience, expanding our knowledge considerably and making many new friends. The flight took us to New Delhi, where we were met by British Council officers and transferred to a good city centre hotel. I think this short break had been arranged as a consolation for not visiting Goa and also to aid our transfer back into more civilised society. There were visits to see the various tourist attractions, but by then we were ready to return home to our families and friends and so ended an eventful chapter in our lives. I had lost two stone in weight and Veronica was quite shocked when she saw me. Although I had hospital treatment in India on two occasions for stomach upsets, I was able to quickly resume my duties and responsibilities at the College. Not so for Colin, who was very ill for several weeks and unable to return to work.

Cleveland Technical College 1975–77

Nationally the nature and provision of education and training was undergoing a major structural change. The Report of the Haselgrave Committee of Inquiry into Technical Education had recommended the creation of the Technician Education Council (TEC) and the Business Education Council (BEC) to take over the organisation for national certificate and diploma qualifications. These two organisations became operational in 1974 and colleges had to respond quickly to the changes in curriculum content and assessment methods. My department was only concerned with TEC qualifications in building but other departments in the College had to deal with BEC qualifications.

As I had anticipated, Norman Greenwood had carried out the plans for the new session meticulously and he had introduced the changes that had been agreed at the end of my first year. Student numbers had remained steady with solid support from CITB and Wimpey's Training Centre. A proportion of our students travelled from as far afield as Whitby and many lived in remote parts of the North Yorkshire moors. This meant that those who lived in the North Yorkshire local authority area had to seek permission to cross the border as Cleveland local authority could claim recoupment from the host authority for the full costs of the courses. As the nearest North Yorkshire college was at York, there was usually no difficulty with obtaining approval. However, we soon began to experience resistance from North Yorkshire for the Whitby students who were being told to attend courses at Scarborough College. The issue of recoupment was national and led to disputes in many parts of the country, especially in more urban areas where there was more competition between colleges.

Together with the recoupment issue there were accusations of 'poaching' of students that was also an issue for the other heads at Redcar. They regularly accused Longland College in Middlesbrough of approaching students who had been enrolled with attractive offers. The colleges were only eight miles apart and a dual carriageway linked the two towns. The main residential areas were approximately mid-way between the colleges so that competition was inevitable. The local education authority officers held meetings with the College principals to try to get agreement of catchment areas, but with little effect. So the LEA proposed to rationalise provision across the four towns of Redcar, Middlesbrough, Stockton and Hartlepool as each local college offered similar courses to the others. The debate centred around the river Tees, with a proposal that specific courses should only be offered in one college in the north and one in the south. Whilst this was agreed in principle, the detail led to a furious debate. Inevitably, colleges would lose courses and staff members would either be made redundant or would have to move to the College selected to undertake the specialism. For construction courses south of the river, a decision had to be made to make Redcar or Middlesbrough the centre. Both colleges had craft and technician courses although Redcar had the CITB approvals and more craft students. However, Longlands College, had stronger technician programmes and had the exclusive specialism of structural engineering. When the debate began it was apparent that Longlands was the strong favourite to become the construction centre which would mean that my job would disappear and my team would be transferred to Middlesbrough. But as the local authority officers extended their investigation to employers and the CITB, Redcar case became stronger and eventually I was called to the education offices and invited to become head of a joint Department of Construction based in the two colleges with the object of transferring the Longlands equipment and staff to Redcar over a two year period. Structural Engineering stayed at Longlands and the head of department retained his status.

I held meetings with the Longlands craft teachers to discuss the decision and, with the assistance of Norman, got their backing. It was a lukewarm response initially, but when they observed the better resouces at Redcar, they became more enthusiastic. Two of the older members of staff who could have been very difficult were offered either early retirement or a responsible position at Redcar. The additional student numbers raised the new department into a higher grade. That was some recognition of the increased workload that I had to undertake and I had to work more closely with CITB and the local employers in the expanded area of South Cleveland. I had several key employers on the Departmental Advisory Committee and the chairman, Harry Peacock, was a member of the College governing body and highly respected in the construction industry. It seems that Harry and the regional director of CITB had strongly supported Redcar's case to be the construction centre and I was grateful for their support.

Veronica and I were expecting our first child in July 1975 and our respective parents were very excited in becoming grandparents for the first time. We had an Easter holiday in Tunisia and enjoyed a relaxing time in the warm climate. I continued playing cricket with Middlesbrough Second Eleven and enjoyed a good season, missing only one game to attend the Annual Reunion at Huddersfield. I also continued with the Reserve Army with weekends running instructor training at Huddersfield and a summer camp at Deepcut running courses for NCOs. I had given up refereeing just before leaving Huddersfield as the requirements from the various league secretaries had become too demanding.

Our GP in Skelton had arranged for the baby to be delivered in the local cottage hospital, but as the summer began, Veronica started to experience high blood pressure and it was decided that the maternity hospital in Middlesbrough would be more appropriate. This proved to be the case as the baby had to have an assisted birth. This proved traumatic for our baby boy, Andrew, and he was transferred to intensive care for several weeks before we were allowed to take him home to Skelton. He had been born on 29 July, our third wedding anniversary, and he soon began to flourish and grow strongly. Andrew's blond hair and good looks gained him a lot of attention and his photo appeared in the local paper after a reporter had attended the Skelton WI Summer Fair. We had our first family holiday at a Ruswarp Hotel near the River Esk, a short distance from Whitby. Andrew had started to walk confidently and enjoyed the gentle walk from Ruswarp to Whitby. We were always welcomed at Forest Lodge in South Littleton and Veronica made several trips with Andrew to stay with Vera for short periods. I often stayed as well during holiday breaks.

During 1976 onwards, I became actively involved with NATFHE, not only as the Cleveland College Branch chairman but also on the Cleveland Committee and as the NATFHE representative on the Cleveland Manpower Services Commission (MSC). The other college representative was the principal of Kirby College in Middlesbrough. I had been invited to join the local CSE Moderating Committee and attended meetings in Sunderland and Newcastle. There were several meetings every year in London and the only way of getting to a morning meeting in the capital was to travel on the overnight sleeper from Darlington to King's Cross. Veronica would drive me to the Saltburn Station where I caught a local train to Darlington to change for the 2330 train that arrived into London about 0530. Passengers were allowed to stay in their sleeping compartments until 7 a.m. and then I walked into the Great Northern Hotel for a bath and breakfast before setting off for the meeting.

It was during a meeting with regional heads of building departments in 1977 that I overheard a conversation about an opportunity at Leeds College of Building. I knew the College principal Jack Place quite well as he had maintained a close link with Huddersfield through Jim Pratt and Eric Tuxworth. Apparently, Jack's vice principal, Sam Brown, had died unexpectedly and there was speculation on who would be in the running for the vacancy. At that time I had not considered moving from Redcar, but I did discuss with Veronica the possibility of applying for the post. I had developed an ambition to be a principal and the next move would be to obtain a deputy's post. With so few specialist building colleges in the country it seemed too good an opportunity to miss, so I submitted my application. I was delighted to be short-listed and invited to attend a two-day interview at the end of April. Jack met all the candidates and explained that the loss of Sam Brown had been a great shock to him and he had delayed seeking a replacement until the Leeds LEA had insisted that the post be filled. The first day was mainly visiting all parts of the College and its annex in Cross Green. The main college in North Street was quite new and had excellent facilities for the construction students. I rang Veronica that evening saying that I was very keen on obtaining the post, as everything seemed to be an improvement on the facilities at Redcar.

The chairman of governors was Stanley Deavin, who was also deputy chairman of the regional gas board. He chaired the interview panel and was supported by Jack, other members of the governors and Stuart Johnson, the director of education. The interviews were held in the boardroom of the College and Stanley gave me quite a grilling, but Jack and Stuart were more sympathetic and I felt that I had performed reasonable well. After all candidates had been interviewed, there was a relatively short delay before I was invited to return to the boardroom where Stanley offered me the post and I accepted it. Jack had asked me to wait and as soon as the panel had left, he invited me into his office. He seemed very pleased with the appointment and congratulated me on the interview. He said that Stanley found it difficult to believe that I had been involved in so many educational activities and had gained such a broad grasp of the FE sector. I found this rather curious, as I had always assumed that ambitious people would all be willing to involve themselves in a broad span of relevant interests associated with their profession. As it was customary to give a full term's notice, it had been agreed that I would commence my new post in September 1977 and Jack suggested that I could call in to see him during the preceding months. Veronica was pleased with my news and we realised that this would mean another move only four years after the last one. I met with Laurie Robinson the next morning and he seemed pleased for me and wished me well. Norman and the department staff called in and offered their congratulations, as did the other heads of department.

The summer term was a bit of a blur with so many issues to address. House hunting in Leeds and visits to the College of Building as well as a full programme of Cleveland College activities and regional meetings. I managed to fit in about fifteen cricket matches but did not achieve many decent scores and found myself playing a few games for the third team. I did not realise it at the time but this was to be my last season of competitive cricket, which had started twenty-five years earlier. Veronica and I had selected a house in Oakwood on the east side of Leeds, quite near to Roundhay Park. It was about three miles from the centre of the city and from the College with easy access to the A58 road towards the northeast. After a last minute hiccup with the sale of the Skelton property, the sales were completed and we were able to move to Leeds before the start of the academic year.

CHAPTER 6

Leeds College of Building
1977–82

I N 1977 THERE WERE STILL several local authorities that organised
their further education along monotechnic lines. Most of the larger
cities had several specialist colleges, including a building college. In
addition to Leeds, there were colleges of building in London
(Vauxhall and Brixton), Liverpool, Manchester, Birmingham, Nottingham, Sheffield (Shirecliffe) and Hertfordshire (St Albans). In
Scotland, Glasgow also had a college of building. However, over the
next ten years most of those authorities moved from a monotechnic
structure to single large institutions.

Leeds College of Building proved to be a revelation to me
compared to Redcar. Jack Place had been principal for twenty years,
originally appointed to be head of the Branch College of Building,
then the renamed college. He had presided over ancient school
buildings that had been adapted for vocational education and it had
been in recent years that funding had been made available to
demolish the old school buildings in North Street and replace them
with a purpose-built college. Jack had a practical building background
and Sam Brown had been an architect and their combined skills had
ensured that the consultant architects had produced an environment
that was very appropriate for modern construction vocational
education and training.

When I had first visited the College as a tutor at Huddersfield, I
had been impressed by the excellence of the facilities and most
construction heads of department envied them. The College was
built around the workshops. The brickwork and plastering areas were
located on the ground floor in a large open area with sufficient height
to construct a two-storey dwelling. Adjacent to this area were the
workshops for shop fitting, wood machining and carpentry and
joinery. Roof slating and tiling courses were adjacent and to the rear
and the mechanical engineering workshops for plumbing, gas fitting

99

and heating and ventilation were to the rear of the building. The first floor corridor overlooked the workshop area and provided excellent views of the craft activities. The library, classrooms and laboratories were on the first floor looking outwards. Also on the first floor was the management suite and boardroom. The boardroom overlooked North Street and the park beyond it. There was a sitting area outside the boardroom and the offices of the principal, vice-principal and their secretary were opposite the boardroom. The offices of the heads of department were accessed through a door from the seating area. On the top floor was located the refectory, the staff common room and more classrooms and laboratories. The whole building was compact yet had sufficient space to meet all of the educational needs of the students.

The other colleges in the city when I was appointed were Kitson College (Engineering), Park Lane College (Business Studies), Jacob Kramer College (Art and Design), Thomas Danby College (Catering), the College of Music, Leeds Athletic Institute, Joseph Priestley Institute and Wetherby Institute. The other college was Airedale and Wharfedale College in Pudsey, which had been part of West Yorkshire prior to local government reorganisation. Unlike the other colleges in the city it was multi-disciplined and offered engineering, business studies and other assorted courses. This inevitably led to disputes between colleges when the LEA was allocating resources. The principals were an interesting group that met frequently together to discuss matters of mutual interest. George Hume at Park Lane had been in post for as long as Jack but I found him to be quite cynical at times and his humour could be malicious. Jack Cooper of Kitson College was also an experienced principal and after an initial stiffness, I managed to develop a good working relationship with him. Dr Boffy at Thomas Danby was relatively new and did not have the drive or confidence of his more experienced peers. On the other hand, the newly appointed principal of Jacob Kramer, John Robb-Webb, was more relaxed and easy going. Joe Stones at the College of Music was a real character and a talented musician who was partial to a glass or two of good wine. Hugh Johnson at Airedale and Wharfedale was often on the defensive but I got on well with him. In my early days I did not see much of the principals from the three institutes and the LEA closed Wetherby and the Athletics institutes soon after my arrival. Graham Binks was the first principal that I met from Joseph Priestley.

Jack had four heads of department, three of whom had been with him for many years. Les Jacques was head of Building Services and I soon recognised that he was the person that Jack turned to for advice. Les was a gentle person who seemed to be liked and respected by everyone in the College and I often popped into his office for a friendly chat. Tom Priestley was responsible for Timber Trades and he had a very different personality to Les. He took everything very seriously and carried out his responsibilities meticulously but with little humour. (It was some years later I discovered that Tom had been seconded to Holly Bank for several years.) Harry Chell was responsible for Fabric Trades and he was a 'hail fellow, well met' kind of person who was popular with his staff but he often upset Jack. David Anderson was the fourth head and he had recently been appointed for General Building when Sam Brown became vice principal. Sam had originally held both posts until the College was told that the VP had not to be a dual post. David was as keen and enthusiastic as one expected from a new post holder and we soon established a good working relationship. There were sixty-seven teaching staff plus the tutor librarian and twenty-nine support staff led by registrar Mary Siddons. Jack was always referred to as Mr Place by all staff and some would insist on using 'sir'. I found this rather unnerving at first and soon persuaded the heads to call me Peter.

On my first morning of the autumn term, Jack called a full staff meeting in the lecture hall, which was off the main entrance hall of the College. The seating was tiered with a projection booth to the rear and a demonstration bench at the front. Jack assembled the heads of department at one side of the stage and I sat next to him near the centre. Jack gave a welcome to staff, including some new members. He made several comments about new developments and then introduced me and, without warning, invited me to address the assembled throng. I suppose I should have expected this but I had to furiously think of something appropriate to say to the expectant audience. Happily, I did know quite a few of the people from my days at Huddersfield and although I do not recall my comments, they were sympathetically received and Jack seemed pleased that his new protégé had not let him down.

During the first month I was introduced to most of the middle managers and many of the teaching and support staff. Jack and I regularly had our morning and afternoon breaks in the staff common room, rather than in our own offices. The staff appreciated this and we did not experience any unwanted canvassing from individuals. I met with officers and advisors of the LEA and soon started to appreciate that Leeds had a good team of professional officers that reflected well on Stuart Johnson, the CEO. Max George was the finance officer who dealt with colleges and he could not have been more helpful in providing support and guidance. Leeds had a system of assistant directors for each sector and over my time at Leeds we had several FE assistant directors who were first class in every respect. I recall David Wadsworth and David Cracknell who both progressed to a chief education officer post in other LEAs. Jim Heaton was the senior advisor for FE and John Burnill was his deputy. They were also good colleagues who gave colleges support whenever necessary.

Staff development was a high priority for the Leeds LEA and it had its own residential centre at Bramley Grange on the east side of the city. At the beginning of October I attended my first Bramley Grange residential programme, which was for new staff to the authority. This gave me an opportunity for contact with a full range of officers and a good introduction to the Leeds educational scene. Stuart Johnson opened proceedings and for the three days we were usefully engaged. The LEA had also submitted my name to attend a Department of Education and Science (DES) Senior Staff Programme for 16–19 Education that was aimed at people who had recently been appointed to schools and colleges in the region. The initial meeting was held in the second week in October and was mainly an induction to the programme to the next nine days spread over four months and ending in mid-January. It was my good fortune to acquire a place so soon after appointment as many of my fellow course members had been waiting for over a year. The programme comprised visits to higher education institutions, colleges and sixth form centres together with visiting speakers and discussion groups. It was a well-organised course and I found it most useful in making many new contacts in the region.

During October, I attended the Construction Heads Conference at Holly Bank and experienced my first meeting of the College governing body. At Redcar only the principal had attended governors' meetings but Jack had requested that I should attend at the College of Building meetings and this had been agree by the Board and the LEA. I had been vaguely aware of the DES 7/70 circular regarding College Governance but not sure of the detail. Jack had given me a copy and I noted that the DES recommended that the composition of governors should be one third from educational sources, one third from related industry sources and one third from the community that the College served. LEAs often used the first and third categories to appoint councillors and their nominees so that they could have a strong influence on the governors' decisions. This was certainly not the case in Leeds. The construction industry regarding LCB as its college and there was a strong presence of the ten regular attendees from all strands of the industry. The educational representatives comprised the head of civil engineering from Leeds Polytechnic, a University of Leeds nominee, a secondary teacher, the regional director of the CITB, four staff representatives and two students plus the principal. As Leeds LEA had the overall responsibility for the College, there were six councillors on the Board and the clerk to the governors was designated as the director of education. In practice, the assistant director for further education undertook the duties with a LEA administrator taking the minutes. At my first meeting I was co-opted onto the Board together with another industrialist. Stanley Deavin, the chairman of the governors, was a very experienced businessman and conducted the proceedings skilfully getting through the agenda in a democratic and purposeful manner.

That first term passed quickly and I also managed to fit in three Reserve Army weekends, two instructor training sessions at Huddersfield and a weekend at Stafford Hospital relating to my new RAOC Laundry and Bath Unit responsibilities. In November, I attended a Bramley Grange conference and a Construction Heads of Department Conference in London. I had maintained my commitment to CGLI and attended a Foundation Certificate in Construction meeting at Bolton College of Education (Technical) and a meeting of the G Course in Construction in London. Jack and I had developed a good relationship and we worked closely together on preparing budgets and strategic planning. He explained that each college had to produce an annual report for the Further Education Sub-Committee of the LEA and the chairman and principal of each college had the opportunity to present the report to a group of councillors and officers. The report for 1976–77 had been completed and Jack had briefed me on its contents prior to the meeting at the education offices. He had spoken to the chairman who had agreed that a request should be made that I be allowed to attend the meeting and the director had agreed. I was totally unaware that this was unheard of and there were rumblings from the other colleges but I attended and continued to attend over the next four years. I always suspected that the other principals were not keen to have their deputies present as they wished to keep them in the dark about certain issues.

In 1977 the Government created the Further Education Curriculum Review and Development Unit, later known as the Further Education Unit (FEU). The unit was established with broad terms of reference for reviewing provision, making recommendations to fill gaps, undertaking development activities and disseminating information. Geoffrey Melling was seconded by the HM Inspectorate to be the founding director for its first three years when Jack Mansell became its director. In its early days FEU was heavily involved in supporting Unified Vocational Preparation (UVP), a joint scheme of the Education and Employment Departments for giving education and training to young people in low-level work which traditionally did not offer those opportunities.

I was soon up to speed in the new year with another Bramley Grange residential conference. I had developed a good working relationship with John Tull, the director of Bramley Grange and this was the basis of many technology-based conferences over the coming years. The conference was immediately followed by a weekend of military training with the Stafford Field Hospital. It had been decided that my Laundry and Bath Unit would support the Field Hospital on an exercise in Sennelager, Germany, in July and it was necessary to develop good links with the TA military hospital staff to ensure a mutual understanding. The following weekend was also devoted to the AER, with a study period managed by headquarters staff and included a dinner night on the Saturday. Either side of that weekend, I had two CGLI meetings in London. One was my first meeting of the Specialist Subjects Committee and the second was the annual moderating committee of the Construction Supervisory Studies Committee. I had become the chairman of this committee having handed over the mathematics paper to my Leeds colleague, Ted Judkins. In February, I had my first meeting of the Leeds Technical Education in Schools Committee. Deputy director Chris Tipple chaired the committee and he always gave the impression of being a very enthusiastic overgrown schoolboy! Another first was a meeting of the College staff welfare committee that tried to address issues raised by the teaching and administrative staff. The staff unions were represented and invited to bring forward appropriate issues other than conditions of service or contractual issues. Jack dealt with most of these issues expertly and the meetings usually ended quite harmoniously with promises to address the issues.

Over the years, I had developed good links with various members of Her Majesty's Inspectorate (HMI). At Huddersfield it had initially been mathematics inspectors but later I worked with construction inspectors and also engineering and science inspectors who ran summer schools at Holly Bank. HMI had a responsibility to inspect colleges on a regular basis; this was achieved through full inspections that occurred occasionally and by the College inspector who usually developed a friendly relationship. In most cases this tended to be more advisory than inspectorial. Howard Wainwright had been the staff inspector for construction and on his retirement Peter Wilmore has taken over the top job. Just before my appointment at Leeds, the College had been subjected to a full inspection by HMI and I had arrived at a time when Peter Wilmore was presenting his report. It was customary for the Staff HMI to brief the principal in advance of the formal presentation to the College governors and Jack has requested my presence at the briefing. My previous experiences of Peter had always been cordial but on this occasion he showed a different side of his character and it was one of the very few times that I saw an angry Jack Place. I thought that most of the briefing reflected positively although it did include criticisms that clearly upset Jack. There was a sharp exchange of words and Wilmore made it very clear that Jack would have to accept the report, as its contents were non-negotiable. As I expected, the governors listened carefully to the presentation of the report and asked several questions, but it was quite clear that they had formed an opinion that the report was quite acceptable and fair. From my point of view having a fresh independent report, as a tool for my introduction to the College, was most useful.

I always had a healthy respect for HMI. After appointment they were carefully prepared for the job over a period of one year before being allowed to be an independent inspector linked to colleges and included as part of a full inspection team. This professional approach ensured a consistent application to the inspection process. They had much autonomy when carrying out their duties and could not be over-ruled by ministers or DES civil servants. Indeed, I was aware that some inspectors were often invited to prepare speeches for ministers on their specialist areas.

My AER instructor-training programme had attracted interest from RAOC CVHQ, which was the AER headquarters. My approach was so different from the rigid regular army training manuals that the senior officers felt it could be helpful to them to attend one of my programmes at Huddersfield. I suspected that at least two of them who were not too far from retirement thought that attending such a course would be useful to their futures. I was asked to provide a programme covering two weekends for a group of senior regular and AER officers. My team included Brian Gannon, who was also an RAOC TAVR captain and principal lecturer in staff development at Barnsley College and Keith Evans, who had been a senior warrant officer in REME and was running courses at the REME Training Centre in Bordon. Brian, Keith and I had been working together as a team for several years and our different approaches and experience produced very successful courses. The two weekends fell in February and the Colonel Commanding CVHQ and the TAVR commanding officer, Bob Manders, also decided to attend. I had warned Jim Pratt that I would have some 'top brass' attending and he took it upon himself to notify Ken Durrans, the rector of the polytechnic. By this time the College of Education was part of the polytechnic and Ken turned up on the Saturday evening and joined in the conviviality. Later, he had to be helped to his chauffeur driven car after trying to keep pace with the rate of drinking of the seasoned military tipplers! Everyone seemed to enjoy the weekends and my team received fulsome praise in the Commander's briefings later in the year. In April I had to join a reconnaissance group to Sennelager, Germany, in preparation for the army exercise in July. I had to travel to Brize Norton for the flight on Saturday morning and my group had less than a day to examine the vast area that we would be using. The field hospital expected to remain static once a suitable location had been agreed and my unit would be adjacent to it. I had some misgiving about that assumption as my experience had taught me to be prepared for any eventuality. The recce was completed and preferred areas were identified and we hoped for good weather in July.

The post-Easter holiday period was traditionally the time when the departments held their prize evenings. Each department had so many donated prizes from the construction industry that it was not thought practical to have a full college ceremony. The first prize giving for the year was for cleaning science students. Cleaning science was part of the Building Services Department but the students were all mature and mainly drawn from public sector staff in education and hospitals. It was a small but cosy evening with John Daniels, the course tutor, directing proceedings. The General Building Department held the next awards evening quickly followed by a joint event for the Fabric and Timber Departments. These were very well attended events and it was pleasing to see many parents, friends and governors present. I always believed that these events were excellent PR for the College but, more importantly, the students gained so much from this public recognition of their achievements.

After Easter I was invited to attend a Bramley Grange College Conference that debated the future of the Leeds LEA and its various institutions. This was an interesting day and various scenarios were aired and discussed. For a relatively new person in the LEA, I thought that this frankness was very refreshing and challenging. I suspect that some of the participants were seeking to expand their empires whilst others were fretting about their futures. At that time the Conservatives were the controlling party but their reign was to be short-lived.

Although I was no longer involved with League cricket it was pleasing to find that the College had an enthusiastic number of staff members who played friendly matches during the summer term. It was a pleasure to join the team on several occasions when college commitments permitted. Regardless of success on the pitch the College members joined the opposing teams in a convenient hostelry for liquid refreshments and convivial conversations.

I was surprised to receive an invitation to the retirement party at Redcar for principal Laurie Robinson. He had not given me any indication that he would be retiring early but when asked to say a few words, I was willing to respond. It was a pleasant evening with colleagues past and present wishing Robbie well. He made a relatively short speech and seemed a bit overcome by the occasion. He and his wife had decided to move to Scotland and they did so very soon after that evening. The following weekend was the Huddersfield FSA Reunion and many people mentioned Robbie, who had attended the first pre-service course in 1947. He had also been an external examiner for many years and he was very popular with the Huddersfield staff. The reunion usually marked the end of the academic year for teaching staff and therefore it was a time for relaxing and 'letting the hair down' (for those that had any hair left). I had to return to college for a two-day Bramley Grange staff development conference followed by a one-day safety course at Beckett's Park. The last two weeks were participating in the AER exercises in Sennelager with my Bath Unit supporting the field hospital.

1978–79

The autumn term commenced with the traditional enrolment week, welcoming new and returning students. This was always an extremely hectic period for the teaching staff that had only one week after enrolments to revise the pre-planning that tended to be either too optimistic or too pessimistic. Classrooms had been initially allocated on predicted enrolments, but as there were always swings and roundabouts with some departments doing well and others falling short of target; horse-trading had to take place to ensure all groups were accommodated before the first week. I had experienced the enrolment period as a lecturer and as a head of department but my role as a vice-principal was rather different. I found that it fell to me to arbitrate between the departments, who tried to retain the rooms that they regarded as 'theirs'. Section leaders were the worst offenders and they would insist that they were sure that they would reach or exceed their targets with late enrolments. In the good years, when demand was high, each morning and evening of the first week would present accommodation problems and all senior staff had to be on call to respond to any potential crises. The College of Building was very susceptible to the state of the national and local economy as the construction industry was regarded as a barometer of success or failure. I suspect that it was this volatility that was beyond the control of the College that had led to the establishment of a strong link course provision at the Cross Green annexe. These courses had replaced the former pre-apprenticeship courses that had been very popular but had faded with the raising of the school leaving age to sixteen.

The first LEA event of the year was held at the Queens Hotel in City Square where I attended a one-day Industry-Education Conference that had been organised by a group chaired by Chris Tipple. After the conference I had to drive to Deepcut for a long AER weekend to deliver an instructor training session. With a large LEA such as Leeds there were many local committees and I occasionally attended the Links Courses Committee that included head teachers, principals and advisers. There was a sensitive issue over funding and the LEA accepted that it would compensate the College for this work without transferring resources from the schools. October was a popular month for conferences and I attended a 16+ Counselling Conference and the annual Heads of Construction Conference at Huddersfield.

On Saturday 26 October 1978, the College provided facilities for groups of young people participating in the Duke of Edinburgh Awards Scheme. The grassed area in front of the College, the foyer and hall were all used to capacity to show the range of activities carried out in the scheme. The Duke of Edinburgh was making a personal appearance to meet students and present awards. Jack insisted that I should be in the group that welcomed HRH along with the director of education, scheme organisers and Jack as principal of the College. The Duke spoke to each person in the welcoming group in the main entrance before meeting the students in the hall, which was adjacent to the entrance. I was the last person to be presented and the Duke asked me about the College and after I had given him a quick response he expressed an interest in having a look at the workshops. His officials were alarmed as they would be working to a strict timetable, but HRH insisted and Jack and I took him to the first floor landing where he could look down on the various practical activities.

During all this activity, Veronica had taken Andrew down to South Littleton to stay with Vera during the half-term break. I travelled down on the Friday evening to pick them up and I was alarmed to see Andrew looking very pale and being carried. I expressed my concern to Veronica who said the boy had been off-colour during the week. On our return, we took him to our local GP, who immediately referred Andrew to hospital for tests. Before the day was out, we knew the worst: a virulent form of leukaemia had struck down Andrew, and his chances of survival were not good. We had an agonising week during which Andrew was given blood transfusions and had drugs pumped into him. He died on Saturday evening, leaving us distressed. I could not have received more support than that which was offered from the College and the LEA. Stuart Johnson invited me to his office to express his commiserations and asked if Veronica would be interested in returning to teaching, as there was a Home Economics post vacant at a school in Pudsey. Veronica applied for the post and was appointed to Crawshaw School, about ten miles from the city centre. This meant that we could both have a work commitment that would distract us from our sad loss.

The rest of the autumn term was a bit of a blur, with the usual round of national, regional and local meetings, including two AER instructor training weekends at Holly Bank. Veronica and I had a meeting at Seacroft Hospital with Dr Bailey who had supervised Andrew's treatment and we were given assurances that the chances of a similar illness, if we had any more children, were extremely unlikely. The Christmas break helped us to reflect on the future and Veronica's return to teaching.

January and February provided plenty of snowfalls to make travelling difficult and I had to make the journey to Pudsey to collect Veronica from school when all the buses had stopped running and driving was very tricky. Although the College prepared an end of year report for the local authority, it had not previously prepared development plans. In 1979 a plan was prepared for the governing body and was broadly welcomed by the members. The plan was used as a discussion paper at a residential teaching staff conference that was held at Trinity and All Saints College, Horsforth, in September, prior to enrolment week. The work of the College during the 1970s had been heavily influenced by new curriculum developments by the Technician Education Council (TEC) and City and Guilds. Also, the Construction Industry Training Board (CITB) directed building craft programme requirements and all these initiatives had demanded a fresh examination of teaching programmes, methods and techniques.

Later in the year, I had managed to renew my interest in computer technology to assist educational administration. The only computer at Cleveland Technical College had been a mainframe that had been donated to the College by ICI. Only one member of staff was allowed to use it and only for a limited period as the amount of electrical energy needed to power it caused a dimming of the lights in the College. Desktop computers started to appear on the market in 1977 with machines such as the Pet Commodore, Olivetti, Apple and Research Machines 380Z. My interest in computer aided administration (CAA), stemmed from contacts with Huddersfield staff that had been exploring timetabling possibilities. My financial work with Jack had helped me to identify two areas that I believed would benefit from computer support. The main areas were the manage-ment of the College budget and commitment accounting. At that time the LEA received hand written order forms from the College that were typed onto five-copy carbon-forms in City Hall before sending the original to the supplier, three to the College and retaining a copy centrally. At the College, a copy was sent to the department head and two were retained in the office. Heads maintained a manual account of the transactions, as did the general office. The second area that I identified was the method of dealing with part-time staff contracts and payments that was also a lengthy manual process involving the LEA, college administration and heads. I discussed the possibilities with Jack and he gave me his enthusiastic support to attempt to find a solution. At that time, the LEA finance officer who dealt with the College had an open mind on the issue, but asked to be kept informed of progress.

The College had purchased a 380Z but its storage capacity was too small for administrative purposes. I met one of the RM sales staff and she invited me to visit the Research Machines premises in Oxford where I had the opportunity of observing the manufacturing process and the new equipment that was being developed. Resulting from the visit, I requested the purchase of two 380Z computers with eight-inch disc drives; one machine for my use to develop the software and one machine to train the office staff. Thus began an exercise that would span more than eighteen months. I had to decide on a program language, as I did not believe that my experience with Fortran and Algol was compatible for the microcomputer. So, on advice, I settled for Basic as the most appropriate language. I had to fit in this development exercise within the constraints of my normal vice-principal's duties and the several committees to which I had been appointed. Some of the work was done at the College in the evenings but most was done at home, mainly at weekends. The robust nature of the 380Z helped to influence the decision on microcomputers for educational purposes and the College purchased several machines.

At that time I was the only senior manager in the Leeds further education service with any expertise in computing and I was persuaded by the other VPs to offer them some hands-on training and this eventually led to sessions for the principals. I often attended conferences at Bramley Grange and, if I was giving a presentation, I always tried to incorporate some computer technology instead of transparencies on an overhead projector. With the assistance of John Tull, I was able to link several computers together in the conference room so that all the members of the audience could see at least one of the screens that were showing the graphs and diagrams of the presentation. During 1979, a computer assisted administration group (CAA) was established at Huddersfield by some of my former colleagues and I was invited to join the group. My project was noted but it did not match with the other projects, which were mainly associated with student-based administration. This was not really surprising because all of the other members of the group were practitioners rather than senior managers.

Veronica had become pregnant and was expecting a baby in September. We decided that we needed to have a good holiday at Easter and I booked a trip to Tenerife to find some sun and fresh air. It was a good break, the only slight setback was that our trip to Mount Teide had to be cancelled because of Veronica's morning sickness. In the summer we spent some time at South Littleton with Vera and relaxed in the slower pace of Cotswold life. I had to fit in my Annual AER training that was held at CVHQ Headquarters in

Deepcut. Helen was born on 14 September 1979 and there was great rejoicing within the family and our colleagues were also very pleased and supportive. The term had already started and when Veronica was admitted to the maternity ward at St James' Hospital, I had to make regular visits with the support of Jack.

The College had experienced a good year and the growth in student numbers was reflected in the appointment of some additional staff. Jack chaired all teaching staff appointments and I was also included on the panel along with the head of department, representatives of the appropriate sections of the construction industry and one or two members of the governing body. More senior appointments involved the chairman of governors and LEA officers. Being a monotechnic college ensured that we attracted good candidates and deciding on the best candidate was often very challenging. When he chaired a panel, Jack allocated specific areas of questioning to each member of the panel and it was expected that each candidate would receive a very similar experience. Over the next two years, Jack had several major operations for bowel cancer and when he was away I was acting principal and had to chair several appointment panels. I recall the only occasion that I had a serious disagreement with a member of the governing body was when I was chairing a panel. One of the candidates was clearly weaker than the others but it had always been Jack's policy that each candidate was given their full quota of questions. When I invited the governor to ask his questions, he declined, saying that he did not have any questions. I was quite annoyed and made the point after the panel adjourned. The governor was quite surprised when I took issue with him and at the end of the year he resigned from the governing body.

1980–82

Throughout the year, I was involved in several Bramley Grange conferences, either as a conference member or organiser. I had been invited to join the YHAFHE Consortium meeting that was involved in teacher training and staff development for the region's colleges. Frank Barr was a key member of this group and I enjoyed the meetings. My City & Guilds commitments continued and I was now chairing two moderating committees: the 600 series Construction

Supervision and the G Course in Construction. They usually involved three meetings during January and February. The Leeds vice-principals had formed their own group and this had not been welcomed by some of the principals. I had spoken to Jack and he agreed that it would be useful for the VPs to meet and share views. He made the point to the other principals that as they met regularly he could see no reason why the deputies should not get together professionally. Stanley Deavin had been chairman of the College governing body for the last three years and that was the end of his term of office. I had developed a great respect for him and I had learned much from his skill at handling meetings. To mark his retirement from the governors, he invited Jack and I to lunch at the Old Swan Hotel in Harrogate and we had a very pleasant meal and expressed our thanks to Stanley for his time and commitment to the College.

In October, the Under Secretary of State for Further Education, Mr Roy Walker, visited the College on a fact-finding tour and his observations were very complimentary. The following day I was a guest at the annual dinner of the Institute of Building (Yorkshire Branch) held in the Merchant Taylor's Hall in York. It was a splendid evening with good food and good company in fine surroundings. I had been invited to join the Huddersfield Polytechnic Teaching Practice Assessors Panel and my first meeting was in November at Huddersfield. It was a pleasure to meet with former colleagues and to have an opportunity to observe the changes that had been introduced since I left Huddersfield in 1972. The panel members were drawn from colleges within the catchment area of the Polytechnic and they were mainly principals and vice-principals. I enjoyed several visits to local colleges accompanying one of the College tutors. The report back sessions in the following spring were usually managed professionally and grades for students were thoroughly discussed before decisions were made.

The new year started with a City and Guilds residential workshop in Wakefield to review the syllabus of the 600 series modules. Later in January I commenced the programme for potential principals and vice-principals at Coombe Lodge. Most of my fellow course members were already vice-principals but there were some heads of department and two principals in the group. This was a two-week intensive programme with some lectures and seminars but mainly projects and assignments. The group members were divided up into teams for some of the projects and I was teamed with Tony Jeans, vice-principal of GLOSCAT (Gloucester and Cheltenham College of Arts and Technology). Our project involved an in-depth examination of Stroud College and we spent some time at the College observing and meeting with the principal and some of his staff. We had to produce a comprehensive report and present it to the rest of the course members, tutors and the Stroud College principal. He took our criticisms quite well and I was fairly certain he was aware of many of the issues we had raised. I felt that I had benefited from the course and also the opportunity of meeting colleagues from around the country with similar problems. The course was not compulsory and several of the participants had been in post for many years and wished they had attended sooner.

March was a hectic month with City and Guilds meetings in London, a regional vice-principals' conference, two days of meetings of the Teacher Training assessors and a residential staff development conference that I organised at Bramley Grange. I also had two meetings of the former students' association at Holly Bank and a regimental dinner night at RAOC CVHQ at Deepcut. This was my 'dining out' event as I had decided to resign from the TAVR after twenty years of service. I had been awarded my Territorial Decoration (TD) and had risen to the rank of captain but there had been no opportunity to gain promotion to major without committing much more time to the army. I had no regrets. I had made many friends and developed a lot of skills and knowledge, particularly in leadership, but the demands of the College job and the potential to move forward in my career made the decision easy.

My involvement in using computers to support education administration and teaching continued to expand and I was invited to join the Northern Region Computing Group. The YHAFHE computer steering group was meeting more frequently and proposals for projects were considered. Although external funding was a problem, enthusiasts did much work on a voluntary basis. I was increasingly involved in staff training with computers and my two main programmes for college administration were beginning to be used. The commitment accounting programme had taken me over a year to design and develop. I gave demonstrations to the principal, heads of departments and administrative staff, making amendments when they put forward constructive suggestions. The finished product was presented to the assistant finance director for Leeds LEA, Max George. Max was very enthusiastic and used his influence to persuade the LEA to allow the College to use the system to generate its own orders and maintain a local accounting system. The new system speeded up the previous order process by cutting out the LEA, which now received two copies of the order forms that were generated in the College. The computer software produced reports at a college, department and section level so that Jack and I had an overview of all spending and the heads and section leaders could monitor their own budgets. Inevitably, there were some teething problems, mainly with the printer that produced the orders as it struggled to cope with the volume of work and the five-ply continuous order forms. For the first few weeks I monitored every part of the process, fine-tuning whenever necessary. Other colleges visited us to observe the system and were keen to purchase our package but I decided not to allow this to happen. Not because I was protecting my ideas but because the product was bespoke and had been written by me and it would have been extremely difficult for another college simply to run and maintain our programme. The part-time teacher budget and contracts programme that I produced was more modest and took much less time to develop. It seemed to streamline the process to the satisfaction of heads and administrative staff.

The end of term was again signalled by the Huddersfield reunion weekend and by my brother Richard's marriage to Jill in early July in Surrey. We had a family outing to Goathland, one of my favourite areas, when working for Holiday Fellowship at the Marske Centre. We also enjoyed the Leeds Show at Roundhay Park as well as the Harrogate Annual HIFI Show in the central hotels.

Jack Mansell's appointment as director of FEU led to a change in direction of the work of the unit. Jack had been the chairman of a key document produced by FEU called *Basis for Choice* that led to the introduction of the Certificate in Pre-Vocational Education (CPVE) as well as having a great deal of influence on the DES. It had influence in curricular terms in three ways:

(a) it suggested a national framework into which and around which many existing programmes could be fitted;

(b) it suggested a common core spelt out in specific objectives, but which recognised that processes were involved in learning as well as products;

(c) it went for a profile which reflected a curriculum-led philosophy of assessment.

FEU had a useful budget to encourage colleges to bid for funds to develop ideas in specific areas such as post-sixteen youngsters with special learning needs, adult training issues, women disadvantaged by the production of negative stereotypes, new technology and marketing. Another issue that was addressed by FEU was the lack of support for staff and curriculum development in FE at the institutional level.

Whilst I had spent a considerable amount of time on the administrative programme, my main interest was seeking new solutions to support student learning. Ever since my year as a student teacher at Huddersfield when I became involved with programmed learning, I had visions about students learning at their own pace, in their own time and on demand. The introduction of affordable 'mouse-computers' seemed to me to present the opportunity that I had been waiting for over the last eighteen years. I used the YHAFHE Computer Steering Committee to float the idea of a regional project to pilot computer based learning materials and there was support from some of the members. It was about this time that I was approached by the Department for Education and Science to serve as a founder member on the Further Education Unit's (FEU) New Technology Group. Jack Mansell was the group chairman and members comprised civil servants, HMI and invited people from further and higher education. The first meeting was in November 1981 at Elizabeth House in London. The group considered papers from the department and proposals from institutions for projects. The group monitored the progress of approved projects and ensured that the outcomes were published and circulated to colleges and higher education. The output of educational research in general from FEU was considerable and at that time technology was just starting to get underway. I took the opportunity to put the YHAFHE proposal to the group and it received a severe grilling. The proposal was deemed far too ambitious by most of the members but Jack Mansell decided to support it and in due time thirty thousand pounds was allocated to the project. This was the largest sum allocated to a single project and I recognised the responsibility I had to Jack to justify his confidence.

The project aims and objectives were sent to every college in the Yorkshire and Humberside region and I was delighted with the response. Whilst the project aimed at producing learning packages, the underlying concept was a staff development programme involving as many college staff as possible in the production and evaluation of a new form of assisted learning. The project was entitled 'Computer Based learning in FE – A Staff Development Model'. The first phase of the project involved the design and development of computerised learning materials across a wide range of further education subject areas. The second phase involved field-testing the materials in other colleges. The YHAFHE steering committee established a project committee to oversee the complete process. I had agreed to be the project director and Joe Waters, director of computing at Bradford College, was appointed as chairman. There were eight subject areas to be developed and each subject had a development team. There were about seventy people involved in Phase One of the project and about 130 participated in Phase Two. The project commenced in 1982 and took two years to complete. Sheffield Polytechnic's print unit was commissioned to produce the computer discs and the supporting materials and the complete package was offered to colleges at a modest price. The materials produced were displayed on 22 June 1984 at the National Launch at Leeds College of Building attended by three hundred representatives. The speakers included Mr Roy Walker of the DES and Jack Mansell of the FEU. I wrote the report for FEU and it was published in 1985. In his covering introduction, Jack Mansell stated:

> Computer Based learning (CBL) remains something of a mystery to many FE teachers. This report describes how a region involved some two hundred teachers in coming to grips with the concept, how over sixty of them actively participated in producing courseware and how that material was tested. In describing the product and processes associated with this project, this document removes a little of the mystique and introduces readers to a source of greater clarification.

During this period, the government introduced new curriculum into the FE sector.

The Department of Education and Science (DES) opted for the FE-inspired Certificate of Pre-Vocational Education (CPVE) rather than the Certificate of Extended Education (CEE) for youngsters staying on beyond the school-leaving age without academic or vocational commitment. Not long after that the government introduced a New Technical and Vocational Initiative (TVEI), under the Manpower Services Commission (MSC) (part of the Department of Employment (DE) group), to infuse the fourteen to sixteen curriculum with subjects and activities relevant to the world of work. This raid on the DES empire shocked the colleges less than it did the schools for FE had become used to intervention by the MSC, which used the lever of offering funds to those who would follow its bidding in providing training courses, especially for the unemployed.

Jack Place and I had discussed the concept of an extended college year to meet the needs of the construction industry and our proposal had been accepted by the governors and approved by the Education Committee of the Leeds City Council. The new arrangements commenced in September with a slightly modified staffing structure to accommodate the 'extended college-working year'. It was also in this year that we submitted proposals to extend the annexe at Cross Green Lane. This involved the provision of a roof over the open inner quadrangle area to provide additional workshop space and it was completed the following year. During 1982 the government approved the New Training Initiative (NTI) that was launched by the Manpower Services Commission. One of the objectives of the NTI was to introduce the Youth Training Scheme (YTS) that provided school leavers with a year of training as a foundation for work. The scheme came into full operation in September 1983 and it had a significant effect upon the work of the College.

The 1981–82 year was critical for Leeds College of Building. Jack Place, who had been its principal since it opened in 1960, was sixty-five on 1 April 1982 and he had to retire by 31 August that year. This meant that the College governors had to start the process of appointing a new principal to take up post on 1 September 1982. I had no great expectation of being appointed, as it was not customary to appoint a deputy to a principal's post. The view taken then was that 'a new broom' would bring in new ideas and enthusiasm to the job.

When the post of college principal was advertised early in the new term, Jack urged me to apply and, although I had some misgivings, I followed his advice. I was invited to attend an interview on 22 and 23 April. I was not unduly concerned about my short-listing as it was usually seen as a courtesy to interview internal candidates. I was surprised when I met the other candidates that included Gordon Grant, the head of civil engineering at Leeds Polytechnic, together with heads of construction departments. As no other vice-principal had been included (I did not know if any had applied), I began to realise that my chances of success were much greater than I had anticipated. Being on home territory is a big advantage for an internal candidate and I felt that I had performed well at the interview on the second day. There was a delay of about thirty minutes after the last candidate had been interviewed before I was invited back into the boardroom to be offered the position of principal with effect from 1 September 1982. Jack was delighted with the outcome as we had worked so well together over the last five years and the governors and LEA officers congratulated me warmly.

I rushed home to share the news with Veronica and we celebrated. We had already had some good news a little earlier in the year when Veronica confirmed that she was expecting another child in the summer and we could reflect upon 1982 as a memorable year. Two weeks after the interviews I attended the Annual Heads of Construction Conference at Huddersfield and I was flattered by the many good wishes that I received. My old friend and colleague, Jack Hall, principal of Shirecliffe College in Sheffield, seemed particularly pleased for me. I fulfilled my teaching practice assessment duties for Huddersfield in Accrington, York and Grimsby, and, at the same time, engaged in planning Jack's retirement party, which was to be held in the restaurant of Thomas Danby College on 6 June. It was a great occasion with so many of Jack's colleagues from around the country, as well as from Leeds and the Yorkshire region. The director of education, Stuart Johnson, gave the main speech in which he extolled Jack's virtues. Jack was presented with a full set of golf clubs to enjoy in his retirement. There was an emotional response from Jack who had devoted most of his working life to further education and the College in particular.

As my post of vice-principal was now available, the governors advertised the post shortly after my appointment. The timing meant that interviews could not take place until the summer and therefore if an appointment was made it was unlikely that the successful candidate could commence his duties before January 1983. The interviews were held on 30 June and David Roberts, head of department at Manchester College of Building, was appointed. I had known David for several years, initially when he was head of department at Dewsbury College and I had been a CGLI assessor for one of his courses, and later through the Heads of Construction Conferences. As Manchester would not release David early from his contract, I had to seek an internal appointment to fill the post for the autumn term. Les Jacques was the senior head and I had a great respect for him. He indicated that he had contemplated retirement but that he would be delighted to accept my offer. The other two older heads, Tom Priestley and Harry Chell, had decided that they would like to retire at the same time as Jack and that gave me the opportunity to establish a new senior management team.

Normally, the annual reunion of former students at Huddersfield marked the start of the summer vacation, but I was still heavily involved with the regional project and meetings at FEU and City and Guilds in July. Veronica and I took Helen to Veronica's parents' home in Retford for a few days, whilst we had a short break including our tenth wedding anniversary meal at the Mansion Restaurant in Roundhay Park. Two days later Edward James was born in St James's Hospital on 1 August – Yorkshire Day.

Chapter 7

My First Years as a Principal

A T THIS POINT IT IS WORTH recording the system of further education and the role of the principal prior to those appointed after 31 March 1993. Further Education was part of the responsibilities of local education authorities that owned all of the College buildings and employed all the staff. They also controlled all of the finance associated with the College and allocated resources on an annual basis in line with the recommendations issues by the Burnham FE Committee. This was a national committee controlled by the Department of Education and Science and included representatives of local authorities and teachers' unions. It laid down formulae for determining college staffing numbers and salary scales and the number of hours that a lecturer should teach per week, with reductions for more senior grades, which allowed a local authority some discretion on a scale within certain limits. Burnham also made recommendations on the salaries of principals, vice-principals and heads of department. Most local education authorities selected the mid-point within the recommended scales, but some were more generous and others rather mean. Colleges did not have their own bank accounts so that all financial transactions had to be monitored and processed by the authority's treasury section.

The role of the principal was therefore primarily as an academic leader with management duties delegated by the LEA. Many LEAs delegated significant authority to their further education sub-committees that in turn allocated responsibilities to the College board of governors that could delegate some of its duties to the principal. However, as the LEA was well represented on the Board of Governors, it could not delegate all of its responsibilities. For example, staff appointments were the responsibility of the governing body that usually had an appointments sub-committee. In most colleges this sub-committee would only make appointments at a senior level and the principal would be responsible for teaching and support staff appointments. If the principal wished to restructure the management of the College, any changes would have to be approved by the governing body. The clerk to the governing body was the director of education and therefore the control of agendas and record of meetings so that the LEA could restrict the governors if it wished. On the financial side there were directives on capital and revenue expenditure with a cap imposed on capital items that could be ordered by the principal. This was usually a modest amount and was only fifty pounds when I was first appointed as vice-principal. These strict practices were rigidly enforced and it had been a brave move on the part of Leeds LEA to allow me to develop the commitment account computerised package and to print our own orders. The limits placed upon the principal's responsibilities did not restrict him (her) of participating in local, regional, national and international related educational activities and I took full advantage of the opportunities when they were presented.

Further education had been male dominated for most of the twentieth century. Not really surprising as engineering had been the predominant subject area, particular in the post war years as the country had to replace the huge loss of skilled labour in the manufacturing industries. All the principals tended to have engineering or technical backgrounds and the only females in colleges tended to be in administration, 'office arts' or catering. This practice was still true to a large extent when I became a principal. Even in Leeds with its specialist colleges all of the principals and vice-principals were men. However, colleges were expanding their portfolios and a greater range of subjects was being offered. Whilst engineering was contracting, business education was one of the fastest growing areas along with catering, health education, childcare and hair and beauty therapy. Construction had always had a significant role in multidiscipline colleges although few people with a construction background became principals of such institutions. The College of Building was also male dominated with not a single female on the teaching staff. Not surprisingly, there were very few female students except on the technician courses.

With Les Jacques as acting vice-principal and two of the other heads of department retiring, I had moved quickly to appoint David Stanway to the Building Services post. David had been the principal lecturer in the department and I rated him highly and the governors agreed with my recommendation. I had decided to merge the two building crafts departments into one and had advertised nationally. The successful candidate was Reg. Rose and he took up his post in January 1983 at the same time that David Roberts joined the team. The teaching complement was then eighty-two, plus the management team, with an administrative staff of thirty-four that included a large team of technicians supporting workshop and laboratory activities. I knew all of the staff quite well, having worked closely with the departments over the last five years. Also, by taking a break in the staff common room on most days, it helped to establish personal links other than purely academic. I had also been in the practice of observing the teaching skills of most of the staff. It was relatively easy to observe practical sessions, which formed a significant part of the work of three of the departments. Classroom observation was a little more sensitive but most staff seemed happy that I was taking an interest in their work.

During my five years as vice-principal I had been able to assess the strengths and weaknesses of the College establishment. Compared to my experiences elsewhere I was pleasantly surprised to note an extremely high level of competence and commitment amongst all of the staff members. In addition to an experienced management team the College was fortunate to have a very strong team of middle managers in John Daniels, Don Croll, John Cowie and George Birkett. Indeed, when I assessed the lecturer and senior lecturer members it was difficult to identify any obvious weaknesses. My optimism for the future of the College was further reinforced by knowing that Mary Siddons' team of administrators, technician and caretakers comprised equally enthusiastic and competent members.

My appointment had been well received by the staff. Also, many of the local construction firms and associations had extended their congratulations to me. Jack had usually been invited to attend events organised by employer's organisations in the region as many had their headquarters in Leeds. My first invitation was to the Institute of Plumbing Annual Dinner and Dance in October and Veronica and I had an enjoyable evening and made several new friends. The NFBTE Annual Dinner and Dance followed in November and was equally enjoyable. With the September enrolments having been successfully completed and timetables adjusted to the peaks and troughs that are so familiar to further education, I was able to take stock of my priorities for the coming year and to reflect on longer term planning. Having worked so closely with Jack, who had been keen to allow me to be involved in all aspects of college management, I did not feel that dramatic reorganisation was necessary but I did intend to introduce changes within my second year.

I decided to join the Association of Principals of Colleges (APC) during my first term. Jack had refused to join and he had not explained his reasons to me. I felt that meeting with colleagues with similar issues to resolve would be an advantage. The APC was a national organisation with a council and annual conference but my immediate interest was the regional structure. The Northern branch of APC included Yorkshire and Humberside, and the North East – covering an area from the Scottish Border to North Lincolnshire. There were four meetings per year of the regional committee, two hosted at York College and two at Darlington College. APC national council was comprised of representatives from the regions and all of its duties and responsibilities were carried out on a voluntary basis by acting principals. In addition, APC, as the only independent representative body for the FE sector, was invited by many national organisations to nominate principals to be members of their main committees. This meant that at virtually every meeting of our regional APC committee there was a request for volunteers to serve on a national body. In practice, almost every principal in the country would be on at least one such committee.

The Leeds principals had their own group and I was warmly welcomed to the meetings by my new colleagues. It was a busy term with the regional FEU CAL project taking up a fair amount of my time in working with the participating colleges and attending FEU and YHAFHE meetings. Within the Leeds authority, there were meetings of the careers service, a CEIL conference at Beckett's Park, the Link Courses Standing Committee and a staff development conference at Woolley Hall.

1983 commenced with a full diary of commitments. I had arranged a one-day conference for my new management team and a week later held a two-day staff conference at Bramley Grange to share the details of the planning with all of the staff. Leeds LEA was working closely with the Manpower Services Commission (MSC) and I attended an MSC workshop in the education offices. The main thrust was the development of the Unified Vocational Preparation (UVP) programme and I was involved with a group at Sheffield Polytechnic as well as with the Leeds group. David Roberts had taken up his post as vice-principal and he had persuaded me to give a presentation at the Manchester College of Building weekend staff development seminar. This was held at the Palace Hotel in Buxton and I was asked to share with their management team the IT initiatives that had been developed in Leeds. Travelling over the Pennines in February can be challenging and this was no exception. However, the hospitality and the comradeship were very enjoyable and made the effort worthwhile. Jack Hall also invited me to Shirecliffe College to share ideas and tactics in influencing the development of construction education. Jack was serving on several national committees that enabled him to put forward ideas that could be beneficial to the FE sector.

I was an automatic member of all of the College's departmental advisory committees that met in the spring and autumn terms. These committees comprised representatives of industry who were willing to give up some of their time to advise a department on a range of relevant issues. I tried to attend every meeting as the links with industry could be enhanced through those meetings. Each head of department had a different style of managing their advisory committee and, although I did not want to be prescriptive, I was keen to see that the chairman of each committee was a representative from industry rather than the head himself.

I had attended a number of courses at the Coombe Lodge Staff College in Blagdon, mainly to assist with my personal development as a head of department and then as a vice-principal. My first conference at the Staff College as a principal was a three-day event specifically aimed at principals with an objective of future developments. Whilst I enjoyed the overall experience, I was surprised at the number of aging colleagues who regarded Blagdon as a rest centre rather than for personal staff development. Certainly the atmosphere in the remote rural setting was more suited to a holiday than serious endeavour. Nevertheless, I did believe that it offered an ideal location to set the problems of the day to one-side and concentrate on future issues. As the development of computer aided administration became a mainstream activity, I became a regular presenter and expert witness at many Coombe Lodge events during my years at Leeds.

Just before the end of the spring term I made teaching practice assessment visits to local colleges with Bill Squires to observe in-service teachers. Veronica and I decided that we should make the most of the two-week Easter break so we had a week at Blackpool and a week at South Littleton. Edward was still a small baby but Helen was old enough to enjoy the seaside and the Cotswold countryside.

The summer term started with a two-day staff development conference at Bramley Grange and was followed by the usual round of committee meetings locally, regionally and nationally. In May I attended an FEU meeting at Elizabeth House. The agenda was too long to be completed in the available time and diary commitments did not allow for a follow up meeting to cover the outstanding items. It was decided that we should try a teleconference that would enable decisions to be made without the long journey to London. This was my first experience at teleconferencing and it seemed to work quite well as long as the chairman kept control of the business. The end of my first year as principal of Leeds College of Building was celebrated with a wine and cheese party for all of the staff and it provided me with an opportunity to meet retired colleagues and to make presentations to those colleagues who were retiring that year. It was good to see Jack Place looking well and enjoying his retirement. The family enjoyed a week in Blackpool at the Imperial Hotel and then a further week at South Littleton. I found it necessary to spend a good deal of the summer vacation at the College to finalise budgets and to prepare plans for the ensuing year, the latter to be submitted to the members of the LEA FE sub-committee for their consideration.

It was in July 1984 that I accepted an invitation from the Royal Society of Arts to become a Fellow. That decision would eventually involve me in regional activities in Yorkshire and the North East as well as a stint on the National Council.

1983–1984

The first week in September involved a welcome and induction for new staff and a full staff development day to bring all colleagues up-to-date with developments and targets for the year. The local authority had restructured governing bodies of the colleges and an

Inaugural Meeting was convened for mid-September. Fortunately, Leeds College of Building escaped any major changes with Arthur Crocker re-elected as Chairman and Peter Bewell as vice-chairman with hardly any changes of the membership. At the end of the month, I was involved in a three-day residential staff development event at Bramley Grange involving most of the colleges.

At that time, the high unemployment rate amongst young people nationally indicated that there would be a continuing need for the Youth Training Scheme courses and the College became fully involved in the provision of those courses. The development of this work led to a review of the College departmental structure and in 1984 a Vocational Preparation Department was established to coordinate the Youth Training Schemes, link courses, foundation courses in construction and courses for the unemployed.

The CITB had been urging building departments in colleges to consider introducing the extended college year. As the construction industry traditionally worked for fifty weeks of the year with two weeks off over Christmas and the New Year, there was resentment in the industry, particularly from smaller companies, that apprentices should not expect school holidays when they attended college. The CITB schemes at the time allowed for full-time attendance in the first year to ensure that the apprentices had a full range of practical experiences that were not available when working 'on the job' with a company. The CITB had invested financially in all its appointed colleges and was keen that the tools and equipment that it provided should be used throughout the year. At the Annual Heads of Construction Conference, this issue had been pursued and received a mixed reaction from the colleges. I was of the opinion that it was difficult to argue against the case made by the CITB, especially in a construction-based college. Jack and I had introduced modest extended year programme and I prepared a paper for the senior management team to extend the system and gained the support of the heads in principle as long as the existing conditions of service could be maintained. The paper went to the governing body and, as I expected, the industrial members were very enthusiastic although the staff members had reservations. Detailed meetings were held with the staff and eventually there was an agreement. The local authority had no objections so I agreed to draw up a plan to implement the changes.

In October the College received a visit from the Secretary of State for Education, Sir Keith Joseph, who also happened to be my local MP in Leeds. He was particularly interested in work-related, non-advanced further education as well as technical and practical activities. He had a family interest in the construction industry and so he could demonstrate his understanding when talking to the students and staff on many courses during his visit to the workshops. He briefly discussed the FEU project with me. (I later learned that he read all FEU documents, much to the discomfort of his civil servants.) At the end of the visit, Sir Keith expressed his satisfaction with the work of the College. The visit was discussed at the November meeting of the governing body and they were delighted with the outcome. It was also a topic raised a few days later when Veronica and I attended the NFBTE annual dinner and dance, as everyone seemed to seek some reflected glory from the visit. In the period leading up to Christmas the regional CAL project dominated much of my time as the deadline was fast approaching. There were extra meetings of the YHAFHE sub-group and a meeting in London of the FEU New Technology Group. By mid-December I was ready for a break.

Christmas and the New Year were over-shadowed by my father suffering a series of strokes and I kept dashing up to Sunderland to visit him in hospital. He died at the end of January and I felt the loss deeply as he had been very supportive and reassuring throughout my life.

The pressure to complete the regional CAL project had intensified with more meetings and mini presentations of the various products. FEU held an IT conference in March and I had to give a presentation on the project. There were as many cynics as there were enthusiasts in the audience and I had to patiently explain the philosophy behind the project. The final floppy discs and documents were conveyed to Sheffield Polytechnic's Pavic Unit that had been commissioned by FEU to produce and distribute the package. The final package of staff development materials was quite substantial with virtually every vocational area having examples of software. A price had been agreed between FEU and the producers and this may have limited the number of colleges that were willing to purchase the package. However, there was a good take up of the materials and they were well received by most of the colleges. The following weekend was the Huddersfield annual reunion and it provided a much-needed break for me from the pressures of the Project. July started with an FEU IT group meeting, quickly followed by an IT conference at Gloucester covering another FEU sponsored project for which I had been acting as adviser.

Veronica and I took stock of our situation with an enlarged family and economic stability thanks to my promotion to principal. It seemed a good time to move into a larger property and we were fortunate to purchase a detached house in Whitechapel Close only a short distance from our Barlby Way home. We moved during the summer and quickly established ourselves.

1984–1985

After a short family holiday in the Vale of Evesham, it was back to college for the start of another academic year. The usual frantic exercise of enrolment went relatively smoothly, partly thanks to CITB providing a good recruitment to most of the building craft courses. The Leeds principals started the year with a dinner at a local Greek restaurant and most of my colleagues attended. Three days later I hosted a meeting of Leeds principals but little corporate good seemed to emerge. This was perhaps understandable as each college tended to have different issues associated with its specialist areas. I had no difficulty understanding the problems of Hugh Johnson of Airedale and Wharfedale College and Bob O'Brien of Kitson College as we all had mainstream vocational students. John Robb-Webb at Jacob Kramer, Joe Stones from the College of Music and Graham Binks from Joseph Priestley Institute always seemed to have other matters of priority, whilst George Hume of Park Lane College rarely agreed with anyone and Brian Boffey of Thomas Danby College usually had very little to contribute. Despite this, we had a further two meetings in October to deal with issues identified by the Leeds LEA. It had always been a pleasure to work with the officers and politicians of the local authority, even after a change in political control when the Conservatives lost in the local elections to the Labour Group.

However, over the next two years it became apparent that there was a political desire to transform further education in the city from a monotechnic structure to a single college structure. This was not really surprising, as this pattern had been adopted by most of the larger cities in England such as Manchester, Liverpool and most recently Sheffield. The treatment of the senior staff in the monotechnic institutions at the time of the restructuring had been harsh in some cases and this fact tended to influence the views of the Leeds principals in deciding their tactics. It was also about this time that the deputy director for education, Chris Tipple, was seconded to a national post and he was not replaced. Instead, the chairman of the Education Committee, Councillor Driver, moved into the deputy director's office. I suspect that the director of education, Stuart Johnson, did not favour this.

When George Hume retired from Park Lane College, David Eade, who had been rapidly promoted internally to vice-principal the previous year, replaced him. David had been well known in local and national FE circles as a prominent member of NATFHE and a member of its National Executive. He had little time to adjust to his new status before George Mudie, the Leeds Labour Leader of the City Council, co-opted him to head up the team that would advise the authority on the proposed restructuring. The Leeds principals decided that they would look at the emerging proposals and prepare their own recommendations to provide a professional view as opposed to a political solution.

All the normal activities had to continue and I attended meetings locally, regionally and nationally. There were also the social engagements that I had inherited with the principal's job as a guest at dinner/dances hosted by the construction industry employers groups. The employers were aware of the proposed restructuring and were totally against any move that would close the College of Building. However, with the closure of Shirecliffe College in Sheffield, Leeds had the only monotechnic structure in England and I had to warn the employers that it would be a hard fight to resist the national trend. As building employers were traditionally associated with the conservative party it seemed that they would not get a sympathetic hearing when they approached the local authority.

My involvement with the Further Education Unit's New Technology Committee had continued and I often received a phone call from Jack Mansell before a meeting asking me to chair it as he had another commitment. This was the case for the first meeting in 1985. At the meeting a visit to the Federal Republic of German (also known as West Germany) was announced and I was invited to represent the FE sector and another member of the committee was invited to represent higher education. The object of the trip was to visit companies and education establishments to observe the progress in introducing new technologies into the learning situation. Germany operated 'The Dual System' for post compulsory technical education, which meant that large industrial companies had a further education college attached to them for the training of their apprentices. The visit was scheduled for March and was to be led by Roy Walker, who I had met when he visited Leeds College of Building in June 1994. Also in the UK party were two HMI, Malcolm Himsworth, the Staff HMI for business and computing and Ernie Haiden, HMI for mathematics and computing. Both were members of the FEU Committee and I flew with them from Leeds/Bradford airport to Heathrow to meet up with the London-based members of the party.

We landed at Kohn airport and were taken by car to the Beethoven Hotel in Bonn, which was the capital city of West Germany. We had an initial briefing meeting in the Department for Education before commencing a series of visits. The first visit was to Troisdorf Vocational School, a relatively short journey north of Bonn. The vocational school was linked to a local company and it was well equipped to provide the specific training needs of their apprentices. There was little sign of any new technology in use and the teaching was very traditional. In the afternoon we travelled to the Nobel Dynamic Training Centre, which was another example of the Dual System and there were some modest examples of the use of technology in the training situation. The following day we visited the factory of Beyer AG in Leverkusen. We were shown into the boardroom of an impressive building, which was the headquarters of this multinational company. After refreshments and an introduction to the company we were shown the training facilities for the office-based staff, which were equipped to the highest standards. We were also shown a training suite for computer-based staff that had a range of the latest models and peripherals. At about 2 p.m. we were escorted to the management dining room for an excellent lunch. The discussions around the table kept us occupied for the rest of the afternoon and we returned to Bonn with some food for thought.

The next morning we set off for Essen for a full-day visit to Essen Adult Retraining Centre. This was a government-funded centre providing a range of vocational skills, especially for light engineering and clerical work. It claimed to have good links with local industry for work placements and employment. We had a conducted tour of the facilities and an opportunity to talk to the trainees and instructors. We enjoyed the visit and could see some parallels with schemes in the UK. The next two days were spent in discussions at the Department of Education in Bonn. On the first of the two days there was a seminar for the UK delegates to share experiences and prepare notes for the feedback session to the German officials on the following day. In the afternoon we visited the British Council offices to see its resources and how it promoted the UK in Germany. In the evening we dined together in Bonn. On the second day we were located in a lecture theatre that was equipped with headphones and translators so that presentations in German could be shared almost instantaneously in English. The presentations by the German government representatives and our response from Roy Walker were carefully edited so that no one could take offence at any of the comments. However, the HMI, the HE representative and I had been asked to give a practitioners view and we were much more robust in our praise and criticism. To their credit the German officials accepted our comments in a good spirit and agreed that our criticisms had been fair. They commented that we had a big advantage in having teacher training facilities for post-school education. In the evening we were entertained at the Beethoven Halle (Concert Hall) where the Beethoven Orchestra gave us a Beethoven Concert. We had the following morning to do some shopping in Bonn before flying from Kohl to Heathrow and then to Leeds Bradford.

After City and Guilds had restructured the FTC in Construction and developed the Construction Supplementary Studies qualification, I had been invited to become chairman of the examinations moderating committee for the eight subjects and Jack Hall had become the chairman of the projects moderating committee. With building technology changing there was a need to review the syllabus for most of the subjects and I hosted a weekend at Bramley Grange to update the schemes. The qualification had become popular with over 2000 UK candidates and several hundred candidates from India and Africa. I was to continue to be chairman of the committee until 2005. Meanwhile, in the area of technician qualifications, the Business and Technician Education Council (BTEC) replaced TEC and BEC in 1984.

I had inherited Paula Chadbourne as my secretary when I took over from Jack Place and found that she was very competent. She had amused the staff members when the cricket team was short of a member and she volunteered to bat in a motorcycle crash helmet. She had decided to marry a soldier and Veronica and I attended her wedding shortly after she resigned from the College. One of the aspects of further education that had caused me some concern over the years was the attitude of teaching staff to administrative staff. LEAs had probably introduced the terms 'academic' and 'non-academic' but this had encouraged an unhealthy division between the two elements of the institution. I did my best not to use the word 'non-academic' and let my views be known throughout the College. In practice, several of the administrative staff members had stronger academic qualifications than the teaching staff members, which I gently pointed out from time to time. I took the view that all the employees of the College had important roles to play in the well running of the institution and that college social events had to be open to all staff. At Leeds the senior administrative officer was the registrar and Mary Siddons fulfilled that role throughout my time at the College. She was very competent and reliable and I always found her to be supportive of any proposals that I was developing.

My interest in the application of new technology to support learning and administration in colleges had led to invitations to speak at conferences, especially at the Staff College in Blagdon. The director was particular keen to run two-day courses on Management Information Systems as the College was seeking to launch FEMIS, the further education management information system. With the expertise and support from Ken Deciacco, my senior IT staff member, I pushed ahead with developing computer networks for students and introduced a touch-screen monitor in the main entrance to enable visitors to access information directly. I suspect that we were the first UK college to attempt to introduce this technology that proved quite successful and created a lot of interest amongst students as well as visitors. Over the next few years I travelled regularly to Blagdon and enjoyed the involvement with the staff team. My first engagement was in July 1985 and several days later, Veronica and I attended our first Royal Garden Party at Buckingham Palace. We had a wonderful day enhanced by hot sunny weather. The Garden Party brought a busy month to an end as, in addition to the trip to Blagden, I had a two-day construction conference at Thames Polytechnic, a two-day staff development residential at Bramley Grange and an APC Regional Conference at Beverley.

The new academic year started with a two-day staff conference, which enabled me to set the scene for the ensuing year and to update colleagues on changes and local and national developments. It was also a useful introduction exercise for new members of staff, who often felt a bit nervous, particularly if they were new to teaching in further education. The teaching staff establishment had increased to eighty-seven and it was important that this growth was justified by a good enrolment. Fortunately, the enrolment sessions went reasonably well and jobs were secure for another year. I had been heavily involved with the Leeds Careers Committee and I attended a National Careers Association Conference in Eastbourne in mid-September. The rest of the autumn term followed a pattern of meetings at local, regional and national venues. I had been invited to become a member of YAHFE Council and enjoyed my first meeting of this strategic group in November. I had also been involved directing another FEU project that involved the impact of technology on construction education. This was relatively small compared with the Yorkshire regional CAL project, but it helped to maintain the momentum within the construction sector of colleges. I made a report of progress at the FEU New Technology Committee in November.

1985 was the Silver Jubilee of the College of Building and the governors, with the agreement of Leeds LEA, commissioned Jack Place to produce a short booklet on the history of the College over its first twenty-five years. Jack was delighted to be involved again and together we dug out documents that assisted his research. The outcome was an excellent summary of the key points over the period and it was illustrated with some interesting photographs. It included a graph showing the steady growth in the workload of the College. At its formation in 1960, Jack had a teaching staff of nine supporting an enrolment of about eight hundred students. By 1983, I had a full-time teaching staff of eighty-six and a student enrolment of four thousand. The graph also highlighted the volatility of the construction sector and its impact on the workload of the College. After a steady expansion over the first seven years, the College experienced almost a static period of about seven years followed by a rapid growth for three years, a drop for three years and then a period of steady growth. In addition to the booklet there was a Silver Jubilee Day Conference with national and local speakers. For the Jubilee Award Ceremony, I invite Robin Bullough, the Examinations Secretary of City and Guilds, to present the prizes.

The restructuring of colleges in Leeds project had been developing over the year and a meeting between the Leeds LEA and colleges took place in late November to discuss progress. It was becoming apparent that the views of the colleges were likely to be ignored and that a single college solution was the preferred outcome at a political level. This meeting served to sharpen the issue with those principals who had not taken much interest in the developments to date and it was resolved that the principals group should sharpen up their own paper to inform the debate. So 1985 closed on the realisation that change was likely to be imposed and, if the Sheffield experience was an indication then most, if not all, of the current principals would lose their jobs.

With all my other commitments, I found that January 1986 was heavily booked. There was the 'Apprentice of the Year' competition committee meetings, followed later in the month by Leeds Apprentice Merit Awards in the Civic Hall, a 'Training the Trainers' day at Bramley Grange, a YHAHFE Council half-day, a day in London chairing the CGLI 'G' Course Moderating Committee, a College advisory committee and a full day meeting on two-year YTS schemes at Airedale and Wharfedale College. I seemed to have little time to devote to my principal's duties in college! Fortunately, February was a quieter month and I was able to catch up with events in the College. My only significant committee during that month was the FEU IT Project Committee, which met at Gloucester College of Arts and Technology (GLOSCAT) site in Cheltenham. I had been acting as an FEU nominee on two projects at GLOSCAT and had developed a close working relationship with Chris West who led both projects. Just before the Easter break, FEU organised a national IT conference in London to raise the awareness of colleges to the challenges that were beginning to emerge. I was one of the speakers at a well-attended event.

We took an Easter family break of five days at the Imperial Hotel in Blackpool and, despite the chilly late March weather it was a good break and an opportunity to spend some quality time with Veronica and the children. The new term started with the College prizegiving ceremony. Previously, each department had held its own event but I had persuaded the heads to consider a college event so that all the governors and parents could see the full scope of the work of the College. It was an excellent evening and I felt that I had made the right decision to consolidate the events. The following day I had to dash down to Portsmouth for a FEU IT meeting, a long journey by train.

The Leeds LEA published its consultative report on the reorganisa-tion of further education in the city and it was a substantial document. The evidence prepared by the College principals was placed at the very end of the document and this was interpreted as a slap in the face for the principals. This document, together with a feeling that after nine years at Leeds College of Building it would be time to look for a new opportunity, led me to apply for three posts of principal in other colleges.

My first application was to Hull College of FE and I was invited to attend a three-day interview at the College. Eight candidates attended and the plan was to select three at the end of day two for short-listing. Two days before the interview I received a phone call from the current principal, who I knew from APC and other meetings. He said that the interviews were going to be a charade as a local candidate was the preferred choice of the chairman. I found that difficult to believe as Hull was a large college and its governors should be looking for the best candidate. I knew several of the selected candidates that included my Leeds colleague Bob O'Brien and Doug Hardacre, principal of Keighley College, who hailed from Hull and was keen to return there. On arrival the candidates were given a conducted tour of the premises that included buildings well away from the main campus. Many of the buildings were in a poor condition and did not provide a good environment for learning. After the tour we were divided up into small groups and then 'interviewed' by a variety of college personnel that included governors, teachers, students and support staff. Whilst this may appear an inclusive method of getting the views of a wide selection of interested people, in fact most of the panel members seemed embarrassed by the situation and struggled to articulate relevant questions. The internal candidate that I had been warned about did not attend the site visit and departed immediately after each group interview without making contact with the other candidates. If I had doubted the retiring principal's view I was rapidly becoming suspicious and so were the other candidates. At the end of day two, I was almost glad not to be included in the final three as I had not been impressed by the buildings or the chairman of governors who seemed arrogant and uncompromising. We found out two days later that the internal candidate had been appointed. He lasted less than two years!

My second application was to York College of Arts and Technology where George Hardgreaves was retiring after many years in the post and where I had experienced eight weeks of teaching practice in 1963. I was invited to a long-listing interview at County Hall in Northallerton, together with about fifteen other applicants. The interview was with the officer and adviser for further education, both of whom I had met on regional committees. I was one of six people short-listed for a two-day interview at the York College campus. One of the six obtained another post before the interview and a reserve candidate was added. I knew two of the other applicants, including Bob O'Brien for Kitson College. Bob and I had observed our rivals and we had concluded that most of the candidates were worthy but, including ourselves, there were two others that we felt may be offered the job. We were wrong and a little surprised when David Mason, the reserve candidate, was offered the post.

My third application was to Darlington College of Technology, which I had visited several times on teaching practice from Huddersfield and more recently at APC regional meetings. There was to be a two-day interview process for the selected six candidates and at lunch on day two it was anticipated that three candidates would be short-listed for a final interview. I received a lot of banter from my

Yorkshire colleagues when they heard of my short-listing. 'Was I a member of the Labour Party?' 'Was my Co-op card up to date?' together with similar observations. I was not deterred by these comments and arrived at Darlington ready to do my best and with the experience of the two previous applications I felt I was fully prepared.

On day one we met the existing management team, led by retiring principal Dick Exelby and the Durham County LEA officers, followed by a conducted tour of the College. We enjoyed a pleasant meal in the College restaurant and I had time to weigh up the opposition. There were only three principals in the group and I wondered if that had been a reflection of the people who had applied. On the second day, the morning was devoted to interviews before the full governing body with the director of education in attendance. The candidates assembled in the principal's office that was adjacent to the boardroom where the interviews would be held.

I had not been warned of the 'Durham system' of interviewing but I was soon to be enlightened. Ten minutes before a candidate was due to be interviewed they were taken to a separate room where an officer presented a piece of paper with a number of questions on it. The candidate had ten minutes to consider the questions and prepare answers that they would give to the panel. The panel may or may not ask supplementary questions when the candidate finished speaking. I was given the paper with three questions and told I should speak for about fifteen minutes. The questions were fairly generic and I had little difficulty in fitting my prepared answers to the questions. On entering the boardroom, I was faced with over thirty people crammed around two long tables with a semi-circular head table, with the chairman facing me at the other end of the room. She welcomed me and invited me to answer the questions. After I had spoken for the proscribed period, I sat back and was pleased to receive several supplementary questions that allowed me to expand my views.

The candidates had lunch together before being told that three had been selected. There were, in alphabetical order, Keith Byfield, principal of Bishop Auckland College, Clive Constant, deputy principal of New College Durham and me. As the first two were well established in Durham I did wonder if I was making up the numbers and that those who had pulled my leg about a job in Durham may have been correct. The same procedure followed in the afternoon, except that we had new questions and were allowed twenty minutes to present our answers. As I was last in, I wondered if the level of concentration of the panel was falling and so I decided to give a vigorous performance. Again, I received several questions before being invited to withdraw. The three candidates waited in the principal's office for a short time before the deputy director for FE announced that I was to be offered the post. The director of education, Derek Sewell, met me to offer his congratulations and to inform me that it was one of his last duties as he was about to retire.

Between the three interviews I had to continue my responsibilities in Leeds. We had made a successful bid to host the National SkillBuild Competitions at the College in summer 1987 and plans had been carefully drawn up to ensure that every craft area would be set up to the high standards that would be expected. I had attended numerous competitions over the last fifteen years and I had a good understanding of the standards to be achieved. I had three meetings of the FEU IT working group in London before Christmas as well as speaking at a residential IT conference at the Staff College. 'Work related non-advance further education' (WRNAFE) was the current flavour of the year and Leeds held a one-day conference at Airedale and Wharfedale College to promote the concept.

The College had offered short courses on an informal basis to the construction industry for several years but a short course prospectus for 1986/87 was launched to formalise the process. Stan Troy was the co-ordinator for the programme and he organised nine of the programmes with tutors Don Croll (6), Jeff Watterson (4) and Adrian Dent (4).

My interest in IT regionally and nationally had not limited my enthusiasm for promoting ITC in the College. I had realised that to influence the majority of the staff of the value of embracing the technology, I needed an enthusiastic role model on the staff to lead the way. During the two-year staff development project, which had involved two hundred staff in the region, I had met several people who I thought would be suitable. The person who had impressed me most was Ken Decciaco from Bradford College and I was delighted when he applied when the senior lecturer post was advertised at the College of Building. He was duly appointed and soon fulfilled my desire to see an ICT champion leading the innovation. We were one of the first colleges to have a computer network for students. I had been able to maintain my links with RM and they had produced a 480Z model that could be used as a workstation and this formed our first modest network. When the BBC announced its Acorn Micro-computer in late 1981, it set the educational world alight. At about the same time, BBC launched its Computer Literacy Project. The graphics, sound and music capabilities of the Acorn opened up the potential applications well beyond the earlier microcomputers. An Econet System became available for BBC Computers and we took this opportunity to develop a networked computer room in the College. I was particularly pleased that several of the construction workshop staff had expressed an interest in having a microcomputer in their workshops for the use of staff and students.

1987 started with a two-day IT conference in London. My FEU working group made a presentation to the full New Technology Committee and it was well received. March was a critical month for FE in Leeds. There was a meeting of the All Party Working Group to consider the document. A week later I had a meeting of the College governing body and all of the members were alarmed at the direction that was being taken by Leeds City Council. There was a proposal that the industrial members would use their contacts and influence to try to preserve the College of Building identity during the consultation period. The proposals were discussed at a regional APC meeting and whilst there was sympathy for the Leeds principals, it was clear that there was no optimism for a change of direction. There was also a joint APC meeting between the North East and North West branches at Oldham College that simply took the view that the monotechnic system was no longer relevant. It was shortly after I had accepted the post at Darlington when the restructuring proposal collapsed. There were various interpretations for this but it seems that David Eade had upset the leader of the Council to such an extent that David had been taken off the project and returned to his duties as principal of Park Lane College. The plans were kept on ice for quite a long time before being quietly dropped. It was too late to change my mind about the Darlington post for I had decided that I needed a new challenge that would be provided in a large multi-discipline college.

National Vocational Qualifications (NVQ) were introduced in 1986 and YHAFHE organised a regional conference in May to raise awareness and encourage debate. There was also a meeting of the YHAFHE Construction Committee. I attended my last meeting of the College of Building governing body, which was immediately followed by a meeting at Bramley Grange. I was grateful for the fulsome praise and best wishes that I received from the governors, who had given very generously of their time to support the College. My final responsibility at Leeds College of Building was to host the National SkillBuild Competitions. This took place in early July and lasted three days, commencing with a formal official opening by Mr Raman Subba Row, the former England cricketer, with an audience of civic dignitaries and leaders from the building industry. Thanks to the huge commitment made by the workshop staff and managers, the event was a great success and in the closing ceremony the College received praise from all of the speakers. I was full of pride when giving the closing address and I left the College on the crest of a wave.

David Roberts was appointed acting principal as my post had not been advertised due to the uncertain future of the College. David had to wait about two years in an acting capacity before Leeds LEA agreed that his position should become permanent.

CHAPTER 8

Darlington College of Technology

Autumn Term 1987

VERONICA AND I HAD ONCE AGAIN had to begin searching for a new home for the fifth time since we were married. The Darlington area, including North Yorkshire, offered a wide range of properties, but we were keen to live within the town. This was partly for my benefit but mainly to ensure that the children had easy access to local schools. Having looked at many properties, we settled on a new small housing development about a mile from the centre of the town. The house we chose could not be completed before February 1988, which meant I would have to find some accommodation for about five months. Fortunately, my mother in Sunderland was pleased to accommodate me so that in a typical week I would spend four nights in Sunderland and three in Leeds.

Taking over the responsibility for a college significantly larger and more complex than Leeds College of Building was quite a challenge. Whereas LCB was a monotechnic with a staff of less than one hundred within an education authority with eight colleges of further education, Darlington College was multi-disciplined, with over four hundred staff. Although it was one of five colleges in the Durham LEA, it was the only FE College in Darlington, which was the largest town in the county. During my first week, Chris Horne, the assistant director for FE, spent some time with me in which he indicated that there was much to do. He referred to the College as 'The Sleeping Giant' of the county and that there was an 'inbreeding culture' in appointing staff. He also explained that the county's preferred structure was tertiary colleges and that East Durham College (formerly Peterlee) and Derwentside College (formerly Consett), were part of the first stage. Darlington should have been the third tertiary college with the merger between the College of Technology and Queen Elizabeth Sixth Form College that was being progressed during my interview for principal. It appeared that the then Deputy

Director of Education, Keith Grimshaw, had visited the sixth form late in the summer term to promote the merger and had received such a rude response that no further progress was made.

I had asked to see the financial reports for the last two years, as only partial information had been made available at the interview. The College registrar Bert Lowcock, who had been at the College for many years and was nearing retirement, provided this information. I found the figures very depressing when compared with the relatively generous funding in Leeds. Over eighty per cent of the budget went to staffing costs, leaving modest amounts for building maintenance and materials and equipment to support student learning. I arranged with the College engineer to give me a full tour of all of the College buildings. The original college had opened in a purpose-built stone structure in 1897 in the centre of town but had been moved to the Cleveland Avenue site in the late 1950s. Previously, the site had been occupied by the girls' high school and the original school building remained, surrounded by college buildings dating from the 1950s, 1960s and 1970s. Two later buildings had been added. One had been sponsored by the CITB and was exclusively for the training of building craftsmen, the other was a detached block at the farthest end of the site, housing the library on the ground floor and art and design courses on the upper floor. All the post 1950s buildings had flat roofs and when I inspected them with the engineer, I was not surprised to learn that most of them leaked in wet weather. There had been little maintenance for several years. The workshops varied considerably. As expected the CITB building was in good condition with excellent facilities and a welcoming environment. The engineering workshops were poorly ventilated and cold in the winter. Most of the equipment was ancient and one large workshop had a single contraption covering most of the floor area. This turned out to be a wind tunnel that had been bought many years ago by an ambitious vice-principal and had hardly been used. The construction workshops were a little better but still inferior to the equipment at Leeds College of Building. At the front of the building, with its own independent entrance was a small, attached structure that was occupied by the county careers service. After a few months the careers service vacated the premises and the PICKUP Unit was based there. PICKUP (Professional, Industrial and

144

Commercial Updating) was introduced by the DES to encourage colleges to provide courses and other services in technologies and management for local firms. A former Darlington industrial liaison officer, Gordon Merry, had been appointed as the College publicity and liaison officer and PICKUP was one of his responsibilities. The unit was renamed as 'Services to Business' and by 1987 its turnover had reached £130,000 from cost recovery courses and services.

The inspection of the classrooms and laboratories did not raise my spirits. The classrooms on the ground floor at the front of the building were amongst the worst I had witnessed in comparison to the many colleges that I had visited as a teacher-training tutor. The desks were ancient and the blackboards had little of their original surfaces and no attempt had been made by teaching staff to improve the ambience of the rooms with some posters or models. On the upper floors there was not much improvement and the chemistry labs were old fashioned and unwelcoming. By the time I had completed my tour I was deeply depressed and was not surprised at the lack of enthusiasm that I had witnessed from the staff members as I had moved around the buildings. I had seen no signs of any computers on my rounds and was informed later that the three or four machines were kept securely locked away. I made a promise to myself that there would be a phased programme of improvements to the learning environment, with an emphasis on open-access facilities. With the modest resources at my disposal I had no idea when I could make a start but I set about drawing up a list of priorities.

I then turned my attention to the senior management team of vice-principal and five heads of department that I had inherited from Dick Exelby. There were an interesting group of six men; three in their early sixties with long service at the College and three who were relatively recent recruits. My vice-principal was Doug Boynton who had joined the College a year earlier having been head of engineering at Wearside College in Sunderland. Doug was a local man whose parents still lived in the town and I soon recognised that he would be my main ally in making the changes that were desperately needed to improve the experience for students. John Davies was the head of department of business, accounting and journalism, Peter Pearson was head of department of catering, health and fashion and Selwyn Morgan was head of science and humanities. These three had been at the College for many years and were trying to make the most of their modest resources in attempting to do a professional job. Bob Twitty was head of the department of construction and art and design and Alan Dixon was the head of the department of engineering, a post he had held for one year. My first impressions were that Bob and Alan would be easier to convince than their more established colleagues. The senior administrative officer, registrar Bert Lowcock had been promoted internally several times before arriving relatively recently in his current post. Bert was a likeable chap and nothing seemed to upset him or surprise him. He informed me that he would be sixty-five before the end of the year and that the LEA would require him to retire on his birthday. The principal's office was near the front entrance to the College with the boardroom across the corridor. I was told that management meetings had traditionally been held in the principal's office. I made it clear that I wished future meetings to be in the boardroom and that decisions would be recorded. My new colleagues agreed with my assessment of the state of the College but there was no optimism that I could make any difference in the short term. It was implied that Dick Excelby's early retirement was due to his despair after having his bids for resources turned down year after year.

Despite the negative observations, I soon identified some positives at Darlington College that gave me some hope. Firstly, the students were relatively well behaved and well motivated, which was partially attributed to the influx of students from rural areas and also the high proportion of older students who had a calming influence on many of the youngsters. The other positive that I soon identified was that most of the staff were committed to their students and strove to provide the best educational experiences despite the poor surroundings and facilities. However, there was at least one exception when I received an anonymous sheet of duplicated paper containing outrageous allegations against the previous management of the College. The sheet was one of several that had been produced on a Banda duplicating machine in the College and pinned to noticed boards in each department. This anonymous person produced several similar abusive sheets over the following month and I was included in some of the slanderous comments. The matter was discussed with the senior managers who were all as upset as I was but they had no idea of who would resort to such tactics. Selwyn Morgan confided in me, implying that there were only two people in the College that were sufficiently literate to produce the standard of grammar used on the sheets! The sheets stopped by the end of October but I retained the evidence until I retired.

Enrolment of students took place during the first week in September, which always seemed odd to colleagues in the other education sectors where students number were known well in advance of the start of the academic year. However, the risk was not too great as most of the full-time students had been recruited and the slight variations were due to last minute changes of mind. In respect of the part-time courses, all those directly supported by local companies or training boards would have been discussed with heads of department and numbers agreed. The unknown areas were some vocational courses that were dependant on individuals enrolling and the large number of non-vocational classes that were very popular in Darlington. Full-time students commenced their programmes in week two of the term and the part-time courses began in week three so that staff had a little longer to sort out any issues caused by shortfalls or excesses.

The Durham County LEA kept a much tighter control over the colleges than I had experienced elsewhere. The director of education convened 'the Principals' Conference' at least every month to monitor the colleges' activities and to convey directives from the Council. During my first week at Darlington I attended a meeting at County Hall together with the principals of the other six colleges. It was chaired by Chris Horne, assistant director for Further Education. I had the opportunity of meeting my new colleagues for the first time at that meeting. Keith Byfield of Bishop Auckland College who I had met at the interview, Laurie Turner, (New College, Durham), Chris Hughes (East Durham, Peterlee), Louis Crecsi (Derwentside), Consett) and Alan Hetherington (Houghall Agricultural College), Durham) made up the team. Joe Willis and Wes Gargett supported Chris Horne at all the meetings and specialist officers, including the director of education, would attend as necessary. At that first meeting there was a discussion regarding the outturn for the previous year, as colleges had been required to submit their statistics regarding students to enable the calculation of establishments for the current year in accordance with the Burnham Committee report. County Durham's interpretation of Burnham was less favourable than in Leeds, thereby generating a lower number of staff and graded posts for a similar level of work.

College funding was based on the academic year September to August, although the county had to operate on financial years April to March. The colleges did not have their own bank accounts and carry over from year to year was not permitted. The colleges could only offer courses that were approved by the Northern Council for Further Education (NCFE) that was based in Newcastle. Applications to run a new course had to be submitted well in advance of the proposed start date so that the Approvals Committee had time to consult LEAS and colleges that may be influenced by the application. In practice, Durham and Newcastle colleges kept a tight grip on their respective portfolios by challenging anyone who put in a bid regardless of the geographical distances involved. For example, only Newcastle College was allowed to run performing arts courses and New College had exclusive rights to travel and tourism courses. In addition to the Principals' Conference on 4 September, there were two more during the month and a further three in October, reflecting the controlling influence of the county over the colleges. During the first week in October, the county called the principals together for the 'enrolment clearing house'. This was an opportunity for the colleges to share low enrolments in specific subjects and to discuss possible combinations to accommodate as many students as possible. It sounded great in principle but in practice colleges were reluctant to identify areas with low enrolments as they hoped late entries would enable viable groups to be formed.

Another local issue that had little impact on students in Leeds but was a problem in the Northern region was the restrictions of the 'extra district fees'. The regulation required local authorities to pay for the further education of students residing in their district, so that a student who wished to study at a college outside the district had to apply for permission from their local authority. With Darlington College being only one mile away from the North Yorkshire boundary and quite close to the Cleveland boundary, there were many cases where those authorities refused permission and offered the student a place at one of their own colleges on a similar course.

There were instances of students living just on the North Yorkshire side of the border being instructed to travel to Northallerton or even York that involved them in considerable travelling distances. Darlington was the nearest town to Catterick Garrison, a large army base that would become the largest military garrison in Europe during my time as principal. Army personnel seemed to have no problems taking courses at the College but their wives and children did. I found out at a later date that many avoided the 'extra district' problems by giving an address of a relative in Darlington when they enrolled.

Being somewhat shell-shocked by my early experiences, I perhaps should not have been too surprised when I attended my first meeting of the College governors. In 1970 the Department of Education and Science had issued Circular 7/70, which gave advice to LEAs on the constitution of governing bodies. The preferred model divided the Board into three groups: one-third of councillors or their nominees, one-third from educational interests, including staff and students, and one-third representatives from the community, including representatives from the industries that supported the College. Darlington governors consisted of fifty per cent LEA nominees, mainly councillors and with one of them acting as chairman with a casting vote, it ensured that they could remain firmly in control. There were two representatives from industry who were very supportive, some local community people plus two staff and two student members. I had the ex-officio position of principal. The councillors were transported from County Hall by a minibus or coach and about one hour was allocated for the meeting that had an agenda controlled by the officers.

I had intended to prepare a report as had been my practice at Leeds but was told that a verbal report would be better as the councillors would not have time to read my paper. County Councillor Mrs Moorhouse, who had been elected at the last meeting before I joined the College, did not turn up and indeed I did not see her again. So Lewis Gordon, the vice-chairman chaired the meeting. When I was invited to speak by Lewis, the councillors were already looking at their watches and as they had shown little interest in the preceding business, I decided to confront them head-on with the problems of the College. After less than two minutes I was interrupted by a councillor and asked: 'What piece of equipment are you asking for,

HALF A CENTURY OF FURTHER EDUCATION IN ENGLAND

Principal?' I was amazed at the remark and responded firmly (and politely) that he had not grasped the thrust of my presentation. I then enquired when the governors had last visited the College to inspect the buildings and learning facilities. From the silence it was apparent that most of the members had never been in any room other than the boardroom. The meeting was quickly closed and the councillors departed to the transport. The other members stayed behind with the officers and thanked me for my efforts. The two industrial members told the officers that I must be allowed to present a paper at all meetings and that time limits should not be imposed to restrict discussion. They also wanted a visit arranging as a matter of urgency. The officers were sympathetic but were not confident that they could arrange any of the requests. Apparently, councillors received an attendance allowance for governors meetings as well as the committee meetings in County Hall and if the College board took longer then they would miss a meeting and lose the income from following meetings. Lewis Gordon was not a councillor and lived locally. He had been the head teacher of Humersknott Comprehensive School but had retired early on medical grounds. He was an LEA nominee but he was sympathetic to the points that had been raised and agreed to work with the officers to find a compromise.

As it happened, Lewis did not have to challenge the councillors. Another moneymaking venture for the councillors was the attendance at appointments panels and the first vacancy that came up at the College was an administrative post. At Leeds I had been given delegated powers to make teaching appointments up to senior lecture grade and all administrative appointments except for the registrar. In Durham every appointment was a governing body appointment and all the members were invited to attend. Again, the coach arrived and disgorged its contents and almost thirty people were sitting around the horseshoe-shaped table with a seat at the end for the candidate. I could understand such an arrangement for appointing a principal but for a junior member of staff this was ridiculous and intimidating for the candidates. The candidates were subjected to exactly the same procedure that I had experienced. However, when a candidate ended their presentation, I started to cross-question them to determine rather more than the 'Durham method' had deduced. So instead of each candidate receiving ten minutes in some cases the time more than doubled. I was aware of the growing irritation amongst the councillors and after the second candidate had left, I was told that Mr Excelby never asked questions. I gently reminded them that appointing staff members was one of the most important tasks and each candidate was entitled to a proper hearing and searching questions. When the last candidate had left the room, the chairman stated he would take a show of hands to elect the successful candidate. I interjected to insist that there should be a discussion so that members could share their views. Clearly, this had not been done in the past as it took up more of their valuable time. But I persevered and Lewis agreed. It was clear that one of the weaker candidates was known to some of the members and they were trying to get that person appointed. I made it clear that I could not agree and identified the person who I believed to be the strongest. This was supported by several of the other members and it was then agreed. I received a call the following morning from County Hall informing me that it was unlikely that councillors would be attending future appointment panels. The overall outcome was that most of the councillors not only avoided the appointments panels but also stopped attending board meetings.

I was therefore left with a core of Darlington councillors, namely Jim Skinner, Ron Flowers and Stella Robinson from the Labour group plus Louis Gordon as a nominee of the County Labour group together with Sheila Brown and Philip Stanford Bewley from the Darlington Conservative group. Sheila had been on the College governors for many years and she was also a member of the County Council. I had encountered Philip during my initial teaching practice at Shipley College in 1962.

Having lived and worked in the North East region for twenty-seven years, I had a good knowledge of the regional economy and the rapid changes that had occurred in recent years. The region had been a key participant in the manufacturing expansion during the industrial revolution. Like many parts of the country, engineering was a large part of the economy and most of the students in FE colleges were following craft or technician education programmes. The Crowther Report, 'fifteen to eighteen', of 1959 included statistics showing students data and engineering numbers were greater than the total in the rest of the other areas. Darlington had a wide range of manufacturing industries, such as railway locomotives, Whessoe Engineering producing large steel components, Darlington and Simpson Rolling Mills, Cleveland Bridge (structural engineering), Chrysler Cummins (engines for vehicles) and Darlington Chemical Company that became DARCHEM (chemical engineering). I was told that Whessoe alone had up to one thousand engineering students at the College at its peak. It was therefore obvious that engineering would be the largest department in the College. At the time of my appointment, railway engineering had disappeared and Whessoe was a shadow of its former self. All the other companies were experiencing contraction and eventually the Rolling Mills and DARCHEM closed completely.

There was some compensation in that the new town of Newton Aycliffe, some seven miles from the College, had several smaller light engineering companies and they had formed a training consortium known as South West Durham Training that worked with the College and provided a useful stream of students. However, there was competition for those students from Bishop Auckland College and New College, Durham. The department was still offering a very wide range of craft and technician programmes in almost every area of engineering although numbers were modest in several areas. The HNC and HND programmes remained quite strong and with the advanced craft programmes this gave the department a solid block of advanced FE work.

Darlington had secured the provision of journalism training thanks to the influence of Harold Evans when he was editor of *The Northern Echo*. This was the same Harold Evans who was editor of the *Sunday Times* from 1967 to 1981 before moving to the US to be editor-in-chief of *The Atlantic Monthly Press* and later editorial director of *US News and World Report*. Journalism was part of the department of Business, Accounting and Journalism and it was located in an annex in Trinity Road, a short walk from the main site. I was particular interested in this section as it had been granted all of the capital monies allocated to the College for the year and they had decided to spend it on a computerised editing system. After looking at the proposal and the proposed equipment, I asked that the decision be reviewed but was told that the order had been placed and approved by my predecessor. I was not amused and my fears proved justified as the system did not achieve its stated outcomes and was rarely used.

This section offered professional training courses for journalists in print and radio and undoubtedly achieved high standards but I was concerned that that there was a reluctance to expand the portfolio to younger students. The pattern of attendance of the existing programmes showed that there was spare capacity to do more and I was keen to see a programme for full-time students. This was resisted for a short time before I made it clear that it had to happen. I soon learned that the staff members in the section were a law unto themselves. They had all been professional journalists and some of their old habits had followed then into FE. Some frequented the bar in the Arts Centre at lunchtimes often accompanied by students and I again made myself unpopular by outlawing that practice. The advantage of journalism programmes to the department was that they were all classified as advanced FE and together with some of the management programmes they formed a significant scope to exploit the Burnham Grading regulations that determined the numbers of senior posts. Whilst journalism had the capacity to expand, the area of banking that was a regional provision in the College was in terminal decline and closed during my first year. This left a group of staff that had to be retrained to work in other areas of the College or to seek redundancy or early retirement.

The Catering, Health and Fashion Department had expanded rapidly. I was well aware of the high reputation of the catering section as I had dined in the restaurant on numerous occasions when the College had hosted APC regional meetings. There was a strong element of staff with Army Catering Corps experience and their skills and discipline ensured high standards were maintained. The relationships with the industry were also excellent and I was keen to see that the section should be encouraged to expand. The fastest growth section was Health, which also included child-care and nursing courses. Another strong area was Hair and Beauty with a talented team of enthusiastic staff. Traditionally, the College had been male dominated but most of the growth areas were attracting females and that was particularly true in this department. Fashion mainly attracted adult students on non-examination programmes and again I was keen to explore the possibilities to include fashion in the full-time provision.

The Department of Science and Humanities was the smallest unit and was trying unsuccessfully to compete with the sixth form college for GCSE and A level students. Like most of the workshop resources, the science laboratories were dated, poorly equipped and an unpleasant smell pervaded the corridors. Evening classes for adults seeking to pick up single subjects or to study a language of a country they wished to visit were very popular and compensated somewhat for the low numbers in the full time programmes. This was the only department that had purchased any computers and I found that the three machines were locked away in cupboards when there were no students in the room. There was no college strategy concerning the purchase of hardware or the application of technology to programmes in general.

The Construction, Art and Design Department was an interesting combination and I saw no signs of collaboration between the two sections. The construction section offered a full range of craft and technician programmes as well as professional programmes. Along with the advanced craft and HNC programmes, they produced a strong pool of advanced FE work. The art and design section was based on the top floor of the library block. Its main daytime programme was a BTEC National Diploma and when I arrived, I inherited a dispute between BTEC and the College over the quality of the provision for full-time students. Resolving this issue needed a good deal of diplomacy as it soon became evident that the quality of several members of the teaching team was sub-standard and the BTEC assessor in particular had singled out one teacher. The College had already recruited students to commence in the new term and the first year students were expecting to commence the second year. However, without the BTEC approval the courses could not continue. There was only one member of the teaching team, Hilary Midgley, who had emerged unscathed from the assessor's report and she was not keen to be dragged into the dispute. Fortunately, being the good professional that she obviously was, she agreed to take over full responsibility for both years of the programme as long as the other teachers were not involved. Happily, BTEC accepted this solution and some good part-time staff were recruited to support the permanent staff member. The staff that had been criticised were sidelined and eventually left of their own accord. The remaining work of this section was non-vocational and the resources were well used in the evenings.

In addition to the commitments within colleges and the LEA, I found that there were other meetings that I was expected to attend. I attended my first meeting of the Regional Manpower Services Commission in Newcastle and met the regional manager Gordon Nicholson. APC had asked me to represent the Association on the Heating and Ventilating Contractors Association (HVCA) and I attended my first meeting in London in October. The Durham LEA had a local office in Darlington and the officers arranged regular meetings with the secondary head teachers and the two college principals. My first meeting with this group was in October at the Teachers' Centre in Northgate. On top of that was a special meeting concerning the CGLI 600 Series in London, two separate conferences organised by the Northern Council for Further Education (NCFE) in Newcastle and a Staff College Conference at Wetherby.

I had taken stock of the current situation and was wondering if I had made a dreadful mistake in leaving the relative calm of Leeds for the chaos in the North East. I called the heads of department together and informed them that I intended to have a full review of all aspects of the College and that it was likely to lead to major restructuring. The format would be a series of off-site meetings with the heads to thrash out all the details and to produce a solution that would be implemented in the next academic year. Needless to say, my proposal was not greeted with unanimous enthusiasm. However, I had previously briefed Doug Boynton and he gave me his full support. The first meeting was held at the Walworth Castle Hotel in November and I presented my impressions of the College, identifying all the problems that had to be addressed whilst acknowledging the poor resource base allocated to it by the LEA. I gave all of the team an opportunity to put forward their personal views and there was a significant level of agreement with my assessment of the problem. We now needed to address the solutions.

There were two positives that I experienced during my first term at Darlington; the first was the Darlington Lecture Association that held eight monthly lectures between September and May in the College hall. The second was the Tate Vin evening that was organised by the catering section staff. This provided an opportunity for the College to show off the skills of its students to an invited dinner audience and a gourmet meal with wines was served. With each student looking after a table of four guests, a team of judges assessed the talents of the youngsters and the winning student was presented with the wine taster spoon that was hung around the neck and the student was entitled to wear it whenever they were on duty in the restaurant.

The Christmas vacation in Leeds with the family provided a welcome relief to the first term of trials and tribulations. The house sale was secured and everything was in place to move to Darlington in early February.

January began with a Principals' Conference at County Hall and there was a further meeting during the month together with a private meeting of the principals. I had instigated a county colleges group to look into the impact of the new technologies and the first meeting of the Electronics Communications Working Party took place at Neville's Cross on 6 January. Also, during the first fortnight I had a three-day DES Conference in Birmingham. All this extra activity meant that my second Away Day with the management team at the King's Head Hotel was delayed until 20 January. Progress was slow and I had to hide my frustration and try to maintain an optimistic approach. In view of the lack of progress, it was agreed to hold a two-day residential session in early March.

On 1 February 1988 the family moved from Leeds to our newly-built house in Hadrian Court and within a relatively short time Veronica had sorted out all the rooms to made the house feel welcoming for all the family. The children had been accepted at St. Augustine's Primary School which was a short walk from the house and they soon settled into the welcoming atmosphere of the school. On 2 and 3 February the LEA had called two more Principals' Conferences, which meant I had little time to support Veronica at home. During the next two weeks I started to make my plans that I intended to present to the management team at the residential and at the same time to work on financial statistics that I had discretely received from Chris Horne. The statistics showed the funding for each of the Durham Colleges over several years and I soon identified that if Darlington had been funded on a similar basis to most of the other colleges it should have received approximately £1m more per year. This revelation confirmed my worst suspicions and I confided first with Doug Boynton and then with Lewis Gordon. Lewis was not too supportive, as, I suspect, he did not wish to upset the county councillors that appointed him to the College and other governing bodies. I therefore had to request a personal meeting with the County Chief Executive Kingsley Smith to discuss my problems with the LEA.

When my request came to the attention of the education department, I received a visit from the county treasurer's officers, who tried to convince me that the College was not being treated badly. However, they could not argue against their own figures and also they did not provide me with convincing evidence that the other colleges deserved more resources than Darlington. (I discovered some time later that most of the educational establishments in Darlington were also experiencing discrimination. It was suggested to me that when Darlington had its own LEA several years previously it had invested heavily in education and the schools and the College had better facilities than the county schools at the time when the merger took place.)

Eventually I was invited to attend a meeting at County Hall. Kingsley Smith had invited the director of education, Keith Grim-shaw, his deputy, Keith Mitchell, and the director of finance to attend. I was invited to present my case that was supported by a document that I had previously circulated to them. After the presentation, Kingsley Smith invited Keith Grimshaw to respond and he gave a rambling discourse that lacked any hard facts. Keith Mitchell also made several observations. The CEO then turned to the director of finance who simply said that, 'Mr Shuker appears to have a strong case'. I was thanked for attending and invited to leave. The outcome was an adjustment to the College budget for the following financial year of a sum close to my request. At that time I was delighted with the outcome but unfortunately the LEA did not incorporate the additional sum into the base budget for the College and the battle had to be renewed two years later.

My work at Leeds on computer-assisted administration had roused interest around the FE sector. The FE Staff College at Coombe Lodge had approached me to participate in a two-day conference in mid-February and I had agreed to make a presentation. The conference was well supported by colleges and LEAs and my presentation led to a lot of questions. As a result of that experience I became a regular participant in Staff College conferences on MIS (management information systems) for several years. In March I was invited to give a presentation at an IT conference at Weston-Super-Mare. It is perhaps worth pointing out that I received no fees for my professional contributions at the Staff College or for any of the other external commitments at which I had been invited to participate.

The Technical and Vocational Education Initiative (TVEI) first began as a pilot scheme in 1983 and was expanded nationally in 1987. The programme was introduced in an attempt to improve the allegedly low quality of vocational education and training that was claimed to be handicapping commerce and industry in the competitive 1980s. The late 1970s and early 1980s were marked by rapidly rising unemployment and the decimation of important sectors of the economy. The Northern region was keen to promote TVEI and a regional conference was held at Beamish Hall in late February. The seventeenth century Beamish Hall was a former residence of the Shafto and Eden families but had been converted into a residential conference centre that was mainly used by the Durham LEA schools. Most of the colleges in the region sent a delegate as TVEI was perceived as a potential area for growth. I quite enjoyed the day and made several new contacts.

I had raised the issue of MIS at the Principals' Conference and officers in County Hall had discussed it. The outcome was a meeting of interested parties in County Hall and I was asked to comment and several officers in the administration also made contributions. There was no firm proposals agreed at that time but there was recognition that this was a key area that needed to be monitored.

I held the residential senior managers' seminar over the next two days at the Kings Head Hotel and we had a major breakthrough by the end of the second day. My proposal to move from a departmental structure to a part matrix solution had been hard to sell but I persisted and eventually it was agreed to designate the heads as assistant principals with the following roles: curriculum, students, staffing, buildings and resources, and research and development. Areas of responsibility were allocated to each role and broad job descriptions were produced. The departments were to be replaced by schools and as the College had many principal and senior lecturers that I believed would benefit from some middle manager responsibilities, I was keen to see quite a large number of schools initially. The five heads were invited to write down their first preference for the new positions on a piece of paper and to pass it to me without revealing it to anyone else. Amazingly, each head had selected a position that was not requested by a colleague. The look of amazement on their faces will remain with me for many years and I think that my credibility rose several notches that day. John Davies had selected curriculum, Peter Pearson had selected staffing, Bob Twitty had selected buildings and resources, Selwyn Morgan had selected students and Alan Dixon had opted for research and development.

I should have guessed that this solution was just too perfect and shortly after our successful residential, Doug Boynton dropped in to my office to tell me that he had applied for the post of principal at Telford College. He said it was a speculative application to 'test the water' but a few days later he informed me that he had been short-listed for the post. The evening of his interview he rang me at home saying that he had been offered the post and he did not know if he should accept it. Although the last thing I wanted was to lose such a good deputy I told him to go for it and he did. I was keen to try to find a replacement for Doug as soon as possible and convinced the governors and the LEA to advertise without delay. The response to the advertisement was disappointing but a short-list was produced including Bob Twitty, the only internal applicant. Interviews took place in late May and it was clear to me that there was only one possible applicant that could do the job and that was Margaret Armstrong, who had held senior appointments in several North East colleges. However, the governors were determined not to support me so I insisted that the job be readvertised and they reluctantly agreed. I regarded Selwyn Morgan as the senior of the existing heads and asked him if he would take on the duties of acting vice-principal as it was unlikely that we could fill the vacancy before Doug's departure. Earlier he had indicated to me that he had intended to retire at the end of the year but had agreed to cover the VP duties until an appointment was made. The second interviews were at the end of May and again I had reservations about identifying a suitable candidate. However, the Board was not in any mood to delay and chairman Lewis Gordon backed Alan Dixon who was the internal candidate. Although I felt that Alan lacked the experience that I would have preferred, I accepted the majority view that he was the best candidate.

I had raised the question of the College Academic Board with the registrar and I had the impression that it did not meet very regularly and he seemed far from enthusiastic about my proposal to have a meeting every term. As the governing body met in March, I thought it appropriate to have a meeting of the Academic Board in the morning before the Board met. I had inherited Dick Exelby's secretary Diane Muckle and she was proving very efficient and quickly found the file of minutes of the last meeting of the Academic Board. After studying the minutes I began to realise why the registrar was reluctant to convene a meeting. However, it was clear from the terms of reference that the Academic Board should meet on a regular basis and therefore the Board needed to be managed to make it a more relevant body within the College. I changed the format of the agenda and asked the heads of department to produce papers or to submit information to me to be included in my paper so that the Board members would have an opportunity to study any of management's proposals. As it was the first time that the Board had met since my arrival there was some curiosity on how I would chair the meeting. Consequently, there was a good turn out of the members. However, the meeting was a disappointment to me as only managers made any contribution although Dick Armstrong, the NATFHE representative, who was also a member of the Governing Body, did make several sarcastic observations. After the meeting I felt that little had been achieved and that it was an issue to be addressed to make the Board more effective. Just before the Easter break, I was invited to the official opening of the Information Technology Staff Development Centre in Leeds, which had been promoted by Doug Masterton, the IT adviser for the schools sector and a person I had been pleased to work with over the last two years in Leeds.

I had been an active member of APC but had not joined the recently formed Association of College Managers (ACM) that was recruiting principals, vice-principals, heads of department and other senior managers. Some of the principals in the Northern region and the Yorkshire region had joined and it was agreed to hold a joint meeting of the members of the two regions. A meeting was held in York in April and the champions of both organisations expressed views. At that time I felt that the long established APC offered a good forum for principals to meet and discuss sensitive issues with the knowledge that there would be no indiscretions or leaks to embarrass members. The outcome broadly reflected my views and few principals changed their minds. ACM had offered free membership to APC members and I attended a further joint meeting at Bradford in May.

Chris Horne, the LEA assistant director for FE had obtained another post in Derbyshire and was leaving the authority at Easter. I was sorry to see him go, as he had been very helpful to me in recouping some additional financial allocation to the College. The principals dined him out at a pleasant bistro in Bishop Auckland and we had a good evening, which also helped to cement my relation-ships with the other principals. Chris was to be replaced by Mike Daubney who proved to be a very different kind of officer who tried bullying tactics at Principals' Conferences.

May was an interesting month that started with an invitation to the Awards Ceremony at Leeds College of Building and I was delighted to attend with Veronica to see my former colleagues and many students as they received their well earned awards. Veronica and I were also invited to the Open Day at Houghall Agricultural College, an annual event that attracted many visitors to observe the work of the College and purchase some of the produce. This was followed by a three day IT conference at the Staff College where I gave another presentation.

The restructuring of the senior management team had led to the division of the departments into schools and the heads of schools were appointed from existing principal and senior lecturers. I had decided to make the schools quite small initially so that the management of the staff teams would not be too onerous for the new heads and eventually we finished with twenty-four schools. During the second week in June, I arranged for all the heads of schools and the assistant principals to attend a residential staff-training seminar at the Teesside Airport Hotel. This proved to be a popular event and brought to my attention the fact that many of the heads of schools had not met many of their colleagues, which probably contributed to the rigidity of the departmental system.

With Selwyn Morgan's pending departure, I appointed Tom Harker, a principal lecturer, to the acting post of assistant principal (students). Tom had a reputation for having a lively sense of humour and often acted as master of ceremonies at staff social events. When Bert Lowcock had to retire from his post as registrar, we found an able replacement in Michael Wood who had been an assistant registrar at Newcastle Polytechnic.

Mike Rowarth was the principal of Newcastle College and he was also the regional secretary of APC. I had known Mike for several years and he contacted me regarding the proposed merger of Hertfordshire College of Building and St Albans College by Hertfordshire LEA. As I had experience of a building college and a general-purpose college he asked me to be the APC representative at a meeting between the LEA and the governors of the two colleges. I reluctantly agreed as I had very little knowledge of the political implications and no experience in that type of negotiation. I was invited to attend an evening meeting at St Albans in late June. The chief education officer had sent me some papers about the proposals and I met him briefly before the meeting commenced and he indicated that the College of Building governors were strongly opposed to the merger.

The meeting became heated with the College of Building governors feeling that 'their college' was the loser in the proposed merger. I listened carefully to the discussions and noted some concessions to the College of Building had been added to the original papers. When I was invited to comment, I realised that I was in a no win situation but I tried to highlight the extra concessions that would ensure that the College of Building governors would have a guaranteed quota of representatives on the new College Board so that they should be able to ensure that construction would not be treated unfavourably. There was a grudging acceptance so that all parties agreed to the amended proposals. After the meeting, the CEO thanked me for the assistance in achieving a suitable outcome and I departed rather late on the long journey back to Darlington. It had been an interesting experience and I would have two further opportunities in the future to support college principals that had asked for the APC for assistance.

The College had an established press officer in Gordon Merry and during the year I had encouraged him to produce a new logo for the

College and to prepare the traditional newsletter to accompany the course information for 1988–89. The logo was a pink 'D' made up of arrowheads going from left to right on a black background and it was generally agreed that this gave a positive, forward-looking image. The newsletter had good, positive content with plenty of photographs that would hopefully attract the people of Darlington to respond by enrolling at the College. The newsletter was produced for several years up to incorporation.

The traditional end of term at Darlington included a summer fête that was held on the College playing fields and involved many activities for staff and their families to get together. Monies were raised for local charities and a large crowd turned up to support the event. The engineering department staff had an annual do and I was invited to join them at the York Junior Unionist Club. This was really an end of year drinking session and an excuse to let the hair down. I had been warned about this event and to keep clear of the people who had a reputation for 'going a bit too far'. Sandwiched between these events was the Huddersfield Annual Reunion and Selwyn Morgan's retirement dinner at the Sutton Alms at Elton that brought an end to my first year at Darlington College of Technology.

1988–1989

During enrolments in the first week of September, I called at Sherwood's Garage in Darlington where Alasdair MacConachie was the managing director. I had met Alasdair several times during my first year, as he was involved in many local activities, including the Lecture Association and the RSA. As Sherwood's was the Vauxhall dealer I had expected Alasdair to try to sell me one of his latest models but instead he persuaded me to buy an Audi 80GL. At first I thought that this was a better all round vehicle but I soon experience minor problems with the car that caused disruption to my heavy college schedule, so I reverted back to Vauxhalls.

I had maintained links with the computing HMIs that I had met on the 1986 trip to Germany as well as seeing them at the FEU New Technology Committee. Malcolm Himsworth, the staff inspector, had decided to organise a visit to France and Germany with a party drawn from colleges and polytechnics. I had been invited to lead the

FE group of twelve and the polytechnics had about thirty places taken mainly by deans of computing. The visit was scheduled to take seven days departing on 11 September in London. The group travelled on a new coach that was hired from a North East company, the first leg being to Essen in Germany via a ferry from Dover to Calais.

We visited a variety of training establishments in Essen, Düsseldorf and Cologne and observed fairly traditional methods of teaching in well-equipped buildings. We met apprentices who were employed in major companies with a training college attached to the workshops and adults being retrained in engineering. Motivation appeared to be good but we were disappointed not to see any evidence of innovative use of learning technologies. We were informed that plans were being considered to purchase computers to support computer-aided design.

The second part of the trip was to Grenoble University in France, which was a long journey by coach. The coach had two drivers, one of whom had experience of travelling in Europe but the other had not driven outside of England. The drivers had decided to avoid driving on roads that carried a toll charge and that resulted in some interesting diversions, including crossing over the border into Switzerland. We had been travelling for several hours on motorways when the coach broke down and we were stranded for almost twelve hours before a replacement part could be located and delivered. The forty-five passengers were far from happy as the temperatures were quite high and the air conditioning on the coach was not working. It was dark when we arrived in France and we insisted that a stop was made for an evening meal as it was obviously going to be too late for a meal by the time we expected to arrive in Grenoble. Malcolm Himsworth stopped the coach in a small town and gave firm instructions that he wanted us all back within forty minutes. In the FE group we were lucky to have John Gray, vice-principal of Basford Hall College as he was a competent linguist and could help his colleagues to decipher the menu. All of the FE team returned on time but the polytechnic deans came straggling in over thirty minutes late having enjoyed a three-course meal and there were some ill feelings from the FE members and HMI.

Eventually, we arrived at our accommodation in Grenoble in the early hours of the morning and Malcolm reminded us that we were to meet the director of the university at 9 a.m. and that he expected all to be present. Given that this meant only three hours' sleep, it was surprising that all but one of the members turned up on time. The university visit was of little interest to most of the FE team but the polytechnic deans seemed to enjoy the experience. The final leg of the visit was to Paris and the journey was uneventful until we arrived at the hotel. One of the HMI had been nominated by Malcolm to carry out all of the administrative duties and she asked us to stay in the coach whilst she checked to see if the hotel was ready for our party. I do not know exactly what she observed in the hotel but she raced out saying, 'It is a brothel! We cannot stay there'. Malcolm calmed her down and eventually rooms were made ready for occupancy. The overall impression of the visit was that the UK was probably ahead in terms of developments in computer applications to learning and administration based upon the small sample we had witnessed. However, the main benefit of the visit was the close working and understanding that had developed between the FE members. After the visit the college members organised a residential weekend seminar at the Walworth Castle Hotel, near Darlington, to consider the implications of the visit for the UK further education sector. It was agreed to establish a voluntary organisation to encourage college staff to share examples of good practice.

Immediately following the visit I was faced with two more journeys to Derwentside College in Consett and Peterlee College in East Durham for Principals' Conferences that were called in respect of enrolments in the colleges. The principals had persuaded the officers, including the new assistant director Mike Daubney, to rotate the venue for meetings. This was really a political move rather than making life easier but I felt that it did balance the power between LEA and colleges more fairly. The following week Darlington College had been selected to receive a visit from Lord Young, Secretary of State for Trade and Industry, and despite his reputation for being abrasive, I found the visit interesting and potentially useful.

I had been concerned at the lack of student support services at the College and after some negotiations with senior colleagues it was agreed to establish a 'Student Services Unit' to provide advisory and confidential services for students. In 1990 the unit was revised to become the 'Client Support Unit' with a more clearly defined remit to support students (and potential students) from initial enquiry to entry to the College, during their studies and, on completion of their studies, to assist them to progress their career goals. I also approached the local clergy to establish an independent part-time service that I called the 'chaplaincy'. Three of the local churches responded with Father Bob Spence taking a lead role.

The rest of the autumn term required me to focus on the new management structures and to assist the senior post holders and the heads of school to work in harmony for the benefit of the students. I had established a good working relationship with some of the head teachers in the town, especially Dela Smith who was head of Salters Lane School which provided education for students with severe learning difficulties in the age range two to nineteen. Dela was the first head to approach me and welcome me to the town. She expressed a desire to raise the aspirations of her pupils by establishing a Youth Training Scheme (YTS) for the older pupils but her initial efforts had not been supported by the Manpower Services Commission. I had agreed to give her whatever support that she required, including link course opportunities in the College. Some of my colleagues were alarmed at the proposal and were convinced that the College was not the right place for such youngsters. However, I did get some support from one or two of the vocational schools and links did eventually begin. There was a small team at the College that covered post-school special needs students but I had not been impressed by the standards achieved or the attitude of some of the teaching team and I did not perceive much interest in this area from senior staff. In addition to Dela there were two other head teachers from the other Special Needs schools in the town, together with representatives from the LEA. Eventually, Dela's persistence paid off and she did succeed in getting her YTS scheme.

As a response to the objectives of 'Furthering Education for All' the college promoted the National Adult Literacy Scheme with a full-time co-ordinator and a team of part-time staff and voluntary tutors. The College secured special funding to establish, in a former staff room, a fully equipped and staffed Adult Learning Centre that was opened by Alan Wells, Director of the Adult Literacy and Basic Skills Unit (ALBSU). Alan was very impressed with the facility as he had been highly critical of the general approach of FE colleges in addressing adult literacy. In 1991 the College was one of the first to be awarded the ALBSU 'Quality Kite Mark' for its work with adult learners.

There were seven secondary schools and a sixth form college in the town and a previous Darlington administration had restricted post-compulsory education to the two colleges and the catholic school that had a small sixth form. This arrangement ensured that most of the pupils in six of the town's secondary schools had access to unbiased careers advice with no pressure to stay in a local sixth form. The LEA held meetings of the Darlington secondary heads and college principals on a regular basis and I found that the meetings were fairly positive and friendly. Austin Brooks was head teacher of Longfield School and he invited me to the school's Awards evening and Veronica and I enjoyed the evening and the many more that followed. Mary Bowles was the principal of Queen Elizabeth Sixth Form College and we met occasionally to exchange information, although at that time there was little overlap in our respective educational provision. Mary concentrated on O and A level courses for school leavers whilst our modest provision in that area was aimed at adults. Carl Ottolini was head of Haughton School and he regularly invited me to school events. David Henderson was head of Hummersknott School, located in the affluent West End of the town and I also met him from time to time. The four remaining heads at Carmel RC school, Eastbourne School, Branksome School and Hurworth School were friendly but seemed to be in no hurry to invite me to their schools. At that time the LEA linked Newton Aycliffe with Darlington to form the South West Durham area. Therefore, the two Aycliffe secondary schools of Woodham and Greenhead attended meetings with the Darlington schools.

Dick Excelby had represented APC on the NCTJ (National Council for the Training of Journalist) Board and I seemed to inherit the annual visit to London. The meeting was at the end of November in Bloomsbury and consisted of editors, National Union of Journalists (NUJ) representatives, educationalists and officers. The first part of the meeting passed uneventfully with the business being briskly conducted. Then there was a break for lunch that included some modest sandwiches and snacks. However, this was more than compensated by the array of alcoholic beverages and by the time I reached the table most of the members were clutching their own bottle of wine or spirits! I helped myself to a glass of wine and chatted to some of the members. When it was decided to resume the meeting after about an hour of steady drinking, an official presented members with a plastic cup as apparently the glasses were not to be taken into the meeting room. The plastic cup was to allow the drinking to continue during the second half of the meeting. I can say without any fear of contradiction that the remainder of the meeting did not take long and few would be able to recall the decisions taken. I decided not to attend another meeting of the NCTJ.

The winter term started with an induction programme for new staff. I had included this element in the College policy on staff development when it became apparent that departmental boundaries had limited integration of staff across the College. I took the opening slot to set the scene for the rest of the induction programme. This at least ensured that new staff would be likely to recognise me in future! I had also arranged for a two-day management training session at Walworth Castle in January to keep the pressure on senior managers in their new roles to ensure that progress was being made and monitored. January was also the first opportunity that I had to participate in a national bid for European funding for IT. The meeting was held in the Polytechnic of Central London and I had my first experience of the complexity associated with this exercise. There was a meeting of the Darlington Industry Committee, which met at the College and had been formed from the RSA initiative 'Industry Matters'. Alasdair MacConachie seemed to be the driving force and he had gathered a mix of business people and educationalists together to discuss issues of the day and to visit local companies that appeared to be operating well. I had a number of City and Guilds appointments during this early part of the year; firstly, two visits to London with the 600 Series Moderating Committee and two visits from Jim Pratt and Norman Phillips, who were regarded as key planners for the Institute for Construction Technician programmes. Norman had been head of building at Carlisle College and he had been promoted to vice-principal and then principal at the same college.

Management information systems were being actively discussed in many quarters but I had been disappointed with the slow progress in implementation. However, the county established a MIS Committee for FE Colleges and it met regularly to identify computerised systems and to estimate costs. I was a member of the committee, which meant more meetings at County Hall but none of my principal colleagues felt sufficiently confident to become directly involved. Angus Byrne, who was employed as an advisor by the LEA to have an overview of IT issues was also a member of the committee and we got on very well. There was also a regional MIS group that met under the direction of the NCFE in Newcastle and again I found myself elected to serve on that committee by the region's principals.

Although I had spent a considerable amount of time implementing MIS systems, I had not overlooked the need to develop computing in the curriculum. We had taken advantage of the DES Education Support Grant (ESG) initiative to enhance the provision of computing and Information Technology by purchasing equipment for our first Open Access Centre. There were one hundred computers by late 1988 and that would quickly double, with most of the computers being networked. At the time there was much scepticism amongst the teaching staff who would probably have preferred to see the money spent on other items, but the students enthused about the facilities and it was clear that these improvements were having an influence on the increased number of students enrolling at the College.

In early February I introduced another innovation in the College when I held a full staff meeting in the College hall. This was open to all staff, both teaching and support staff. This was a further dimension to my staff development vision and an attempt to keep all staff informed directly by me of current and proposed events that would have an influence on them. The majority of the staff seemed to appreciate the opportunity but I had the feeling that some of the longer serving staff felt it was quite unnecessary – no doubt they preferred to remain in ignorance.

I had been elected to serve on the Council of the Association of Colleges of Further and Higher Education (ACFHE) that represented colleges and polytechnics across the country. It had been formed in 1893 and most institutions subscribed to it. Its council meetings were held in the main buildings of the Polytechnic of Central London and there was a two-day annual conference that was well supported. Clive Brain, Principal of Swindon College, was the honorary secretary of ACFHE and he was highly regarded by his colleagues. My good friend Chris West had moved from GLOSCAT to Swindon to be Clive's vice-principal and he enjoyed working with Clive. Anne Limb, then Principal of Milton Keynes College, was also on ACFHE council and I was impressed by her contribution to the debates.

The Maastricht Treaty or the Treaty of the European Union

The European Community (EC) had embarked on a program popularly referred to as Europe 1992. The aim of the program was to achieve a unified European market that would overcome the economic stagnation and unemployment of the early 1980s and improve the position of EC members in the global economy. In 1985 the European Commission proposed almost three hundred specific reforms that would reduce trade barriers between EC countries by 1992. In Darlington it was agreed to form a 1992 Committee with a view to raise awareness with local business and the community in general. I had been invited to join the committee and it met frequently. To launch the concept, two conferences were held in the Town Hall during February and, as expected, the debate raised all of the old issues both for and against Britain joining the EU. Clive Owen, the Darlington Chief Executive, chaired the early meetings but I was invited to take over the chair in 1990. The intention was to have a conference within the Darlington community each year leading up to 1992 and Tony Blair, who was the local MP for Sedgefield, had agreed to speak at the launch of the first conference in 1989. Stephen Hughes, who was the MEP for County Durham and lived in Darlington, had also agreed to participate.

With Alan Dixon being appointed to the vice-principal post it left a vacancy for the post of assistant principal for research and development. The interviews were held in late February and I was pleased when the governors agreed to appoint Dr Graham Best to the post. Graham had a strong background in research and he was willing to take an innovative look at how he could interpret the remit for the benefit of students and the College. He was interested in the European developments and agreed to explore possibilities of European funding to promote some of our developments. He did not take up his appointment until September but he made several visits to the College to discuss his ideas with me before then.

I had always been enthusiastic about recognising the success of students. At Redcar and Leeds there had been either college or departmental award ceremonies with local employers donating prizes for specific awards. At Darlington I was informed that the practice of award ceremonies had ceased fourteen years ago and that the county councillors were not in favour of these events, as they believed they encouraged unhealthy competition between students. At a meeting of the governing body in late 1988, I had informed the members of my intention to reintroduce a College Award Ceremony in 1989 and I was not surprised when a prominent councillor told me that he did not approve of such events. I politely informed him and the other Board members that I was not seeking their permission and that I hoped that they would attend the Ceremony and support the students. My secretary, with the help of some of the longer serving members of the College, recovered many of the trophies that had been donated by local companies, together with a number of beautifully made medals that had been presented to the College by a large regional engineering company to recognise excellence in technician engineering courses. I had also written to several local companies and was delighted with an enthusiastic and generous response from most of them. The heads of section were invited to identify students who merited recognition for their work, commitment and attitude during the year and a comprehensive list was produced.

The Awards Ceremony took place in April and the hall was filled to capacity. Only Louis Gordon in his capacity as Chairman attended from the LEA nominees. He had the support of the two industrial governors and the two Conservative councillors. On the advice of Alasdair MacConachie, I had invited John MacFarlane, who was a senior director of ICI and lived in Darlington, to present the awards. The format of the evening commenced with a welcome from the Chairman, a short presentation by me to highlight the successes of the year, the presentation of awards by John MacFarlane followed by a short address by him. The evening ended with refreshments in the students' refectory. The students and their families as well as the staff and guests enjoyed the event. The following day there was a meeting of the Academic Board and I was pleased with the members' positive reactions to the evening.

The 1988 Education Act required LEAs to delegate significant responsibilities to colleges. The government had indicated to LEAs that there should be more financial responsibilities delegated to colleges and this was referred to as 'Local Financial Management'. Most local authorities and that included County Durham had not traditionally delegated any responsibilities to their colleges. All orders for equipment and materials had to be processed through the county treasurer's office. Colleges did not have bank accounts and the amount of petty cash was strictly controlled. The county held a Local Financial Management seminar at New College, Durham, in late April and it soon became clear that there was little enthusiasm from the officers for any of the government's proposals. Laurie Turner and I as principals of the largest colleges spoke strongly in favour of freeing up some the restrictions but not all of our colleagues seemed too happy about having greater financial responsibilities. This made it relatively easy for the officers to 'divide and rule' and little progress was reported. However, after further discussions a concession was agreed on 'carry-over', which allowed colleges to carry forward surpluses or deficits from one financial year to the next. This brought to an end the rush to spend as the end of the financial year approached in April. The only principal who was not happy with this decision was Keith Byfield as Bishop Auckland had a reputation of overspending most years without being penalised. In talking to colleagues at APC and ACFHE meetings it was apparent that some LEAs had been more enlightened than Durham. The comprehensive coverage of the 1988 Education Act was not fully appreciated by the majority of people in the FE sector. Secretary of State for Education Kenneth Baker had set in motion the impetus for the Further and Higher Education Act of 1992 that led to the incorporation of colleges and a parting of the ways with local authorities.

4 May 1989 was an important day for me when the group of FE IT practitioners who had been on the visit to Germany and France in 1988 met in London as Founders of SCITFE (Standing Conference for IT in FE). This rather clumsy title was chosen on the advice of HMI as it reflected the use of 'standing conference' in the polytechnic sector. In addition to the FE representation there was Staff HMI Malcolm Himsworth. We were informed that the DES FE section had given us its full support and it had approached some key

industrialists who could be interested in providing some initial sponsorship. Don Libby, the senior civil servant with a responsibility for FE had taken the lead in supporting this initiative and he had approached Barney Gibbens, Chairman of the SEMA Group and Founder Master of the Worshipful Company of Information Technologists. They offered to arrange the meeting and Chris West and I met with the group to give them an overview of our proposals and they seemed interested and implied that they would be amenable to sponsoring some of our activities.

It was agreed to have a two-day setting up meeting of SCITFE at Preston Polytechnic later in the month and I was invited to be the founder chairman. The dean of computing at Preston Polytechnic had been very supportive of our proposals and had offered to host the meeting and provide whatever technical support we might require. We formed an 'executive group' comprising me as chairman; John Gray, Vice Principal of Basford Hall College in Nottingham; Chris West, Vice Principal of Swindon College; and Harry Langstone, an IT advisor to Avon and Somerset LEA. We set a target to hold our first annual conference in October and each member of the group agreed to take on some areas of responsibility. Chris suggested that the conference should be held in Bristol and that was agreed. The recruitment of colleges to membership of SCITFE was modest initially but with the active support of the DES and the HMI the numbers started to increase. Some of us were not happy with the SCITFE title and before the conference agreement was reached on a new name – National Information and Learning Technologies Association (NAITFE) – that we believed reflected the purpose of the Association. The inclusion of 'National' in the title indicated our intentions to recruit colleges from Scotland, Wales and Northern Ireland as well as the English colleges. John hosted a council meeting at Basford Hall College in July and the conference took place at the Grand Hotel, Bristol on 24/25 October 1989. All of the preparation, including the preparation of promotional materials, was handled by the small team meeting at John Gray's home in North Muskham, near Newark.

The NAITFE activities did not deflect my attention from the business in the College, as there was still much to be done to rouse 'the sleeping giant' to provide the quality of education that the local students deserved. My educational philosophy owed much to my experiences at Huddersfield where I had worked with a team of committed professionals striving to practice what they preached. I had no doubt that the most important people in the College were the students and that is was the responsibility of all members of staff, both teaching and administrative, to support the students and maintain a good quality learning environment. I was not comfortable with the 'lecturer' label used by DES and local authorities to describe the teaching staff as it reinforced views that lecturing was the approved method to encourage learning. I had observed some poor lessons during my time as a teacher trainer and, sadly, Darlington was no different. I made time during the week to quietly visit different curriculum areas to observe the interaction between staff and students and whilst most of the workshop sessions were of a good standard, the classroom sessions were often dreadfully boring. Most staff at Leeds College of Building were teacher-trained but the same was not true at Darlington, despite the opportunity of in-service training at Durham. I found that most of my senior colleagues agreed with my views but there had not been any pressure applied to untrained staff to address their deficiencies. It was agreed that the College would take up its full quota of places at Durham in future and that every effort would be made to recruit new staff that were fully qualified.

As I had been granted much more autonomy in appointing staff now that most of the councillors had opted out, I introduced more liberal selection methods that would hopefully identify the best candidates more effectively. I ensured that I chaired most of the appointments panels for administrative and junior teaching positions and that appropriate senior members of staff were also involved so that the representative from the LEA could have little objection with our choice. I was keen to appoint younger people to the staff and thought that we should look towards our own full-time students as possible recruits to the administration. To achieve this I proposed that the College establish a number of trainee positions for clerical staff and I had support from the governors. However, the county personnel officers were not supportive as this was unprecedented in the authority. Eventually, after much discussion with councillors and education staff it was agreed to permit the College to appoint up to two trainees. This resulted in several appointments over the next

23. Darlington College Enterprise Centre 1990 – Student trying out the new facilities

24. Construction in Schools Project 1991 – Presentation of £50,000 cheque being signed by the local manager of the NatWest Bank, with project chairman, Bob Carnell

21. Lord Mayor's visit to Leeds College of Building 1980

22. Jack Place

25. *Humber Bridge visit by Brno Technical University Students with Bridge Master Malcolm Stockwell – July 1991*

26. *Retiring chairman Lewis Gordon receives a clock, made by the construction department, from new chairman, Geoff Nichol 1992*

27. With Roger Ward and college principals for an EU briefing in Dusseldorf, December 1994

28. Hotel and catering students celebrating another successful Tate Vin evening

29. Firthmoor Presentations by Frank Robson, Mayor of Darlington

30. Prime Minister John Major presenting the crystal Charter Mark December 1995

31. *With Pat Gale and the Charter Mark at the Darlington College stand*

32. *Visit of HRH Prince Andrew, with the Lord Lieutenant, students and Angus Byrne*

three years and included the appointment of Gaynor Dobie who would eventually become my secretary and PA.

When I was at Leeds I had been invited to join the RSA Yorkshire Regional Committee and had served for three years before moving north. It was in 1989 that I received a phone call from Derek Sewell, who had been the director of education when I was appointed at Darlington, inviting me to join the RSA North East Regional Committee of which he was chairman. To make my first contribution, I hosted a committee and dinner at the College two weeks prior to the RSA regional AGM where I was formally elected to the committee. Little did I know at the time that it would be eighteen years before I would gracefully resign from the committee.

CHAPTER 9

Widening Horizons

1989–90

IN SEPTEMBER I JOINED A GROUP of business people from the Teesside area on a trip to Strasburg to visit the European Parliament. The flight from Teesside Airport included an address by a government official on the opportunities that we should be taking up to become bigger players within Europe. The visit was useful with an opportunity to meet MEPs and civil servants who provided some interesting information and answered our questions. This was all linked to the 1992 target date and was one of several initiatives in the sub-region.

Another interesting development was the involvement with the Catterick Garrison. This was fifteen miles south of Darlington and in North Yorkshire, but the military personnel regarded Darlington as its local college and despite the objections from North Yorkshire LEA, soldiers attended several of our courses. Pat Gale, who lived in Richmond and was employed by the DES nationally, had approached me to enquire what we were doing about 'the abandoned wives of Catterick'. This referred to the many young women who had married soldiers and had later been abandoned at Catterick when the soldiers were moved to another posting. These women were generally lacking a good education and as a result were not able to find employment in the Catterick area and did not have resources to move back to their home areas. The Army had some local education facilities at the garrison but they were only meant for military personnel. Some of the officers' wives had provided some support but there was clearly a need to establish a more permanent arrangement.

Setting up a Darlington presence in North Yorkshire was not going to be straightforward and I had meetings with an area education officer who was not optimistic about my plans. A short time later I had a meeting with Fred Evans, the chief education officer for North Yorkshire. Fred was much more down to earth and recognised that Darlington College was better placed to respond to the garrison's needs than the county and he gave me his support. This was the beginning of a fruitful partnership with the garrison as it was one of the largest communities in the county but mainly ignored by the rest of the county. This enabled the College to bid for a government grant to enable it to launch the 'ROUTES' learning programmes. One hundred and fifty wives enrolled in the first year and Anita Cook was given the task of running the programme. The successful outcome of the programme led to a greater demand from the military and civilian communities for more local further education facilities. We negotiated with the Army to use a small detached brick building in Horne Road that was accessible to people living in the garrison or in Colburn village where many of the 'abandoned wives' could be found. The Army property team could not have been more helpful and ensured that the building was upgraded and a prominent sign was installed on the front of the building bearing the title 'Darlington College at Catterick'.

I had met with the garrison commander and his deputy and established a good working relationship. The commander had been to the College and was keen to see more collaboration. I was invited by the Royal Signals Regiment to attend one of their dinner evenings and it took me back to my National Service and AER days. I was challenged for not wearing my Territorial Decoration Medal at the dinner and I must admit I had not even thought about it.

In November I achieved my first goal of introducing information technology into the College on a larger scale by opening a drop-in Open Access Centre on the ground floor of the College. It had cost £80,000, the bulk of the capital funding for the year but it set a pattern for the forthcoming years and started a mind-change amongst staff and students. I had invited Llew Aviss, UK personnel director of Fujitsu, to be our guest of honour at the official opening that was covered by the local press. I regarded Llew as a key industrial partner who had the position and personality to influence local industrialists and he made some very complimentary remarks about the new centre to the local journalists. I had negotiated a good deal with Research Machines who had supplied the computers and peripherals for the networks in the centre and the popularity with the students was quickly reflected in the heavy use of the centre. A little later in the academic year, we opened the COLTEC Suite, a room in the former girls' high school block that we converted from a typical type writing and shorthand room into a centre that had a range of the latest machines and equipment used in business administration. This was to be a student-centred resource where they could practice their skills with staff in support.

In December there was a two–day residential staff development conference at Walworth Castle, a trip to Birmingham to speak at the Polytechnics Standing Conference in IT and a presentation to the East Midlands FE council's MIS Conference in Loughborough. I also attended the Tate Vin competition run by the catering school.

Into the nineties

The local authorities held a North of England Education Conference annually during the first week of the year, just before the start of term. I had received invitations to previous conferences but had not been able to take up the offer. However, as Newcastle Council was hosting the1990 conference I decided to attend. The conference was held in Newcastle City Hall and lasted two days. This was a grand setting and I quite enjoyed the conference even though the bulk of the sessions were related to school education.

Alan Wells, the chief executive of ALBSU (Adult Basic Skills Unit), had invited me to be a member of one of his advisory committees and this was the start of a long association with Alan and his organisation. The rest of January included two meetings of the Principals' Conference, two meeting of the county MIS group and meetings of the county IT group, the Darlington Committee for Industry, the 1992 Forum and the governing body. I had one trip to London to represent the APC on the Heating and Ventilating Contractors Association Council and a Saturday morning on Derby station with John Gray and Chris West planning the next steps in the evolution of NAITFE and to plan the committee meeting in February.

Meanwhile, the work of the North East Regional IT group led to a regional conference at the Ramside Hall Hotel and this attracted representatives from most of the colleges in the region. The response was encouraging but I was disappointed with the general ignorance and cynicism amongst many of the participants. Local commitments outside of my college responsibilities continued to expand with another visit to Catterick Garrison to maintain the momentum of the earlier visits and the regular meeting of the 1992 Committee. Principals' Conferences continued at about two a month and the Darlington Committee for Industry was expanding its activities. My third week in February was spent in London with three days at City and Guilds and the Annual ACFHE Conference.

The very active school of catering regularly entered students into regional competitions and I was invited to one of those events in Newcastle organised and sponsored by NORGAS. It was an excellent evening with all the students performing well and I was especially pleased as Darlington students gained top marks.

The regional RSA Committee had alternate meetings in Newcastle and Durham with Hatfield College hosting the Durham meeting. Perhaps as a result of the link, I was invited to dinner at Hatfield College by the Master, Professor James Barber, to discuss issues of mutual interest. It was a pleasant evening with a new experience at dining at the 'high table' but despite friendly discussions it was difficult to identify any obvious common ground between our respective institutions.

Bob Twitty informed me that he had accepted the post of vice-principal at Wigan and Leigh College and that he wished to be released early from his contract so that he could start after the Easter break. Bob had been a conscientious and reliable manager even though he had taken a lot of criticism for his selection of pink paint on the external pipe-work as part of our attempts to brighten up the external appearance of the College. 'Twitty Pink' became the in-joke for several years before and after Bob left the College. I saw little benefit of hanging on to Bob until the summer and advised the governors and the LEA to release him and to advertise for a replacement. This did not interfere with the management residential seminar at Walworth Castle, as I was determined to further cement the new management structure and to encourage the emerging sense of co-operation between the assistant principals. Bob Twitty was not the only person leaving the county. Chris Hughes had resigned from East Durham College to become principal of Gateshead College and that meant two dining-out events in one week.

There was the usual Durham appointments procedure and six people were short-listed for the assistant principal's post. There were no outstanding candidates but I had identified a person who I thought had the necessary skills and would compliment the rest of the senior management team. However, Lewis Gordon had been attracted by a larger than life character named Chris Watson who was doing a similar job at Huddersfield Technical College. Chris claimed to have done every job at Huddersfield and that he was the principal's right hand man. I was suspicious as I was aware of some of the peculiarities that had gone on at Huddersfield and I was also concerned about how his flamboyant outlook would stand with the rest of the team. I raised my concerns with the Appointments Board but Lewis was keen to make an appointment and, in effect, over-ruled me and Chris was appointed. To be fair, during his time at the College, Chris did make some useful contributions in several areas but his overconfidence caused concerns in a number of areas.

The LEA had restructured the FE colleges governing bodies and I took the opportunity to organise an evening meeting for the new members and I was quite pleased with the changes. There was a good attendance of governors at the Annual Awards ceremony when Lady Diana Brittan was our principal guest and presented the awards.

The summer term started with a trip to Bournemouth where I gave a presentation at a two-day IT conference. I travelled by train as I had an ACFHE Council meeting in London immediately after the conference and the journey would have been too long and difficult by car.

My involvement with the Darlington Lecture Association had led me to meet Peter Ridley, who was editor of the *Darlington and Stockton Times*. He had been trying to establish a schools' public speaking competition in the town for several years but had received little support. When he mentioned the idea to me, I felt that it should be supported and I backed his presentation to the Lecture Association Committee. I offered the use of the College hall and the provision of refreshments and the *D&S Times* offered a contribution towards the prizes. Despite some reluctance the majority of the committee agreed to support the event and to make a contribution to the costs. Peter Ridley, with some support from the College, did most of the work to persuade the Darlington and Newton Aycliffe schools to partici-pate. After careful consideration it was agreed to only include public sector schools and all nine schools signed up to participate in the first competition on 8 May 1990. Peter acted as chairman for the evening and I assisted with the presentation of the awards. Alasdair Mac-Conachie, who was a past president of the Lecture Association, gave the vote of thanks. It was a very successful evening with excellent performances from the young students and it was agreed to make it an annual event.

I had been keen to introduce a child-care facility at the College and there had been support from most of the members of the governing body. However, there was resistance from the County Council, much to my amazement. Durham MP Hilary Armstrong must have been told of the difficulties I was facing and she used her considerable influence to speed up the process. The outcome was a conversion of the former caretaker's house at the front of the College. This had been empty for several years and there had been resistance from several quarters that this provision should be retained. However, Councillor Jim Skinner stated at the Governors meeting that the Darlington Council was not in favour of 'tied housing' and that they would support the venture. The house had a steep staircase that was deemed dangerous for young children so that all the facilities had to be on the ground floor. This allowed the upper floor to be used as an office and the storage of records and spare equipment. We eventually received planning permission for a nursery, limited to the use of children of staff and students and it would open at the start of the academic year. Alan Milburn, the prospective labour party candidate for Darlington, and Hilary Armstrong visited the nursery in March 1992 and expressed their delight at the facilities and the quality of the staff.

Alasdair MacConachie introduced me to Darlington Rotary Club which met for two hours on each Friday. Austin Brooks, head at Longfield School, was the only other educationalist member of the club and so I met a number of people from Darlington that I had not come across before. The legal profession was well represented, as was the medical profession, but the majority of the members belonged to local retail and professional companies. Fr Bob Spence of St Augustine's Church was well known to me and I soon established a link with Geoff Nichol, who was the chief executive of Darlington Memorial Hospital and he had told me he had been a member of the College governing body in the past. The venue for the meetings was the Coachman Hotel, adjacent to the railway station but this would change after two or three years when the Dolphin Centre restaurant became the regular venue. For most of the year the two-hour session started with lunch followed by a speaker although in the summer holiday period we dispensed with the speaker as so many members were missing. With the work pressure on key business people increasing it became difficult to recruit new members to a luncheon club, even on Fridays. Over the years the average age of the members steadily increased and a significant proportion had retired. During my early days, the club organised a visit to RAF Leeming to see the Tornado Regiment. This was an excellent visit and I really did enjoy the experience.

During the summer term there was a joint North East/North West APC regional meeting at Blackpool College where principal Mike McAllister welcomed us. This was immediately followed by a three-day residential IT workshop in Derby hosted by a company that was developing self-learning packages for industry. John Gray and I had been invited to attend and I found the content interesting and whilst it was not directly related to FE colleges, I could see the potential for the sector. Two days later I drove to Swansea for the ACFHE Annual Conference that was very well organised and I found it to be one of the best that I had attended.

As the end of term approached there was the usual activities associated with ensuring that students who were leaving had all the necessary documentation and support. Registers had to be finalised and checked before submitting to the LEA for inclusion in its calculations for staffing and resources for the following year. I took the senior managers on a staff development day to bring them up-to-date on IT matters and my targets for September. I followed this up with an in-house staff development day that involved all staff. I visited the National SkillBuild competition, which was hosted by Workington College on the west coast of Cumbria. At the end of July, Veronica and I had the honour and pleasure to be invited to a Royal Garden Party at Buckingham Palace for a second time. It was a marvellous day with glorious weather and a fitting ending to a very satisfactory year for the College and me.

The College had its own newspaper and Gordon Merry asked me to produce an article for the August edition that would be distributed in the town and be issued to new students, so I produced an article entitled *The College as a Community Resource*:

Darlington College of Technology, as a major provider of further education and training in the region, has many roles to play in supporting the needs of the local community.

The physical resources of the College have been improved and more readily meet the demands of local industry, commerce, community groups and individuals. The range of courses and learning opportunities has been expanded to provide flexibility and permits the College to accommodate most methods of attendance.

A Client Support Service is being introduced to enable potential students to receive personal, rapid and reliable advice and to ensure that all our opportunities are equally available. The unit will also offer to assess prior learning so that credit may be given for previous academic and industrial experience.

The extensive range of full-time courses, which includes GCSE, GCE 'A' as well as 'AS' subjects, BTEC, City and Guilds, RSA and other vocational awards has been extended to include technical courses in Nursery Nursing, Fashion (Clothing Technology), Social Care and Information Technology. Full time students are now entitled to a core curriculum in addition to their academic and vocational studies. This core includes a European Studies element together with a European language, relevant information technology skills, and work experience with a local employer and personal tutorial support.

The well-established Youth Training Scheme (YTS), managed by the College, offers a range of vocational opportunities leading to a national qualification and employment.

Students who commence a two-year course in September will complete their studies in 1992 – a very significant year, heralding the Single European Market. The rewards will be considerable for those who are prepared academically and technically to take advantage of the many employment opportunities, which will be created. However, the prospects are gloomy for the unskilled and unprepared.

There is an increasing number of openings at the College for adults whether employed, retired or seeking employment. The recently developed open access facilities in Office Skills, Information Technology, Multi-skilling and Enterprise enable people to book these services at times to suit themselves between 9am and 9pm daily.

The College crèche is available to support women who have had a break from employment to raise a family and who wish to update their skills or develop new ones. For those needing to brush-up their literacy and numeracy skills, the well-equipped Adult Basic Education Unit offers a personal and confidential service. The College makes a further contribution to the community and the local economy by offering a range of services to business and industry to help to update the skills of the existing workforce.

The new Governing Body, which includes many representatives from employment interests, will be keen to see the resources of the College used effectively and efficiently to meet the needs of local residents. The College aims to offer the Darlington and District community a QUALITY service.

The Training and Enterprise Council (TECs) were local bodies established in England and Wales in the early 1990s to administer publicly-funded training programmes, replacing the former Manpower Services Commission. The first group of nineteen TECs was launched in 1990. TECs managed various schemes including Youth Training (formerly known as the Youth Training Scheme) and the early Modern Apprenticeship scheme. They also promoted training and business enterprise with local organisations. TECs operated as private limited companies and reported on their progress to their regional government office.

Darlington came under the Durham TEC with Fred Crowe as its chief executive and colleges were expected to work closely with their local TEC. Inevitably, college catchment areas did not take account of TEC areas and in my case, the Catterick Garrison came under North Yorkshire TEC. This meant involvement in local committees in two sub-regions and increased the number of meetings that had to be covered. The first committee that I was invited to attend was the Construction Sector Working Group, which met in the TEC offices in Darlington. Bob Carnell, a local builder, was invited to chair the group and I was nominated by the principals to represent the colleges' interests. The first meeting in October 1991 was an introduction to TEC officers and the members from industry and training interests. The TEC had a substantial budget to promote training in its area and this ensured good attendances at meetings. In the early days the group concentrated on surveying the existing construction training and education provision in the Durham TEC area and to identify areas of under-provision. It also had a remit to promote the construction sector in schools in particular and the region in general as it was believed that the image of the industry did not inspire able young entrants. It was in this area that most of the energies of the group were directed in the early years. The TEC did not have its official launch until 25 October. This was held at the Ramside Hall Hotel and all the principals attended together with many interested parties throughout the county.

I had two ACFHE meetings in October, a council meeting in London, quickly followed by a regional committee at Wetherby. Thanks to my links to IT HMI, I was invited to a DES IT meeting in Pudsey at the DES regional office. I was there in my capacity as chairman of NAITFE and Malcolm Himsworth, the Staff HMI, for business and computing was also present. It was quite a useful meeting and the nods and winks about a White Paper followed by an Education Act in 1992 were signalled.

I had not been neglecting my college responsibilities with all the external commitments. The state of the buildings in Cleveland Avenue and the quality of the educational environment had been a major concern. Plans were in-hand to strip out all of the awful classrooms on the ground floor at the front of the building and to replace them with a learning centre. There was also an opportunity to release a large workshop that had housed the obsolete wind tunnel that had been sold for a useful sum. After discussions with the interested parties, the available space was converted into an enterprise centre with a range of areas set up for different activities to encourage ideas for potential new businesses.

I had approached the leader of Durham County Council to see if he would perform the official opening ceremony and he had accepted. On 10 October C.C. Don Robson arrived and was accompanied by Darlington's Labour candidate, Alan Milburn, and the Durham MP, Hilary Armstrong. I had appointed Ian Billyard, a lecturer in building, as the enterprise centre manager and he had made a good job of designing and staffing the centre. Don Robson was fulsome in his praise during his address and there is little doubt that politically this exercise was very useful to the College. The centre provided resource-based learning opportunities in desktop publishing, computer-aided fashion design, catering, hairdressing, languages, electronics and reception work. After the ceremony, Don

Robson confided in me that this had been the first time for eight years that he had been to Darlington. I was quite astounded as Darlington was by far the largest town in the county. He explained that the labour councillors in Darlington were very different from those in the rest of the county and he left the rest to my imagination.

The following day I had the opportunity to visit The White Rose Club at Catterick to participate in a presentation ceremony for the successful students on college courses in the garrison. This was to be the first of many such happy occasions where the students were given public recognition for their academic success and many would progress to higher qualifications. After the ceremony I was invited to stay to lunch and met several people from the garrison that were delighted with the involvement of the College and pressed me to consider further developments. We had been using some vacant Army accommodation and some support from the Army Library Service but I was advised that a more permanent location would be preferred. This led to the negotiations with Carol Browne, the new head teacher at Risedale School. Carol had an adjacent building that was under-used and she was willing to negotiate for the long-term use of the facilities. I met with Carol and her chairman of governors and we agreed arrangements for a pilot year.

NAITFE's second Annual Conference was organised by John Gray at the Royal Hotel, Nottingham, which was conveniently close to Basford Hall College. The three-day event was well supported by sector representatives and by the IT industry that, as well as sponsorship, provided stands to display their latest products. John had arranged transport for course members who wished to visit his college to view the developments in IT. The format for the 1990 conference set the pattern for many future conferences. Starting after lunch on a Sunday and ending at Tuesday lunchtime, gave two evenings, the first for regional or special interest groups to meet together and the Monday evening for the conference Dinner with guests and industry representatives. I hosted the follow-up council meeting in December where there was general agreement that the conference had been very successful and the North East members of the Council offered to organise the 1991 conference. There was a meeting at New College, Durham of the NAITFE North East region the day prior to the

Council meeting to plan their own programme and to host the National Conference.

The Northern Council for Further Education (NCFE) organised regional events as well as being a Regional Examinations Board and I attended two of their events before the end of the year 'Managing Quality Improvement in FE' was held at the Blackwell Grange Hotel in Darlington and it made a change not to have to travel up the A1 road again. The other NCFE meeting concerned the requirement for college governor training that met at the Newcastle offices of NCFE. This was quite a revolution in the sector as traditionally governors, who were mainly LEA councillors or nominees, had not thought it necessary to be trained to do the job. However, the changing culture with colleges taking more responsibility for financial issues together with the hints from the DES of greater autonomy in the near future required some training to be available. NCFE had been charged by the DES to design a programme of training that could be delivered regionally and locally and a committee was set up to co-ordinate the process.

Many of the additional activities that I had picked up since arriving at Darlington had either been national or regional. One of my first local activities was to be invited to join the Board of the Darlington Business Venture that had a remit to assist and support small businesses. It had several premises that could be let to fledgling companies to set up workshops or offices and it offered legal and business advice. I had some quiet reservations about joining the DBV Board as I had little experience of small businesses but I attended regularly and offered advice when I thought it appropriate. Members of the Board included Councillor David Lyonette, Ian Stevenson, a local solicitor and Barclays Bank manager, David France, who was chairman.

My links with the construction industry were still strong and the regional manager for Fairclough's, who I had known in Leeds, invited me to present the Apprentice awards at the company's Annual Prize giving at Hardwick Hall. It was a pleasant evening and it was good to see the pride in the youngsters when they received their awards. I was also invited by the editor of *The Northern Echo* to the launch of their CD-ROM at Newcastle Civic Centre. This was the first regional newspaper and possibly the first UK newspaper to make its archived news available in that format. On the social side, I hosted the Durham principals to a Christmas lunch in the College restaurant and on the last day of term we held a carol concert for staff and students in the College hall.

1991

There was a busy start to the year. Chris West had resigned his post as vice-principal of Swindon College and had become the chief of ECCTIS 2000, which was an organisation for the collection of data and data management in the UK educational and training sectors. He was expected to progress its quality and develop its use by all who could potentially benefit. In 1990 ECCTIS Ltd was seventy per cent funded by the government and by the end of 1994 ECCTIS was operating as a full self-funding service, serving over 750,000 students at 4,300 CD-ROM access points. Chris had invited me to join the ECCTIS 2000 Committee and I attended my first meeting on 8 January 1991. Immediately after the meeting, I travelled to Stourport to attend a two-day residential DES MIS Conference before returning to London for a meeting of ALBSU's Training Strategy Committee.

On returning to Darlington, there was a spate of local and regional meetings commencing with the Durham TEC Construction Sector Working Group, two meetings followed by a visit to the BETT Exhibition at the Barbican Centre and a meeting of the ACFHE Council. I then had three days to concentrate exclusively on college issues before the opening of a new chapter in my professional life.

CHAPTER 10

Opportunities in Europe

T HE LATE 1980s SAW A 'velvet revolution' taking place in Eastern Europe with many of those former communist countries seeking to distance themselves from the influence of Russia. The European Union had been communicating with these countries and offered to establish training grants to encourage partnerships between higher educational institutions in Eastern Europe with EU higher education institutions. Fortunately for FE in the UK, the EU recognised FE within the scope of higher education and Graham Best and I had discussed the possibilities of establishing some contacts in the East. Graham had sent letters to several universities in some of the countries and he received an early response from a university in Czechoslovakia. As a result of an invitation to visit and approval for EU funding, Graham and I set off on 22 January 1991 to fly from Teesside to Heathrow and onto Prague to visit the Brno Technical University. The first impact on us was the freezing conditions at Prague airport and the close inspection of our documents at passport control. After collecting our cases we met representatives from the university who took us to a large car that transported us on the long journey to Brno, the second largest city in the country. The frost-bound countryside through which we travelled was devoid of any form of life. We were told that all animals had to be kept inside during the harshest months of winter. We arrived in the evening and were taken to a large hall of residence that was to be our accommodation over the next three days.

The educational link in the university was with the Faculty of Civil Engineering and after breakfast we met the dean who took us to meet the rector. We were warmly greeted and offered coffee, cakes and a shot of potent brandy, which we felt obliged to sample. Language differences were overcome by the assistance of an English tutor who accompanied us throughout the visit. The university seemed to offer a good traditional environment of higher education but there was no indication of new technologies being used to support the learning process. Graham and the dean thrashed out a Memorandum of Agreement for further collaboration between Brno and Darlington and the rector and I duly signed it at the end of the visit. Despite the very cold weather we enjoyed this first venture into Eastern Europe. The university and hall of residences were maintained at high temperatures and we found that eating out and local gifts were very reasonably priced. We hoped that our agreement would lead to further EU funding to enable exchanges of staff and students for several years. Indeed, the funding was secured to enable four Brno civil engineering students to spend three months at Darlington, partly on work placement and partly using the College's technology resources.

Some time earlier I had moved the established 'Services to Business Unit' in the former careers service office with Les Baker giving up his head of school duties to become the director of Industrial Relations. Initially, the unit was designed to support local small businesses with full cost training and to assist the heads of schools to establish better relationships with local companies. As the College involvement in international activities, especially in Eastern Europe, expanded so the opportunities for Services to Business rapidly changed. By 1993 the unit had achieved ISO 9000 status for the quality of its operation and its annual income had increased to £260,000. With the advent of incorporation the unit became a wholly-owned subsidiary company of the College Corporation and was renamed 'Quadrant', with its own Board. In addition to the traditional work, Quadrant also embraced the catering school and the hair and beauty school as both produced an income by selling services to the general public.

At the end of the month I had a visit from the Catterick Garrison commander, Brigadier Martin Roberts and Colonel Chris Jarvis. Garrison commanders changed regularly, usually about every two years. This meant that I had to repeat the introduction on a regular basis. Brig. Martin seemed very keen to see the College and garrison working together and he had been impressed by the progress in recent years. He was aware of the difficulties that the College faced working out of its LEA area and also out of its TEC area. The Army was not perceived by the North Yorkshire TEC as needing any training support from its resources and indeed, when I visited the NY

TEC offices in York, I was surprised that the Garrison did not appear on its map of the county. I pointed out that the population was greater than most of the towns in the county and that many of the people were not army personnel. I hoped that this might cause a rethink amongst the TEC staff. I was invited back to the Garrison in March to be given a conducted tour and to learn of the ambitious plans for the future developments. In April, I was invited to give the Annual Army Lecture to the Institute of Electrical Engineers, under the title 'Learning at a Distance – a new form of Education'. This was potentially quite a challenge as the audience included many very senior army officers from the Royal Signals and REME. However, it was well received and the text was published in the Army's *Quest* magazine.

The beginning of February involved a flurry of Durham County activities commencing with a private meeting of the principals, a Principals' Conference and then a meeting of college principals and chairs with officers at County Hall. I followed this with a two-day residential management seminar at Walworth Castle Hotel to brief my team on the issues that had been raised and to plan our response to the challenges of increasing responsibilities. John Davies and Peter Pearson reminded me that they would reach retirement age in the following year and they were already planning for their retirement. In many respects this was fortuitous, as it would create an opportunity to bring in at least two new managers with the energy to take the College forward and give me more support. A week after our seminar there was a two-day residential management conference at the Three Tuns Hotel held jointly with New College, Durham. This was a great break with tradition as New College had benefited from a more generous allocation of funding from County Durham LEA and had rarely mixed professionally with the other colleges in the county. The break-through was mainly due to Laurie Turner and I having established a good relationship and had met from time to time to discuss issues of mutual interest. The Three Tuns event enabled our senior managers to explore common ground and to identify areas of mutual collaboration.

This local activity was followed by five out of region events, commencing with a NAITFE Council meeting at Bradford College and a presentation to a YHAFHE Conference at Woolley Hall. As I was still a member of ACFHE Council I had to attend the Annual two-day Conference at the London Tara Hotel, quickly followed by two days of moderating with City and Guilds and a meeting of ALBSU's Strategy Review Working Group.

The College had strong links with local industry and particularly with engineering companies. One company that had worked closely with the College was Presswork Metals Ltd and its owners, Reg and Sue White, regularly visited the College to monitor the progress of their trainees. In March I was invited to their premises in Newton Aycliffe to present proposals for a new full-time BTEC diploma course in engineering for school leavers. Sue had recruited several other engineering employers and it was a useful event. This would not be the only time that Sue helped to promote the course. She also supported a presentation at the Newbus Arms Hotel in July and persuaded local MP, Michael Fallon, to give the event his backing.

NAITFE had established a regional framework and in several regions initiatives were in evidence. In the North East there was a core of enthusiasts and they held the first NAITFE Regional Conference in Boldon. This two-day event was well supported and I was delighted that colleges were beginning to take the impact of IT on colleges seriously.

The National Council for Education Technology (NCET) was a government funded quango to promote the use of IT in schools and colleges. However, the main emphasis and most of the funding was aimed at the schools sector. There was one FE representative on the NCET Board and I had been approached to fulfil that duty for three years. My first involvement was to attend two national NCET conferences in London and Birmingham in mid-March. I met the new chief executive, Margaret Bell, who had been recruited from British Telecom, and I felt sure that I could work with her. The chairman was Heather Du Quesnay (Jon Richards took over later) and the membership of the committee was made up of institutional representatives, the school sector staff HMI of computing, sector organisations and advisers from the DES. Owen Lynch represented the primary education sector and was a head teacher in Cumbria. Sandra Davies represented secondary education. Owen, Sandra and I often found we had issues in common on which we could collaborate. I also met Ruth Gee through the committee and our paths were destined to cross many times over the next twenty years. Another useful contact was Barnaby Gibbens, who was a leading industrialist and a supporter of NAITFE. The NCET offices were based in Warwickshire University buildings in Coventry and my first attendance at a Board meeting was not until October 1991.

Following up the success of restarting the College Award ceremonies, I had discussed the idea of introducing a Higher Awards evening to specifically recognise the significant amount of higher education work that was taking place at the College. This time I experienced no opposition and the first ceremony was held in the College hall on 22 March 1991 and Oliver Coulthard, deputy director of Teesside Polytechnic, was our guest of honour. It was a very successful evening, with many of the students clothed in academic dress and I have to admit that much of the success was due to Chris Watson who managed the support team of staff. There was an Academic Procession with accompanying music and the staff and governors wore academic dress. As well as being a splendid evening for the students and their families and friends it was excellent PR for the College.

I had been working with the Durham TEC Construction Working Group to consider ways of raising the profile of the industry with school pupils. In April we launched the 'Construction in Schools Project'. This was quite a high profile event held in the College hall with MP Michael Fallon being a keynote speaker and the local manager of NatWest Bank presenting a cheque for £50,000 to launch the project. Stan Bell, who was a senior lecturer in brickwork at the College, volunteered to take a leading role with the Project and over the next few years he organised initiatives in several schools in the town. Some of the most successful initiatives were in primary schools where the youngsters really seemed to enjoy the activities and some, when completed, became an asset to the school. It was difficult to assess the long-term effects of the Project when many of the pupils were so young, but at least they gained knowledge of the industry and developed some useful personal skills.

After Easter, Graham Best, Adrian Dent and I embarked on our second visit to Eastern Europe with a four-day trip to Hungary. Adrian had moved from his role in construction and was a key member of Graham's team. He had developed a track record of successful bids for EU money. We flew into Budapest and were taken by car fifty miles south to the town of Dunaujvaros, which had a population of 50,000. The name could be interpreted as 'new town on the Danube' as it had been built in the 1950s on the banks of the Danube River. As with our visit to Brno, we had received a response to our requests for partners under the EU scheme to link Eastern Europe with the EU countries. Our host was Dunaujvaros Polytechnic, which was housed in dilapidated buildings near the centre of the town. We were informed that the Polytechnic had been promised new premises in an area that the Russians had occupied as an army garrison, but at the time of our visit the Russians had not left the site. At the polytechnic we were surprised to be surrounded by mobile TV cameras from a local TV station and the eager reporters captured our every movement and comments.

Eventually, we escaped the attention of the media and met with the Polytechnic rector and his senior staff. We were taken into a lecture theatre with a group of staff already waiting for us and we were invited to give a presentation. This came as a surprise but fortunately I had brought some view-foils to use with an overhead projector and I had placed them in my briefcase in the event of such an occasion. Although the town reporters had left, we still found ourselves confronted by TV cameras operated by polytechnic staff but we simply tried to ignore them and concentrate on a presentation in English to a mainly Hungarian audience. We had an English interpreter, Charles Chibe, who appeared to be quite competent and would accompany us for the rest of the visit. This practice was normal for all of our expeditions into Eastern Europe and we could only trust that our messages were being accurately transmitted to the audience. We noticed that the staff members were mainly men, perhaps not surprising in an institution teaching mainly engineering. With the exception of the senior managers, most of the men wore shabby casual clothing with 'designer stubble' before it became popular! Initially, we put this down to the relative poverty but when we were introduced to the staff of a feeder secondary school, we noted that all the female staff members were immaculately dressed and their male colleagues aped the appearance of the polytechnic staff. The ladies seemed delighted to have us visit them and they took us to an interesting cellar restaurant one evening for a pleasant meal with lively company.

Whilst I managed the PR, Graham and Adrian strove to draw up an acceptable joint statement setting out the outcomes from the visit and future partnership activities. This was essential to ensure we received the EU grants for the trip. As with the Brno visit, we felt quite exhausted with the non-stop round of meetings during the four days and we left Hungary feeling that a useful link had been formed, although full benefits would not develop until the polytechnic had moved to its new location and expanded its student base. In the meantime we had made a useful contact with Dunaferr, a large factory complex for the Hungarian steel industry.

There was a lot of activity at that time resulting in many meetings both in and out of college. This was partly due to the increasing realisation of the impact of new technology on college administration and learning and the steady push for change that was coming from central government. The county's post-sixteen planning group met again but little progress was made because of all the vested interests. Schools with sixth forms made it clear that they would fight to retain them and the LEA's attempt to rationalise was thwarted. The county's FE MIS Committee struggled to make progress with identifying a suitable system for all colleges and I seemed to be the only principal that could see any virtue in making a decision. The Principals' Conference still met at least twice a month and there were also private principals' meetings to discuss tactics but relationships were strained as Mike Daubney, assistant director for FE, was much more difficult to work with than his predecessor. The new director of education, Keith Mitchell, had little interest in FE and attended no more than one Principals' Conference a year. He always had an excuse for not visiting Darlington College and I found that very disappointing. The Darlington/Newton Aycliffe meeting of principals and head teachers with the local LEA officers was little more than a coffee morning with thin agendas and little enthusiasm to address big issues.

There was the annual ACFHE conference in Glasgow in June that preceded a pre Euro-week breakfast meeting at the College. Euro-week opened with a concert in the Dolphin Centre given by the police band and this was followed by several events in the town with the College and schools participating enthusiastically.

It was during this period that I had a key NAITFE meeting hosted by the DES in Elizabeth House. Don Libby, the senior FE civil servant had convened the meeting with NAITFE officers and Barney Gibbens, who was chairman of the SEMA Group and would become the founder chairman of the Information Technology Livery Company. It was a useful meeting and Barney agreed to support the next NAITFE annual conference and assist with any other issues. Perhaps more importantly, the meeting cemented the good relations with the DES and thereafter there was always a DES observer at NAITFE council meetings.

Back at the College there was the annual meeting of the 75th Trust. This had been established in 1972 by Darlington Council to celebrate the seventy-fifth anniversary of the College. There was a sum of money that had accrued sufficient interest to allow the Trust to allocate several hundred pounds per year to educational activity in the College. The Darlington Building Society held the Trust money and its chief executive served on the committee. The current chief executive was Peter Rowley and he helped to shortlist the bids that were made by the teaching staff. There were always far more bids than could be met from the modest fund and the meetings often lasted quite a long time.

The facilities of the library were greatly enhanced with computer terminals linked to the College network, giving access to learning programmes and information sources on disk as well as traditional printed media. An area of the engineering workshops was modified to create a computer aided design centre with state-of –the-art facilities that were initially used by traditional draughtsmen being retrained to safeguard their jobs in a rapidly changing workplace.

There was also the College fête in June when family and friends gathered together on a Saturday to relax and enjoy the activities that had been booked by the small team of enthusiasts. Diane Muckle, my secretary, was always at the heart of these social events and Mike Horam was a tireless worker for this specific event. The school of catering could be relied upon to serve up a good barbecue.

There were several interesting events in July with the arrival of our first EU sponsored students from Brno Technical University who would spend three months in work placements and in accessing the computer facilities at the College. As they were all civil engineering students, I arranged to take them on a visit to the Humber Bridge. Bridge Master Malcolm Stockwell had been a colleague of mine from

Dorman Long and he had also played cricket with me for Stainsby Old Boys. Malcolm spent most of the day with us, giving a conducted tour of the towers and the complex technology within the roadway sections that monitored all movements of the structure. It was an excellent visit and I later encouraged some of the staff members at Darlington to take their students to the Humber Bridge.

Probably because of my European links, a few days later I was invited to participate in a cruise on the River Tyne that hosted a number of international visitors to the region. I was introduced to two senior education officers who were based in Bratislava in the Slovakian part of Czechoslovakia. They had heard about the College's involvement in Brno and were keen to involve us in an EU funded research project in the northern part of the country and I expressed some interest and awaited an invitation.

The pre-college enrolments for September, particularly for full-time programmes, were proving to be much higher than we had anticipated and it was clear to me that the budget allocated in April for 1991–92 would not be sufficient to cover the additional costs for the projected additional twelve full-time groups of students. When I had negotiated a deal during my first year at the College, I had anticipated that the additional amount would be incorporated in future budgets but that had not been the case and once again I anticipated a head-on clash with the LEA. In 1988–89 the enrolment had been 9,019 students, including 767 full-time students and by 1991–92 the enrolments were expected to be 11,000 with 1,000 full-time. The local press – *The Northern Echo* and the *Darlington & Stockton Times* – had picked up the story and the College received some excellent publicity, which certainly helped to eventually obtain a settlement from the county that was fairly close to the £200,000 I was seeking.

By this time of year most of the staff had departed for their summer break but I had an invitation to visit the official opening of the Macmillan IT College in Middlesbrough, which had been directly funded by the government without the approval of the LEA. Although it had the title of 'college' it was really an eleven to eighteen school in a run-down part of the town where it was hoped to provide state-of-the-art education to less fortunate youngsters. All the other local LEAs had sympathised with the Middlesbrough LEA and had instructed their staff not to attend the opening. I did not get involved with local politics and decided to attend. I enjoyed my visit and complemented the head and his team on the quality of the resources and the welcoming atmosphere in the school. I was also impressed by the smartly dressed and courteous conduct of the young pupils.

A meeting of Durham principals was convened to agree bids for staff development funding for the next academic year. There was always much less money available compared with the ambitions of the colleges. Indeed, some colleges could have used all the funding on their own submissions. Inevitably, the outcome was unsatisfactory for all colleges but this was quite normal. I had an ACFHE council meeting in London and then Jim Pateman from ALBSU called in to see me about some proposals he hoped I could support. I was invited to the Blackwell Grange Hotel by the Darlington Business Venture to participate in the launch of Business Link, another government initiative to encourage small businesses and DBV had secured the contract for Darlington. The family took a short break to Carlisle in August with a day trip into Scotland. On our return we had a day trip to the North Yorkshire Dales Centre in Danby.

1991–1992

The new term started with the usual round of Principals' Conferences and, in addition, Veronica and I had the pleasure of being invited to 'Beating Retreat' at Catterick Garrison, preceeded by drinks and snacks in the Officers' Mess. I had an exploratory meeting with Clive Owen, the chief executive of Darlington Borough Council, regarding several issues. One in particular concerned the future of the College if the government gave colleges freedom from LEA control. I flagged up the need for some new premises and my desire to encourage and expand the higher education work in the College. Clive hinted that there had been a tract of land earmarked many years earlier in the event of a university being established in the town. When Teesside Polytechnic became the designated HE institution in Middlesbrough, Darlington realised that its dreams of becoming a university town had vanished. We did discuss possibilities including a site adjacent to the main railway line on the east side of the town and also the conversion of properties, including the Arts Centre adjacent to the sixth form college. I was not impressed with the railway site and decided to consult on the suitability of the Arts Centre. This building had originally been the Darlington College of Education and it was still held in trust. Solicitor Ian Stephenson and his father, who had been closely associated with the Trust, indicated that there would be a preference to return the building to an educational use. However, after much debate it was decided that the College could not meet the costs involved in converting the building.

It was in late September 1991 that Graham Best and I set off for our third visit to Eastern Europe. Our colleague Angela Harris, Director of Training and Enterprise, who also had expertise in educational research, joined us. This was the follow-up to the cruise on the Tyne with Slovakian educationalists and we flew into Vienna from Heathrow on 21 September. We were met by one of the people that I had met in Newcastle and an official car drove us to the Slovakian border where we were confronted by a long queue of traffic that was being held up by security guards. We were told that the reason for the queue was the corruption of border officials who expected bribes from foreign visitors. When we reached the front of the queue, our driver spoke roughly to a guard who quickly ordered the gate to be opened to allow us to pass without further delay. We drove to Bratislava, which at that time was not particularly attractive and seemed in need of a good clean up. It was a Saturday and there seemed to be little activity. We called in briefly at the education offices before being taken to a hotel in the city. The hotel we were booked into was squalid and despite the warm weather I was reluctant to use the shower as it was filthy and swarming with insects.

We survived the night and on Sunday morning we were picked up by the driver and our guide and set off for the long journey to the High Tatras Mountains situated in the northern part of Slovakia, on the border with Poland. We stopped at an agricultural college in Piastrani, where the principal met us and provided a sumptuous meal mostly made from local fresh produce. This raised our spirits, as our experience to that point had been discouraging. After a couple of hours we took our leave and headed north arriving in the town of Martin.

At that time Martin had a population of about 60,000. It had a particular importance from a historical and cultural point of view in

Slovakia. In the nineteenth century, a turning point in Slovakian history, Martin was the centre of cultural life in the country. It became the symbol and the center of a national movement which founded the 'Matica Slovenská', a foundation devoted to education and culture, literature and the arts. Several remarkable monuments can be found in Martin, amongst which are the Matica Slovenská building, the National Museum, the National Cemetary and the Janosik Fountain.

As it was rather late when we arrived we were taken to our accommodation for the four nights we would be staying in Martin. The Bratislava official had made an arrangement with a local printing company to use its guest accommodation that proved to be clean and comfortable. The following morning we awoke to glorious views and found overselves surrounded by the towering peaks of the Tatras Mountains. It was soon apparent why Martin had been selected for the research. Although small, the town supported a gymnasium school, roughly equivalent to an English grammar school, a specialist engineering college and an engineering training centre. The engineering college was similar to the former monotechnic colleges in the UK and provided an academic setting for the practical skills. The training centre was predominently craft-based and involved mainly workshop activities. All three institutions drew their students from a wide area and they provided hostel accommodation for those who did not live locally. We started with a visit to the gymnasium and found a well resourced institution with polite students who were well occupied with academic and sporting activities. The facilities were traditional and lacked the technology that our students had in Darlington but there was little doubt that their students were gaining a good education. The same was true at the cngineering college. Traditional workshops and classrooms and a feeling of purpose gave us the impression of a well run establishment. The training centre had more up-to-date equipment and the students seemed to enjoy their courses. The head of the centre was quite a character and prided himself on his fitness and sports prowess. Judging by his physique I had no reason to doubt his claims.

Graham and Angela made a start on the research project whilst I established links within the various organisations. A trip to Žilina had been arranged to visit its higher education institution. It would appear that it had lost its university status during the velvet revolution and was eager to rebuild its reputation to regain its former glory. Žilina is a city located in the centre of Northwest Slovakia at the confluence of the Vah and the Kysuca. By population, it is the third largest city of Slovakia. The most well known monument in the city and the surrounding areas is the Budatin Castle, located to the north of the town, above the two rivers. We spent an interesting day meeting people and discussing possible EU bids for exchange visits.

The Bratislava education official was keen that we had opportunities to see the local places of interest and he arranged with the colleges and our driver to make time within the working programme. Not far from Martin is a traditional Slovakian village, restored and set up as a museum. It offered the visitor in a pastoral setting, the beauty and simplicity of popular architecture from past centuries. We enjoyed a short visit to the village and at the end of the tour our host invited us to try one of the local delicacies in the museum café. It was apparently a cheese dish created from local sheep's milk and the smell was awful and the taste was beyond description! Whilst we surreptitiously tried to discard the offending morsel, our host tucked into a second helping and was surprised when we politely refused to join him. The excellent local beer, however, helped to wash away the taste of the cheese. We also had a visit to the ski slopes. This part of Slovakia was a ski resort during the winter months and we were informed that it was very cheap compared with the rest of the European skiing resorts. Although it was late summer the weather on the top of the mountains was chilly and after admiring the views we were pleased to get into the car for the tortuous return journey down the mountain.

On our last day in Martin, the staff arranged for an evening out. During our stay, two female teachers of English had acted as our interpreters and we had developed a good relationship. They were keen to arrange exchange visits for students and staff and Graham briefed them on the various EU schemes that could provide financial support. We set off in our transport and visited a school of music to the south of Martin where we were entertained to a delightful concert. We then drove on and arrived at Rajecké Teplice, a spa town with several spas. We were taken to one of them and found, to our embarrassment, that we were expected to participate in one of the treatments. Without any swimming costumes we tried to wriggle out of the invitation but our host was insistent and the spa staff produced three costumes for Graham, Angela and me. These costumes were not the most flattering as they looked to have been worn many times and were very baggy, particularly on Angela. It was single-sex treatments so that Graham and I, together with our host, were taken to a very hot pool with yellowish steam rising around us. After three minutes we felt that we had enough exposure but our host continued to relish the experience and we suffered for another few minutes before getting out. We had a cold shower and retired to the dressing cubicles where we saw Angela looking very embarrassed. I sat for several minutes, sweating profusely and feeling a little faint. Soon our friends from Martin hunted us out and we retired to a local restaurant for a pleasant meal. The following day we travelled the long journey back to Vienna for the flight to the UK. I hardly had time to unpack before attending a meeting on the NAITFE Council the following day.

A general election was anticipated in 1992 and Darlington's current MP, Michael Fallon, was hoping to be re-elected. However, the Labour party had selected a strong candidate in Alan Milburn and he had visited the College on several occasions. He approached me with a view to host a party of local North East Labour MPs so that they could see how a progressive college was functioning and preparing for the future. I had agreed and Alan brought along seven MPs who seemed to be interested and asked some challenging questions. One of the MPs was Derek Foster, who represented the Bishop Auckland constituency and he had been a minister in a previous government and I was destined to meet him on numerous occasions in the region in the coming years. It was shortly after the visit that the College journalism school was invited to produce the *Town Crier*, the Darlington Borough Council magazine that was periodically de-livered to 40,000 homes in the town. Jon Smith, who I had been delighted to appoint from the *Times* newspaper, had taken on the role of editor and journalism staff and students combined to produce a much more lively publication than the previous editions. The leader of the Council, John Williams, reserved the right to have the final decision on what was included and in the early editions there was little to change.

In 1986, following the publication of the *White Paper Working Together: Education and Training*, the National Council for Vocational Qualifications (NCVQ) was set up. NCVQ developed a framework of NVQs for eleven occupational areas. In parallel, the government funded the Industry Training Organisations (ITOs) to develop the occupational standards on which NVQs were based, with awarding bodies developing the assessment and quality assurance arrangements to criteria set by NCVQ. The objects were to encourage worker motivation and raise performance and efficiency. Questions had been posed about employer's attitudes to the qualifications and their lack of involvement in qualification design. The outcome was a plan to develop qualifications that were skill and competency driven, and designed for the workplace so that required skills could be expressed in performance criteria objectives and standards. It was hoped to target eighty per cent of the workforce. A clear ladder of progression was introduced from NVQ level 1 (very basic) to NVQ level 5 (post graduate). Much of the drive for this came from Prime Minister Margaret Thatcher. Alongside the NVQs, that were meant for part-time study, were introduced General National Vocational Qualifications (GNVQ) that would replace the existing national and higher national certificates. By 1991 there were different views about the value of NVQs and in my interest area of construction there were serious reservations about the level 2 craft qualifications that were seen as a 'dumbing down' from the traditional CGLI craft certificates. There was also criticism of the NCVQ for failing to recognise the crucial importance of the assessment and verification process as well as creating a complex and bureaucratic system. It was at the end of September that I attended a regional NVQ conference at Neville's Cross Centre, Durham, which gave an opportunity for colleges to express their opinions. Not surprisingly there was far more criticism than congratulations. After people had expressed their opinions there was a more constructive debate on how things could be improved for the benefit of the learners and the industries.

The government had published its White Paper on its proposals for further education reform and regional conferences were held throughout the country to receive the views of colleges. The North East event was held in Newcastle in September and the Durham principals had held a meeting in the morning prior to the regional meeting. There was broad support from most of the colleges that were represented although there were some reservations about a complete break from local authority control. I spoke strongly in support of the proposals, as did most of the principals from the larger colleges. However, there was a lot of unease from several principals about the potential unknown threats of losing the protection of LEAs and a certain lack of confidence that their colleges could survive in a more competitive environment. Obviously, the LEA officers were not enthusiastic as their jobs would be under threat and also in the North East region that was a stronghold for the Labour Party, the proposals from the Conservative government were unlikely to be received enthusiastically. However it was clear that the White Paper had been broadly welcomed and that legislation to bring about the incorporation of colleges would be introduced in 1992.

I was already thinking about the structures I would need to put in place to cover administrative responsibilities that were currently held by the LEA. The need for efficient financial management was top of my agenda and I made some tentative soundings when I attended Darlington Rotary Club. Alasdair MacConachie and Geoff Nichol were both interested in the future of the College and suggested that I contacted Peter Armitage who was a partner in KPMG. I spoke to Peter and he suggested that one of his team members might be interested in working for the College. I met his colleague, Debbie Leigh, who was a chartered accountant and ran one of the auditing teams at KPMG. Debbie was married and was considering raising a family but the job requirements at KPMG were not conducive to that. She said she would be interested when the College was ready to make an appointment.

Over the next two months I attended my usual national committees such as ACFHE, NAITFE Council; NCET Council, NCET Training Committee, A DES Conference at the Langham Hilton Hotel and local meetings organised by NCFE and the FEU. The topic of removing colleges from LEAs was high on the agenda and simply raised more questions than answers. APC organised a special regional Incorporation Conference at Bretton Hall College that attracted many principals. The NAITFE Annual Conference at the end of October at the Copthorne Hotel in Newcastle provided some relief from the agonising about the future of colleges. The hotel had recently opened and we were the first large conference to make a booking. The North East NAITFE Committee had rallied round to assist with the local arrangements and it was an excellent conference in every respect. Key decisions were taken to appoint a chief executive and to consider making NAITFE into a limited company with charitable status. There were other numerous activities at that time. NCFE and CGLI were setting up a joint initiative; my old friend Robin Bullough of CGLI and Isabelle Sutcliffe, deputy chief executive of NCFE, were leading and I joined the working party. At about the same time an Eastern European Working Group was set up in the region and I found myself invited to its meetings.

During the year I was president of the Darlington Lecture Association and I had assisted in arranging for Elizabeth Esteve-Coll, curator of the Victoria and Albert Museum and a former Darlington High School girl, to give the November lecture. The president's role was to introduce the speaker and at the end of the presentation to give the vote of thanks. As Elizabeth had not been keen to take a fee for her services, we had arranged for a large bouquet of flowers to be presented instead. In my enthusiasm to extend my thanks to Elizabeth I forgot about the flowers that were hidden behind the curtain and they were not discovered until Elizabeth had departed. Fortunately, Elizabeth was spending the night at her mother's home in Darlington so Veronica and I took the bouquet to the house and we were invited in. We then enjoyed a most pleasurable hour discussing issues of mutual interest and Elizabeth became a good friend.

There was a spate of local events which included a Young People's Conference at the Ramside Hall Hotel, a newly constituted Durham Hardware MIS group, a forum for local directors, Darlington Business Venture AGM, an industry committee visit to Darlington and Simpson Rolling Mills and two invitations to local secondary schools. I was invited to attend the official opening of Fujitsu factory at Newton Aycliffe by the Queen and the Duke of Edinburgh that included a visit to parts of the factory. I also attended the degree ceremony of Teesside Polytechnic at Middlesbrough Town Hall. I hosted a one-week visit of staff from the Martin colleges from Slovakia who were keen to build on our earlier visit to their country. The last event of the year was the happy occasion of the Children's Christmas Party in the College hall, attended by many children and grandchildren of the staff.

CHAPTER 11

1992 Preparing for Incorporation

THE YEAR STARTED WITH A TEAM from IBM giving a presentation to the Durham MIS hardware group at the Durham University Mountjoy Centre. At that time the county was hoping to adopt a system that all colleges would use and the LEA could collect college data centrally. I had to go along with this approach even though I felt sure that the LEA was unlikely to be involved directly with colleges after incorporation. I held a two-day college management seminar at Walworth Castle Hotel to bring the team up-to-date with developments nationally and regionally. I was keen to listen to their views prior to a Principals' Residential Conference the following week that was also at Walworth. At the second conference there was an attempt to get a broad agreement about a collective approach but several of the principals from the smaller colleges were still hoping that incorporation would not be introduced before their retirement. A regional conference in York the following week went over much of the ground that we had covered locally but the overall climate was very positive towards change.

The College published the third year report of the 1988 Three Year Development Plan and a *Northern Echo* reporter interviewed me on its contents. The reporter was particularly interested in the plans to extend the College year and I had to expand my views on a fifty-week opening and the availability at weekends. The report also included the intention to increase opportunities for students to have a pick and mix approach to their courses. The action plan within the report referred to links with other European countries and upgrading to the buildings.

In Darlington, the Business Venture opened its Business Information Centre and I gave a presentation to the Darlington Soroptimists. I had a visit from the College HMI, Peter Craddock, accompanied by HMI Bill Hill and the next day BTEC commenced its Quinquennial Review of our HNC programmes. I was invited to a meeting of the Cleveland principals as many of our students travelled from within the Cleveland area and discussions on the future of FE after incorporation suggested that Darlington would have a stronger attachment to Teesside than County Durham. I did not necessarily subscribe to that view but I hoped to retain good relations with Durham whilst expanding into Teesside and North Yorkshire. It was useful to compare Teesside attitudes to that of Durham principals and I found them to be mostly positive. At the end of the month NCFE organised a conference at Blackwell Grange Hotel with Sir Bill Stubbs as the main speaker. Bill was earmarked to lead the organisation that would take over the funding role from the LEAs and therefore getting an insight into his views at that early stage was very helpful.

Alan Wells convened an ALBSU conference at Centrepoint in February and it proved a useful forum for cross sector activities in supporting basic skills developments. I was taking a keen interest in the evolving MIS debate, both regionally and nationally, and HMI Ernie Haidon suggested that we should visit Sandwell College, which was supposed to be a trendsetter in that field. It was an interesting day in observing how that college was approaching the various issues and the costs associated with the implementation of their electronic register system. The Sandwell visit was quickly followed by a further three trips to London; firstly the BTEC advisory board for construction and then the two-day ACFHE annual conference. The conference officers reminded members that the Centenary of the Association would be in 1993, which was likely to coincide with the introduction of incorporation and members were asked to consider if the occasion should be celebrated. The third meeting was the annual CGLI Moderating Committee for Construction Supervision. As chairman I had to ensure that within two days the eight papers were thoroughly assessed and, if necessary, modified. The examiners formed part of the Moderating Committee so that they could present their papers and could argue the case if the independent members sought to make changes or challenge the accuracy of the questions. Quite often it was left to me to receive amended papers that had needed modification after the meeting before resubmission to the C&G officers.

The Durham TEC was trying to keep ahead of the game and it launched its Business Advice Centre at a gathering of business people and educationalists at Lumley Castle Hotel. Most of the Durham principals attended before dashing off for a meeting at Bishop Auckland College. These meetings had increased to about three a month as colleges became more anxious about the pending changes and the LEA officers were manoeuvring to retain their jobs and responsibilities. The banking world was also taking an interest, seeing opportunities for new customers and the Nat West Bank organised workshops for FE colleges at Selby Fork Post House Hotel in early March.

The following day I took Gareth Davies, the IT Manager for Newcastle College, to a NAITFE council meeting at Dudley College. Gareth was an active regional representative of NAITFE and had assisted with the National Conference in Newcastle and with North East regional events. With the support of John Gray and Chris West, I had appointed Malcolm Himsworth as NAITFE's part-time chief executive. Malcolm had retired from the Inspectorate and his senior position had been taken over by Ernie Haiden. Malcolm had undertaken the task of setting up the limited company and gaining charitable status. We also agreed to establish a wholly owned subsidiary company to be the trading arm of the parent company. This was achieved remarkably quickly and the companies were established by May.

The second College Higher Awards ceremony was also a great success. I had invited Anne Wright, the Vice-Chancellor of Sunderland University, to make the presentations and to speak to the audience of students, staff, families and friends. From my point of view this was part of a plan to establish links with several universities in the region. We already had work with Durham University in the field of nursing and health care and there was an improving relationship with Teesside. With my former link with Huddersfield we had developed in-service teacher training provision. A few weeks later we held the College Awards ceremony with County Councillor Don Robson, Leader of Durham CC, as the principal guest.

International links began to flourish and I welcomed a group of Hungarian visitors from Dunaujvaros Polytechnic and Dunaferr steel works, who were staying in Darlington for two weeks. There were few financial benefits from such visits although the EU grants covered most of the expenditure, but I had taken the view that the Eastern European partnerships would have benefits to our respective students and staff in sharing ideas and cultural interests. I therefore always set aside some of my free time, often at weekends, to show the visitors the local places of interest as well as the beauty of the countryside in South Durham and North Yorkshire. We also had visitors from Italy, Germany and France.

Another aspect of the approaching incorporation of colleges in 1993 was the issue surrounding college assets that were currently owned by the LEAs. With this in mind, NCFE organised an assets and property conference to explore the issues. For those of my colleagues who had not given such issues any thought – and I suspect that was the majority – the prospects of becoming a property and land owner as well as the employer of all of the staff seemed to come as a big surprise and I suspected that this conference led to several principals starting to look for early retirement. Of course at that stage discussions were hypothetical. The APC regional committee meeting at York in mid-March simply highlighted the anxieties of several of the members that attended. I convened a senior management residential seminar at Walworth Castle to update the team and to identify priorities to prepare the College for the anticipated changes. With both Peter Pearson and John Davies due to retire, there was a priority to seek new academic leaders to fill the gap and particularly to appoint a capable finance director to take on the key role of setting up systems and managing the cash flow. The traditional funding methodologies via the LEAs would be replaced by direct funding from the government agency to be named the Further Education Funding Council. Colleges would be responsible for ensuring that income was sufficient to meet all expenditure and to build up reserves year on year. Colleges would have to appoint their own bankers, auditors and solicitors.

The Further and Higher Education Act was approved by Parliament in March 1992 with full implementation set for 1 April 1993. Some people regarded the constitutional changes of polytechnics to universities as the most significant action part of the Act but from my point of view the impact on further education institutions would influence far more people. The polytechnics had enjoyed significant independence for some time whilst colleges were still linked to local education authorities, most of which had not delegated any of their powers. Colleges had just over a year to prepare themselves for the huge responsibilities that would transfer to them and at that time there were significantly more students in the FE colleges than in higher education institutions. Some of the responsibilities to be conferred on colleges are listed below:

(1) A further education corporation may do anything (including in particular the things referred to in subsections (2) to (4) below) which appears to the corporation to be necessary or expedient for the purpose of or in connection with the exercise of any of their principal powers.

(2) A further education corporation may conduct an educational institution for the purpose of carrying on activities undertaken in the exercise of their powers to provide further or higher education and, in particular, may assume as from the operative date the conduct of the institution in respect of which the corporation is established.

(3) A further education corporation may provide facilities of any description appearing to the corporation to be necessary or desirable for the purposes of or in connection with carrying on any activities undertaken in the exercise of their principal powers (including boarding accommodation and recreational facilities for students and staff and facilities to meet the needs of students having learning difficulties within the meaning of section 4(6) of this Act).

(4) A further education corporation may –
 (a) acquire and dispose of land and other property,
 (b) enter into contracts, including in particular –
  (i) contracts for the employment of teachers and other staff for the purposes of or in connection with carrying on any activities undertaken in the exercise of their principal powers, and
  (ii) contracts with respect to the carrying on by the corporation of any such activities,
 (c) borrow such sums as the corporation think fit for the purposes of carrying on any activities they have power to carry on or meeting any liability transferred to them under sections 23 to 27 of this Act and, in connection with such borrowing, may grant any mortgage, charge or other security in respect of any land or other property of the corporation,
 (d) invest any sums not immediately required for the purposes of carrying on any activities they have power to carry on,

(e) accept gifts of money, land or other property and apply it, or hold and administer it on trust for, any of those purposes, and

(f) do anything incidental to the conduct of an educational institution providing further or higher education, including founding scholarships or exhibitions, making grants and giving prizes.

(5) The power conferred on a further education corporation by subsection (4)(c) above to borrow money may not be exercised without the consent of the appropriate council, and such consent may be given for particular borrowing or for borrowing of a particular class.

The LEA governing bodies were to be replaced by further education corporations with a composition that strongly favoured membership from local industry and commerce and with no requirement to include lea or student members. Principals were to be designated as chief executives and to be an ex officio member of the corporation, although they could choose not to take up the offer. The powers of a corporation are shown below:

Constitution of corporation and conduct of the institution

(1) For every further education corporation established to conduct an educational institution there shall be –

(a) an instrument providing for the constitution of the corporation (to be known as the instrument of government), and

(b) an instrument in accordance with which the corporation, and the institution, are to be conducted (to be known as articles of government).

(2) Instruments of government and articles of government–

(a) shall comply with the requirements of Schedule 4 to this Act, and

(b) may make any provision authorised to be made by that Schedule and such other provision as may be necessary or desirable.

(3) The validity of any proceedings of a further education corporation, or of any committee of the corporation, shall not be affected by a vacancy amongst the members or by any defect in the appointment or nomination of a member.

(4) Every document purporting to be an instrument made or issued by or on behalf of a further education corporation and to be duly executed under the seal of the corporation, or to be signed or executed by a person authorised by the corporation to act in that

behalf, shall be received in evidence and be treated, without further proof, as being so made or issued unless the contrary is shown.

The Further Education Funding Council for England (the Council) was set up in July 1992 as a new statutory body created under the Further and Higher Education Act 1992. Its main statutory duties were to ensure that all reasonable needs for further education in England were met and that the quality of FE in England was assessed. The Council operated through setting a funding and policy framework within which colleges were able to respond to local needs for further education. The Council's funding system was intended to rewarded cost-effectiveness and be related to individual student activity with elements of funding available for the initial entry and guidance costs, teaching costs and to recognise student achievement. In 1992 the Secretary of State for Education set a target for the sector of achieving growth in student numbers of twenty-five per cent over the three years from 1992–93 to 1995–96, while making significant efficiency gains. During that period the College saw its enrolments increasing to 12,215 students of whom 1,299 were full-time, representing an increase of thirty-five per cent over three years and 69.4% over five years.

The first FEFC chief executive was Sir Bill Stubbs with his headquarters in Coventry, although offices were also used in London. Sir Bill made it clear that he wanted all of the colleges to collaborate in advising and assisting in setting up procedures that would be acceptable as well as workable and a number of committees were established. I was invited to join the Statistics Group, which was charged with identifying strategic indicators to enable FEFC and the colleges to establish common objectives and priorities, especially for funding. Dr John Capey, Principal of Exeter College, was appointed as chairman of the Statistics Group and there were several other principals from FE and sixth form colleges in the group. In addition, there were officers from the Statistics Branch of the DES and FEFC officers together with a representative from the Welsh FEFC. The first meeting of the Group took place on 30 April 1992 in Metropolis House, London, and it was the beginning of a series of meetings that started with an overview and progressed into much greater detail.

Three sub-groups were established to investigate issues and I was invited to chair the PIMS (performance indicators and management statistics) sub group.

The College was paid a big compliment by the FEFC when it was selected to be one of forty to be studied in detail. The outcome was to be a report showing examples of good practice that would be sent to all colleges in England. The report covered many areas but in particular management and computer management information systems.

After Easter the chairmen and principals of the region's colleges met at the Ramside Hall Hotel to discuss the issues of incorporation and it was clear that most of the chairmen were against the changes. This really wasn't surprising as many of them were either local councillors or LEA representatives. I had decided to embark upon a series of eight seminars to brief the staff of the College on the implications of incorporation and to rehearse my views on the threats and opportunities that would challenge us in the near future. The first seminar was on 8 May and by the end of the month all the staff members who were interested had attended. Like the chairmen of governing bodies, many of the staff members were apprehensive and those nearing the end of their careers made it clear that they hoped that early retirement would be an option. I did my best to give an optimistic view whilst not concealing that until the method and level of funding had been resolved we would not be able to plan with any certainty.

One of the key requirements in preparing for incorporation was to establish a 'shadow governing body' that would work with the principal to prepare the College to take on the full responsibilities from 1 April 1993. I met with Alasdair MacConachie and Geoff Nichol who I knew through Darlington Rotary Club, and we drew up a list of possible members, broadly reflecting the advice of the department. We had to include people with financial and legal experience as well as people from local business and industry. There was no requirement to have representation from the County Council or local councillors although I felt that there would be some advantage in maintaining some form of link with the councils who were major employers and potential customers.

Alasdair and Geoff had both agreed to be on the new Board and we quickly identified Ian Stephenson, a local solicitor, to cover the legal aspects. Denis Gatfield from Hydro Polymers and John Parsons from DARCHEM were quickly identified as major senior managers from industry along with Sue White from Presswork Metals and David Kelly from *The Northern Echo*. Dela Smith, head teacher of the local school for special needs and Oliver Coulthard, deputy director of Teesside Polytechnic, were recruited to provide educational input and Alan Dodd, a local chartered surveyor, was included to advise on buildings. Clive Owen, a local chartered accountant, agreed to serve to offer financial and accounting advice. This formation group then decided that local councillors should be included and invited Sheila Brown, who was on the existing board and was a Durham County Councillor and a Darlington Borough Council Councillor representing the Conservative party, together with John Williams who was leader of the Darlington Labour Group. The voluntary sector was represented by Don Hill. At a much later date, when the College extended its activities into North Yorkshire, County Councillor Carl Les was nominated by North Yorkshire County Council to represent the growing market in the Richmondshire area. Also, the Catterick Garrison commander was invited to join the Board. The final area was to decide on college representation. The principal would be, by virtue of the Act, also the chief executive of the College and an ex-officio member of the Board. It was decided to include two staff members, one from the teaching staff and one from the administrative staff and one student. That completed the membership of the Shadow Board, which meant for almost a year I would have to service two parallel groups of governors. The new group had the task of assisting the principal to appoint staff and service providers that would be needed in the incorporated college and to lay the foundations for the future of the institution.

The first professional appointment was Debbie Leigh from KPMG as finance director as it was agreed that getting the right financial structures in place was essential. My second priority was to seek a personnel professional as I anticipated that this would be the most challenging area during the early years and I planned to press this upon the Shadow Board. The County Council had already started to woo the colleges with offers to service many of the administrative responsibilities that they were currently controlling but would have to pass over to the colleges in April 1993. I saw that taking up the offer was an easy short-term solution and resolved to try to establish external provision well before the hand-over. However, most of my colleagues went for the soft option and did a deal with the county.

In the first week of June, Graham Best and I embarked on another trip to Eastern Europe with a visit to Svishtov Economic University in Bulgaria. We had flown into Sofia and the university's international director Agop Sarkissian greeted us. He drove us the considerable distance to the university situated on the south bank of the River Danube with a view over the river into Romania. Agop introduced us to the rector and other senior staff. It was apparently quite common in Eastern European countries for the university staff members to elect the rector for a prescribed period, usually five years. The Svishtov rector had only recently been elected having previously been a relatively junior professor and I suspect we were the first international visitors he had received. We had an interesting week and Agop was an excellent host taking us to see some of the local places of interest. Svishtov had a wide range of specialist technical schools and we visited the catering school where Agop's wife was the head teacher. Some of the students lived many miles from the school and had to stay in the school's accommodation; this arrangement was common in several Eastern European countries. Agop worked with Graham to draw up an agreement for cooperation between the university and Darlington College, which the rector and I signed. At the end of the visit we returned to Sofia and Agop gave us a conducted tour of the city. This visit proved to be the start of a most robust partnership leading to many EU projects, funded under the Tempus Scheme that would develop over the rest of the decade, involving a network of several Eastern and Western European countries.

I had a day to recover from the Bulgarian visit before chairing a NAITFE council meeting at Lincolnshire College of Agriculture, followed by hosting a lunch at the College for head teachers from North Yorkshire schools who were taking an interest in the activities of the College as they had become aware that incorporation would bring an end to county boundaries. In practice, the College offered little competition to the schools' sixth forms as traditionally their students who did not wish to follow the A level route had travelled to one of the North Yorkshire colleges and a few had found a way to cross the county border into Darlington. The greater threat to them was from the Queen Elizabeth Sixth Form College, which would also become incorporated in 1993. Consequently, we had quite a convivial lunch and new contacts were formed. In the afternoon I took the train to Birmingham to attend the three-day annual conference of ACFHE. This was quite a nostalgic gathering because ACFHE Council had decided that it would not be appropriate to continue in the new incorporated sector with two new national bodies emerging to represent colleges. So on the eve of its centenary, its long service based upon voluntary commitment from senior college managers, came to an end. The two leading lights during its latter years were chairman David Bradshaw, principal of Doncaster College, and secretary Clive Brain, principal of Swindon College.

Darlington's Euro-Week ran in mid-June and included a European Showcase at the Dolphin Centre that was intended to appeal to young people and local industry. The College stand included catering demonstrations by the staff and students. There was also a Music and Fashion Show. Although I was still chairman of the Darlington Committee I had a busy programme during that week that included a NAITFE Curriculum Group meeting in Birmingham at the Motor Cycle Museum, meetings of FEFC and the NAITFE MIS Group in London and a personnel conference in London organised by the Hay Group. Locally there was a meeting at Teesside University to discuss our proposed degree in journalism.

1992 was the ninety-fifth anniversary of the opening of the College and it was suggested that there should be some modest celebrations with a view to gather ideas for the centenary in 1997. Chris Watson took on the role of coordinator and there were a series of summer activities that started with an impressive fireworks display and climaxed with a procession from the College led by Scots pipers followed by staff and students and a cavalcade of classic vehicles through the town centre. Time capsules were buried in the College grounds, containing names and addresses of almost every Darlington resident together with a collection of college magazines. This created a mild diversion from the stresses invoked by the pending incorporation.

The main emphasis during July was preparing for incorporation. FEFC had organised regional meetings with Coopers and Lybrand to brief colleges on the financial implications and the need to engage appropriate accountants and auditors. In Darlington there was a meeting with the chairman of the Education Committee and council officers to discuss the implication for the town. Fred Crowe, the chief executive of Durham TEC, invited the Durham colleges to a meeting at Bishop Auckland College to explore changes in relationships. The County Council invited the principals to County Hall to discuss the issues arising from the transfer of property and to identify any problem areas. It was clear at the meeting that the county was most unhappy with the prospect of losing all the land and property that was currently used by the colleges and most of us left the meeting anticipating that there would be a conflict over some of the buildings, particularly those which had joint usage. For the College I could foresee problems with the Larchfield Sports Centre that was used part-time by our students, as there was no sports provision on the Cleveland Avenue site. There was also an issue of the Abbey Road playing field, which was used by the College and the sixth form college and the three annexes in Trinity Road, two used by the College and one by the sixth form. There was a Watson Burton presentation at the Gosforth Park Hotel in Newcastle dealing with the legal issues and the need for colleges to ensure that they appointed appropriate legal firms. I held a day and a half incorporation planning session on 23/24 July and this was followed in the evening by a meeting of the Shadow Corporation Board.

At the end of the month, when most staff members were on holiday, the Durham principals met to review the situation and to share hopes and fears for the following year. Laurie Turner and I felt that our colleges were of a sufficient size to quickly adapt to the advantages of incorporation and to move away from the services currently undertaken by the LEA. Most of the other colleges felt threatened, particularly by the national predictions that small colleges would not survive. As I had much work to do over the summer, we managed a one-week family holiday in August, based in Walsall with visits to Ironbridge, Shrewsbury, Birmingham and Evesham.

In September, the College experienced another good enrolment with a significant increase in full-time students, slightly offset by a fall in some vocational part-time courses owing to the recession that was affecting the construction and catering industries in particular. The overall increase was about five per cent. The enrolment procedures were computerised for the first time and a laminated identity card, with photograph, was issued to each student. The cards were valid for one year and had a bar code that gave entry to open-access areas. A month later, Graham Best launched the 'Student Passport' to 1,500 full-time students. This contained the student's ID card, essential college information and a large capacity computer disc to be used for storing valuable data and projects created on the College computer networks.

The next six months were dominated by the plans to implement structures and procedures to cater for the demands of incorporation. The Shadow Board had established a committee structure to handle the detailed negotiations and appropriate appointments for internal and external services that had been performed by the LEA. The Board had agreed with me that there should be a clean break from Durham LEA whilst preserving good relations with a potentially important customer in the future. Geoff Nichol had been appointed chairman and Denis Gatfield vice chairman. The initial sub-committees included the Finance and General Purposes Committee, the Personnel Committee and the Physical Resources Committee. As the composition of the Corporation Board included people who were not known to one another, I persuaded them to have a short residential conference with a view to establish relationships. This took place at the beginning of October and despite the criticism of the Scotch Corner Hotel venue, the event proved to be very successful. I was particularly pleased as new members to the College environment probably benefited most and were able to convince their more experienced colleagues that they had much to offer. I had been invited to speak on BBC Cleveland radio in Middlesbrough on the changes to the FE sector the day before the conference and it led to some interesting feedback from colleagues and the general public that had little knowledge of the new responsibilities of their local colleges.

Later in the week we had the first meeting of the Personnel Committee and I had the full support of the members to appoint a personnel director as soon as possible to commence the establishment of systems and procedures that were currently the responsibility of the LEA. The LEA was offering to provide pay roll services but I was convinced that a clean break was essential. Debbie Leigh had been appointed as finance director and soon after, Simon Cassidy was appointed as personnel director. At a national level, the Colleges Employers' Forum (CEF) had been established to represent colleges and to advise on salaries and conditions of service. Roger Ward was appointed as its chief executive.

The legislation allowed colleges to determine their own staffing structures and salaries that had previously been guided by the Burnham Committee and applied by LEAs. CEF hoped to provide colleges with detailed guidance on these issues and to negotiate nationally with the various trade unions that represented the employees. However, the ultimate responsibility for salaries and conditions of service was the Corporation Board that could adopt or ignore the recommendations of CEF. Thankfully, the pensions of staff were safeguarded; the teaching staff would continue to be part of the Teachers' Pension Scheme and administrative staff would continue to be part of the local authority schemes. The Association for Colleges (AfC) was formed to provide the professional services to colleges and Ruth Gee had been appointed as its chief executive. From the outset there were tensions between the two bodies and overlapping areas of their services exacerbated this. There were mixed views in the sector about the two organisations with both having champions, but after several years, the outcome was a merger to create the Association of Colleges (AoC). The more aggressive Roger Ward eventually won the war of words and was appointed the chief executive of the new body.

At the end of September, I was invited to give a presentation to an ADSET (an organisation for careers and guidance professionals) conference at the Viking Hotel in York. In the light of the major changes to FE, ADSET was keen to ensure that its members were well prepared to give advice to school leavers and to fully understand the new environment of the changing sector. I did a quick overview of the before and after impact of incorporation on the colleges and then spent some time on the information requirements that the college would need to operate as a successful business as well as providing accurate information to FEFC, the TECs and other funding providers. I stressed the importance of management information systems using the latest technologies, as in my view, paper-based systems would not be able to cope with the mountain of information that would have to be collected and retained.

With so much activity being created by the pending incorporation, it would have been easy to set aside domestic issues but I felt that I needed to maintain my interest and influence and continued to attend the regular meetings and events of the Darlington Business Forum and the Darlington Business Venture as well as the almost weekly meetings with Durham principals. At this time I was also on the APC Board and attended an Extraordinary General Meeting in London and in the middle of October I chaired the Annual three-day NAITFE Conference at Blackpool, which had been supported by the North West NAITFE Committee. At the end of the month, the Shadow Board was involved in three days of interviews to appoint internal and external auditors and for payroll services. An FEFC directive had required colleges to appoint auditors from different companies for internal and external audit. The Board appointed Deloitte Touche as internal auditors and Ernst & Young as the external auditors. The search for payroll services were conducted in conjunction with some of the other colleges and the interviews were held at New College. The LEA put on a brave effort and certainly won over several of the smaller colleges but we decided to appoint a national agency to provide the service. Barclays Bank had been developing a close relation with the college for some time and I knew the local business manager, David France, as a fellow Rotarian. The Board did appoint Barclays Bank for a number of good reasons but perhaps its involvement in local activities in the town was a key advantage.

November started with an NCET Committee meeting in London. I had requested that meetings should be held in London rather that the NCET headquarters in Coventry because it was easier for most members to travel to London. I had developed a respect for Margaret Bell, the chief executive, who was very capable and willing to battle with the DES officials over budgets and allocation of resources. The following day I attended a meeting of the FE/HE Liaison Committee, which was hosted by the University of Teesside and it included the Cleveland colleges and invited Durham colleges. This was soon followed by a day at Ramside Hall Hotel where principals and chairs of the new shadow boards met to discus issues of common interest. The group met again the following week when Gordon Scott, chair of East Durham College Shadow Board and a member of the CEF

Board, gave a briefing on national issues and their probable impact on colleges. It was a useful meeting and good preparation for a regional CEF meeting the following day at the Hallgarth Hotel.

Up until this time, the European Social Fund (ESF) had been handled through the LEA and colleges that wished to take advantage of this money had to bid through their local LEA. Under incorporation colleges would be able to make their own bids to the ESF. In 1993 a Durham ESF Committee had been established by the colleges to consider bids for the post-incorporation period and to consider individual and joint submissions. The first meeting was held at Houghall College in November and I soon had doubts that it would last as little common ground was identified.

APC had nominated me to be its representative on the CGLI Policy Committee for Education and Training (PCET), which was one of the most important committees of the institute. I attended my first meeting in London in mid-November and quite enjoyed the experience although John Barnes, the director general, did not impress me. The following week I had two meetings in Birmingham; at the first I gave a presentation on behalf on NAITFE to the heads of computing in universities at the Holiday Inn. On the following day I attended a meeting of the APC Council. At the end of the month I welcomed a small group of staff from the Martin colleges in Slovakia.

December started with an excellent World Class North Yorkshire Conference in York and I was particularly pleased to be invited by the director of education as this was recognition of Darlington College's developing role in the north of the county. Later that week the Corporation Board Appointments Committee selected Simon Cassidy as director of personnel. I attended a meeting of NAITFE's CMIS Conference at Basford Hall College, Nottingham, before travelling on to Birmingham for the first FEFC National Conference at the NEC. All principals were expected to attend and so there was a large gathering to hear Sir William Stubbs set out the FEFC's plans for the sector. The overall message was very clear: colleges would have the opportunity to thrive in an entrepreneurial environment that was free from LEA control but those that did not succeed in managing their finances would be in danger of closure or take-over. During one of the intervals, John Gray and I met with Sir William and his deputy Roger McClure to press the case for a top down approach to MIS systems in colleges as we felt that if colleges were left to make their own decisions, there would be the potential for chaos in co-ordinating data nationally. We received a curt response and it was made very clear that colleges would stand or fall by making their own decisions. With hindsight this decision probably cost the sector millions of pounds in wasted time and energy chasing the many providers that suddenly appeared to offer MIS software.

This pre-incorporation period had led to local interested parties beginning to woo colleges and I am sure this was generally a positive development. The new Catterick Garrison Commander, Brigadier John Almond joined me for lunch and I gave him the conducted tour of the College. Just like his predecessor, he was very enthusiastic to develop stronger links between the College and the garrison and we discussed possible extension to our current involvement.

There was an important meeting of the national Assets Board in December where principals were informed of the process of appeals against LEA decisions for transferring assets to colleges. I also had a visit from Mike Guggenheim and Barry Williamson, former colleagues from Huddersfield who wished to discuss the possibility of franchising teacher-training courses to the College and I expressed my enthusiasm to participate in the scheme. So ended a hectic period of activity and I think that all the senior managers felt that they had earned their Christmas vacation.

CHAPTER 12

1993 Into Incorporation

THE NEW YEAR STARTED WITH A visit from the Education Assets Board to the College. During the visit I stated the College's case for the transfer of the Larchfield Street Sports Centre and the two annexes in Trinity Road. There was a debate about the Abbey Road playing field, which was jointly used by the College and the sixth form college, as the latter had made a bid for sole ownership. The Board pointed out that there could not be joint ownership and that they hoped that the two colleges could arrive at a mutual agreement. The sixth form was also making a bid for the property that they used in Trinity Road and part of the Arts Centre, which they used for some of their drama studies classes. Louis Gordon, who was still chairman of the outgoing Board of the College, was the vice chairman of the Sixth Form Board and he had indicated that he hoped to stay with the new Sixth Form Corporation Board. This clash of interests resulted in the College eventually having to concede the Abbey Road playing field to retain the two buildings in Trinity Road. The LEA was reluctant to release the Larchfield Street Sports Centre and after arbitration with the Assets Board they gave in with the stipulation that the College had also to take ownership of the Gladstone Street Sports Centre that required major expenditure to make it safe for sports activities. The constraint on Larchfield Street was that the College should safeguard the current use of the local sports groups that rented the facilities in the evening and that the caretaker would be transferred to the college establishment on his current salary. These conditions were accepted although the salary of the caretaker was similar to that of the head caretaker at the College.

The Darlington Business Venture was going through a crisis at this time with serious accusations being made against the chief executive. A meeting of the Board was convened and it set up a disciplinary committee to hear the allegations. I was asked to be a member of the committee that met within a week of being established. The committee agreed that the charges against the chief executive were substantiated and recommended dismissal, which was endorsed by the Board. Alan Coultas, whom I had met in his capacity as manager of an IT centre in Middlesbrough, was appointed as the new chief executive and we worked reasonably harmoniously over many years.

As well as the usual round of local meetings early in the year, there was a visit from the Radio Journalism Authority (JACTRAJ) that validated our courses on a regular basis. The College was one of a handful of centres in the country that was authorised to offer the qualification and we were keen to remain the only centre in the NE region. The panel consisted of some lively characters and I had been warned that they enjoyed making centres sweat over their decisions. On this occasion I was happy with their report and continued approval but less pleased when I discovered the cost of the validation exercise! Over the years I had less happy experiences and some battles to maintain their approval despite investing significant resources into upgrading the facilities.

The other unusual event was an invitation from Longfield School to consider a franchising agreement with them. I had known the previous head teacher, Austin Brooks as he was also a member of Darlington Rotary Club, but he had retired and his successor was seeking to establish a closer relationship with the College after incorporation. Unfortunately, the initiative did not materialise as the head teacher's family did not settle in the area and they returned to Wales.

It was about this time that Clive Owen, chief executive of Darlington Borough Council invited me to his office to discuss the proposals for unitary status which would, if approved, take Darlington out of County Durham control and give it powers within its own designated boundaries. Clive was testing out the proposal with local vested interests to advise the Darlington councillors on the measure of support. I indicated that I thought that the new Corporation Board would be in full support of the proposal although there would need to be comprehensive discussions on the implications for local companies and services.

I attended a NAITFE organised conference at Bourneville College debating the new GNVQ in Information Technology. I arranged a meeting with Sheila Andrews from City and Guilds on the GNVQ developments to discuss the input that NAITFE could make in the

IT area. I had a meeting with Mike Johnson of CHEST (Combined Higher Education Software Team) that commissioned and distributed learning materials. I had first met Mike on the HMI visit to France and Germany in 1988 and he was keen to develop links with the FE sector. The next day I took a train to Birmingham to make a second visit to Sandwell College that had made good progress with introducing an MIS system that included electronic registers.

I had maintained a good relationship with Dela Smith, head teacher of Beaumont Hill Special School since my arrival in Darlington. Link courses and progression into appropriate FE courses for her students had been developed and I had appointed George Hollis as a senior lecturer to lead in that area. In February 1993 Dela and I organised a special needs seminar at the College and it was very successful in raising interest in this area.

I welcomed Agop Sarkission and his colleagues from Bulgaria, who were making a first visit following our earlier trip to Svistov. The object of the visit was to further develop the projects that had been identified in Bulgaria and to acquaint the visitors with the educational developments in the College. The College hosted a European seminar breakfast to start a day promoting Europe in the town. It was well attended by key people from industry and commerce. Later in the day we held an audio conference with our twinned partner college in Amiens in which students from both colleges participated. I have to admit that my French was so rusty that I stayed on the periphery of the debate.

In February, *The Northern Echo* invited me to contribute to a weekly article entitled 'My Week', in which a local person would outline a typical week on their working life. The following is extracted from the article:

> I enjoy everything I do. I'm very fortunate. Because of the incorporation of colleges, which means the college becomes responsible for its own affairs with the effect from 1 April I have to spend a lot of time out of college – at least two or three days a week at present.
>
> Though the travelling is tiring the actual involvement is very exciting. I have to meet a lot of people. I chair a lot of committees both national and regional. It's giving the college as high a profile as possible because we're in a competitive situation compared to four or five years ago when all we did was determined by County Hall

regardless of community need. That's all changed. The college and its governors can determine the priorities. But it means a lot of committees.

Last week was a typical one for me with 15 to 16 hour days. On Monday I travelled to Birmingham to speak at a conference on GNVQs. I was back in time to organise college visits to Holland and Romania. Then I attended the committee meeting of Darlington Lecture Association. The mail had to wait until 9pm.

On Tuesday I talked to the college branch of the National Association of Teachers in Further and Higher Education then visited Haughton School as chairman of the South Durham Forum for Education and Industry. By 2pm. I was back to talk about the role of the college in the development of a community radio service in Darlington. Then I agreed the distribution of the annual report and the new director of personnel, Simon Cassidy, came to talk about his duties.

On Wednesday, I had a chat with the Finance Director, Debbie Leigh over further financial details requested by the FEFC. Then I met Darlington Borough Council's chief executive and the town's headteachers to discuss the council's ideas for education within its bid for unitary status. At lunch I entertained colleagues from Teesside University and the principals of the six Cleveland colleges, where we considered the franchising of degree courses and a partnership scheme. Then I held another meeting to explore the possibility of influencing the main computer suppliers of software to colleges.

Thursday saw me on a train to London for a meeting of the advisory board of ALBSU. A short walk from Holborn to Tottenham Court Road to arrive at the London offices of the FEFC for more talks on computer software. I returned to college to face a mountain of mail and just managed to get home before the children went to bed.

I chaired the Academic Board on Friday for the last time in its present form before April's changes then dashed to the railway station for the Birmingham train. It was 50 minutes late. When I got there I chaired a meeting involving private and public sector interests in information technology – we agreed to a pilot scheme to develop the training of teachers in the use of computer networks. It was nearly 3.30pm when I got back into Darlington so I decided to go straight home to the family.

The Funding Council began to fund colleges on 1 April 1993 and the method of calculating the amount due to colleges was very different to the Burnham Committee Report method that had been used by LEAs. Another factor was the growth projections of student numbers in accordance with government plans envisaged at twenty-five per cent between 1993–94 and 1998–99. At first I was quite pleased with the new methods as it appeared that Darlington College would receive significantly more revenue monies for the existing workload. However, when FEFC completed its calculations it became apparent that the range of traditional allocations to colleges across the country varied so widely and that to introduce the new methodology immediately would certainly lead to distress to the traditionally well resourced colleges. It was therefore agreed that there would be a gradual move over several years so that eventually there would be a level playing field. As Darlington had been relatively badly treated by County Durham LEA, I was bitterly disappointed with the modest increase that was allocated to us. New College, Durham, that had been more generously treated would continue to enjoy a margin in excess of £1,000,000 for a similar workload to Darlington.

As staffing was the largest item of expenditure at almost eighty percent of the total, I decided to have an away-day seminar with the senior managers to consider the options. The new corporation was aware of the situation and it had urged me to reduce the ratio from eighty per cent to a target to be agreed. In my own mind I felt that sixty per cent could be achievable but it would take several years unless compulsory redundancies were implemented. Having Simon Cassidy in the team was useful, as he had produced a schedule showing the distribution of staff by grade. It became immediately obvious that the seven principal lecturer posts that had been generated by the Burham method were not sustainable with the new method of staffing and, similarly, the number of senior lecturers with no management responsibilities had to be addressed.

The next international visit was a five-day trip with Graham Best to the Netherlands to collaborate with Eindhoven University. We flew from Teesside into Schiphol Airport and then took a train to Eindhoven where we were accommodated in an excellent hotel in the city. The city was dominated by the Philips technology industries that produced many of the electronic goods familiar in UK homes. The university was already involved in several EU contracts with Eastern European countries and it was seeking a UK partner to conform to the new regulations. It had a large contract with Romania to provide three-monthly placements for their university students in Western Europe and as a result of our negotiations we secured a small share of the work. The contract was with Bucharest Technical University for four students per year. They would spend part of their twelve weeks attached to a local industry and the balance in the College improving their English language skills and using the college technology that was well in advance of the equipment in their own institutions. Earlier we had a similar successful contract with Brno Technical University and therefore this new contract was quickly established. What we had not envisaged was that in the second year, Eindhoven University, with little warning, asked the College to take on twelve instead of the agreed four students and this stretched our resources to the limit.

With incorporation only a month away, I felt comfortable that the College was moving in the right direction to take advantage of its new responsibilities. However, there was one change that the government was introducing that I had not supported and that concerned the new inspection process. The Act stipulated that FEFC would be required to set up its own inspectorate that meant that the existing team of FE HMI would be disbanded. I suspected that civil servants in the Department of Education had persuaded ministers to make the change as I had witnessed several occasions where MPs preferred the views of HMI instead of those of the civil servants. My respect for HMI had been built over many years, starting with Huddersfield where I met specialists in construction, engineering and mathematics and at Leeds, where I was mainly involved with the full construction team. All of those people had been recruited from the FE sector with first hand experience of teaching and management. Their training was thorough and their judgements were reliable. I had further experience through my work at Darlington where I met a much wider range of specialist inspectors and also with NAITFE, where I was closely involved with computing HMI. Indeed, I had appointed Malcolm Himsworth, a former staff HMI for business and computing to be the first chief executive of NAITFE when he retired from HMI. Some of the redundant HMI agreed to join the FEFC inspection team but those who were nearing retirement or were not impressed by the new arrangements decided to take early retirement.

One of those was the current staff inspector for mathematics and computing, Ernie Haidon, who I had known for some time and he also lived in Darlington. Our paths were destined to cross in the years ahead.

The final month under Durham LEA started with the last Principals' Conference at County Hall and it was a rather nostalgic affair with most of the officers that we had worked with over the years calling in to the meeting. Several of them were uncertain of their future as the FE sector had been supported by quite a large team of staff. There was also a meeting of the South West Durham Head teachers and principals with the Darlington based officers.

APC held a regional meeting in York and there was a view that the regional branch should be split into a North East branch and a Yorkshire and Humberside branch. The reason given was that the FEFC was setting up regional offices in each area and that it would assist with sorting out local issues if APC mirrored their organisational structure. I spoke against the proposal, partly because I had served in both sub-regions and had seen the advantages of the experience of the larger group and also the fact that the NE Region had fewer colleges. No decision was made at that meeting but in due course the decision was made to split into two smaller regions. I chaired another meeting of the NAITFE Council at Basford Hall College and then chaired the first meeting of the FEFC's Performance Indicators and Management Statistics Group (PIMS) in London.

There was a final meeting in March of the outgoing governing body followed by a dinner to record thanks to those who had given so much service to the College over many years. A few days later we held the Annual Awards Ceremony and Louis Gordon acted as principal guest and presented the awards to the students. The College links with Bulgaria were further strengthened when I was invited to the Bulgarian Embassy in London to have lunch with the Ambassador and to discuss further collaboration between his country and Darlington.

1 April 1993 was the official transfer of powers from the LEA to the Corporation Board and I became principal and chief executive of the College by virtue of the Act. I arranged for a staff lunch to mark this momentous occasion and impressed upon the staff that there would be opportunities for the College and that it was up to all of us

to strive to make Darlington College an excellent centre for learning and a first choice for students. Whether we liked it or not, colleges would be expected to be more efficient and that those that succeeded would be duly recognised and rewarded. Inevitably, there would be competition between colleges as the former restrictions were either removed or relaxed so allowing colleges to enlarge their portfolios of learning programmes. In particular I had in mind the potential of the sixth form college to move into several vocational areas that had been the exclusive responsibility for the College. With Easter being in early April, most of the staff departed on the following day for two weeks vacation. I had a meeting with the Durham principals before having a few days at Milton Keynes and London with the family that allowed me to attend a PCET committee at City and Guilds.

I had a meeting with the college branch officers of NATFHE and it was not surprising that they were not looking forward to incorporation. There had been signals coming out of NATFHE Head Office warning of redundancies, changes in conditions of service and a freezing of salaries across the sector and I could not give any guarantees to the officers at that time as it was too early to assess the full impact of the imposed changes. The Colleges Employers' Forum (CEF) had been briefing colleges and it was preparing new draft contracts for colleges to adopt that staff would be expected to sign. Simon Cassidy and I had discussed the draft contract and it had been presented to the Personnel Committee for consideration. The harsh message to teaching staff would be a significant reduction in vacation entitlement, although in the short term I did not expect it would be implemented. The College already had an extended college year for CITB sponsored students and for other apprentices, but the view of the future was a greater use of college premises and resources outside of the traditional college year. I had been an advocate of this principle for a long time, as it had always seemed to me that the traditional college year was a serious waste of public resources during the fourteen weeks of vacation.

The other significant proposed changes were to the staffing structures with more grades with shorter salary ranges and the termination of automatic progress through salary bars. Again, it was difficult to argue against this as the progression regardless of performance had not encouraged initiative and often led to complacency. There would be safeguards for current staff with regard to the latter points, but when the Corporation Board approved the new contract all the staff would be expected to sign it. The FEFC had made funds available to allow for an early retirement/voluntary redundancy scheme and this was welcomed by many of the older staff members that were quite fearful about the whole concept of incorporation. The big advantage to the College of the scheme was the opportunity to shed senior posts that could not be justified in the new organisation and would free up some of the staffing expenditure to invest in improvements to the buildings and upgrading of equipment.

There were seven principal lecturers whose salaries were almost as much as that of an assistant principal and the immediate task was to find them a suitably challenging job or to persuade them to take early retirement. The principal lecturers comprised Angela Harris, who had been appointed to replace John Davies as director of learning programmes; Fred Lawson, who was the oldest of the PLs and had previously been appointed as director of staff development (he was happy to take the early retirement option); and Peter Tickner, who had led the journalism section but had not seemed to me to be particularly happy with some of his colleagues and he left the College for another appointment. Sue Rawlinson, of whom I held in high regard, soon found a senior appointment elsewhere, eventually working for the British Council. This left me with Tom Harker, who had acted as an assistant principal (students); Adrian Dent, who had followed me from Leeds; John Rosser, who had led on business management and Les Baker, who was a long serving member of the engineering staff before taking the PICKUP management development post. Tom also had an interest in a private nursing home and he decided to make that his full-time job, John took on the role of staff development, Adrian worked with Graham Best on the R&D and Les continued in his business management development role.

The departure of Peter Tickner enabled me to recruit a new head of school for journalism and Sue Campbell was appointed. Sue had been a journalist on *The Northern Echo* in her early days and she was now editor of an upmarket journal in Hong Kong. She brought good leadership and enthusiasm to the school of journalism that went from strength to strength.

Prior to incorporation the senior management team had been referred to as the 'principalship'; this was changed to 'executive' and 'Executive Committee'. My excellent secretary, Gaynor Dobie, became my personal assistant (PA) and registrar; Michael Wood also took on the role of clerk to the corporation. This was somewhat controversial as the FEFC advice was that the clerk should be independent of the college management. It was eventually resolved when Michael moved on to another job and the Board appointed an independent clerk. The corporation decided to establish a wholly owned subsidiary company, 'Quadrant', that would be allowed to seek new full-cost business and accrue profits that would be transferred to the corporation from time to time. A separate Board was set up for Quadrant and it included the corporation chairman and vice chairman in its membership. Les Baker was appointed as the Quadrant director with Graham Best as his line manager. I moved all of the international work into Quadrant, as it seemed the obvious centre to bid for EU monies. It was also agreed that the college restaurant would be part of Quadrant as it could trade and hopefully make a small surplus on its activities. Eventually, the hair and beauty salon also came into Quadrant as it handled cash from the public.

My new executive team consisted of Alan Dixon as deputy with the following assistant principals: Debbie Leigh (finance), Simon Cassidy (personnel), Graham Best (research and development), Angus Byrne (telematics), Chris Watson (resources), Angela Harris (curriculum) and Tom Harker (student issues) until Pat Gale was appointed in January 1994. Pat had worked as a lecturer at the college many years earlier and she had been involved in national and regional activities in recent years. Angus Byrne had been a computer adviser employed by Durham LEA and I was delighted to secure his expertise and knowledge of the wider education community. Incorporation had generated a lot of interest locally and I was invited to several organisations to talk about the effects of incorporation on education within the town and I enjoyed lively discussions with those groups.

Although Chris Watson and I did not always have the same priorities, his role in identifying the most urgent areas of the College for improvement was important. FEFC had been allocated capital resources to disperse to colleges to recognise the under funding of repairs and maintenance in the sector over many years. We had a visit from the Hunter Surveyors, who had been commissioned by the FEFC to survey colleges to identify urgent repairs and maintenance and then to recommend an appropriate sum. Our initial allocation was about one million pounds and Chris produced a list of urgent repairs that including replacing all of the flat roofs that had leaked every time it rained and an upgrade to the heating system, especially in some of the workshops areas. I was particularly concerned about the former girls' high school building that was in the centre of the newer college buildings. Whilst it was structurally sound, it was in poor decorative order and better use could have been made of the existing space. We opted to replace some of the existing kitchens with a large open plan kitchen based on industry standards and to convert the old hall into a dining room with one hundred covers that would be open to the public plus an adjacent area for a Bistro for staff and students. There was also an opportunity to construct a mezzanine floor above the Bistro area to make a large room for meetings or private study. Chris quickly sorted out the plans and implemented the proposals to at least put a more positive side to the staff members with regard to incorporation. During a second phase of capital improvements with a similar allocation of money, he managed plans to make Larchfield Sports Centre more suitable for the needs of our expanding Sports Science and Uniform Services courses that were based at the annex.

Malcolm Himsworth had been a strong influence in pushing NAITFE forward since he was appointed part-time chief executive. The Board had discussed a permanent location for the company offices and David Roberts at Leeds College of Building agreed to offer two rooms for that purpose. It suited Malcolm as he lived on the Eastern fringe of the city and administrative staff were appointed to support him. Board meetings were held in the college boardroom that had photographs of the two previous principals on the wall – Jack Place and me!

In late April the Teesside Partnership was launched. This was a consortium consisting of the University of Teesside and all of the Teesside Colleges, including Darlington College, with the option to invite other colleges by agreement of the founding colleges. The primary object was to collaborate on higher education courses as most of the colleges had some higher-level work. The university had not given up its HND and HNC work, unlike some of the former polytechnics and therefore there was an overlap of provision. A few days later I met with Derek Fraser, the new vice-chancellor of the university and he was keen to maintain the links with Darlington and to have a senior colleague on our Board.

May commenced with the Annual two-day conference of APC at the Swallow Hotel in Birmingham and immediately afterwards I travelled to London for the BTEC Advisory Board for Computing. The APC Conference was the usual lively affair but there were a few familiar faces missing and a lot of concerns from colleges that were alarmed at the low level of funding that had been allocated to them. The London colleges had always been very generously treated by ILEA and they had negotiated a gradual reduction over a long period to bring them into line with the average for the sector. This meant, of course, that those who had been treated badly would continue to suffer low funding for quite some time before they reached the mid-point.

In early May, Graham Best and I flew to Romania to visit Bucharest Technical University as a follow-up to our visit to Holland. Whilst Graham was negotiating with the university staff, the professor in Civil Engineering took me to visit the University in Iasi, a short flight northeast from Bucharest. Iasi is the second largest city in Romania, in the region of Moldavia. My host was keen to show me the facilities for measuring earthquakes in the engineering laboratory and after the visit we had a tour into the attractive local mountains.

We returned to Bucharest the following day and I met with the team of staff that would be involved with supporting the university students that had been selected for attachment to Darlington. We talked to our new friends about our links with Svishtov and suggested a meeting between the two universities during our visit. There seemed to be a bit of reluctance but when I explained that a joint project between Bulgaria and Romania with UK support would probably be very acceptable for EU funding, the meeting was agreed. Four of us travelled by car over dreadful roads to the north bank of the Danube and Agop and his colleagues from Svishtov crossed the river for the discussions. It seemed a positive meeting and Graham and I left with the hope of a new contract with the EU. Our visit lasted seven days and we did manage to see some of the places of interest in the city.

I had a day to recover from the flight before a two-day residential conference in Birmingham for the ALBSU Advisory Committees to discuss issues and identify priorities for the future. This was a particularly useful experience as it brought people from other ALBSU groups together to brainstorm issues. Princess Anne was the Patron of ALBSU and she often visited the residential events as well as taking a leading role in the Annual Conference. The following week NCET held a two-day workshop in London to review progress and establish priorities for the immediate future. I enjoyed both of these events as it gave me much more time to explore issues in depth without the pressures of time-limited meetings.

Between these two events, I was invited by the Durham principals to give them a briefing at Durham County Cricket Club in Chester-le-Street on the situation regarding the progress on performance indicators that I was chairing for the FEFC. As I had a PIMS meeting in London the following week, I was able to present my colleagues with an up-to-date account of developments and the likely impact on the colleges. Since my days at Leeds, I had not been surprised at the lack of computing and mathematical skills amongst principals and that lack of understanding was patently obvious with most of my Durham colleagues. However, I did think that they grasped the message of the need for national statistics and benchmarks to set targets and measure progress. The meeting was also useful to me as the PIMS meeting was preceded in the morning by a meeting of the full Statistics Group and I could feed back some views to the membership.

I was determined that the DES statisticians would not impose unreasonable performance indicators (PI) on the sector. They had produced working papers to try to manoeuvre the PIMS Group into accepting a long list of indicators. I insisted that there should be a short list of key indicators and most of the sector members supported me. The eventual outcome was identifying six primary PIs and I was quite pleased to achieve my target. However, over the next weeks the statisticians negotiated several sub-PIs for each primary PI. It was the best compromise I was likely to get. The next work of the group was to identify a list of management statistics, but at that time it was not deemed a priority and my group did not meet for several months to consider the issue. One of the senior FEFC officers that took an interest in the Statistics Group was Geoff Hall and I quite enjoyed some of our exchanges and debates.

The month of June was filled with meetings, local, regional and national that reflected the levels of activity in the sector. The CEF held a regional briefing meeting in Leeds and Roger Ward stressed the need for colleges to make progress on implementing the new conditions of service for staff and the options that were available to exert pressure on those unwilling to conform. It was an uncomfortable meeting for many principals who, like me, were still members of NATFHE and could see the prospect of strikes arising from this activity. I had eventually to resign from NATFHE, after thirty years' membership, when the Darlington College NATFHE branch officials made my continuing membership untenable.

On my return from Leeds, there was a more positive experience with the establishment of the Darlington Construction Centre, a development that had been encouraged within the County by Jane Richie and supported locally by the CITB and Durham TEC. Bob Carnell, a local builder and chairman of the Durham TEC Construction Committee, had been the founder chairman since 1991 and Stan Bell, the college senior lecturer in bricklaying, was still the organiser. The target group continued to be the primary school sector and there were some excellent construction projects produced by several schools.

The following day I travelled to Coventry where FEFC had agreed to host a NAITFE CMIS meeting. Keith Duckett had joined FEFC from the private sector to bring in much needed expertise on computer technology and he was to prove a long-term friend of NAITFE's. I was out of college again the next day with meetings at the Ramside Hall Hotel, a regional principals' meeting in the morning followed by a briefing from AfC in the afternoon. This briefing prepared us for the three-day AfC Annual Conference in Chester at the start of the following week.

On Saturday there was a special occasion when Sir Leon Brittan, vice president of the European Commission, came to the college to present one of our students with a 'European Award to a College Student'. The young lady who received the award had submitted her application and had been selected from a large number of other students for this prestigious award.

I hosted a meeting with Lynn Howe, who was in charge of the FEFC Northern office in Newcastle, to discuss several local issues. This was quickly followed by a visit from Carol Brown, head teacher of Risedale School in Catterick, and we formally agreed the use of some additional rooms at the school to expand the permanent base within the garrison. The centre was opened at the end of May to provide courses in business administration dental surgery assistants, hairdressing, community sports leadership, languages, catering and training for work.

The next week started with an APC regional meeting at Askham Bryan College on the outskirts of York. We met there because David Mason, principal of York College, had decided to no longer host APC meetings. We had a good meeting and an excellent lunch in very pleasant surroundings. I returned to Durham to meet with Laurie Turner and Gordon Scott, a member of the CEF Council, for a confidential briefing on the latest developments and to advise Gordon on the views of local principals and governors.

Despite my encouragement, teleconferencing was rarely used and video-conferencing was still on the horizon, but FEFC did organise a teleconference on 22 June that saved me a trip to Coventry. After the teleconference I had lunch with Jeremy Beeton, chief executive of Cleveland Structural (formerly Cleveland Bridge), who wished to discuss a range of training requirements for his staff. The meeting proved useful and I maintained good links with Jeremy for several years. It was back to London the following day for a Coopers and Lybrand project supported by FEU.

My plans to develop more student supported learning progressed with the official opening of an Open Access Computing Centre in the college library. I had worked with Research Machines (RM) to ensure a good deal for the college whilst the company hoped to gain some publicity and more sales from the project. Margaret Bell had kindly agreed to perform the official opening ceremony and there was good support from the Corporation Board and the press. It was opportune that I hosted a Council meeting of NAITFE the following day and my colleagues were duly impressed with what was certainly one of the first such facilities in the FE sector.

Another important development involved the school of journalism that had been offering professional one-year full-time courses in print and radio journalism for many years as well as a one-year international journalism course that was supported mainly by Scandinavian students. The college had recruited Jon Smith, who had been chief sub-editor of the *Times* newspaper, and he led an initiative to establish a degree in journalism. The college had to find a university that was willing to validate the degree and after several discussions, Teesside agreed to validate the course and the first intake commenced in September. The month finished with yet anther meeting of the FEFC Statistics Group in London and a visit from FEFC national officers to discuss a European Regional Development Fund bid that we had submitted.

I set aside all of the following week for a management seminar to thrash out the issues of incorporation that still needed to be resolved. I was aware of the limitations of the group and I had to do my best to try to raise their motivation to meet the various challenges that we were facing. It was necessary to resolve issues relating to the support staff establishment and to consider if any of those services could be contracted out without losing the quality of service that was expected. There was a meeting scheduled with the chairman and vice-chairman of the corporation to discuss the new contracts and I needed to be able to give an accurate assessment of progress. Angus had been addressing the problems with the existing telephone system and he had identified a state-of-the-art system that he believed would best meet our needs. I had to leave the group for a Durham principals' meeting with David Hall, the new chief executive of the Durham TEC. He had decided to establish the TEC office in Darlington, much to my pleasure, but I am sure that County Hall was not amused.

The following week I welcomed the rector and other visitors from Bucharest Technical University. The first group of students from the university would arrive on the 19 July for four months and the rector was keen to see our facilities and to re-assure himself that the students would have a valuable experience during that time. I had meetings throughout July and up to 6 August before taking a family holiday in Bulgaria, where we met Agop and his son, Emile. Agop had hinted to me when he visited Darlington that he would like his son to further his education in the USA or the UK and his appearance on this occasion was a complete surprise. I talked to Emile and I was impressed by his excellent command of the English language and his experience at a specialist IT school. I indicated that I was sure the college could accommodate him on a BTEC National Diploma course if he could obtain the necessary visa. I should not have been surprised when Agop assured me that he had already put the wheels in motion! They spent two or three days with us before returning home.

At the end of the college year, my report included the following statistics:

Total enrolments 12,215, equivalent to 2,850 full-time students
Examination entries 7,732 with a pass rate of eighty-four per cent
Total income of £8.345m

CHAPTER 13

Adjusting to Change

FEFC HAD SET CHALLENGING GROWTH TARGETS of twenty-five per cent over the next three years for the FE sector and I was conscious that our expertise was limited in high-profile marketing. Although Graham Best had made a good effort to produce a more attractive prospectus I feared that local prejudices would favour the sixth form college that was considering moving into more vocational areas. We had worked hard to raise our profile with the local schools, not only in Darlington but also in North Yorkshire where the County Council had agreed to provide support for their residents who wished to travel into Darlington to study. In this respect we had the advantage over the sixth form college as the County did not support travel into Darlington for their GCSE and A level courses. Another aspect of the FEFC target was its link with budget allocations and the threat to 'claw-back' funds if a college fell short of its agreed target. The provisional approved applications for full-time courses showed an increase in most areas and when formal enrolment was completed we had a healthy increase in both full-time and part-time programmes.

During the first week in September, during the fruitful enrolment period, Simon Cassidy and I attended a seminar organised by KPMG in Manchester that offered advice on personnel matters, particularly in respect to the current changes in staff conditions of service and transfer of staff between organisations. Most of this information was familiar to Simon but I found it useful to confirm some of the legal issues that had been discussed in principals' groups were on the right lines. However, it was becoming clear that there would not be a uniform implementation of the CEF contract as a number of colleges with higher traditional levels of funding were able to water down some of the more radical proposed changes.

Our international interests had expanded into Russia, thanks to a long-standing relationship between the Durham County Council and the State of Kostroma. Regular exchanges between the two had taken place over several years and had included school visits. Earlier in the year the college had been invited to fill a last minute vacancy on one of the visits and Rod Harris, head of school for business and finance, had volunteered. During the visit he made links with two higher education institutions in the city of Kostroma, the technical university and the teacher training college and both had expressed an interest in some form of partnership. I had decided to follow Rod's visit with an invitation to the two institutions and we hosted a visit in September. The people from the technical university were particular interested in our 'Services to Business' unit run by Les Baker and there seemed to be a potential project to seek external funding that was duly successful and led to a useful long-term relationship with Kostroma.

September was a traditional month for national meetings following the vacation period and I travelled to London for two meetings of the BTEC Advisory Board for Computing and Information Studies, the ALBSU Advisory Committee and the FEFC Performance Indicators and Development Group (PIDG). NAITFE's activities were also increasing and I chaired an F&EP meeting in Leeds and a Council meeting in Dudley where principal Gordon Hopkins was an enthusiastic supporter of NAITFE. I also attended an ADSET Conference in York. ADSET was involved with information and guidance services and my interest was their ambition to utilise information technology to improve the existing systems. This period of external activity concluded with two days with NCET in Coventry, commencing with a Council meeting followed by a workshop to explore new developments in educational technology. I had suggested that NCET Council should consider using the emerging technologies such as videoconferencing for some of its meetings. This would reduce the amount of time travelling for some of the meetings in Coventry or London. Although I believed that NCET should be taking a lead, I had no support from the other members.

Locally the Darlington Business Venture had recovered from the traumas of the dismissal of its chief executive and at the next Board meeting there were positive signs of good progress. Fujitsu, the Japanese electronics company, had opened a large microprocessor manufacturing plant in Newton Aycliffe. The plant had provided a lot of highly skilled jobs for the area and the college had developed good relations with the chief training officer who directed students to the college. Veronica and I were invited to a Fujitsu sponsored event in Durham Cathedral that included classical music followed by refreshments, mainly sushi. Two days later I attended a briefing at New College by the FEFC on the proposed inspection process that did not fill me full of confidence although it would be more structured with a full inspection of each college every four years.

I attended my first ALBSU National Conference at the Queen Elizabeth Conference Centre in London and listened to a knowledgeable presentation by Princess Anne. At the weekend there was the Corporation Board Residential Conference at Redworth Hall Hotel and this again proved to be a very beneficial meeting for the Board members and for me. The residential allowed us to explore areas that could not be developed fully in formal meetings and those members who were new to the Board or who had little prior knowledge of FE had the opportunity to raise questions to clarify issues that were not clear to them.

In the following week I had a meeting of the FEFC Statistics Group and then took the train to Heathrow to join David Hassell, head of the school of computing, on a flight to Porto to visit a new international partner in Portugal. This was our first link involving computing students and it opened up opportunities for exchanges over several years. The college's contact in Porto was English teacher Maria. She had arranged an excellent programme for our visit and she had organised accommodation in a pleasant hotel in the city, a short drive to the college. The college principal spoke no English and (as you would expect) we spoke no Portuguese, so we relied heavily on Maria to provide communications. David and I gave short presentations to the staff and we were given a conducted tour of the buildings and met students who were likely to be involved in the exchange visits.

Darlington Council was twinned with two towns and because of the considerable publicity that the college had enjoyed in the local press with its current international partnerships, I had been asked by a senior councillor to explore possibilities for civic links with other countries. Therefore, on the following day we visited the Department of Education in Porto and talked with senior officials about formal links with Darlington. However, it soon became clear that they had already been approached by several large cities in the UK who were keen to link with one of the new members of the EU that were beginning to benefit financially from that status. In the afternoon Maria took us to visit the buildings of the Porto Chamber of Commerce and we were overwhelmed by its size and opulence as I had experienced much more modest facilities in the UK. I had wondered how an English teacher at a local college had so many influential contacts and when I broached the subject with Maria she admitted that her husband was currently the president of the Chamber of Commerce and that she came into regular contact with most of the senior business people in the city. At the weekend Maria arranged for us to visit the Sandeman Porto Cellars, famous for its fine port wines. The company had been founded in 1790 by a Scotsman, George Sandeman, and it had developed to be one of the major producers of this fortified wine. As it was Sunday and most places were closed, Maria had arranged for the finance director of the company to give us a private conducted tour of the cellars with an opportunity to sample some of the various vintages. After the tour, much to our delight, we were taken to the Douro River and boarded the Sandeman boat for lunch and a short cruise up the river. It was an excellent meal with some wonderful wines to accompany each course. It had been a splendid day and we were quite exhausted by the time we returned to our hotel. We returned to Teesside the following day.

It was at the end of October that the corporation's appointments panel was convened for the first time to appoint an assistant principal (students) and Pat Gale was successful in her application. I think that some of the panel felt that the two-day process was rather excessive but having witnessed the cavalier methods used by Durham LEA, I was determined that this method would be more likely to weed out the weaker candidates. November started quietly with a meting of the South Durham Forum for Education and Industry, but then the pace heated up with a dash down to London for a Centre of Economics of Education Conference at LSE before catching a train to get to the North East RSA AGM in Newcastle.

The following day I drove to the Crieff Hydro Hotel in Scotland to give a presentation to the Scottish Colleges IT Conference and stayed until Friday to participate in the discussions and to promote NAITFE. The Scottish colleges had also been granted incorporation, as had the Welsh colleges, but they had their own FEFC structure that was taking them in a slightly different direction from England. NAITFE had been working hard to recruit colleges in Scotland and Wales and there had been some successes. Tom Wilson, principal of Glasgow College of Building and Printing, had been a loyal supporter and had encouraged the other principals to join, but distance and inbuilt prejudice had been a problem. On Monday I welcomed the Bulgarian Ambassador to Darlington and took him to meet a gathering of local business people and local councillors to enable him to promote business opportunities for UK firms in Bulgaria.

The NAITFE Annual Report for 1992–93 was published in the autumn and this was the first report since becoming a charitable trust. As chairman I was delighted to have a very strong council comprising five principals, five assistant principals, a chief executive and four IT co-ordinators. The Council members were also directors of the company and they all embraced their new responsibilities enthusiastically. With a strong membership of FE colleges, generous industrial partners and well supported conferences during the year I could report a healthy state with respect to our finances. Another pleasing factor was the four specialist groups and five active regional groups that were dealing with the challenges of emerging technologies to colleges at national and regional levels. Collectively these groups involved over sixty college practitioners who brought their expertise to be shared and disseminated.

I hosted John O'Neil, the new head teacher of Carmel RC School, which was the only secondary school in the town to have a sixth form. I had met him previously at various local gatherings but he had tended to say little. He was obviously anxious about the impact of incorporation on his sixth form, but as most of his work was based on GCSE and A levels, he recognised that the threat was likely to be from the sixth form college. At that time Mary Bowles had decided that incorporation was not her scene and had resigned and David Heaton had been appointed to the sixth form college from a similar post in Barrow. I had worked harmoniously with Mary but Jim O'Neil was not the only one to wonder if the QE6FC would expand its portfolio to increase the competition in the town. The next day I hosted a regional APC meeting with lunch in the restaurant and in the evening we also hosted an RSA lecture and dinner. This was all good business for the school of catering.

I had maintained my links with Yorkshire principals and YHAFHE and I was invited to address a YHAFHE Conference on the development of new technologies and its impact on further education in particular. It was a well attended event and I hoped that the earlier pioneering spirit in the county would be continued by some of the new principals. I also tried to promote the forthcoming NAITFE National Conference. This three-day event was held at the Brittania Hotel in Docklands, London, and the venue had been agreed following mild protests from southern colleges that the previous conferences had been in the north of the country. The problem that had not been identified was that the light gauge railway that connected central London to Docklands did not run on a Sunday, our usually starting day, so delegates had to use taxis instead. Other than that slip-up, the conference was very successful and Malcolm Himsworth was duly congratulated on his organisation.

The developing links between Teesside University and the colleges strengthened when the principals of the colleges were invited to participate in the university's degree ceremonies in full academic dress and with a designated place in the procession and on the platform. There had been a meeting of the partnership the previous week and the vice-chancellor had expressed a wish that we would attend the ceremony and there was a good response to his invitation.

At the end of November, Jack Place and David Anderson paid me a visit at the College and I was delighted to see them and note how well Jack appeared to be after twelve years of retirement. Jack had been stationed at Middleton-St-George during the war when it was an RAF station and he was keen to visit it again. It was now Teesside Airport but the general surroundings had not changed significantly and he enjoyed his trip 'down memory lane'. There was also another touch of nostalgia when I invited two of the former long-standing governors, John Bishop and Bill Rewcastle, to join me for lunch as some recognition of their support for the college and especially to me during those early years under Durham LEAcontrol. The year ended with the usual round of local, regional and national meetings, but the highlight was the Higher Awards evening with Professor Derek

Fraser as the principal guest. The Christmas holiday was a welcome break from the rollercoaster of constant activity and challenges of the first nine months of incorporation.

1994

There was no relaxing in the new year with two FEFC meetings, the Statistics Group in London and the PIDG in Coventry. The chairmen and principals of Durham colleges met at New College to review progress and share concerns usually relating to finance and personnel. I enjoyed a day and a half at the BETT Exhibition in London that had expanded as the interest in IT in education had spread rapidly and the number of suppliers had also grown to meet the new demands. Primary and secondary education dominated the exhibition stands but there was plenty of interest for further education. RM had a large stand and I met with some of their representatives.

The Darlington Employers' Forum, consisting of council officers and members as well as representatives of the public, private and voluntary sectors, had started to flex its muscles and wanted to make an impression on some of the big issues that faced the town. The deputy leader suggested that the Forum members should see some of the problems in the Firthmoor Estate area that had a bad reputation for crime and vandalism. Consequently, on a Saturday morning we boarded a bus and were given a conducted tour of the estate and I was pleasantly surprised at the general good quality of the buildings. The tour finished at the community centre, where we met local residents who wished to impress upon the visitors that Firthmoor did not deserve its reputation and that most of the problems were localised on a small number of families. The Forum members were impressed by the visit but seemed to have few ideas that would help to improve the wellbeing of the residents. I contacted the head teachers of the Firthmoor primary and junior schools with a view to establishing a learning centre on the estate that would aim to attract young women with poor basic skills who would be unlikely to attend the college. In due time a centre was opened and it became popular and very successful. One of my relatively new members of staff, Ruth Bernstein, who had joined the college from the London region, expressed an interest in being involved with the learning centre. Her experience and commitment quickly won over any reluctance on the part of the local people and the centre flourished. I visited it from time to time and I was delighted by the enthusiasm and rapid progress that had been made by most of the learners. The long-term success was that several of the women progressed from the centre and then onto the college and then higher education.

There was a launch of the Northern Consortium for Child Care and Education at Darlington College with Steve Broomhead, principal of Bishop Auckland Technical College acting as chairman. The idea stemmed from the discussions within Durham Social Services and lead to the introduction of an NVQ in Child Care and Education in 1992. Darlington College had the most students in this area and I was invited to make proposals on behalf of the countywide consortium to implement the new qualification. Dorothy Meadows, a member of the Darlington College staff, was appointed as the co-ordinator.

I attended another meeting of the CEF in Leeds where the colleges were again urged to finalise the new employment contracts and to avoid watering down some of the main requirements. Simon and I had been meeting with NATFHE branch officers but we seemed to be making little progress so we had set up a series of small group seminars in February with heads of schools, teaching and support staff. This was to explain the contract to the staff members and to discuss the long-term implications for the college if the situation was to develop into an extended dispute with industrial action. Most of the heads of school had decided to support the new contract and had been discussing the issue within their teams. Eventually, with a degree of reluctance, most of the staff agreed to accept the contract without any of the variations that were being agreed in some of the region's colleges. A small group of older members of staff decided not to sign the contract and stayed upon the 'Silver Book' contract until retirement. Outside of the sector I noted that people were amazed that the staff had agreed to forgo their fourteen weeks of paid holiday and to accept the seven weeks in the new contract. In those early days the college rarely had need to implement the contract in full as the extended college year was still in its infancy and a significant amount of work was linked to full-time courses that operated between September and June.

The last week in January was earmarked for the excellent World Class North Yorkshire conference in Harrogate, a NAITFE Council meeting in Leeds, an ALBSU meeting in London and two days with City and Guilds. Oliver Coulthard was leaving the University of Teesside and I had asked the vice-chancellor to designate another senior colleague to serve on the College Corporation Board. He recommended Geoff Crispen, who would be taking over Oliver's duties. I met Geoff over lunch and was impressed by his frank, open style and he agreed to join the Board.

The FEFC held its second two-day Annual Conference at the Birmingham Conference Centre. Delegates were expected to book their own accommodation and I selected a hotel reasonably close to the railway station rather than the more popular choices adjacent to the conference centre. There was a certain amount of relief that the sector had survived the transformation and was adapting to the relative freedom of incorporation without any casualties, so far. FEFC officers set out their plans for the future, emphasising the importance of hitting the government's growth targets. At the plenary session it was the usual suspects who leapt to their feet to ask the obvious questions of Sir Bill Stubbs, who was more than capable of providing answers.

I hosted another group of Russian visitors from Kostroma, who were staying for three weeks as part of a training programme with Les Baker to develop their skills and ideas in supporting local businesses. I took them to a Rotary meeting and for a meal at Walworth Castle Hotel, as well as inviting them to join a European breakfast meeting with local business people. This development had become the largest undertaking of all of the international links and I was hopeful that it would start to generate a useful income strand.

There was an unexpected request for me to act as chairman for one of the Bishop of Durham's retirement lectures. David Jenkins had been an academic with controversial views about Christianity and when he announced his retirement he expressed a wish to give a series of lectures around the county. Two were scheduled for Darlington and David Heaton and I were invited to act as chairmen. The Bishop and I had a brief discussion before his presentation on how he wished me to deal with questions and then he began to address a full attendance in the central hall of the Dolphin Centre.

He talked non-stop for about forty minutes, ranging over several issues, and I noted some puzzled faces in the audience as they struggled to follow his complex arguments. When it came to questions, I pointed out that there was about twenty minutes for questions. A gentleman posed a question to the bishop based upon points that he did not understand from the lecture. David stood up and his reply lasted for most of the twenty minutes and seemed to leave the questioner even more confused than before. I looked across at David, who had made it very clear to me that one hour was the limit, and he implied that I should bring the proceedings to a close. My vote of thanks was greeted warmly and the bishop received a good round of applause. If some of the audience thought they would have a private word after the lecture, they were mistaken as he made a quick departure.

Despite all the activities with FEFC, it should not be forgotten that the TECs were still active and I found myself involved with Cleveland TEC and North Yorkshire TEC as well as Durham TEC. I attended a meeting of Cleveland TEC at its offices in Middles-brough and in addition to all the principals there was a significant number of private training providers present. I knew most of the college principals through the APC but had not met the four sixth form college principals, making a total of ten Cleveland colleges plus Darlington. Because of this fragmentation in Teesside it meant that Darlington was the largest college in the group, which could have made things difficult but I was made to feel very welcome and they seemed to appreciate my knowledge and willingness to challenge the officials whenever necessary.

I returned to college for a meeting of the Finance and General Purposes Committee (F&GP) that was considering the current financial statements. One of the important positive changes that had been introduced by FEFC was to move away from the traditional financial year starting in April that had been a regular problem under LEA controls, to a financial year coinciding with the academic year. The colleges now received their allocated resources on a monthly basis, at the beginning of the month so that Debbie could place some of the monies at the bank on short-term interest rates. Additional funding for capital or special projects was made by negotiation with FEFC. This made the reports to F&EP more understandable and coherent. After discussions with the chairman and vice chairman of the corporation, I had set a target to reduce the staffing budget from eighty per cent to sixty per cent over a five-year period on the basis of greater efficiencies and increasing income from a variety of sources. We had already increased income from work with the TECs and the contracts with the EU for international activities had also grown strongly. Most of this additional income was channelled through Quadrant and its own Board which provided reports to the F&GP through Debbie.

The following week I spoke at the BACH (British Association of Construction Heads) Annual Conference in Nottingham. I had been involved with BACH during my time at Leeds College of Building and had maintained links via its president, Jack Hall, former principal of Shirecliffe College in Sheffield. I was asked to speak on the impact of technologies on construction education, a subject that I had developed over several years. Despite all the work that I had done in Leeds, through FEU and YHAFHE to develop learning materials in all areas, including construction, I was disappointed that so many heads of construction departments were still opposed to the innovations that technology could bring to their staff and students.

Having a full-time personnel director had many advantages and Simon and I regularly met to share ideas to improve the opportunities for staff to develop their expertise or to make them more efficient in their work. One innovation was the induction programme for new staff that lasted a week and allowed them to meet all the key staff and adjust to the college environment. In addition to senior managers, the new starters met union officials and the safety officer. I tried to speak to new starters on their first day but other commitments often meant it was later in the week before I could meet them. I used that opportunity to give the new staff members an overview of the history of the college, the current situation and then to outline our ambitions for the future. Simon had introduced a confidential feedback form to allow the new starters to give their views on the induction and this proved to be useful in making minor amendments for the next series of presentations.

March started with an APC regional meeting in Doncaster, followed by a visit with Graham Best to the Bulgarian Embassy to meet the Bulgarian Ambassador again who wanted to maintain the momentum of his visit to Darlington. The following week Graham and Mike Cox represented the college at a trade fair in Hong Kong that was opened by Chris Patten in his capacity of governor of Hong Kong. Meanwhile, I was a guest at a dinner at Headlam Hall Hotel hosted by the solicitors, Latimer Hinks, who had been appointed solicitors to the college at incorporation. This was one of the largest practices in the town and it could therefore offer a wide range of legal advice on the issues that the college may require. During the same week I gave a talk to the members of the Darlington Retired Teachers' Association who were very interested to hear about incorporation and its probable influence on education in the town. I tried to convince them that the change should lead to significant improvements in the range and quality of educational opportunities for youngsters leaving secondary education.

I attended my first meeting of the newly formed North Yorkshire Construction Group that had been established by North Yorkshire TEC. It had realised that Darlington College did most of the construction education and training for companies in the north of the county and it made sense to invite the college to be a member. Another new group that required my attendance was the Durham County Development Group that met at County Hall and was seen as a critical committee to identify issues and advise the Council. There was a large gathering of people that included the college principals, the TEC chief executive and various officers of the county. I did regard this as an important group and made every effort to attend the meetings and if I were not able to attend I would ask Alan Dixon to substitute for me.

In the evening the executive group dined out: John Davies and Peter Pearson who were retiring after serving the college for many years. Both had continued until they reached the age of sixty-five although it would probably have been in the interest of the college for them to retire a year earlier to allow their successors to be in post for the start of incorporation. The Annual Awards ceremony with Stephen Hughes, our local MEP, as the guest speaker provided a happy end to the spring term and staff departed for their Easter vacation, thankful that we had survived the first full year of incorporation.

Debbie was giving me optimistic reports on the college finances as I was aware that some colleges were struggling along without a professional accountant. There were meetings of the Business Venture and the Employers' Forum, and Teesside University invited me to be a guest at a Middlesbrough home game at Ayresome Park. This started with a pleasant lunch with another three people, one of whom was the university's host and two other guests. Refreshments were provided at half-time (just as well as it was a chilly day and it was much warmer in the restaurant) and more drinks after the match.

Our little nursery unit had flourished with all of the places being filled and it was a nice idea to plant a sapling adjacent to the outside open area to commemorate its anniversary. I was asked to do the honours surrounded by the youngsters and staff members and it was one of my more pleasant and satisfying duties.

Another pleasant event was the annual dinner with head teachers from the local secondary schools. I had introduced this prior to incorporation and it was such a success that it had become a regular feature. I do recall that on the first occasion, when I was welcoming the heads in the college boardroom, all but one of the heads had arrived in their smart suits with their wives in cocktail dresses. We were just about to go into dinner when Bob Dingle, head of Eastbourne School, arrived in a woolly sweater, much to the consternation of his colleagues. If Bob was embarrassed he gave no indication and carried on as normal. Needless to say, at the dinner the following year he conformed to the dress code set by the others! I had enjoyed a good working relationship with the local head teachers, and the annual dinner at the college for heads, deputies and partners had become a firm fixture in the diary. One of the more able heads was Carl Ottolini, who I had regarded with great respect and I was very sorry when he had to retire prematurely on health grounds from Houghton School. His replacement was Sheila Potter who had a totally different outlook and distanced herself and the school from any collaborative initiatives such as the public speaking competitions and the annual dinner.

In May I attended an initial meeting at Darlington Town Hall to discuss the Single Regeneration Budget (SRB). The SRB began in 1994 and it brought together a number of programmes from several government departments with the aim of simplifying and streamlining the assistance available for regeneration. SRB provided resources to support regeneration initiatives in England carried out by local regeneration partnerships. Its priority was to enhance the quality of life of local people in areas of need by reducing the gap between deprived and other areas, and between different groups. It supported initiatives that built on best practice and represented good value for money. The types of bid-support differed from place to place, according to local circumstances. To obtain funding, organisations had to demonstrate that their bid met one or more of the eligible objectives. For example:

(a) improving the employment prospects, education and skills of local people;
(b) addressing social exclusion and improving opportunities for the disadvantaged;
(c) promoting sustainable regeneration, improving and protecting the environment and infrastructure, including housing;
(d) supporting and promoting growth in local economies and businesses.

SRB partnerships were expected to involve a diverse range of local organisations in the management of their schemes. In particular, they should harness the talent, resources and experience of local businesses, the voluntary sector and the local community. Schemes should offer support to build the skills and confidence of the local community so that it could play a key role in the regeneration of their areas. I was pleased to be involved in the SRB group as I was well aware of the low participation rates in continuing education in the Darlington and South Durham that led to low levels of achievement and skills in the area.

It was also about this time that I visited the Town Hall to participate in a discussion about the Darlington Local Plan that was required by the government to indicate the long-term intentions for town planning. It was an interesting debate as the officers had already drawn up their proposals for our consideration. There were reservations regarding the proposals to develop sizable areas of the Green Belt on the south side of the town, but overall, there was a consensus in favour of the main thrust of the Plan.

I led a NAITFE team in a meeting with the National CMIS Board (College Management Information Systems), which was chaired by John Rockett. His group had concentrated on liasing with specialist

CMIS staff in colleges but as the infrastructure demands for learning centres needed to be planned with the administrative systems, John had noted that NAITFE had its own resources committee that was also involved with MIS. This proved to be a crucial meeting and eventually led to a merger of NAITFE with the NCMIS Board. At a later meeting of the NAITFE executive group it was agreed to change the NAITFE name and John Gray suggested NILTA (National Information and Learning Technologies Association) which was agreed and probably avoided any accusations that NAITFE had made a take-over for the NCMIS Board.

A few days later I attended a three-day EMIS conference in London, organised to debate the many issues that were causing headaches within colleges as the demands for more detailed information from FEFC required colleges to install expensive management information systems. As mentioned earlier, NAITFE had tried to persuade the FEFC to direct the sector towards a common system, and its refusal had led to the inevitable confusion of multiple suppliers chasing colleges with systems that were not compatible with their rivals systems. The former Staff College at Blagdon had developed a product called FEMIS that was adopted by several colleges, including Darlington. Fretwell Downing has secured a share of the market but the overall picture was that there was no leading provider. NILTA had been invited by FEFC to assist in drawing up a specification that all of the providers would have to follow and Malcolm Himsworth had been heavily involved in that task. Although FEFC had allocated money to enable colleges to purchase an MIS system, the colleges were faced with the heavy expenditure of employing MIS officers and input staff to run the system. At Darlington I could rely upon Angus Byrne to take the lead in this area and he set up an MIS team adjacent to the finance department. Angus had already installed a new college-wide telephone system to replace the antiquated system that I had inherited and with the overall responsibility for rapidly expanding computing facilities he had a key role within the management team.

On returning from London, I had the irritating duty of dealing with the Radio Journalism Validation Panel that seemed to take great pleasure in presenting me with a lot of criticism about equipment and accommodation before granting us approval for another year. I suspected that the staff fed this information to the panel members and I found this unprofessional, though not surprising. The school of journalism had been based in the Trinity Road annexe and I was aware of the slack habits of some of the staff who seemed to spend more time in the Arts Centre bar than they did in the college. I had therefore decided to transfer the school into the main building and had charged Chris Watson with the task of creating radio and TV studios, together with suitable classrooms for the journalism programmes. With a bit of imagination and change of use of some of the rooms and under-utilised space, Chris had produced a solution, which was grudgingly accepted by the journalism staff. As the facilities were far superior to the Trinity Road site, I could only assume that the complaint of the staff members was a perceived loss of freedom to roam.

Graham Best had succeeded in gaining EU funding for a new partner in Kosice, the second largest town in Slovakia. So in June Graham and I departed from Teesside Airport to Prague via Heathrow and then by car to Kosice Technical University. We spent a full day at the university, meeting the city's chief executive and university staff with the object of highlighting areas to commence the collaboration. The university seemed to be traditionally well equipped but lacked the latest computing technology so this was one area to explore, the other main area was 'services to business' that had been popular with most Eastern European universities that we had visited. There was time to explore the centre of the city in the evening before discovering an excellent restaurant where we had a superb meal for a ridiculously low price. The following day we travelled north by train to Žilina, which had lost its university status and was looking for western partners to improve its reputation and credibility. We met three of the staff members, some of whom knew of our existing links with Martin. After the meeting we travelled by car to Martin to meet old friends, to visit the historic theatre and to dine in the Martin Hotel. We spent the following morning in Martin visiting the three colleges before returning by car to Žilina to meet with the deputy mayor and deputy chief executive together with the director of the Chamber of Commerce. This delegation reflected the local concerns about the future of their university and the hope that we could help in some way to assist it to regain its full status. I am not sure how much we contributed to recovering its university status, but it was eventually reinstated in November 1996. We returned to Martin in the evening and then back to Žilina the following morning (Saturday) for further discussions before our return to Darlington in the late evening. I needed Sunday to recover and on Monday I picked up a new car from Sherwoods garage.

I had two days to sort out the correspondence and issues that had been raised during my absence before heading to London for the first NILTA European conference in Docklands. This was an initiative that had been taken by John Gray who had strong links with Slovakia and had invited some of his contacts to the event. I also arranged for a small group of Darlington College's international partners to participate. Through Malcolm Himsworth, NILTA had established links with a Dutch organisation with a similar role to NILTA in the Netherlands and they sent a small team to join us. The three-day event was very successful and I was optimistic that more UK colleges would become involved in an area of activity that was heavily dominated by the higher education sector.

For funding purposes the EU regarded FE as higher education but this had not been recognised by most colleges and it had left the field open to universities to capture the bulk of the large pot of money aimed at developing inter-European collaboration through education. I do not think there was another college in England with as many partners as Darlington had established over the last three years. We had strong links with five Eastern European countries plus the partnership with Kostroma in Russia. In the West, we had links with five countries and this would expand to ten over the next few years. I know that some of my colleagues did not share my enthusiasm for the international links and this included some of the Corporation Board members. I had decided to participate personally with the initial visits to new partners because I was aware of the status conscious nature of European universities. In most Eastern European universities the teaching staff members elected the rector for a proscribed period. This often resulted in a relatively junior professor being thrust into the top job with minimum preparation. I knew that staff from UK universities rarely met rectors and I anticipated that if the head of a UK institution was making the visit the rector would be obliged to welcome that person. This had proved the case on each visit that we had made and it ensured that any agreements were signed by both rector and me before our departure.

A new activity was the launch of YITTY (Young IT Technician of the Year). Malcolm Himsworth had been approached about a NILTA involvement in identifying a candidate to represent the UK for a new IT competition at the Skills Olympics. Mary Barker, one of my new computer staff, had taken an interest in this and had offered to organise and run a North East regional heat to identify a suitable candidate to go forward to a national competition. Darlington College hosted the event in an open access area on a Saturday and we were pleased to see many colleges entering students. The winning student was from New College, Durham, and Mary agreed to act as his trainer to prepare him for the finals in London. I had enjoyed the competition and decided that I should attend the UK final that was to be hosted by IBM. Most of the regions had entered candidates and Mary and I were delighted when our local boy was announced as the national winner. Although the event was designated as a test event at the Skill Olympics, it was still a great achievement for our candidate to progress to the finals and then to win the gold medal in Lyon, France.

In July I attended a government hosted conference in London in which the minister and senior civil servants made complimentary remarks to the college representatives for the progress since incorporation and laid out their hopes and ambitions for the sector. I gave a presentation on the progress of performance indicators to regional college representatives at Houghall College and then dashed back to college to attend the Beating Retreat at the garrison with Veronica. As usual the evening commenced with drinks and refreshments in the Officers' Mess where we chatted to military and local dignitaries. We were now being treated like important guests with comfortable front row seats to enjoy the music and the marching.

Many colleges were considering outsourcing some of their services and I had been persuaded to consider outsourcing the cleaning contract for the college. I had some reservations as the college environment had been well serviced by our current staff and I was a little uneasy about any of them losing their jobs. However, there was a successful bidder who agreed to employ all of our existing staff and the service did appear to maintain the high standards that were expected. Durham TEC hosted a conference at the Hallgarth Hotel on training initiatives and the next day I welcomed a group of Romanian visitors to the college. Unlike summers past, the FE sector was kept active during the traditional summer holiday period and I found my diary littered with appointments through July and August. We managed to take a family holiday for a week in Watford so that I could combine it with two meetings in London.

CHAPTER 14

Rising to the Challenges

D URING THE ENROLMENT PERIOD, Leon Brittan (now Lord Brittan)
called in to see me regarding our European activities, which had
been steadily expanding year by year. He was delighted to see the
range of partnerships that had been developed and the variety of links
that were supporting student experiences in several of our partner
countries. I attended a meeting of the Business Venture Board, which
preceded the official opening of some revamped premises in Forge
Way for small companies. The facilities were far superior to the
dismal units that the Business Venture managed in Wessoe Road and
we hoped that it would attract more innovative companies to the
town.

I welcomed the new staff members and then had a visit from Mike
Bedworth who I had last seen when he was working for the TETOC
unit that arranged my consultancy in Bhopal in 1974. Mike was now
principal of Kendal College and he was keen to see how we were
handling the demands of incorporation, particularly the gathering and
reporting of statistics. I had an ALBSU Advisory committee in
London and then hosted a meeting of FEFC inspectors who were
interested in the progress we were making with the College Charter.
This was one of the requirements that the FEFC had expected
colleges to undertake to clearly articulate the mission of the college
and the quality of service that students should expect. I had entrusted
the task of producing the College Charter to Pat Gale who had skills
in this area. I was hoping that our Charter would be of the required
high standard to qualify for the Charter Mark that was awarded to a
handful of colleges nationally.

On the following day I set off for a vist to Kostroma with Rod
Harris and Kevin Frame. Kevin was head of the school for business
and management and had been dealing with the training of the
Russians during their stay in Darlington. I had resisted early
invitations to Russia but with the partnership developing well, I
decided to make a courtesy visit. We flew into Moscow and were

transferred the two hundred miles to Kostroma in a car from the university. It seemed a long and hazardous ride on poorly made-up roads with little passing room to avoid a collision with on-coming traffic.

My brief opinion of Moscow, as we drove through the city from the airport, was not enhanced by the diversions and dowdy appearance of the buildings and the general population, but I was assured that there were many good features. Kostroma was quite different. It is an historic city and the administrative centre for the Kostroma region. It is located at the confluence of the Volga and Kostroma rivers and we stayed at the Volga Hotel overlooking the river. I was a bit apprehensive about this hotel as Les Baker had reported that on his first visit he could not sleep in the bed because it was full of bugs. However, the hotel had been given a thorough upgrade and we were quite comfortable. There are some beautiful buildings dating from the sixteenth century when there was spectacular growth of the city attributed to the establishment of trade connections with English and Dutch merchants. It is understandable why the Romanov tsars regarded Kostroma as their special protectorate. The Ipatievsky monastery was visited by many of them, including Nicholas II, the last Russian tsar. We were greeted by the rector, a small wiry man who had a reputation as a all-round sportsman and his deputy, a tall, jovial character, who we had met in Darlington.

We spent a full week in Kostroma visiting local companies and meeting staff and students. The object was to raise the profile of the university within the town as a centre and to support the training of local managers. Darlington College would supply expertise to develop a 'Business Support Unit' at the university with funding from the EU. An agreement was reached and a contract was signed committing the College to give regular on-the-spot support for the university staff as well as providing training in Darlington. We had the opportunity to assess the existing team members who appeared to be keen and willing to accept the challenge. I was impressed by many of the students that we met, by their grasp of English language and their enthusiasm for the partnership.

At the weekend, for some relief from the intensive activities, we were taken to a retreat that was owned by the university to provide short holidays for staff and their families. It was in a pleasant location with chalet accommodation and a variety of sports activities. We were taken to the Turkish baths, which were exceedingly hot and we were pleased to escape into the main swimming pool to cool down. On our last evening the rector hosted a banquet for about twenty-five people set around a large circular table with a raised central portion that rotated so that each guest could access the food as it passed by. Then it was time for the toasts. The rector stood up and gave a short toast and we stood up and drank the toast. Then it was my turn and so on right around the table until it came back to the rector. I foolishly thought that would be the end, but no, he stood up and gave another toast and so it continued until we had completed about fifty toasts. There had been a wide choice of drinks with vodka being very popular with the locals but I noticed that the rector stuck with beer, as did I. Whatever the choice of drink, after so many toasts most people were very merry and we left discretely to prepare for our journey home on the next day.

Inevitably, after a week away from the College there was a backlog of correspondence and decisions to be made. Gaynor had handled most of the issues in her expert manner and it was my good fortune to have someone so reliable when I was out of college so frequently. Gaynor would have a list of urgent tasks that needed to be actioned. Those of my colleagues who covered for me at local and regional meetings would drop in to update me on any news or significant developments that required further action.

Darlington Borough Council had twin town arrangements with Mulheim in Germany and Amiens in France. The College had developed strong links with Siemens Engineering Company in Mulheim and its training college so that exchange visits for engineering staff and students had been developed. The links with the college in Amiens were not as strong and I had encouraged the heads of school to consider developing links, particularly for students studying French. It was a pleasure to welcome Herr Jeckel of the Mulheim College in early October prior to a luncheon meeting with the chairman, vice-chairman and two new members of the Corporation Board. I had found that meetings such as this, over a meal, were often far more productive than those in the office. As soon as the meeting was over, I raced to the station for the London train for dinner with the NCET council members that preceded the AGM and council meeting the following day. I think that Margaret Bell was keen to ensure that all council members were well briefed before the AGM and that there would be no embarrassment for her team. As soon as the AGM closed, I headed for the station for the Darlington train as I was entertaining a group of Slovakian staff and students on their last evening in Darlington after their week's visit to the College.

I had become chairman of the expanding Northern Consortium for Child Care, which was hosted at the College and comprised representatives from Durham colleges, private sector trainers and employers. I was delighted to observe the high success rates of students taking NVQ child care courses.

There was a meeting about the proposed Radio Darlington, which involved a group of people who wished to bid for a licence to broadcast within the town and surrounding areas. I was keen to be involved both actively and financially, as I thought it would provide good experience for our journalism students and our facilities were of a professional standard. The Borough Council and local stake-holders also supported the bid. Unfortunately, the bid had to be withdrawn when we were informed that only thirty per cent of the funding for the radio station could be provided by the public sector and the college and local authority input exceeded that figure. After the busy week, I spent the weekend at the King's Head Hotel with the Corporation Board for its Annual Residential.

I had tried to maintain a weekly senior managers' meeting but the external demands were constantly causing them to be rearranged. Therefore, I spent a full morning with the assistant principals, getting progress reports, solving problems and agreeing priorities. I had a lunchtime meeting of the corporation's Audit Committee that had a general overview of the work of the corporation and then a meeting with Carol Brown at Catterick Garrison to assess progress of college courses on the school's premises. There was a meeting of the Darlington head teachers and principals' group that I usually asked Alan Dixon to deputise for me as I felt it was a low priority. However, as the meeting was at Queen Elizabeth 6FC, I took the opportunity to see what was happening at our nearest rival! Later I joined an interesting visit with the Business Forum to Darlington Building Society and met with Peter Rowley, the chief executive, and his colleagues. In Leeds there was a briefing by the College

Employers' Forum where we were informed of the increasing number of colleges that were experiencing financial difficulties.

Durham County Council invited all the principals to join its Human Resources Working Group which was to take an overview of employment opportunities and to address the pockets of unemployment within the county. The Durham TEC was well represented by several of its officers and it provided statistical information to support the information provided by the county. The intention was no doubt worthy but it soon transpired that the group was developing into a talking shop and principals started to send deputies rather than take up their own valuable time.

Roger Ward, CEO of the CEF, called to see me to discuss our progress with the implementation of the new conditions of service. This was probably because we were one of the few colleges that had adopted most of the CEF recommendations and been able to convince the vast majority of the staff to accept and sign the contract. The small group that chose to remain of the 'Silver Book' conditions were aware that their salaries would be frozen until they retired or signed the contract.

The College had become a member of the North East Open College Network (TROCN), that was based in Teesside University and I was nominally the college representative although one of my colleagues usually attended the regular meetings. However, I had been urged to attend a meeting in November at which a senior appointment was to take place and as one of the candidates was from the university, the chairman was anxious that the appointment had to be seen to be fair.

I travelled to Bracknell for a meeting at the headquarters of ORACLE that provided the MIS software to the college for our financial accounts and I was attended the one-day conference to be given an update on the developments that would affect our system. The following day I travelled into London to attend a meeting of UKERNA (UK's Education and Research Network) which was responsible for the higher educations broadband network, JANET. At that time only higher education institutions had access to this network which meant that colleges and schools were isolated from the wider applications offered by a broadband system. Making the most of the day in London, I called into City and Guilds before attending a Council for Education Technology meeting.

The corporation held its first Annual General Meeting in November and Chairman Geoff Nichol had spent half of the previous day going over the papers with me and Debbie. The meeting went well and all of the questions that were raised were answered to the members' satisfaction. Immediately after there was a normal Board meeting.

A week later I was in Dusseldorf for three days with a group of educationalists from further and higher education to receive a briefing from EU officials on the various funding opportunities for UK institutions. Roger Ward led the small FE group. It was an excellent opportunity to hear at first hand the latest funding opportunities for both Eastern and Western European partnerships and I returned to Darlington with several schemes that I passed to Graham Best to work on. Two weeks later I was in Brussels for a specific briefing from EU officers regarding schemes and proposals that the College was considering. The officers emphasised that these schemes were always oversubscribed by bids from HE institutions and they had years of experience of bidding compared to FE colleges. However, I was not deterred and found the tips useful to feed back to Graham.

I was pleased to welcome Agop from Bulgaria, who was also visiting his son who was now attending the College and proving that he could do the two-year BTEC IT Diploma course in one year. I also welcomed the rector from Kostroma with some of his colleagues.

Bishop David Jenkins was our principal guest at the Higher Awards evening that was again well organised by Chris Watson. Other end of year social events included the Barclays Bank drinks evening, Houghton School Christmas Concert and lunch at Catterick Garrison headquarters with Colonel Mike Dent.

1995

One corporation committee that was a new experience for me was the Remuneration Committee and it was responsible for the pay and conditions of the senior post holders. By definition of the Education Act senior post holders were the principal and vice-principal but I had agreed that it should be extended to include the executive team. Instead of my salary being negotiated nationally and locally applied by the LEA, I had to agree with the Remuneration Committee specific targets, some of which were college-wide while others were more specific to me. Under the LEA scheme and the recommendations of the Burnham Report, the vice-principal's salary was set at eighty per cent of that of the principal and the Corporation Board members took the view that this was overgenerous and that there should be a wider margin to reflect the greater role of the principal with the added responsibilities of chief executive. For the first two years of incorporation there were no guidelines from the CEF and I had to struggle to come to terms with a new skill to negotiate my salary with the chairman and vice-chairman. Geoff Nichol, as the first chairman under incorporation, erred on the cautious side, perhaps understandably. This meant that my salary increased modestly compared with some of my colleague principals who had enjoyed significant rises. It was agreed that my appraisal would form the basis for the salary settlement and in turn, it would be my responsibility for determining the other executive members' salaries within a band agreed with the committee on the basis of my appraisal of them. During the first three years I had some confrontational meetings with Denis and Geoff, often away from the College at a local hotel. They had ideas from their management experiences that they felt should be adopted by me for the College and I disagreed more often than not. Alan Dixon did not fare too well as his salary hardly rose in the early years to allow my salary to become proportionately greater.

With Simon's guidance an appraisal system was designed for all full-time staff members and it was grudgingly accepted by the local union branches. It was during this quiet period that staff briefings were organised so that team leaders were trained to carry out their duties fairly and honestly and that staff were aware of their rights under the system if they were unhappy with their appraisal. I spent a lot of time with Simon briefing the staff and I was sure the effort was worthwhile as there were very few appeals against appraisal ratings. The staff members that had remained on the Silver Book conditions were not included in the appraisal system.

FEFC organised a regional briefing for principals at Boldon and I had a visit from Peter Craddock, the FEFC inspector for the College. The FEFC had introduced a four-year cycle of inspections and as Darlington College had been inspected just before incorporation, it would be in the last group of colleges to be inspected by FEFC. As a former HMI, Peter was a friendly person who was willing to offer advice and answer my questions regarding the first round of inspections. The new inspectorate was also responsible for issues that were not only academic but also related to the financial viability of the institution.

I gave a presentation to all of the full-time staff to highlight national and local changes. I had decided on a restructuring of responsibilities following the departure of Angela Harris. Alan Dixon took over responsibility for curriculum, which included learning programmes and corporate services whilst Pat Gale covered all aspect of learner support including the childcare facilities. Graham Best was responsible for industrial liaison and international activities whilst Chris Watson retained his role as responsible for estate management. Pat, Graham and Chris retained their assistant principal titles whilst the other executive members, Debbie Leigh, Simon Cassidy and Angus Byrne were designated as directors.

I also reported on the current recruitment performance that showed a growth of 5.6% against a target of eight per cent. Full-time enrolments had slipped, mainly because of a fall in science and computing subjects. This had been partly offset by an increase in part-time enrolments. One of the problems was the low staying-on rate in the South Durham area that was twenty per cent below the national average. Sixth forms in schools and Queen Elizabeth Sixth Form College had traditionally taken the bulk of the A level and GCSE repeat students but were now expanding into vocational areas that had been the domain of the FE colleges. We did recruit from all of the seven Darlington schools, but Carmel with its own sixth form and Hummersknott with a high proportion of potential A level students, were proving a challenge. The other challenge was the efficiency gains required by the FEFC of two per cent in the unit of funding for 1995/96, from £18.93 to £18.53 per unit. I also reported on the national state of colleges where six per cent were classified as 'relatively weak' and only seventy per cent were deemed to be 'robust'. Fortunately, we fell into the robust category. The FEFC had also stated that nationally it was holding back £50m (two per cent) of funding to encourage progress on staff contracts. I never tried to hide problems from the staff but I always aspired to raise confidence in what had been achieved and the opportunities that were open to us.

FEFC had its two-day annual conference in Birmingham and later in the month I joined NILTA colleagues for a two-day residential meeting hosted by BT at its technical base in Martlesham, Essex. This was a real treat with an opportunity to see the applications and technologies of the future being tested. NILTA had developed strong links with BT along with RM and Apple who were all major contributors to our funds.

I had been approached by Chris Drew to join the Board of the newly formed Northern Informatics Applications Agency (NiAA). Chris was the chief executive and John Bridge was its chairman. A group of interested people from various backgrounds within the region constituted the Board that was based in Sunderland and had national funding for its small team of staff. I had been invited because of my involvement with the regions colleges in trying to establish the first FE broadband network in the country and I had been bidding for Competitiveness Fund money for BT to construct the infrastructure. I attended my first meeting of NiAA at Sunderland University on 17 February when it appeared that there were a lot of bridges to be built between members before any serious progress could be made. Chris Drew did his best in the early days but eventually it was decided to make a new start and NiAA was re-launched at Darlington College in February 1996 and this was the beginning of a more determined effort to create an 'information society in the North East' and to tackle the divide between the 'haves' and the 'have nots'.

It was in late February that the College's expanded its provision on Firthmoor Estate to build on the previous outstanding successes. Many of the wives and young women that lived on the estate had either left school early or had not succeeding in gaining any qualifications. The centre provided a familiar setting that was not as daunting as having to go to the main site of the College. Sympathetic staff had been specially selected to provide the learning support at the centre and I think that even they were surprised at the enthusiasm and rapid progress that some of the women made in quickly obtaining NVQ Level 2 qualifications. It was soon apparent that many were blossoming in this new learning environment and soon they became sufficiently confident to attend courses at the College and gain higher qualifications. It was really pleasing to note that there was a group of women who were determined to go to university and with the support of Teesside University they achieved their objectives. At the Annual Adult Learners' Day in Darlington, the centre was selected for special mention and the staff and students received the praise that they truly deserved.

With the restructuring and the many other changes and challenges I had decided to hold a residential two days' staff development for the executive team at Walworth Castle. This gave me the opportunity to expand upon the briefing I had given at the full staff meeting and to allow Debbie and Simon to give presentations on finance and personnel matters. Although as a group we were under a lot of pressure to succeed I was pleased with the good humour, skills and commitment that each member brought to the team. I recognised that it was my responsibility to lead and set the pace but without the full involvement of the team we would not have succeeded in achieving most of the targets that had been set by the FEFC and the Corporation Board. In addition to the group meetings I also met each member of the executive team on a regular basis to review their progress and to carry out their appraisal.

In mid-March one of my big projects was completed and officially opened. This was the Function Suite that replaced the former small restaurant and outdated kitchens. I had targeted the oak-panelled hall in the former girls' high school block that had been used as a bolt hole for full-time students and was becoming very dilapidated. The hall was divided by a partition into two areas, the larger part being the Oak Room restaurant for one hundred covers and the smaller area as a Bistro for staff and students. A large commercial-type kitchen had been constructed from three of the original kitchens and a mezzanine floor was constructed over the bistro area to form an additional meeting room.

Whilst Darlington was still our major objective, I was convinced that North Yorkshire was the real opportunity for future developments. The number of students travelling from North Yorkshire had increased since incorporation and North Yorkshire was now providing several buses each day to transport students for the Richmondshire and Hambledon areas.

The FEFC had indicated that capital grants would be available for approved building projects although the government was getting very keen on the PFI (Private Finance Initiative) method of funding. I had a meeting with Harry Tabinor, chief executive of Richmondshire District Council who I had met at Catterick Garrison and he was very interested in the College's plans to develop into the area. He mentioned that the Richmond people had not developed links with Catterick and that they might not support a major centre if it was developed there. He suggested we should also be looking at possibilities in Richmond and he proposed that we should look at the former RC Boarding School which was empty but had large buildings and a lot of land. At a later date I visited the site with colleagues and Alan Dodd, the chartered surveyor on the Corporation Board. The neglected buildings were substantial but we agreed that the cost of conversion to a modern learning centre would be far greater than the cost of the site. Later in the month I met with Roger Grasby, chief executive of North Yorkshire TEC, and he was also supportive of my proposals although he was aware that some of the local schools were concerned that their sixth forms would lose students to FE. In late June I had a meeting with the North Yorkshire head teachers and it was very amicable; their main concern was the influence of Queen Elizabeth Sixth Form College on their potential A level students and they were quite pleased that the College would be able to accept more of their pupils who were seeking a vocational route.

I had a visit from Pat Snell, who was chief executive of UK Skills. I had already agreed that the College would be a founder member as I hoped that the organisation would bring the same enthusiasm as SkillBuild did every year to the construction sector. Geoff Nichol was our principal guest at the Awards Ceremony in mid-March. Geoff was standing down as chairman of the corporation and was due to hand over to Denis Gatfield the following year. The following week the FEFC inspected our engineering courses and a good report was received.

A new initiative was developing in Darlington to raise the interest in the locomotion history of the town. A group calling itself the A1 Locomotion Trust had been set up to build the first steam locomotion for many years. It was seeking funding from the community at large and would be heavily dependent on voluntary assistance in the manufacturing process. There were several older people who had been associated with railway manufacturing who formed a nucleus of talent available and willing to participate. I was approached to see if the College could assist the project by providing any skills or equipment that might be available. Malcolm Price, head of the school of engineering and some of his long serving colleagues identified pieces of ancient machinery that was sitting idle in the workshops that could be released and tools and machinery were eventually transferred to the Trust.

After Easter I participated in a visit to the American Association of Community Colleges (AACC) Annual Convention in Minneapolis. This was organised by the Staff College and there was a coach load of members in the party drawn from senior managers in colleges. Including travel, I was away from College for ten days but the experience in the US was excellent. The convention was huge compared to any event that I had attended in England. The community colleges regarded this as an essential part of staff development and each college had a team of people attending so that there was well over three thousand people at the convention. Our UK group had booked into a large hotel in downtown Minneapolis within walking distance of the Convention Centre. We had two days prior to the commencement of the convention that allowed the group to visit community colleges in the area and I found some of the practices in the colleges very interesting. They seemed to put much more emphasis on student services than we did in the UK and the students seemed to respond positively. However, it was pointed out that we were seeing the best of the colleges and that they were mainly dealing with full-time students.

We had been issued with the substantial programme book for the convention that included as many as twenty-three different presentations taking place simultaneously in different parts of the centre, which meant that trying to choose a personal programme for each day was challenging. There were topics on every facet of further education and I decided to concentrate on the sessions involving new technologies. The convention opened on Saturday 22 April at 4 p.m. with a keynote address by the AACC president, followed by the presentation of awards for the year, including presidents (principals) with over twenty-five years of service – the longest serving had forty years, unbelievable in the UK but retirement at sixty-five was not compulsory in the US. After the opening events we visited the

Academic Marketplace which was full of mainly retailers displaying a wide variety of educational equipment and services. This was fascinating and I returned several times to the marketplace during the convention to talk to some of the suppliers. In the evening we were invited to the Hilton Hotel to participate in a reception sponsored by the Minneapolis Community College System.

On the Sunday morning I decided to support a UK presentation by Ruth Gee, who at that time was chief executive of the Association for Colleges (AfC) and Colin Flint, principal of Solihull College. After a quick visit to the marketplace I attended an internet demo before going to the plenary session on American Pluralism and Identity. This was rather theoretical and I was pleased to go to the afternoon seminar on 'Cybercollege' that had been established by Front Range Community College. This was certainly innovative and confirmed some of my thinking about how I wished the Catterick Centre to develop. The next seminar was on the 'world wide web', that rounded up the day's programme before I attended a reception in the evening at the Hilton Hotel hosted by AfC. At the reception we heard about another reception organised by the National Community College Hispanic Council. It was open until 11 p.m., so we decided to explore. What a contrast between the sedate UK event and the dynamic Hispanic event with singing, dancing and a very hearty welcome to the English visitors. The 8.15 a.m. session on Monday was by Brian Stanford, director of Adelaide College, talking about 'Contemporary Trends in Open Learning Environments'. After his presentation I had an opportunity to talk to him about his ideas and he told me he was having a one-year sabbatical leave and would be spending a lot of time in the UK. I therefore invited him to the North East during his visit.

The highlight for the American participants was the plenary session at 11 a.m. when President Bill Clinton addressed the convention. He had accepted the invitation to attend, as this was the 75th Annual Convention of AACC. There must have been over four thousand people crammed into the centre and he gave a masterful presentation, having the delegates, except those from the UK, on their feet at regular intervals to rapturous applause to his every sentence. It was certainly a memorable occasion and the two following speakers, Robert Reich, Secretary of the US Department of Labor and

Richard Riley, Secretary of the US Department of Education, were totally overshadowed. I wondered if a UK educational convention would ever attract the Prime Minister and two Secretaries of State to speak on the same day. In talking to US delegates later, they confirmed to me that President Clinton did take an active interest in community colleges and that colleges received daily publicity in the national press. It was back to reality in the afternoon when I attended a session on 'Turning the Century – Creating the Transformational Learning Community' and the following session on 'Sharing Resources through the use of Tele-communications'. I attended one further technology presentation before the convention closed at Tuesday lunchtime. It had been a valuable experience although I did have some reservations about the organisation by the Staff College and I decided to raise the issue at the next NILTA Council with a proposition to organise a visit to the AACC in 1996.

I had established a College Innovations Group to bring together a number of staff that I thought could produce some new ideas to enhance the learning experience of students. Graham Best and I had identified a small team and we met occasionally to brainstorm ideas with no definite agenda. Inevitably, the discussions tended to be heavily influenced by the potential of the emerging technologies and the concept of taking learning to the people. After the AACC Convention I was able to distribute some of the materials that I had collected during the visits to colleges and from the seminars that I had attended. This stimulated ideas about student support services and videoconferencing. I also involved the Group in thinking about the proposed Catterick Centre and the sort of innovations that could be included in the planning process.

I had a meeting at a local architects' office to discuss the potential and to explore possibilities and likely costs. I set my mind on opening a centre to celebrate the centenary of the College in 1997 and the corporation supported the proposal in principle. Over the following weeks I had discussions at the garrison with the commander and with Carol Brown. The commander was very enthusiastic but Carol could see the probability of losing useful income if the College had independent facilities. Funding was going to be a key factor as I knew that the contribution from FEFC would be relatively small. There was also the consideration of obtaining a suitable plot of land. At that time I was not sure if we could purchase military land or if we could lease a plot from the Army. The colonel had involved his team in making enquiries from the Ministry of Defence and at the time he asked the team to try to identify suitable sites that would not be required for military purposes. In early June I was taken in an army vehicle to look at several potential sites on the eastern side of the garrison on land that had become heavily overgrown with trees and shrubs. Whilst the sites would have been acceptable, I felt they were a bit too remote from the hub of the garrison and the commander agreed with me.

When Durham LEA handed over the buildings to the College, I was minded to get rid of the two annexes that were used by the journalism and business studies courses in Trinity Road. The new facilities that were being created for journalism in the library wing would release one of the houses and there was a possibility to rent premises in the Business Centre at Morton Park. I had sought advice from Alan Dodd regarding the value of the complete site and his assessment was £350,000, a bit less than I thought, as there was a large area at the rear of the buildings that had been used for sports by the former teacher training college and the tennis courts were still standing. The other issue that would prove to be the highest hurdle was the government's enthusiasm for the PFI schemes for all public sector projects and I had to attend for a whole day being briefed on contracts. In mid-June I was invited to the King's Head Hotel in Richmond to speak to a Richmondshire Partnership group who had expressed an interest in the Catterick plans for the College. I gave them a comprehensive PowerPoint presentation and responded to several questions. I was very pleased with their enthusiastic support for the project and I agreed to keep them informed of progress.

The private finance initiative (PFI) was used to fund major new public building projects, including hospitals, schools, prisons and roads. The Conservatives first introduced the scheme in the early 1990s. Under New Labour, PFI become a major – and controversial – element of private sector involvement in Britain's public services. Since 1997, about £50 billion worth of public-private deals were signed, despite opposition from Labour backbenchers and public sector unions. Private consortiums, usually involving large construction firms, raised the capital finance to design and build a public sector project. They were also contracted to maintain the buildings while a public authority, such as a council or NHS trust, used them. This meant the private sector was responsible for providing cleaning, catering and security services. Once construction was complete, the public authority had to pay back the private consortium for the cost of the buildings and their maintenance, plus interest. The contracts typically last for thirty years, after which time the buildings belong to the public authority.

It was about this time that the cable company Comcast had expanded its operation from Middlesbrough and Stockton into Darlington, having secured a national contract for Cleveland area and Darlington. I was invited to visit the company offices in Stockton to see their facilities and be briefed about the advantages of cable. I could see the longer-term benefits of cable and gave Angus Byrne the responsibility of liasing with Comcast and to consider the potential for linking the College into the network. The downside was the disruption caused throughout the town as every street had to have a trench excavated to allow the cable to be installed.

The College was invited to participate in a meeting with Darlington Council, Durham TEC and Darlington Business Venture regarding the government's proposals to reorganise local government in Cleveland and Durham. It was proposed to abolish Cleveland in 1997 and create unitary authorities in Redcar, Middlesbrough, Stockton and Hartlepool. The proposal for Durham was for Darlington to become a unitary authority in 1998. The current local Darlington councillors welcomed the proposal, which was strongly opposed by Durham. The point of the meeting was to sound out the key players to determine if there was support for the proposal. From my experience with the county I was inclined to support the proposals and the meeting confirmed my view. There were many people in the town that were not convinced as they stated that the town would become one of the smallest unitary authorities and would struggle to meet its full commitments to the community. There was intense lobbying over the next few months until eventually it was decided to support the proposal.

The day after the meeting with the Darlington partners I had an interview with Estelle Maxwell of the *Times Educational Supplement* (TES). The TES did, from time to time, produce feature articles on people in education and I was quite flattered to be selected. Estelle was a skilled professional and we had a lively discussion on a range of issues that she recorded on tape. She had arranged for a photographer to be on hand and he wanted a picture of me in front of the College with the nameplate in the background. Fortunately, it was a pleasant day as, like most professional photographers, he took a long time before he was satisfied. The printed article covered half a page and included a close-up head and shoulders colour photograph of me. There were several inaccuracies in the article but I suspect few people would be aware of them. There was a concentration on my involvement with NILTA and on my views of the impact of technology on further education.

I had tried to keep good relations with the two main unions, NATFHE and UNISON, but the introduction of the new contracts had been a challenge and some of the staff had engaged in one-day strikes in response to instructions from national officials. Regional officials from both unions called to see me during the summer term to try to persuade me to take a softer line than CEF recommended. They claimed that some colleges, and they quoted Newcastle in particular, had compromised but I had to stand firm as the College unit of funding was below the national average and consequently there was very little room to manoeuvre. There were many part-time teachers on the College payroll and I was aware that the only information they were receiving would be via the grapevine and so I offered an afternoon and an evening session to brief the part-time staff on all of the implications of the changes. They were useful meetings, particularly for those who were engaged in a significant teaching load and were heavily dependent upon the College for maintaining their standard of living.

Whilst I still had many external commitments it was now possible to have a regular weekly meeting with the Executive Committee. This was particularly important, as I had necessarily had to delegate most of the day-to-day decisions to the members of the team. The meetings provided an opportunity to share progress and if there were differences of opinion or a problem that had not been resolved I would often need to make the decision. The College hosted the regional Guild of Bricklayers competition that selected competitors for the SkillBuild finals. The College had traditionally done well in both the senior and junior events and I was obviously very pleased when our students won both events.

The regional bid by the consortium of colleges for Competitiveness funding had been successful and the issues surrounding the Competitiveness Fund for the Northern Region started to accelerate as summer approached. There were a series of meetings with BT and colleges and a grand plan to install a broadband network was finalised and the monies allocated. The key meeting in July was held at Durham County Cricket Club ground at Chester-le-Street when every one of the twenty-eight colleges in the region attended. I presented the proposal that showed that the cost of establishing the network, including all of the college links would be covered by the Competitiveness Fund as well as the rental to BT for the first year. There was a debate on how the ongoing costs would be shared and the bandwidths that would be available to each college. The initial bandwidths would be 2 Mb for the larger colleges and 0.5 Mb for the smaller colleges. The outcome was that twenty-five colleges agreed to sign up to the network with the Northumberland Agricultural College and two sixth form colleges deciding not to participate. This was probably a better response that many of us had anticipated. The outcome was also greeted enthusiastically by the FEFC's regional office. I was particularly pleased as this set an example for the rest of the colleges in the country. A few days later I had a meeting with BT to discuss the Competitiveness Fund contract that would have to be agreed and signed by each of the participating colleges.

I gave a presentation on the developments in FE to the senior staff of Sunderland University during their staff development conference at Otterburn Hall. The following day I flew down to Heathrow for an APPLE presentation to NILTA. I had an interesting meeting with the principal and vice-principal of Northallerton College who were worried about the College's proposals for Catterick. Northallerton was a secondary school with a sixth form but, with collaboration between the North Yorkshire LEA and the TEC, the school had an adult education facility and it offered a range of TEC funded programmes. I gave them an assurance that we did not seek to move into the Northallerton area. For one reason: the public transport between Northallerton and Catterick was minimal and the roads were narrow and winding. I had a visit from a BBC reporter who was following up the TES article and Clive Owen of Darlington Borough Council called in to discuss several issues including unitary status and the availability of parts of the Arts Centre. I was invited to attend the launch of the Darlington Economical Development Plan and the Durham TEC AGM.

This was the first summer since the implementation of the new staff contract and this inevitably meant that there would be teaching staff available for part of the traditional holiday period. I had meetings with heads of school to arrange professional activities for staff who were not involved with teaching and to use the time to sort out workshops, equipment and teaching accommodation to bring schedules up-to-date and list redundant equipment. When I had arrived at the College in 1987 all the academic staff, including the principal, took their full entitlement of fourteen weeks leave so that the College was deserted during the vacation periods. I had been slowly introducing the extended college year but the advent of incorporation accelerated the process so that there would be some staff in throughout the summer to deal with potential student enquiries and enrolments of full-time students so reducing some of the frenetic activity in early September.

My diary listed engagements throughout July and well into August including another 'Beating Retreat' at the garrison and Competitiveness Fund discussions with regard to our proposal for a Catterick centre. We had entered into an agreement with the garrison to run a Prince's Trust programme for unemployed young people in Richmondshire. The team leader would be a young army officer, selected by one of the regiments as a form of additional training. We had completed one programme successfully and there was a meeting in August to discuss the outcomes and review the future of the scheme.

In mid August we had a ten-day family holiday in Eire, based in Dublin. We took Veronica's mother with us as she had lost her husband during the year and she wished to make a visit to the land of her birth. We had driven to Stranraer and took the ferry to Larne then drove south over the border to Dublin. We visited relatives in Longford and later had a very long day travelling to Galway for a few hours. It was quite a good break for me and the children seemed to enjoy the experience. Shortly after returning home we all travelled to London for three days to visit the Notting Hill Carnival and enjoy the show *Starlight Express*. Helen and a friend had tickets to visit the National TV Awards and we travelled with her by tube and waited for after the performance.

CHAPTER 15

More Target Setting

1995–96

THE COLLEGE'S TARGET Average Level of Funding (ALF) for 1994/95 had been set by the FEFC at £18.10 per unit and our actual outturn was £18.16, very close to target but there was clearly going to have to be some efficiencies to achieve the ALF target for 1995/96 of £17.84 that would only be achieved by larger group sizes and higher retention rates. The other target that I had to achieve was to increase income from sources other than FEFC, a target that I had proposed to the Corporation Board earlier. One way of achieving this was to increase the number of fee paying students on FEFC funded programmes in addition to the full cost work that was generated by Quadrant. 1st September fell on a Friday and enrolment started on that day and continued through until Saturday – another innovation that proved quite successful with the customers if not quite as much with the staff. With stringent targets to achieve I felt we had to take every possible action to make enrolment easier for the students. I held a full staff meeting after the enrolment period to emphasise the importance of setting targets and achieving them.

I flew from Teesside to Heathrow to meet up with Alan Wells and a small team of officers and practitioners to fly to Canada to look at basic skills education in that country. We arrived in Toronto and stayed in the Royal York Hotel, a beautiful building with excellent facilities. As it was the weekend, our hosts had arranged a coach trip on the Sunday to Niagra Falls and the local district. We had a splendid day, getting soaked on the *Maid of the Mist* boat that takes you very close to the waterfall. The serious business started on the following morning with a visit to Frontier College, which was a national literacy organisation and Jim Page set the scene of basic skills education in Canada. Canada had been selected for the visit as its problems in literacy and numeracy were considered as very similar to those in the UK. They had an additional problem as both English and

French were national languages and all official publications had to be printed in both languages. Each member of the team had a specific brief and mine was to look at the progress in the use of information technolgy to support adult literacy tuition. We stayed together for the rest of the first day visiting several colleges in Toronto and seeing a wide variety of practices and support for learners. There was no shortage of enthusiasm but in some areas the staff did not have much support in terms of materials, equipment and modest accommodation. Two of the people at the Frontier College meeting proved to be particularly useful. Charles Ramsey, the executive director of the National Adult Literacy Database (NALD), gave me specific advice on my programme and I met up with him later in New Brunswick where he was based. Linda Shohet was the director of The Centre of Literacy based in Montreal and she also provided useful support and I met up with her later in the UK.

On the following day the group spilit up and I visited the Institute of Internal Travel, Alphacom and Alpha Ontario in Toronto. These were private organisations that were trying to develop electronic systems for materials to support learning and most of these were at an early stage of development. Later in the day I flew to Ottawa, the Canadian capital, and was met by an official of the Department of Industry who transferred me to my hotel for the evening. My appointment at the department on the following day was scheduled for the afternoon and I had arranged to use the free morning to visit the headquarters of the Association of Canadian Community Colleges (ACCC). The chief executive warmly welcomed me and I had an interesting session being informed of the strengths and weaknesses of the Canadian community colleges system.

I spent the afternoon with several people from the Department of Industry who were involved in the area of basic skills education and they provided me with a lot of statistical information and discussed the challenges of dealing with the problems they faced in reaching out to remote areas where the indigenous population or 'inuits' were to be found. There was recognition of the potential of the developing technologies to take education to the people but the cost of setting up the necessary infrastructure was considerable. I noted that videoconferencing was used on a daily basis between government officers and I was informed that larger companies used that technology extensively to maintain daily contact with colleagues locally and nationally. I spent another night in Ottawa before my next assignment in New Brunswick.

The following morning I flew to Fredericton, the capital city of New Brunswick. I had been advised that the most innovative practices were being developed there and I was looking forward to seeing evidence of that progress. I was met by a small delegation and because I had spent most of the day travelling, I was taken to a comfortable hotel and was entertained by the hosts. I was given a copy of *Driving the Information Highway*, a report of the New Brunswick task force on the Electronic Information Highway dated March 1994. In the opening chapter I read:

> In New Brunswick, we have an edge. Much of the key infrastructure is already in place. A leader in implementing communications technology, NBTel has established a fibre optic ring around the province and now offers digital services to all its customers. This enables every home and business in New Brunswick to gain access to the same high speed digital communications network – a level not found in any other Canadian province or American state at this time.

I thought they could have extended that claim to the rest of the world. At the time of my visit a local broadband connection had been connected to seventy-five per cent of New Brunswick homes delivering services to rural as well as urban customers. With regard to education the report stated that TeleEducation NB was 'providing for the delivery of secondary, college and university courses by audio, video or computer teleconferencing at more that fifty sites acrosss the province'. I found the report stimulating and its recommendations to harness the full potential of the network were at the forefront of current thinking.

In the morning I was taken to the Fredericton site of New Brunswick Community College. Its main site was in Moncton but time did not allow me to travel there. The Frederickton site was predominently geared to job-related training with most of the courses having an on-the-job element. However, what I had mainly wished to see was the distance learning facilities and I met the small team that was developing the technology and the materials to extend educational opportunities throughout this sparsely populated community.

They did not have the infrastructure to provide videoconferencing but they were using teleconferencing to support students on an individual basis. I sat in on a session with a tutor linked to a learner in a remote part of New Brunswick and I was able to converse with both of them to assess the progress that was being made.

I had no doubt of the commitment of the national and local officers and educationalists to make progress in this area and I wished that I had the same support in the UK. The following day was spent with local educationalists and I had lunch with the New Brunswick Government Minister for Education. He was delighted that I had taken the trouble to visit the province as it seemed that most foreign visitors rarely ventured beyond the large cities. My hosts gave me a tour of the city including the beautiful Saint John River. The weather had been kind as it can be quite cold by September that far north. There was no doubt that the visit to New Brunswick was the highlight of my Canadian visit. I flew back to Toronto to meet up with Alan Wells and the rest of the party to exchange experiences before flying back that evening to Heathrow and onto Teesside on Sunday morning. It had been an interesting experience and I produced a substantial report for Alan who was a sceptic when it came to the advantages of technology to support learning.

I had little time to reflect before a meeting of NCET council in London followed by joining a BTEC panel to select the Student of the Year. Because of my diary, the induction of new staff had been delayed and I managed to squeeze it in before a trip to Geneva. I had been invited with several NILTA members and other educationalists to join a day trip to an International Technology Conference and I travelled down to Gatwick the day before departure to meet up with the other delegates. We had dinner at the Gatwick Hilton and stayed overnight with an early morning call. We boarded the flight and taxied away from the terminal building before stopping for the next three hours on the tarmac. Apparently, fog had descended over Geneva airport making landing dangerous and the Gatwick terminal had no spare spaces to accommodate our plane. Eventually, we did take off and enjoyed a shortened day visiting the many stands displaying the latest technology and a variety of gadgets. We returned to Gatwick to spend another night at the Hilton before returning home the next morning.

The introduction of the world wide web in the early 1990s and the emergence of the internet was transforming perceptions in all aspects of life and had accelerated my aspirations for student-based learning. The Education Department's Superhighways Initiative (EDSI) had commissioned NCET in early 1995 to act as the agent in managing the evaluation of EDSI. EDSI consisted of twenty-two educational projects making use of medium and broadband networks and I was fortunate to be party to the evolving technology. I attended an FEFC Conference on 'Information Highways' in London and three weeks later Malcolm Himsworth and I were invited to the launch of the government's consultative document *Superhighways in Education* in Cambridge with Michael Heseltine, the government minister, opening the debate. The document defined superhighways as follows:

> The term 'superhighway' is usually taken to mean a broadband network capable of transferring very large amounts of information – including video, still images, audio and text – at high speed between users. Narrowband networks, for example those linking computers over ordinary telephone lines, are slower and less flexible in their functions. But the digitisation of information, including still and moving images, and the ability to 'compress' that digital information, now means that narrowband networks can carry an increasing range of functions.

SuperJANET was referred to in the document as follows:

> SuperJANET – the Super Joint Academic Network – provides the UK's first education superhighway, and is currently one of the largest high performance networks in the world. Conceived strategically in 1989 as an optical-fibre network to support the networking requirements of the UK research and higher education community, it builds upon the earlier JANET academic network established in the 1980s. SuperJANET currently has two components. A 34 Mbit/s data network interconnects 60 sites across the UK and forms a high performance part of the global Internet. Of these sites 14 are also connected via a 34 Mbit/s multi-service network, which is currently being upgraded to 155 Mbit/s. A plan for the expansion of Super-JANET has been approved by the Higher Education Funding Councils and the connection of an additional 27 sites to the data network has recently been announced.

Further education did get a modest mention in the document as follows:

> Colleges will need to keep pace with education superhighway developments if they are to continue to play their full part in vocational education and training to ensure that the nation remains competitive. In general terms FE colleges are likely to be interested in superhighway developments in order to:
>
> - widen access to provision, including particular specialisms within any college;
> - enrich curriculum content by improved access to resources;
> - foster a more versatile approach to the development of core skills in both academic and vocational courses;
> - promote collaborative ventures with the local community, including employers and schools; and between UK colleges and their counterparts in other countries;
> - gain access to sources of information on vocational needs to improve responsiveness of colleges to changing vocational requirements, both in the UK and Europe;
> - provide information, advice and guidance to prospective students, especially adults wishing to re-enter education.

At one stage I had hoped that colleges could have been accommodated within the JANET network and I knew that individual colleges were having discussions with their local universities to try to link into JANET on a personal basis. In the North East our successful Competitiveness Funded project led to the formation of the Northern Colleges Network (NCN) that would manage the project and I was elected as chairman. Our project was aimed at supporting competitiveness in SMEs that should eventually be able to demonstrate understanding and expertise in:

(a) Acquiring information know-how and good practice by use of the global network;

(b) communicating with markets by email, conferencing and on-line publishing;

(c) managing self-development through communication with learning resources and providers.

A team from Darlington College of Technology, led by director of telematics, Angus Byrne, prepared the proposal which would not only provide the communications infrastructure but would produce a range of services that would be at least equal to those available to the universities. Each participating college had to provide matching funding by installing appropriate hardware to accommodate the broadband infrastructure. Ideally, a college should have provided a powerful server that connected to the cable and then distributed the facilities by an internal local area network throughout the college.

Access to the Internet, World Wide Web, JANET and other services would be provided by the project. I had expected colleges to plan to maximise this major source of information by allowing all staff and students to directly access the network. There was potential for inter-college communications using email and electronic data transfer to examination boards and FEFC. With imagination, transmission of learning materials would enhance opportunities for students who preferred to study at home or in the workplace. Given the student numbers that were currently studying in the participating colleges, it was estimated that a weekly target of 20,500 accesses to the network would be made across the region during the first year of the project.

The regional government office had approved the project and funding that would cover two years of implementation and development. Originally, three specifications were prepared so that each college would have an opportunity to identify the level of infrastructure it could afford after the initial funding ceased. When BT won the contract, it was agreed that the three options could be reduced to two bandwidths: 128 Kbytes/s and 516 Kbytes/s. The government office contracted the project with Durham Training and Enterprise Council, who then contracted with Darlington College of Technology to be responsible for the project management. A regional steering group advised the project managers. The target to ensure that all of the colleges would be on the network by no later than early 1996 was achieved, although delays were experienced with one of the colleges that had been given a microwave link instead of an optic fibre cable. The BT solution was to provide one of their new networking products known as MIPPS, the Managed Information Protocol Presentational Service. The figure shows a diagrammatic representation of the Northern Colleges MIPPS service. The twenty-five colleges were linked to a BT 'point of presence' in Newcastle and

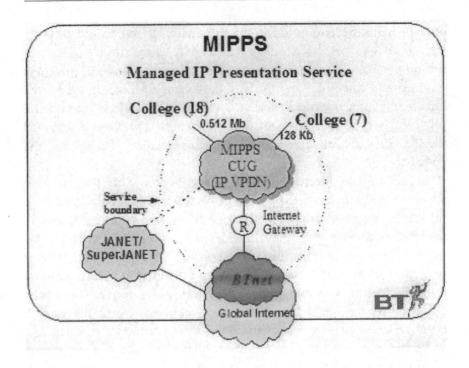

operated as a Closed User Group to enable advanced networking between the partner colleges.

The Competitiveness Fund covered all of the cable installation costs for the colleges and most of the leasing costs in the first year. A second successful bid was made for funding for the second year (1996–97), covering approximately eighty per cent of the cable leasing charges. Those colleges who chose the faster speed bandwidth of 516 kbit/s were committed to an annual leasing charge of about £28,000, whilst the colleges with the slower bandwidth were committed to about £14,000 per year. The total regional funding over two years was £900,000.

Between these two events I had a meeting at the Basic Skills Agency where the visit to Canada was discussed. The three-day NILTA Annual Conference was held at the Queens Hotel in Leeds and attracted a very good response from the sector colleges as most principals had at last appreciated the need to have staff who were competent and up to date with the new technologies. The organisations that supplied equipment and materials to the colleges had provided an exhibition that filled one of the largest rooms in the hotel. We also provide a videoconferencing link to London so that the appropriate government minister could address the conference.

I had to cope with two long sessions with the chairman and vice-chairman who had ideas that did not necessary sit comfortably with me and my views on the direction the College should be taking. I had asked the corporation to establish an International Committee to monitor the activities of the College in that area as I was aware that some members of the Board were sceptical of this activity. However, I had always been able to show that all activities had been externally funded and that the benefits to the students and the College justified the commitment of senior management time.

In addition to the FEFC Inspectorate the colleges were also subjected to FEFC auditors who were interested in the financial management and the efficiency of the internal and external college auditors. Debbie coped with these people remarkably well as she was probably more experienced than they were. However, it did put additional strain on the administration of colleges that were carrying an increasingly large non-productive administration to deal with the demands of FEFC, the TECs and the government. The FEFC auditors were particularly interested in franchised provision. Some of the colleges had achieved growth by franchising education and training provision out to other organisations. The greater use of franchising to deliver provision was said to offer increased value for money and participation of learners. However, it did involve some risks with poor delivery by the franchisee as well as irregularity of expenditure. After numerous complaints, the Funding Council eventually decided to address the issues in 1996. FEFC required colleges to introduce new controls, but if those did not prevent duplication or substitution of funding, the Funding Council threatened to take further action to reduce the risks, or consider whether they would continue to fund this provision. I had decided not to get involved with franchising despite many attractive offers from private sector organisations. I was well aware that some colleges had boosted their FEFC income significanty through franchising and this was having the effect of reducing the ALF for all traditionally delivered work.

The corporation had set up two working groups, one to monitor the Catterick Project and one to oversee the plans for the College Centenary in 1997. I had been optimistic that the proposed Catterick

College would be ready for opening during the centenary year but I recognised that it might prove impossible with the enthusiasm of the government for PFI for part funding new public sector buildings. Both working groups met before the Christmas break and the members seemed satisfied with the modest progress that had been made. A local architectural company, Browne Smith Baker, was engaged to work with the college team to identify a suitable building to be constructed at Catterick. Guy Holmes was the lead partner and I found him enthusiastic about our project. Chris Watson had drafted out some of his ideas and initially his proposal of a central core with open access areas leading away in four directions was favourably considered. However, when we received the views of the North Yorkshire planners it was realised that a simpler building would be needed. The planners, quite rightly in my opinion, demanded a high quality of finish to all external surfaces that would be sustainable over many years. There was also the issue of ventilation in a building crammed with technology. Air conditioning would be an expensive option but it was considered unlikely that natural ventillation could cope with the build-up of heat and fumes from the equipment.

I had the usual spate of London meetings for FEFC, NCET and NILTA but the most prestigious event was the presentation of the Charter Mark Award to the College in London. The Charter Mark was the government's national standard for customer service for organisations delivering public services. It was independently evaluated and assessed and Pat Gale had persuaded the Executive Committee that we should put in a bid to be one of the first colleges to achieve the award. Pat took on the responsibility of putting the bid together and ensured that our student services team was performing to a high standard. We had been assessed and I was delighted to receive the news of our success. The presentation of awards took place in London on 4 December and Pat and I were invited to attend. There were many public sector organisations that had been selected with each one having a stand illustrating its strengths. Prime Minister John Major presented me with the crystal Charter Mark and after the formal proceedings we had to return to the College stand to receive visitors. The Secretary of State for Education Gillian Shephard and local MP Alan Milburn both visited the College stand and spent some time chatting to us.

In the two weeks leading up to Christmas we had a corporation two-day residential, I hosted an APC regional committee and attended a conference in Solihull. There was a meeting of the Durham Informatics Group and I gave an input into a Rural Telematics seminar at Staindrop. Later, there was an enjoyable evening at the garrison with the Prince's Trust Awards to the youngsters who had just completed their programme and on the following evening we held the Higher Awards Ceremony with Dr Christina Townsend, chief executive of BTEC, as our principal guest.

1996

I started the year in London chairing the NILTA Policy Group and stayed overnight at the Park International Hotel so that I could be at the BETT Exhibition at the Barbican Centre on the following day. I had made a presentation at previous exhibitions and on this occasion I gave one on networks. Instead of the usual modest support from FE, I was surprised that I had a full room with many people from secondary education that had heard about the Northern Colleges Network and wanted to know all about it. After the presentation I visited the NCET stand and joined colleagues for lunch. On my return I had a full morning at the Catterick Garrison HQ discussing several issues with the garrison commander and some of his team before returning to Darlington for a meeting of the Durham principals with the TEC officers.

In mid-January I attended the BTEC National Awards at the Institute of Civil Engineers in London before catching a train to Bristol to be a guest speaker at the Annual Conference of the National Association of Business Studies Education (NABSE). The following morning I joined a meeting of the Darlington Borough Council planners regarding unitary status, then back to the college for a PFI meeting. In the evening there was a leaving dinner for Graham Best who had accepted a post at Teesside University. I was sorry to lose Graham as he had been a loyal and dependable colleague during the incorporation transition, despite travelling daily from York until a recent move to the Richmond area. I had cautioned him about the Teesside job and, sadly, I proved to be right as he parted company with them within a relatively short period. Losing Graham meant a serious review of the management structure and in seeking a replacement for Graham I needed someone who could handle the international issues and the Quadrant area of work. I also needed a person who could raise the profile of the College in the local community and to take a key role in the Catterick project. The Board eventually appointed Gary Groom, who had been a middle manager at Barnsley College and who had a good track record in PR. At that time Gary became the youngest member of the executive team and he found that supervising the work of Les Baker in Quadrant quite a challenge. Chris Watson had indicated that he would be interested in early retirement when it was decided to take advantage of an FEFC scheme to assist colleges to reduced staffing costs. Simon managed to work out a package that met the requirements of the FEFC's criteria and also satisfied Chris. I was not particularly sorry to lose Chris as his style did not always fit comfortably into the rest of the team and on his departure his duties were covered by the rest of the executive team. Michael Wood also decided to move on as his original appointment as registrar had become unneccessary with the appoint-ment of a finance director and a personnel director. By resigning he also enabled the corporation to appoint an independent clerk to the Board in line with the advice from the FEFC.

Chris Drew, Chief Executive of NiAA, had estabished several specialist interest groups to try to accelerate progress in the region. I was a member of the Education Sector Group together with a headteacher and a university deputy vice-chancellor. Chris convened the meetings and we often met at Lumley Castle for a breakfast meeting. One of the items discussed was the proposed regional launch of NiAA and it was confirmed that it would take place on the afternoon of 5 February at Darlington College preceded by a rehearsal in the morning.

At the national level the FEFC had set up a committee to look at the use of technology in FE and John Gray was a member. Sir Gordon Higginson was the chairman and in January two national consultative conferences jointly organised by NILTA and CEF were convened to allow colleges to discuss the committee's findings. The report was entitled *Report of the Learning and Technology Committee* but was usually referred to as the Higginson Report. I attended the first conference in London and chaired the second conference in Leeds.

Invitations to attend had been directed at principals as historically most of them had shown little enthusiasm for information and learning technologies. Although several did attend most of the representatives were nominees of principals. This was disappointing as the report was full of good sense and advice to colleges to take on the challenges and opportunities presented by the technology. On my return to College, I hosted a joint College/RSA lecture and dinner with Jeremy Beaton, Chief Executive of Cleveland Structural, talking about the newly constructed Tsing Ma Bridge in Hong Kong.

At the two-day FEFC Annual Conference in London the principals were told that the grant to the Funding Council from the Department for Education and Employment for the financial year 1996–97 would be £3.15 billion. Also the number of colleges in financial difficulty was increasing and colleges collectively had incurred deficits and their financial position had worsened since 1993. 280 out of 452 colleges were in deficit in 1995–96, compared with 214 colleges in 1993–94. It was claimed that the Funding Council's arrangements for monitoring financial health had successfully identified colleges in difficulty and enabled them to work with these colleges to recover their financial health. In this respect, it was important for the Funding Council to receive timely and reliable financial returns from colleges. A briefing visit from FEFC inspectors followed by an interview with a *Northern Echo* reporter kept me active.

It is worth mentioning my approach to the appointment of full-time staff. Throughout my time at Leeds College of Building and during the time that Darlington College was controlled by the LEA, I had either chaired or been a member of every appointments panel. I firmly believed that the appointment of staff was one of the most crucial jobs and that it should be done professionally and competently. There had traditionally been a low turnover of staff at Darlington with many members having served for more than twenty years and I was aware that this could lead to complacency and a reluctance to accept new practices. I therefore made no secret of my intention to recruit young staff for all vacancies.

The corporation had delegated to me the responsibility for appointing all staff below assistant principal. I therefore was in the habit of chairing a panel consisting of Simon or his deputy, the appropriate section leader for teaching posts and a representative from industry. We also introduced some form of skills testing as well as the traditional interviews. With the additional pressures of incorporation and my frequent absences from the College for professional duties elsewhere, I delegated to Alan Dixon the responsibilty of chairing some appointments but even then I was still involved in most panels. This responsibility as well as the overall responsibilty for co-ordinating the College for the regular inspections had made me decide to advise the Board that a specialist assistant principal for curriculum should be appointed. In February we interviewed candidates for the Assistant Principal (Curriculum) post. It had been agreed that the appointment process would consist of two days. Day one would involve a briefing from me and a complete tour of the buildings. The candidates would meet the other assistant principals and the staff working in the area of the appointment and in the evening there would be a dinner with the corporation appointments panel. On the basis of the evidence of the first day there would be two or three candidates that would not be invited to the final interview with the appointments panel. In the case of the curriculum post Sarah Farley was appointed.

There was a full day of PFI interviews for the Catterick College project. This was a hugely time consuming and expensive exercise starting with the production of a full specification for the project and then placing an advertisement in the *European Journal* to invite bids to manage the project. The bidding teams invariably consisted of a partnership of a construction firm, a financial investor and various consultants. They had to produce fully worked up bids that had to be submitted to the College and we had to engage an expert company to assist in the specification and in short-listing the bidders. The corporation panel included the chairman and vice-chairman together with other members with appropriate expertise. Debbie and I were permanent members and I could invite other members of the executive to sit in on procedings. We interviewed four bidders over the day and spent a lot of time deliberating the information presented. Debbie and I were convinced that the PFI philosophy was not relevant to the Catterick situation as there were few, if any, opportunities for commercial activity for a successful PFI bidder in the Catterick community. I also had the impression that some of the consultants advising the bidders were less than enthusiastic. Later in the week I had dinner with Brigadier Peter Lyddon, the garrison commander, to bring him up to date with proceedings.

Following my visit to the AACC Convention in Minneapolis in 1995, I had worked with Malcolm Himsworth to promote a NILTA party to visit the 1996 Convention in Atlanta, Georgia. We had recruited a party of twenty-three people, including chairmen, principals and senior managers from colleges and TECs. I was not aware at the time that AfC was also advertising and that they had recruited a similar number of participants. Malcolm and I have liaised with AACC staff and I had offered to give a presentation as part of the convention programme and at the same time we wished to videoconference the presentation back to Darlington. This has been greeted enthusiastically by AACC as it appeared to be an innovation. I had worked with Durham TEC to prepare a joint presentation with David Lane, a TEC training officer, about the Northern Colleges Network initiative. On 10 April the NILTA group flew from Gatwick to Atlanta and booked into our hotel on the fringe of the city. Atlanta was hosting the Olympic Games later that year and building work and road diversions made travel a bit tricky but Malcolm had negotiated a deal with a local firm that had small coaches, taxis and limousines that we could use as required. Geoff Nichol had decide to accompany me and I was quite please as I hoped that he would see the benefit to me and to the College of participating in the convention. My colleague principal from New College Durham, Laurie Turner and his vice-chairman were also in the party.

On 11 April we were hosted by Georgia State University where we received several presentations regarding education in the State of Georgia. The university had a key role as a hub for telecommunications between all of the State's community colleges, supplying daily broadcasts of learning materials via videoconferencing. We had a conducted tour of some of the university facilities and I was impressed by the layout and equipment in the videoconferencing suites. The following day was at DeKalb Technical College on the Eastern outskirts of Atlanta. This was a large campus of spacious buildings with well equipped laboratories, workshops and classrooms. I could sense the envy in some of my colleagues with the rooms full of modern computers. We met staff and students and had lunch in the communal dining area. We also noticed the significant resources for student services and the vast car parks for staff and students. Most of the students were studying on a full-time basis although there were programmes and facilities for continuing education students that were mainly offered in the evenings.

The convention officially commenced on Saturday but the morning and early afternoon were devoted to local affairs so we attended in the afternoon for the registration, formal welcome and introduction to the events. There were twelve forums running in parallel and we chose to attend the one entitled 'Going Global with Going the Distance' with three panellists leading the debate. On Sunday morning, instead of joining one of the seminars, I chose to visit the Exhibit Hall where the AACC Academic Marketplace was running throughout the Convention. This included a huge gathering of retail and wholesale providers to the educational sector together with several colleges that were engaged in activities they wanted to share with the delegates. This was a fascinating feature and I returned several times to the marketplace during the convention.

I selected one from the eighteen events available at 11.15, entitled 'The Virtual Campus: A Higher Education Transformational Model'. This was a stimulating session that NILTA enthusiasts could relate to. It covered telecommunications technologies, student-centred distance learning programmes and the need for sustained institutional change to transform the culture of higher education. I had another session in the Market Place before attending a plenary session by Richard Riley, Secretary of the US Department for Education. In the early evening our group attended a reception given by the Association for Colleges led by Ruth Gee. Back at our hotel we found people crowded round the TV for the last round of the US Masters Golf Tournament from Augusta, Georgia, with Nick Faldo trailing behind Greg Norman for the Championship. Sipping a glass of beer we watched as Faldo caught up and eventually won.

On Monday morning we took advantage of the complimentary breakfast sponsored by different groups each day, before attending a session entitled 'Riding the Winds of Change: A Fresh Approach to Organisational Culture'. There was a lively multimedia presentation on new leadership strategies and effective training to maximise efficiency. A number of students were included in the presentation and this added extra interest. My presentation with David Lane was scheduled for 14.10 that afternoon and was one of fourteen sessions running simultaneously. The necessary equipment to allow for my PowerPoint presentation and the videoconferencing were in place with seating for about fifty people. It was soon apparent that this was inadequate and by the time I was ready to commence there were at least as many people standing as were sitting. This was quite a compliment for although many of the NILTA team had turned up to support me, the vast majority of delegates were American educationalists. The presentation was well received and the videoconferencing to Darlington College took place without a hitch. I then asked the audience to participate in the three-way debate involving the group at Darlington. This seemed to take them by surprise as it seemed that this was very new to them. The Q&A session went well and as we approached the end of the session, Angus Byrne at Darlington said that they had a special person that wanted to say hello to me. When Angus panned the camera to let us see the visitor I was completely lost for words when I saw my daughter Helen smiling coyly into the camera. The Americans loved it and we finished on an even higher note than expected. The group dashed back to the hotel to change and returned to the Convention Centre for the Grand Reception and Gala Dinner that brought an enjoyable end to a most successful day.

The convention was due to end at lunchtime on Tuesday and we again took advantage of the complimentary breakfast and had a last quick look at the Marketplace. I attended a session entitled 'Empowering the Entrepreneurial Spirit: Doing More with Less', which sounded a bit like the UK system! It covered procurement and support services and provided a model for empowering staff. The concluding plenary session was given by Barbara Reynolds, a columnist of the national newspaper, *USA Today*. In the evening Malcolm, Geoff, Laurie and his vice-chairman and I attended an Atlanta Braves baseball game that seemed to last forever and ended 1–0 after several hours and we were chilled to the bone by the end.

We were due to fly back to the UK in the evening and Malcolm had organised a coach trip during the day so that we could have some experience of Altanta. It commenced with a visit to the King Centre that is the official living memorial dedicated to the advancement of the legacy of Dr Martin Luther King, leader of America's greatest non-violent movement for justice, equality and peace. Later, we admired the skyscraper buildings and the sports facilities and wondered if the Olympic Stadium would be ready for the start of the Games. It was then back to the hotel to change and transfer to the airport for the overnight flight to Heathrow.

The convention had covered the second half of the Easter recess and I had about a week after returning to catch up with all the routine office work that Gaynor had neatly sorted for me. I had a visit by Roger Filby from the Department of Education and Employment (DfEE) who had been commissioned to investigate NCET. As I was very happy with Margaret Bell's management of NCET I gave a positive response to his questions. I guessed that Roger had been told to build up a case for Margaret's removal from NCET, as I knew she was not popular with some of the civil servants. My contribution did not save Margaret and as my three-year term of office as a member of NCET Council was almost complete, I did not expect an extension. In fact, there was a long break without an FE representative on NCET Board after my departure. I hosted a visit the following day from the principal and senior staff of Craven College, a rural college that provided mainly adult education, with its base in Skipton. The principal was keen to adapt to the opportunities of incorporation and having met me through the North Yorkshire TEC group, he hoped to learn from our experiences.

The following week I chaired the first meeting of the newly constituted NCN Board at New College, Durham, and in the afternoon visited the College of Ripon and York St John's York Centre. Later in the week I drove down to Clarendon College in Nottingham where they were actively pursuing a PFI solution to a refurbishment project in the centre of the city. Our PFI consultants were also acting for Clarendon and they had urged me to talk to the principal about her experiences. It was a useful visit and further convinced me that PFI was not an appropriate solution for Catterick. I dashed back to Darlington for the Adult Learners' Awards evening at the Town Hall. There were several college students receiving awards, including recognition of the success at Firthmoor. On the Saturday the College again hosted the YITTY (Young IT Technician of the Year) regional competition with Mary Barker in charge.

There was an important event on the following Monday with the official opening of the Open Access IT Centre by Sir William Stubbs. A videoconference link to the USA had been arranged and an unsuspecting Sir Bill found himself in the novel position of explaining his role to an international audience. At the end of May I had a full day with corporation members commencing with the remuneration committee where I had to argue the case for the executive committee members' salaries based upon the appraisals over the year, as well as striving to maintain my salary at a compatible level with other principals of similar sized colleges. Quadrant Board was next and then the full Corporation Board with a long agenda, reflecting the increasing activities within the College as well as the sector in general. I always produced a Principal's Report for each meeting and added a schedule of my activities since the previous Board meeting. The good news was the twenty per cent increase in full-time equivalent students and achieving an actual Average Level of Funding (ALF) of £15.61 against a target of £17.84 that indicated we had exceeded growth by being more efficient. FEFC had indicated our ALF would be £17.50 for 1996/97, giving us a bit of room to expand.

July started with a meeting of the Northern Childcare Consortium, quickly followed by a first meeting of the Durham County Council People's Group with the TEC taking a leading role. The problem with this group was that it was far too large and with such a broad remit that many of the items on the agenda were of interest to only a few people. It struggled on for several meetings but as members either stopped attending or sent deputies without any authority it was doomed to fail. There was yet another meeting of the FEFC Statistics Group in London and the following day we had a staff lunch when I made presentations to the staff members who were either retiring or moving on to another post.

I was back in London the following day for a very special event in the BT Tower. On a previous occasion I had visited this major London landmark that had at one time had been open to the public but for security reasons it was only used by BT for its own business. On this occasion BT was presenting its annual national awards and Darlington College had been selected for one of the awards. It was a memorable day with lunch in the revolving restaurant at the top of the tower with amazing views over the city. The following week Edward had a week visiting Poland with Hummersknott School.

One of my colleagues on the NCET Council was Owen Lynch who was a head teacher in Cumbria. We were both keen to develop technologies to support learning and I had invited Owen to visit Darlington College. He brought a senior officer from Cumbria LEA, John Harold, and we had a useful day together. At that time we did not know that Owen would succeed Margaret Bell as chief executive of NCET.

Later in the day I made a visit to the garrison to look at proposed sites for the new college building. I hosted a BT IT workshop at the College and in the evening joined a retirement party for John Rosser at Middlesbrough FC's Riverside football ground. This was followed by a day in London with BSA and the following afternoon I gave a presentation to Darlington Employers Forum.

Family holiday 1996

I had been well aware that the work pressures over the last four years had severely restricted my time with the family and we had decided to take a round-the-world holiday in 1996 that would take about four weeks. We flew overnight to Hong Kong for three days, visiting all of the usual tourist sights. The next stop was Cairns in North Queensland for four days. There was so much to see in the area but the highlight was a day on the Barrier Reef and snorkelling in the shallow waters with wonderful views of the coral and fish.

We moved onto Brisbane where we had intended to visit Veronica's brother and family but Tony had obtained a job in Fiji and that complicated our flight plans considerably. However, Tony and Colleen's sons were at school in the area and we did meet them at Nudgee College. We could not get a direct flight to Fiji from Brisbane and had to fly via New Zealand. This allowed us four days to tour the area around Auckland and I was able to see the Auckland Harbour Bridge that I had helped to design in my last year at Dorman Long. The unplanned visit to Fiji to meet Veronica's brother's family was a bonus with a cruise to the Fijian Island of Mana for swimming and snorkelling as well as a trip to Tavuni Fort. The last part of the holiday was in Los Angeles with visits to Universal Studios and Disney World.

CHAPTER 16

Inspection and Developments

INEVITABLY, AFTER FOUR WEEKS leave there were many issues to address at the College and I spent half a day just dealing with the NCN developments. At incorporation the Further Education Development Agency (FEDA), with Stephen Crowne as its chief executive, had been created to replace the FEU and the FE Staff College at Blagdon. FEDA recognised the expertise that was available from the NILTA members and at the end of August there was NCET/FEDA meeting at the Institute of Directors to discuss collaboration in the light of the substantial funding that had been allocated to FEDA for ICT training resulting from the Higginson Report. Ten days later the first meeting of the NCET/FEDA IT Advisory Group was held to determine the priorities and to plan a national staff development programme. I was pleased that NILTA was well represented on the Group.

Locally there was a two-day residential conference for the Durham principals at the George Hotel in Chollerford to consider various strategies for the future of FE in the sub-region. This was in the light of proposed mergers as colleges were squeezed financially by FEFC by the gradual reduction of the ALF and specialist colleges, such as Houghall, were at greatest risk.

There was a further day of interviewing potential PFI partnerships for Catterick with the cost to the College of the whole exercise escalating and the laborious process was increasingly frustrating the corporation members.

The Northern Colleges Network Company was officially launched in September 1996 with all participating colleges having a director on the Board. I was elected chairman and the first Board meeting was held at Chester-le-Street. Durham TEC held a meeting with principals at County Hotel in Durham to give a briefing on proposals and plans for the next academic year. The NiAA Board held its first meeting of the year at Tyneside TEC and I nearly missed the meeting because of a bomb threat at the College that resulted in a police search of the buildings. I was invited to join yet another regional committee called the Northern Business Forum that had decided it should have an educational sector within its structure and my first meeting was in mid-September at New College, Durham.

I welcomed our international PHARE partners to the College in September. PHARE was a EU programme to assist applicant countries from Central and Eastern Europe in their preparations for joining the European Union. Gary Groom and Adrian Dent had worked with some of our existing Eastern European partners to recruit other western European countries to join the partnership and the resulting bid had been successful.

October commenced with a two-day residential management conference that I had convened mainly to ensure that all of the executive team was up to speed with the FEFC full inspection due to commence on 18 November. I had called a meeting the week before to prepare all of the staff members but it was vital that the managers were at their sharpest. Alan Dixon had taken responsibility for ensuring that the mountain of paper evidence that was required by the inspectors had been assembled and that each team member was aware of their own strengths and weaknesses. The inspectors would be looking at all vocational areas and giving grades on a one to five scale, one being the top grade. Colleges with grade 4 or 5 were likely to be re-inspected. We had to set a room aside for the inspectors and Alan had to ensure that a copy of all documentation that they were likely to require was held in that room.

Whilst the inspection preparations continued I had a meeting with Alan Milburn and Geoff Pennington, the Darlington director of education, who had recently been appointed. On Tuesday I attended a briefing for regional principals given by the new FEFC chief executive David Melville. David was a very different character to Bill Stubbs and I had a feeling he would be easier to convince about the importance of technology in learning. There were the routine meetings with North Yorkshire TEC, the NCN Board and the South Durham Forum for Education and Industry AGM but I was happy to let the dust settle and catch up with internal routine. Sarah Farley took up her post as assistant principal (Curriculum). Although it was too late for her to be heavily involved with the inspection detail it was useful to have her in the team to give an independent and probably more objective view on the big issues.

In November I had the pleasure of travelling to Bulgaria as a guest of Svistov Economic University to attend its sixtieth anniversary celebrations. Agop met me and ensured that I had comfortable accommodation in the new hall of residence. At the formal presentation with all of the university staff and guests from other universities in Bulgaria and international partners, the rector gave an address and then invited each of the visitors to give a speech. I had not been given any warning that this would happen and even at that time I assumed that those who were speaking had been briefed. I sat patiently as most of the addresses were in languages other than English, when Agop suddenly nudged me and said, 'it is your turn'. I stood at the podium looking out at the packed hall and made a brief statement about Darlington, its partnership with the university and my pleasure at attending. There was enthusiastic applause, perhaps because I had been briefer than the others! There was quite a party afterwards with a banquet and a display of local wines. Agop suggested that Darlington should negotiate a deal with one of the local wineries to supply the College restaurant and I was not averse to the idea. However, on closer examination it became clear that the costs of transportation would be much greater than the cost of the wine.

In the week prior to the inspection I had two days in London with the Basic Skills Agency and the FEFC PIMS group. An NCN Company development group meeting and the three-day NILTA Annual Conference in Leeds followed. This was Ernie Haiden's first conference as chief executive as Malcolm Himsworth had stood down during the year. Also, John Gray stood down as vice-chairman and Sue Parker took over. I had hoped that John would become chairman as I had felt for several years that I had exceeded my tenure but John, much to my regret, had been reluctant to accept the job. Sue was principal of Harlow College and I hoped she would bring new ideas to a committee dominated by males. The conference ended on Monday when the College inspection was starting and I had to be at the College so I agreed to close the conference by a video-conference link from Darlington.

The FEFC inspectors arrived early morning and quickly settled into their base room. After the formal introductions, I gave an up-beat PowerPoint presentation to the inspection team and then I retreated to let them get on with the job. The inspection lasted all week and involved meetings with members of the corporation and an evening meeting with local people, referred to as stakeholders, who had links with the College. There was also a visit to Catterick Garrison to see the developments and learning programmes. During the inspection I stayed in College throughout in case any inspector wished to see me. On the last day of the inspection the chairman and I received an overview from the lead inspector that gave us some confidence that the College was performing reasonably well. After the stresses induced by the inspection process, there was the anxious period awaiting the official outcome. We had to wait until 13 December for the formal briefing to the Board. The outcome of the inspection was very encouraging with the College being awarded a Grade 1 for responsiveness and Grade 2 for all other cross–college areas including Governance and Management, Resources and Quality Assurance. In the curriculum areas the grade for each observed lesson was displayed in chart form and ranged from forty-two at Grade 1 to fourteen at Grade 4 with rest falling in Grade 2 and 3. To have any at Grade 4 was disappointing and Sarah, in collaboration with the heads of school in those areas, was instructed to provide extra support for the individual staff members. At the special meeting of the Board a few days later there was general approval of the outcome of the inspection although some of the members felt that they should have had a Grade 1 for Governance. What I did not tell them was that the lead inspector had informed me that within the two categories, Management was the closest to the Grade 1 standard but that Governance was not yet strong enough to justify an overall assessment of Grade 1.

There was a meeting of the new NCET/FEDA IT group in Coventry where I expressed my concerns at the relatively low priority being given to a national FE broadband network. Some of my colleagues argued that staff development was the priority but it seemed to me that staff development with dated technology was not very sensible. It was decided to create a number of subgroups to advise the main group on recommendations to send to FEFC and the government.

The following day I met Cynthia Wellbourne, the new director of education for North Yorkshire, to secure her support and understanding for the College to develop the Catterick site. We already had the support from the county chief executive, John Ransford, who had been very enthusiastic when he heard our proposals and promised to urge Yorkshire Forward, the regional development agency for Yorkshire and Humberside to assist with some financial support. After the meeting I travelled down to London to give a presentation on the IT developments in FE to the conference of CRAC, the careers development organisation. Next day was the Corporation Board AGM, which went very smoothly in view of the FEFC inspectors report. The College was on course to exceed its target for 1996/97 of 4500 FTE enrolments and the board supported my proposals for annual growth to 6000 FTE by 2000. There was also agreement to seek to dispose of College accommodation in Trinity Road, Gladstone Street and Archer Street, with some of the income being used to fund the Catterick development.

The College had entered into an agreement with Morrisons supermarket at Morton Park and with the Business Venture to use the Business Centre for some of the management and business programmes, freeing up the Trinity Road buildings for disposal. The facilities at Morton Park were very good and we used some of the larger rooms for staff development or large meetings. It was in December that I held a College PFI day at Morton Park to ensure that staff members were familiar with the concept and advantages and disadvantages if the College appointed a PFI consortium for the Catterick development. The following day the Board members received the official inspection report from the FEFC inspectors that confirmed all that we had discovered informally. In the evening we celebrated the success of our higher education students with the HE Award Ceremony with the Lord Lieutenant for County Durham, David Grant, presenting the awards.

1997

My year started with two days devoted to NCN business that involved identifying potential accommodation for the new company at Gateshead College and New College, Durham. We eventually selected the Gardener's House at New College. On the following day I chaired the panel to appoint a chief officer and the other members included Chris Hughes, principal of Gateshead College. The panel unanimously agreed to appoint Mary Barker, a lecturer in IT at Darlington College, who had a very impressive interview. I was sorry to lose Mary from the College team but I recognised that she was ambitious and had the capacity to go much further in her career.

The next day I travelled to London for the BETT Exhibition and gave a network presentation to a packed audience at one of the FE seminars. Ernie had booked a stand for NILTA and it had attracted a steady stream of visitors from colleges and suppliers.

Yet another IT committee was formed, this time it was the Teesside Innovation Partnership with a link to NiAA. I attended the first meeting at Teesside University, having been present at a NiAA meeting in Sunderland in the morning.

The next day I received a visit from Dan Taubman, who was a national education officer of NATFHE. He was researching the effects of incorporation on the FE Sector. I spent quite a long time with Dan and grew to respect him as a person who appeared to have an open mind and was willing to listen to all sides of the argument. Of course, I had to speak strongly in favour of the introduction of incorporation and the cultural changes that had resulted in a potentially better service to the students. We did discuss the issue of franchising that had become a thorny issue within the sector as a number of colleges had achieved their target growth exclusively by franchising to independent training companies. I was still strongly opposed to franchising and Gary Groom's experience at Barnsley had reinforced that view. The *Times Educational Supplement* had identified several colleges that had entered into dubious contracts and FEFC was considering placing a cap on the amount of franchising that a college could undertake. In 1995 there had been a franchising scandal at Handsworth College but this had not curbed the expansion. Significant numbers of colleges were hoping to expand their franchising contracts to make up student numbers in 1996 despite evidence of widespread mismanagement of franchised courses in the college sector. One of the main difficulties of large-scale franchising was maintaining quality control of courses. But the special committee set up to advise the FEFC had uncovered tensions between free marketeers who wanted to see minimal regulation and those who would have preferred much more stringent rules. Another issue we discussed with Dan was inspection. The inspection arrangements had been well received in the sector. 329 colleges were inspected by the summer of 1996. Strengths outweighed weaknesses in 68 per cent of the curriculum areas inspected and in 64 per cent of cross-college areas but this left about a third of the colleges underperforming.

Later in the month there was the two-day residential conference for corporation members with the executive team in attendance. This was followed by a full day with representatives of BT. In the morning I met them at Catterick Garrison as they were keen to be involved with the College either through a PFI consortium or directly if the College was allowed to procede with a design and build solution. In the afternoon BT met with NCN members to discuss progress with the regional network.

The last week of the month involved a two-day NILTA Working Group residential for brainstorming sessions to provide guidelines for NILTA members. I enjoyed this sort of debate as it allowed the imagination to flow amongst the leading thinkers in this area. I chaired another NCN Board in Gateshead before travelling to County Hall for a People Working Group meeting. In the morning I attended another briefing meeting by David Melville in Boldon and later participated in a Northern Business Forum IT Sector meeting. The NiAA regional launch took place at Darlington College on 31 January, slightly earlier than originally planned. Alan Donnely, a former MEP, had taken over the chairmanship from John Bridge and he and Chris Drew were trying to raise the profile throughout the region. The event was well attended and I did a short presentation following Chris Drew's introduction.

Another major event took place in London in early February when FEDA launched QUILT, its Quality in Information and Learning Technology (in FE), with all the key people present. It was therefore convenient to hold another meeting of the FEDA/NCET network group that I chaired in the afternoon. I stayed in London for the next two days, firstly for a meeting with Roger Ward, who had won the battle for CEF against AfC to become the chief executive of the newly formed Association of Colleges (AoC), then a full meeting of the FEDA/NCET group. Roger Ward had built up a reputation that many principals felt was inappropriate for a person charged with nationally representing the FE sector. My reason for meeting Roger was to explore the possibility of AoC and NILTA working together for the benefit of the sector but it soon became clear that Roger was only interested in expanding his own empire and I left the meeting feeling rather exasperated. On the following day all the principals assembled for the Annual FEFC Conference when David Melville brought us up to date with developments and the chief inspector reported on the state of the sector. It was a fairly up-beat conference led by David Melville compared with the more formal approach of his predecessor. In March we launched Northern QUILT in York.

1997 was the centenary year of the College and the corporation had supported my proposal to celebrate the anniversary with several events by allocating £50,000. It had been decided to publish a history of the College and John Davies had agreed to take on the assignment but he was making very slow progress and when I asked John to give me a detailed report on the current situation it was obvious that it would not be completed during 1997. Indeed, I had to relieve him of the task in late 1998 and commission Ernie Haiden to take over. It was eventually published in April 2000. The actual opening of the original Darlington Technical College was in September 1897 and so we planned to have most of the celebrations in September with Gary Groom taking overall responsibility for the activities with a team of volunteers to support him.

With the addition of Gary and Sarah to the Executive Group I now had a relatively young team to support me in the multitude of issues facing the College. There was an executive strategy day at Walworth Castle to share my perception of the priorities for the year and to try to ensure that the team covered all areas. On a day-to-day basis most of the team were located in the management suite on the ground floor near the main entrance thus avoiding visitors having to travel around the college to some distant staff room. It also meant that the team members were adjacent to me and I could contact them quickly and vice versa. I reflected on the radical changes in staffing since my appointment in 1987. In ten years only Alan Dixon was left of the senior staff that I had inherited and a significant number of middle managers and teachers had retired or moved on. Incorporation was undoubtedly the main cause for the change but also there had been a tradition of staff being appointed and staying in post for the rest of their careers that inevitably had led to a level of complacency and resistance to change. The opportunity for staff members to take early retirement with enhancements to their pensions had been a key factor in reducing the number of older principal and senior lecturers. The demands by FEFC for greater efficiencies had been assisted by the new conditions of service that had enabled managers to organise their teaching staff to ensure that contractual hours were fulfilled and better use made of the accommodation over the extended college year.

Perhaps the greatest change was to the support staffing. Under the LEA, most of the critical administrative responsibilities had been held by County Hall. We had no responsibility for personnel other than maintaining records and sending information to Durham. Similarly with finance, where Jenny Hornby had been the finance officer with a small team that collected money and information and again sent it to Durham. Now I had a finance director in Debbie Leigh and a personnel director in Simon Cassidy, both with a team to support them in their duties. Mick Gossage as head porter had a large team of porters and cleaners to cover the Cleveland Avenue site and the various annexes and Angus Byrne as telematics director had a large team of technicians and materials developers to support the ICT expansion. After Michael Wood's departure, Debbie had become responsible for the administrative staff that supported the executive team as well as her own finance team, Pat Gale's responsibilities as assistant principal (students) meant that she also had a team of administrative staff dealing with student guidance and counselling as well as the crèche. It had been decided that the executive team should have their clerical support locally rather than in an office on the first floor, so when we reorganised the entrance hall to take the reception desk into the centre of the main area, it freed up space adjacent to the executives' offices for the clerical assistants.

In February there were three new committees: The Darlington Economic & Social Steering group and the Darlington Learning Town, both set up by the new unitary authority, together with a College of the Dales group that we had established with the local community. There was an observation that the 'College of the Dales' was already used by Craven College and we eventually quietly dropped the title and used 'Darlington College at Catterick'. I enjoyed another early breakfast at Lumley Castle for a NiAA education meeting before attending a regional FEFC meeting to discuss PFI. The FEFC had been given a strong indication that the government wished the FE sector to use PFI and the FEFC had decided to contribute £50,000 towards the costs of the PFI process. As I estimated that our PFI action would cost in the region of £150,000, it was obvious that our efforts to show that PFI was not an appropriate solution for Catterick as it would leave the College with a £100,000 bill with no advantage to the College.

March started with a two-day FEDA conference in London and the following day I met up with the Catterick Garrison land agents to look at another site that was being offered to the College. This was located on Catterick Road, near to the central roundabout in the garrison and, in my opinion, this was by far the best site we had been offered. The site had originally been used as sidings for the railway line that had long been removed and it was now a large grassed area adjacent to the road and fringed with trees to the South. The commander had already made an approach to the Ministry of Defence (MOD) regarding the situation of the College within the garrison area and he had been authorised to negotiate on the understanding that the price would be modest as long as the site was only used for educational purposes. I had originally anticipated that the College would have to lease the land from the MOD but there appeared to be advantages with owning the land and the property, particularly as there were ambitious plans to establish a business park about a mile away from the college site. The other positive news was the long-term commitment to Catterick by the MOD by establishing most of the recruit training at the Garrison. The MOD eventually asked £200,000 for the site with a twenty years' requirement to maintain an educational presence and we were pleased to accept the offer. The following week there was another full day of PFI interviews. Like the previous days devoted to PFI, the college panel was not convinced that the various consortia could provide the services that we had specified at a price we could afford. I was mainly concerned with the long-term financial burden that I would be leaving to my successor as well as the lack of control that we could exercise if the PFI solution was ineffective. By this stage all of the corporation members were convinced that PFI was not a solution and even our consultants had to reluctantly agree that there was a case to present to the FEFC to reject that solution.

13 March was particularly hectic, starting with a delegation from ICL trying to influence me into buying their products or at least getting NILTA's backing but at that stage I felt I could not make any recommendations. Shortly afterwards I had a delegation from Darlington Borough Council, now a unity authority, led by chief executive Barry Keel with Geoff Pennington, Geraint Edwards and John Buxton to debate a wide range of productive issues involving collaboration between our two organisations. I had developed a healthy regard for Barry and I was pleased that he wished to develop closer ties with the College. After lunch I attended an NVQ presentation before chairing the Childcare Consortium. The following day was the Annual Awards Ceremony and I held a full staff meeting in the morning to brief all members with the current developments. I had invited Dr Nicholas Carey, Director General of City and Guilds, to present the awards and he also gave a lively and stimulating address to a packed audience of students, parents and friends.

The following week I attended the 'World Class North Yorkshire' conference in Harrogate. I always enjoyed this event and I was now feeling less of an outsider and that I had been accepted by most of the North Yorkshire principals who seemed to welcome my input into the various meetings. The next day I was in London to chair the sub-committee of the FEDA/NCET group that was charged with looking at establishing the 'Information Highway'. The group included a variety of college representatives as well as officers from FEFC, FEDA and NCET. The Teesside University Partnership met the next day with the university keen to persuade colleges to transfer their existing HE courses that were directly funded by HEFCE, to the university on a franchising arrangement. It seemed that most of the Cleveland principals, with the exception of the College of Art and Design, were willing to collaborate with this proposal but, as Darlington had a significant number of HNC programmes, I was not inclined to agree. Historically, when it was created a polytechnic, the university had ensured that all of the local HNC and HND work was based in the polytechnic and therefore the Middlesbrough colleges had little work that was classified as 'higher'. I had respect for vice-chancellor Derek Fraser but I was wary of some of his senior managers who seemed to be predators and who were only concerned with their own interests rather than the interests of the partnership.

In early April I attended a three-day RISI Conference at Northumbria University. RISI (Regional Information Society Initiative) was an EU funded initiative and the main source of funding for NiAA. The European Council had written in 1994 that:

> The first countries to enter the information society will reap the greatest rewards. They will set the agenda for all who must follow. By contrast, countries which temporise, or favour half-hearted solutions, could, in less than a decade, face disastrous declines in investment and a squeeze on jobs.

The North of England RISI covered the North East and Cumbria with a population of 3.1 million. The region was near the bottom of the UK economic league table with relatively high unemployment by UK standards. Also, the economic activity rate in the North East was about five per cent lower than the country as a whole. I was well aware of these problems having seen the industrial infrastructure of the region being virtually wiped out in a relatively short period of time. In my youth in Middlesbrough, iron and steel manufacturing, shipbuilding, coal mining, chemical engineering and related industries had provided employment for the majority of the male population. Now there was a heavy reliance on public sector employment and lower skilled jobs. Over the three days of the conference these issues were debated and current progress highlighted, such as the Northern Colleges Network and the JANET HE network. There were other initiatives in progress or in the pipeline but much more had to be done to reverse the downward trend and certainly some ideas did emerge from the event. The Strategic Framework for the North of England RISI was not published until October 1998 due to frustrating delays. The conference was not residential and on the middle day I left early to participate in the College's Centenary Lecture with Sir Leon Brittan as our speaker. It was an excellent lecture and the debate was lively with quite a few anti-EU people in the audience, but Sir Leon's expertise was more than sufficient to win most of the arguments.

The next week I attended an interesting residential conference in Nottingham on the Teaching and Learning Technology Programme (TLTP) in association with NCET. The programme was jointly funded by the four higher education funding bodies, HEFCE,

SHEFC, HEFCW and DENI, who had allocated £22.5 million over three years, starting in 1992–93, for the first phase of the programme and £11.25 million for the second phase at a time when the sector was experiencing a period of rapid expansion. Added to the funding bodies' own commitment of £33 million was the direct and indirect contributions made by institutions to the projects they were hosting. Bearing in mind that higher education had access to the JANET broadband network, I could see the logic in spending such large sums of public money in trying to ensure that staff were maximising the advantages of JANET for the benefit of their students. In FE we did not have access to JANET and a national network was not even on the horizon so I felt that large sums of money spent on staff development without the network was of marginal benefit. Never-theless, NCET was keen to access funding for schools and colleges despite the lack of infrastructure.

On my return from Nottingham I attended a regional launch of Project 2000, a new professional training approach for nurses. The College had a strong nursing team and ran higher education courses in conjunction with Durham University and it was clear that Project 2000 would lead to a significant increase in our workload. Initially, there was good recruitment to the various programmes under this scheme but unfortunately Durham University lost the contract for nurse training to Teesside University. Teesside already had a strong school of nursing and it soon became clear that it intended to take all of the Darlington work away and deliver it in Middlesbrough. This was the second time that Teesside University had taken higher education work from the College. We had developed a degree in journalism thanks to the tremendous commitment of Jon Smith, but it had to be validated by a university and only Teesside was willing to do that even though they had no in-house expertise. However, over a period of time they appointed staff and increasingly infiltrated the programme by demanding that more and more of the course should be delivered in Middlesbrough.

The following week there was an example of college collaboration when the Durham colleges met at the Eden Arms Hotel for a Strategic Planning Day. It was always useful to share experiences and bounce ideas amongst colleagues. There had been four changes of principal since incorporation with John Widdowson replacing Laurie

Turner at New College, Steve Broomhead taking over at Bishop Auckland, David Haulpt at Derwentside and Ian Prescott at East Durham and certainly John, Steve and David were lively additions to the group. At the end of the month I was a guest of Research Machines at their IT Conference in Glasgow where I met up with my old friend Tom Wilson, principal of Glasgow College of Building and Printing, who was still a leading figure in ITC in Scotland.

The next week started with a meeting of the Darlington Economic and Social Partnership in the Town Hall and it was encouraging to see the progress that was being made in a number of initiatives. Next day I hosted a BT Global Network day conference that featured the development of NCN together with other BT initiatives within the educational sector. I held an executive away day at Headlam Hall and completed the week with a Learning Town committee and a NiAA Educational Forum in Sunderland. The Catterick project moved slowly forward with a meeting with the consultants but my target to open a new college in 1997 was now lost and the most optimistic forecast was completion in 1999.

The general election was held on 1 May 1997, more than five years after the previous election on 9 April 1992. The Labour Party won the general election in a landslide victory with 418 seats. Sedgefield MP Tony Blair became Prime Minister and Alan Milburn, who had been MP for Darlington since 1992, was appointed in 1998 as Chief Secretary to the Treasury and a year later he became Secretary of State for Health. At the time there was hope that having key local MPs in the Cabinet would lead to preferential treatment for the north but there was little evidence to support that claim. As a Conservative government had introduced the incorporation of colleges there was some debate that the new government would seek to make changes. I took the view that the understanding of the FE Sector amongst politicians and the civil service was traditionally vague and it was more likely that any major changes would not surface for several years.

15 May was important for NILTA as we launched our 'NILTA VISION' prospectus through a three-way videoconference from Darlington to two other centres in Birmingham and London. Ernie Haiden had produced an elegant document following brain-storming sessions with key NILTA supporters and I was delighted with the quality of the content and the visual impact of the packaging. The

messages to the FE sector were sharply focussed and expressed in a format that was easily read. In hindsight, I believe that this was the most important publication that NILTA produced and most of its recommendations are as valid today as they were in the 1990s. Sadly, many colleges did not get the message and therefore their students did not receive the quality of learning provision and experience that the technology could have provided. I had a meeting at Edexcel in London. Edexcel was formed in 1996 by the merger of two bodies, BTEC and ULEAC (University of London Examinations and Assessment Council), and so my BTEC commitments were held in the Edexcel offices. The next evening I hosted the Darlington senior staff dinner with most of the secondary heads and their partners attending. A North East regional APC meeting was attended by David Melville who gave some complimentary remarks about the NILTA Vision document.

June started with a Basic Skills Agency committee and an FEFC PIMS group meeting in London followed by a two-day APC Conference in Bristol. We had a group of Romanian students visiting the College and I took them to Darlington Rotary Club's Friday lunch meeting and in the afternoon they joined the College staff and students in the main hall to witness the drama students putting on a 'Centenary Show'. The drama and music course had been introduced after incorporation and had proved very popular, as previously similar courses were only available in Newcastle. The show was really excellent and the theme was a potted history of the College, illustrated with music and dance. The students put on two repeat performances to provide an opportunity for all those who wished to see it. I sneaked in on both occasions as it was so enthusiastically performed and I was very proud of the students and the two members of staff who had encouraged them to perform so well. I was particularly pleased to see two of our physically disabled students enthusiastically participating on stage in their wheelchairs.

I had an interesting meeting with Malcolm Read, the chief executive of JISC (Joint Information Systems Committee), who also managed the JANET network for higher education establishments. We discussed the prospects of JANET being extended to the college sector but at that time he was not optimistic about that happening. He was interested in the NCN progress and he mentioned smaller initiatives that were being developed in other parts of the country. I had meetings with Yorkshire principals who were keen to follow the NCN model and in due time they did succeed. However, NCN did experience a set back when the sixth form colleges left NCN in 1997 to form their own network with the support of Sunderland University. I was disappointed, as several concessions had been made to enable the sixth forms to participate in NCN but partly for financial reasons and partly to distance themselves from the FE colleges they chose to split away from the main group. Principals of some of the larger colleges privately expressed the view that we were well rid to the sixth form colleges but I felt that the image of the sector in the region had been damaged. It was the remaining fifteen colleges in NCN that had subscribed to the ADAPT project that was developing sixteen modules of on-line learning materials for SMEs. There were seventy SMEs in the pilot phase and many more expressed an interest in joining when the product would become generally available in June 2000.

George Hollis was my very conscientious senior lecturer responsible for special needs in the College and he had made tremendous progress since taking up his appointment. We had a sizeable number of youngsters with learning and/or physical disabilities and George had ensured that the necessary structural modifications had been made to the buildings to afford access to wheelchairs. Many staff had learned how to sign to assist deaf students in the classroom and software for computers to assist the visually impaired had been introduced. George had approached me to attend a 'Disabilities Conference' in Jesmond, Newcastle, and we went together to listen and share ideas. There were many enthusiasts present but I do not think that George or I gained much from the meeting.

I had maintained a keen interest in the RSA and had been a member of the regional committee for several years. On 19 June I organised a visit for RSA Fellows and guests to visit Catterick Garrison (strictly speaking Catterick is in Yorkshire's RSA Region but their members were also able to attend). The garrison commander had kindly put on a reception at headquarters and, on our arrival at 11 a.m., he gave a short PowerPoint presentation on the history and current state of the garrison before outlining the plans for the future. His comments regarding the proposed college were highly complimentary and I only hoped that I could deliver all that he expected. He had laid on transport so that the visitors could have a conducted tour of the complete site and even I had not appreciated how large it was and all the facilities that were available to the service personnel. The event proved to be a great success and I promised that I would repeat the outing when the new College was opened. In the evening I held a 'vision' meeting with the executive members to keep the team focussed on the steps needed to reach our goals and also to ensure that we were all ready for the Corporation Board meeting the following evening.

Most of the NILTA regions were active, especially in the North East. I kept well away from their meetings but supported the regional conferences that were held most years and often at the Blackwell Grange Hotel. This year it was held at a hotel in Boldon and there was a good turnout of members. I had to leave the conference before the end to attend the Durham TEC's presentation of its Strategic Plan by chief executive David Hall to a large audience of business and college personnel.

I returned to the College to listen to presentations by the Foundation course students who had been on a visit to Pisa in Italy. The enthusiasm of those youngsters with learning difficulties was heart warming as they had gained so much from their experiences and I felt fully justified in encouraging the heads of school to use the many partner institutions that we had established in Europe so that students could benefit from similar exchanges. I believed that many local youngsters had few opportunities to travel and some of them had told me that they had not been out of Darlington. I had therefore set aside a sum of money to provide a subsidy to those students who could not afford to participate in a visit and I made it clear that all full-time students would be eligible for an overseas visit during their two-year courses. The catering school had a long standing arrangement to take their students to Paris and the engineers had links with Mulheim in Germany but none of the other schools had had a tradition of international visits. Construction had established a good link with Martin in Slovakia and other schools were now linked with Portugal, Norway and Greece.

Towards the end of June I chaired a NILTA Council at the FEFC London offices in Tottenham Court Road. The following day Alan

Milburn MP called in to see me and then I met the Investor in People assessor. Simon had been keen to secure an IiP rating for the College and the executive had promised to work hard to ensure that we would meet the standards. From the meeting with the assessor, I was not sure if we had convinced her but in due time we received the approval.

July commenced with a BT FE day in London and I returned in the evening to host a dinner for a party of Romanian visitors. The following day Veronica and I travelled down to Huddersfield to participate in a dinner at the Nags Head to commemorate the fiftieth anniversary of the opening of the College of Education. There was a good turn out and I was pleased to see so many of my former colleagues. We stayed overnight and travelled back the following morning as I had to attend the Remuneration Committee. In the evening Veronica and I were out again, this time to attend the 'Beating Retreat' at the garrison preceded by a cocktail party in one of the Officers Mess's.

John Widdowson, principal of New College, Durham, was a Board member of FENC (Further Education National Consortium) that designed and commissioned educational learning software mainly for the FE market. I had been rather sceptical about some of FENC's earlier offerings having been involved in the FEU project involving two hundred teachers in Yorkshire. John was keen to have my support so he invited me to a FENC Board meeting when it met at New College. Most of the Board members were also principals and I knew some of them from national meetings. I had to admit that they were moving in the right direction with new developments. However, I was still inclined to believe that the materials were over-priced and that it probably would be necessary to offer some 'loss-leaders' to break into the relatively small FE market.

I returned to College for the traditional end of term lunch for all staff and to make presentations to those who were retiring or leaving the College. The next two weeks were relatively quiet and I was able to catch up with most of the domestic issues that needed attention and Gaynor managed to catch up with the usual mountain of filing. During quieter periods I was in the habit of walking round the College to see how we were progressing and to observe the use of the improved facilities. There was little comparison between the College in 1987 and 1997 as in those ten years the learning facilities had greatly improved. New programmes such as sports science and uniform services were based in the refurbished Larchfield Street Sports Centre, originally a TA centre. The journalists had two state-of-the art radio studios, a TV centre and a former classroom converted into a newspaper production office. The catering students had seen their facilities improve with the new dining room and bistro together with a large production kitchen all within the former girls' high school block. Also in the block we had created a studio for the performing arts students and the Coltec Suite for the business administration courses. There were several open access areas, including the library where students could drop-in to use the many computers that had been purchased and two general classrooms and a corridor had been converted into a large open area for Key Skills, where students could get assistance from staff in communications and maths. A foreign language unit was also based in that area. Art and Design had gained a darkroom for photography, a batch of Apple Mac computers for design students and some additional space in the former library for fashion courses. The performing arts students had taken over the former school of catering dining room and they also had use of the hall and the rooms to the rear of the hall. With engineering being in steady decline there was little justification for significant investment in that area but we did add a CAD (computer aided design) workshop and a CAM (computer aided manufacturing) facility with a videoconferencing link to local schools. Construction had benefited from an investment by CITB just before my arrival at the College and only small changes were made to adjust to changing demands for the various craft courses. It was not possible for me to visit all sites during one of my tours so I had to be selective.

In mid-month the Darlington Partnership held a meeting at Corporation Road nursery and the members were able to see the local authority provision aimed at the less well-off people in that part of town. On 21 July I arrived at College at my usual time and after sorting out the programme for the day, I was asked to meet some people in the boardroom. On opening the door I found a roomful of staff wishing me well on my sixtieth birthday! I suspect Gaynor had tipped off the staff and Alison Wallace had masterminded the details. It was a pleasant surprise and I regarded myself as lucky to have so many good colleagues.

It was back to reality in the afternoon to chair an NCN Board meeting at Gateshead College. There was a party of Hungarians from Brno Technical University visiting the College and Les Baker had organised their programme that included a Hungarian evening at Neasham and Veronica and I spent a few merry hours enjoying the music and other entertainment. At the end of the month I attended a BT OFTEL (The Office of Telecommunications) conference relating to the rapid developments in telecommunications and to remind the audience of its role in: (a) promoting the interests of consumers; (b) maintaining and promoting effective competition; (c) making sure that telecommunications services were provided in the UK to meet all reasonable demands.

August had been earmarked to assist Helen to make her choice of university. She had decided at an early age that she wanted to work in journalism and when she completed her GCSE studies at Hummerskott School, she had decided that the BTEC Diploma in Media Studies at Darlington College was more appropriate than A levels at the sixth form college. Because of the strong journalism team at the College it was obvious that our Diploma in Media Studies would lean heavily in that direction and the programme team also offered the NCTJ qualifications that would give successful candidates a distinct advantage in moving into higher education and/or employment. Helen had identified the colleges that were offering the journalism courses that she thought would suit her as she was inclining towards radio journalism as a main option. Consequently, all the family set off via Retford to Barnsley for three nights. This was convenient to visit both Sheffield and Leeds universities over the next two days. We also called in at Trent University's Clifton campus before heading south to Evesham for three nights. This gave us an opportunity to visit Broadway and Oxford before taking the next leg of our journey to Winchester for one night. The following day we continued onto Ringwood for five nights. The main purpose for this location was for Helen to visit Bournemouth University and take their conducted tour but it also provided an opportunity to visit parts of England that were new to all of us. Indeed, we visited Swanage, Corfe Castle, Weymouth and Poole as well as exploring Bourne-mouth. Helen eventually chose to study at Central Lancashire University, based in Preston.

33. NILTA visit to Winnipeg and Minneapolis (Sue Parker, Fred McCrindle, Mary Barker, Sarah Farley) 1998

34. Mother's 90th birthday with family members 1998

35. *Dinner in the College Restaurant with Harold Evans (3rd from L), Peter Shuker, Peter Ridley (Former editor of* D&S Times*), Sarah Farley and Denis Gatfield – December 1998*

36. *Darlington College Executive 1999 – Alan Dixon, Debbie Leigh, Gary Groom, Peter Shuker, Simon Cassidy, Pat Gale, Sarah Farley, Angus Byrne*

37. Alan Milburn MP at the College Charter Mark stand 1999

38. Darlington College at Catterick opens for business September 1999

39. *Darlington College at Catterick official opening by HRH The Prince of Wales with Chairman Alasdair MacConachie, Vice-chairman Ian Stephenson June 2000*

40. *Darlington College at Catterick. HRH Prince Charles meets the customers when he officially opened the Child Care Centre*

41. FE+ Partnership Principals 2000. John Hogg, Alan Old, Tony Sutcliffe, Margaret Armstrong, Peter Shuker, Stuart Ingleson and Dave Wilshaw

42. Retirement event 2001 with Eric Tuxworth, Jim Pratt, Eric Twigg (ex-Huddersfield), Robin Bullough (ex-City and Guilds)

43. Retirement event with Alan Wells and Jaz, Basic Skills Agency

44. Receiving music score from Bryan Robinson

45. With Veronica and The Newcastle Pipe and Drums Band

46. Retirement Dinner at Headlam Hall Hotel organised by the Corporation Board

47. *The family after the OBE Investiture 2002*

48. *Presentation of the Peter Shuker Award to John Gray of PlanAR Research, formerly Principal of Newark & Sherwood and Basford Hall Colleges with Andrew Bird and Peter Shuker 2007*

CHAPTER 17

College Centenary Year

1997–98

I TRAVELLED TO NEW COLLEGE to chair the first committee meeting for a new project called ADAPT. This had stemmed from NCN discussions and would be funded from European monies. I had agreed that Rod Harris, who had been a head of school for finance and accounting, could be seconded to act as project director. He had been responsible for developing the link with Kostroma Technical University in Russia and had indicated he wanted to have a more challenging job than head of school or else he would seek employment elsewhere. As I did not want to lose Rod, the ADAPT project seemed a good way of keeping him actively involved with the College.

Following the deliberations of a committee set up in December 1994, Helena Kennedy QC had produced a book for FEFC in June entitled *Learning Works – Widening Participation in Further Education*. It had been enthusiastically received by the sector and there was an expectation that its recommendations would be implemented to achieve the aim of promoting access to FE for people who did not participate in education or training but who could benefit from it. At the end of August I attended a widening participation meeting in Middlesbrough organised by Teesside TEC. There was little doubt that the book had an impact on colleges, as its many recommendations would lead to changes in FEFC funding to encourage participation in under-represented groups. However, I was not too happy about the encouragement given to franchising as it had already started to distort funding in favour of colleges that had shifted the balance of their workload in a bid to attract 'easy money'. FEFC would eventually see the folly of some of the franchising and impose stricter criteria but for some time those colleges flourished at the expense of the more cautious colleges.

With enrolment starting briskly at the College I began the term at a Durham TEC meeting with the principals and then a trip to

London for the Basic Skills Agency Advisory Group. In mid-September there was a Catterick Project Day to resolve the PFI issue. There had been a visit from the Cabinet Office PFI Unit to try to apply pressure on me to agree to the PFI method but I had patiently explained my reasons and some of the views expressed by financial advisers to the teams that the Board had interviewed. The meeting concluded in a reluctant acceptance that PFI may not be appropriate for the Catterick Project but I would need to obtain the formal agreement of FEFC before moving to the 'design and build' solution that the College preferred. I had to wait until December before the FEFC Estates Team came to see me and gave the formal support we required to proceed.

The following day I hosted a well-attended regional 'inclusive' seminar, based on Helena Kennedy's book. On Friday morning I held my customary full staff meeting to introduce new colleagues and to give a briefing of all the developments that had occurred over the summer and the issues for the immediate future. At midday Darlington Borough Council hosted a lunch for Jacques Santer, the President of the European Union Commission, and I was invited to attend in my previous capacity as chairman of the Darlington 1992 Committee.

The following week had been earmarked for the College's Centenary International Conference and I was delighted with the number of our partner countries that had agreed to attend and in most cases the rector or head of institution was present. I welcomed the guests on their arrival on Saturday and accompanied them on a coach tour on Sunday that included Durham City, Walworth Castle for lunch and, finally, Bowes Museum. They were so impressed with the museum and the weather was so perfect that they indicated a preference to remain there rather than complete the planned tour in Richmond.

The conference started on Monday and I was pleased that several members of the corporation were present as well as John Bushnell, representing the department and Keith Duckett, representing FEFC. MEP Stephen Hughes gave the introductory lecture and Ernie Haiden, who was now part-time chief executive of NILTA, addressed the group on developments in FE and the impact of technology on learning. There was a banquet dinner in the restaurant and the catering students and staff excelled themselves.

I was keen to show off the use of technology in the College and on Tuesday morning we had a videoconference with Adelaide College in South Australia with Principal Madeleine Woolley giving a brilliant presentation on the innovative developments in that state. The buzz around the packed hall was exciting and I gave Angus Byrne a big pat on the back for his efforts in ensuring the technology was robust. Jan Long, the regional director of the British Council spoke in the afternoon and she needed to be at her best to maintain the attention of the audience after the morning's excitement. There was another banquet in the evening with the Mayor of Darlington as the special guest.

The third and last day of the conference commenced with a presentation by Llew Avis, the senior personnel officer for Fujitsu. The performing arts students gave a lively and happy performance to entertain the guests. This concluded the conference and I stepped onto the stage to give my closing remarks and thanks but was interrupted by the Russian delegation led by the rector of Kostroma Technical University and with the aid of an interpreter, he bestowed upon me an Honorary Professorship of his University, complete with gown and mortar board. For a moment I was lost for words and the warm applause from the audience gave me time to recover to thank them for such a gesture. There was an exchange of gifts between the guests and the College and this memorable conference came to an end.

Most of the next two days were in Durham or Sunderland with NCN, two NiAA meetings and Durham principals, but there was a pleasant evening at the Railway Museum where the Darlington Partnership had arranged a dinner on the platform to raise money for the A1 Steam Locomotion project. The other evening was taken up with a Corporation Board meeting where the members were full of praise for the international conference. 1 October was a sad day for me when Gaynor Dobie left the College. She had worked with me for eight years, initially as trainee then my secretary and, since incorporation, my PA. I could not have wished for a more conscientious, hard-working yet always pleasant colleague who could be trusted to keep things moving during the many times I was out of College. Not only was she popular with College members of staff, she was also known nation-wide through all my professional contacts and she had a famous reputation for her cheerful and efficient manner. The executive team dined her out at the Redworth Hall Hotel and she started a new job in London with a company offering English as a foreign language in several countries and in particular Japan. She was working as PA to the chief executive who spent a lot of his time in Japan and Gaynor expected that she would be there for about three months in the year. In fact, it was significantly more than that and she eventually resigned from the job. Debbie had taken over the responsibility for the secretarial staff and she organised a rota to cover Gaynor's duties as none of the girls felt that they could do the job full-time or perhaps they did not want to work for me! The job was advertised and a lady called Heather was appointed as my PA.

I had a visit from a consultant who was investigating the problems in the North East economy for the Regional Development Agency, ONE North East. I gave him a frank view of my perceptions and some suggestions that I thought could make a difference. Richard Appleton, head teacher of Eastbourne School, called to see me about links with his school and we explored several possibilities including running catering courses in the school. Eastbourne's playing fields had been developed into a sports centre for the town as well as for the school pupils and I was interested in the potential for our Sports Science students gaining access to the facilities.

Denis Gatfield was now chairman of the corporation and he regularly called in to see me. He and Geoff Nichol had collectively been trying to get me to make changes that I was not keen to make. One was to remove the office of vice-principal as they insisted that most deputy posts had been dispensed with by industry. This would mean either demoting Alan Dixon or making him redundant; neither option appealed to me as Alan had to stand in for me on my many trips away from College. I continued to resist the pressure but I felt sure that the issue would be raised again.

On 8 October there was a spectacular fireworks display on the College playing fields to commemorate the end of the Centenary Year celebrations. Many students and staff took part and the caterers set up a barbeque to provide refreshments to the assembled throng. I attended the NILTA three-day Annual Conference at the Queens Hotel in Leeds, my tenth conference as chairman.

There were a couple of interesting events in mid-month. Firstly, an invitation to Risedale School for the Opening of the Hall and

Nature Trail and on the following day Helen and I were guests of Comcast at Redcar Races. As neither of us had been to a horseracing event before, we quite enjoyed the experience and even made a small profit from the bookies. Three days later I again enjoyed the views of London from the circular revolving restaurant at the top of the BT Tower on the occasion of the BT FE Awards. It was quickly back to reality next day by another away day grilling by the chairman at Redworth Hall Hotel. Alasdair MacConachie had become vice chairman of the corporation and he tended to avoid these confrontational meetings. There was a change in the corporation membership when accountant Clive Owen resigned and Peter Rowley, chief executive of Darlington Building Society, filled the vacancy.

I started November with a presentation to new staff before welcoming college inspector Les August who was making a routine visit to the College. The following day I flew down to Heathrow to make a presentation to a conference at one of the airport hotels. Later in the week there was a meeting of the APC regional committee at South Tyneside College in South Shields and then an interview on Radio Cleveland in Middlesbrough.

Within the College we had been steadily increasing the access to IT for our students and the most recent innovation was a large open learning support centre on the ground floor incorporating a variety of student services. I had negotiated with the County Durham Lord Lieutenant, David Grant, to secure a royal visit and he had arranged for Prince Andrew, HRH The Duke of Kent, to officially open the Centre. So on 10 November we had the official opening and our media studies students, including my daughter Helen, had the opportunity of covering the event. Prince Andrew was obviously very interested in the technology and spent some time talking to students and viewing the equipment and the accompanying facilities.

This was followed by the three-day AoC Conference in Harrogate and an opportunity to meet up with other principals to discuss the issues that concerned us most, as well as participating in the formal sessions. Harrogate was a good centre for me owing to its relatively close proximity to Darlington. Its conference facilities were excellent and there were sufficient hotels to meet the demands of a large gathering of principals.

The Darlington Partnership had been struggling to achieve its ambitious aims and it had been agreed to reconstitute it. It was then re-launched by Prime Minister Tony Blair. It may have been perceived as a PR exercise by the general public but there had been a need to revitalise the group, particularly when the government was encouraging such partnerships and offering some funding.

It was in mid-November that the corporation started to look at 'Plan B' for the Catterick development. This meant that the PFI option had been resisted and we could move to a 'design and build' alternative. Local architects Browne Smith Baker had been selected to work with the College and Guy Holmes was the senior architect. Some of the earlier ideas for the layout of the building were replaced by a more compact design that I felt would be more appropriate. A provision for childcare had been proposed because the target group included army wives and the 'abandoned wives of Catterick' who usually had children and very few qualifications or skills to help them gain employment. The Ministry of Defence had confirmed its offer for the site for a modest fee on the basis that the buildings would be only used for educational purposes for at least twenty years. Debbie had been looking at all the funding options based upon the estimated cost of the buildings. She had identified support from the FEFC capital fund, the income from the sale of the two Trinity Road properties and Barclays Bank had agreed to a loan to make up the balance. Yorkshire Forward, the regional development agency had also indicated that it was keen to support the project. Interestingly, John Williams, the leader of Darlington Borough Council and one-time member of the Corporation Board, expressed his concern that the proceeds from the sale of a Darlington asset were being used to develop the Catterick Centre. The Board did not support this view and all was set to move forward. Following an invitation to building contractors to tender for the project, the corporation appointed a Northallerton company, Walter Thompson's, to work with our appointed architects to design and build the centre.

As Darlington was now regarded at being part of Tees Valley rather than County Durham, I became more involved with the Teesside colleges, the Teesside TEC and the University of Teesside. I was a member of the Board of the University of Teesside Partnership (UTP) and, as well as participating in degree ceremonies I was also invited to official openings or to visit new buildings. I attended meetings of the Teesside TEC's education committee and became a member of the Teesside principals group that met fairly frequently. The group was less disciplined than the Durham Group of principals and that may have been a reflection of past history, but as most of the members were relatively new to the job I was surprised by the general attitude.

At that time Darlington College was larger than any of the other Teesside colleges and that may have been a reason why I seemed to be welcomed and my views sought on some of the big issues. I had known Mike Clarke, principal of Cleveland Technical College, for some years but he lost the confidence of his Corporation Board and was replaced by the regional director of FEFC, Lynn Howe. However, she did not last long and my old cricketing friend and international ruby player, Alan Old, became principal. Margaret Armstrong had been appointed principal of Stockton and Billingham College when Fred McCrindle had moved to Reading and I had worked with Margaret on NILTA regional affairs and respected her judgement. Alan Clifford had been principal at Kirby College for some time and I had known him through APC. Stuart Ingleson was principal of Longlands College and I considered that he was probably the most astute of the group. However, he did not stay long before taking over a similar post in Preston and his deputy, John Hogg, succeeded him. Tony Sutcliffe was principal of Hartlepool College and I had known him also through NILTA but his interest in technology seemed to have been lost and a person who I thought I could look to for support in ILT was no longer interested. Cleveland College of Art & Design, with principal David Wilshaw, was the odd college in the pack in terms of its specialist curriculum and its significant proportion of higher education work. In additional to the FE colleges there were also four sixth form colleges, excluding Queen Elizabeth Sixth Form College. Howard Clark had been principal at Stockton Sixth Form College for several years and seemed to be respected by the FE principals. Miriam Stanton was principal of Hartlepool Sixth Form College and regularly attended the meetings. The other two colleges, Bede in Billingham and St Mary's RC Sixth Form College, either rarely attended or made little contribution to discussions. There was clearly hostility and rivalry between the FE and the sixth form colleges as the latter moved into traditional FE areas of work.

The College had always tried to work closely with secondary schools in its catchment area and I had visited all the local schools and the annual dinner had helped cement a friendly relationship. In my early years there had been specific collaboration with link courses and Durham LEA was prepared to 'double-fund' these courses by not making deductions from schools while their pupils attended link courses at the College. After incorporation, Durham had reconsidered its position and traditional link programmes had reduced significantly. When Darlington regained its unitary status, Geoff Pennington was keen to see stronger links and introduced the Learning Town group, which I attended whenever I was available. Towards the end of the year there were two meetings of the group and a one-day conference in the Morton Park Business Centre where a wider audience could discuss the proposals from the group.

I had been keen to look at solutions to creating an electronic learning network that was in the spirit of the NiAA proposals but the different funding methodologies did not make this a straightforward choice. With the developing NCN broadband network, I had suggested that individual schools might be interested in buying-in to the network via its local college and Hummersknott School had expressed interest and in due time an agreement was reached. The government had decided to introduce the National Grid for Learning (NGfL) for the schools sector but at this time it was in its infancy and inevitably, there were many teething troubles.

Another technological link with local schools was via a videoconferencing scheme introduced by Denford, a company that was based in Brighouse with a tradition of engineering and the manufacture of CNC machine tools. Denford provided the College with a CNC machine with links to a number of participating schools. The school students would write the software for the CNC machine and this would be downloaded from the school to the College and results would be returned electronically to the school. The VC link enabled staff and students from the College and the school to share information and discuss the outcomes.

I participated in the presentation of certificates to our NNEB students. This qualification was for successful nursery nursing students who had reached NVQ Level 2 or 3 and most of them were either in employment or would quickly find a suitable job. I kept the following day free for the Corporation Board meeting and its AGM as there were many big issues, including the Catterick project, to be discussed.

I travelled to London to chair the FEFC PIMS group. Prior to the meeting I enjoyed a working lunch with BT in the Dorchester Hotel. The following Monday was devoted to Corporation sub-committee meetings, including Staff Development, Personnel, Assets and International. I was pleased to receive a visit from the FEFC Estates Team that was empowered to advise the FEFC on the priorities for capital funding within the sector. It was a relief when the team confirmed their support for Catterick and agreed that PFI was not an appropriate solution in that case. This meant that the College would recover £50,000 of the £150,000 it had expended on the exercise. The Higher Awards Ceremony had Derek Fraser, vice-chancellor of Teesside University, as its principal guest and this was almost the last event of another very full year.

1998

At incorporation, I had agreed with the Board to reduce the proportion of expenditure on staffing to allow more resources to be targeted at physical infrastructure and equipment. We had been reasonably successful thanks to the retirement of several staff members who, after many years of service were at the maximum on their respective grades. However, with the College recruitment of students proving successful by exceeding 19,000 enrolments in 1997–98, so meeting the ambitious government growth targets, additional staff had to be recruited to meet the demands of the changing curriculum and the new courses. A new factor had appeared in the turnover of staff. Traditionally there had been a low turnover with many staff remaining at the College for the whole of their teaching careers. This had started to change with incorporation and although I did not see this as a negative influence, it did lead to an increase in advertising costs and time-consuming interviews. I had maintained the unwritten understanding of the LEAs in advertising all teaching appointments in the *Times Educational Supplement* as well as the local press and occasionally in other national newspapers for specialist posts. I believed that we should recruit nationally rather than limit it to local applicants. I had also preserved the custom of paying expenses to candidates short-listed for interview and to offer removal allowances for successful candidates, provided that they chose to live within easy travelling distance from the College. I introduced these criteria because of my earlier experiences in Darlington when many staff chose to live in remote parts of Durham and North Yorkshire and often failed to attend College in extreme weather conditions. We had a lot of new starters at the beginning of 1998 and it was agreed to split them into two groups for the induction programme.

My new PA could not believe my diary when she found that I did not have a clear day until March. The constant demands of national, regional and local initiatives meant that there was little room to manoeuvre in the event of a crisis. Nationally, I had a NILTA meeting at the Institute of Directors and a Council meeting at RM headquarters in Abingdon. There were two days at BETT, the FEFC principals' annual gathering in Birmingham, a Basic Skills Agency meeting, two days at City & Guilds and a special event in Huddersfield to celebrate the fiftieth year of the Former Students' Association. Within the region there were several meetings of the NCN Council and its sub-committees, meetings with the Durham principals and the TEC, the NiAA Board and a trip to York for a meeting with North Yorkshire TEC. I also found myself on a new group, CIRA. This was the University of Teesside Community Informatics Research Applications and I attended two meeting of the Corporation Board in January and February.

The Catterick Project Group was meeting at least twice a month as we moved to detailed planning and there were two visits from the consultants who had been advising on PFI. The Corporation Board had its residential conference at Catterick, as this was one of the main items of interest.

I had two interesting visitors, Ruth Gee and Ben Johnson Hill. After Ruth had lost the battle with CEF, she had been appointed by the British Council to take a responsibility for technical education. She came to discuss the College's international links and we shared some useful information. Ben's company had been commissioned by the FEFC to carry out a national survey and Darlington College had been selected as part of the sample. Ben spent a lot of time with me, as management was a key part of his investigation, which was not surprising in view of the horror stories of malpractice that were being leaked to the press and did damage to the reputation of the sector as a whole. I had become aware of the wide variation in the quality of the corporation boards and the lack of supervision of over ambitious principals who were abusing the powers bestowed by incorporation. I had been told of colleges where the chairman was self-employed and had a cosy relationship with the principal rather than the professional scrutiny that I had encouraged at Darlington. There were rumours of misuse of funds to provide the principal with palatial accommodation and also of those who used their college's subsidiary company for personal or family gain.

The College received a special visitor in February when Harriet Harman, Secretary of State for Social Security (1997–8) and Minister for Women, came to look at our child-care courses. The visit raised interest with both staff and students and the full-time media students wished to cover the story. Helen had the privilege of interviewing Harriet and her colleagues recorded the conversation.

As the fifth anniversary of incorporation approached, the government introduced the Collaboration Fund. As David Melville stated at a briefing of principals at Chester-le-street:

> Funds have been made available for further education rationalisation and collaboration, and the government is setting the 'culture' for collaboration. The government has refocused and neatly renamed the competitiveness fund a collaboration fund, with £ 25.5 million available in 1998–99. Of this, £15.5 million was to support collaboration between colleges and other partners such as higher education institutions and £10 million was to promote college mergers in support of increased efficiency and effectiveness in the further education sector. Of this £10 million, £7.5 million would support rationalisation proposals – proposals from two or more colleges working together for capital expenditure leading to revenue savings. About ten per cent of the total – £2.5 million – has been set aside to support mergers.

Up to that time there had been little evidence of colleges wishing to merge. Although the Northumberland Agricultual College had been in a severe financial state it had resisted overtures from Newcastle College but eventually agreed to join with Northumberland College in Ashington. Durham Agricultural College was also struggling and with Principal Alan Hetherington reaching retirement it seemed that a merger with New College Durham was the obvious solution. However, East Durham College made an attractive offer and the Agricultural College Corporation Board supported a merger with them. Despite local objections, the FEFC decided to support the merger. In Middlesbrough, Kirby College and Longlands had engaged in tentative merger discussions. Kirby had been formed by a merger with Acklam Hall Boys' Grammar School and Kirby Girls' High School whilst Longlands was a merger between Marton Road School and Longlands College.

The College Annual Lecture and Dinner had Alan Wells of the Basic Skills Agency as its speaker and there was an excellent turn-out for the event. In mid-March I had four events associated with NiAA. We had a Council meeting at Aykley Heads in Durham and then a day's conference for local authorities at the Stadium of Light in Sunderland. It was my first visit to the new football stadium and during the lunch break I joined a party that was given a tour of the facilities. The third event was the first meeting of Tees Valley Informatics, a group that had the support of NiAA to develop strategies for the Tees Valley area. The university had agreed to host the group and Tees Valley Joint Strategy Unit (JSU) had agreed to provide a co-ordinator. I was invited to be a founder member. John Lowther, chief executive of the JSU, was a keen supporter of the group and attended several meetings. The fourth event was a meeting of NiAA's education group, which was held at the Industry Centre in Sunderland.

The Corporation Board had a Search Committee and its main function was to identify potential new members to fill vacancies. Invariably, there was an annual change in the student members but other changes were quite rare. With the developments in North Yorkshire, it had been agreed to recruit two additional members to represent that area. North Yorkshire County Council had nominated County Councillor Carl Les, who was also the proprietor of the Leeming Bar Lodge and Restaurant. The other member was to be the Catterick garrison commander. Both appointments proved to be excellent choices; even though the commander changed every two or three years, each one brought energy and ideas to the Board. Graham Henderson, deputy vice-chancellor of Teesside University had replaced Geoff Crispen, who had been appointed deputy vice chancellor at Thames University, and Councillor John Williams had resigned to be replaced by Councillor Eleanor Lister. When the Search Committee identified a suitable person the routine was to invite the person to the College to have lunch with the chairman and me. This enabled the potential member to fully appreciate the responsibilities and commitment required to fulfil the duties of a Board member.

Alan Milburn, MP, presented the awards at the Annual Awards Ceremony in mid-March. There was a meeting of the Darlington Partnership that had now matured and good links had developed between the public, private and voluntary sectors of the community as a result of its activities. Alasdair MacConachie's energy and enthusiasm certainly helped to drive the partnership. The Darlington LEA invited me to a one-day conference at Branksome School and although much of the business related to secondary education, it was useful to meet heads and deputies and get up-to-date with local issues.

At the end of the month there was a crucial NILTA meeting to appoint a successor to Ernie Haidon who had decided to retire as part-time chief executive. As Mary Barker was one of the short-listed candidates, I felt that Fred McCrindle, who was now principal of Reading College and vice-chairman of NILTA, should chair the meeting at Reading College with me as a panel member. Every member of the panel agreed that Mary was the outstanding candidate and so she became NILTA's first full-time chief executive. This gave me the problem of replacing Mary, who had only been the manager of NCN for about a year. This proved to be easier than I had expected as my old friend, Gareth Davies, applied for the post and was duly appointed.

Alan Hetherington had announced his retirement from Durham Agricultural College and before Easter the principals organised a retirement dinner at a hotel in Bishop Auckland. In the morning we had had a meeting of Durham principals and chairmen to share views on some of the issues that were concerning the sector. It had been quite some time since we had all met and there were some changes in membership. Joanna Tate had been appointed as principal of Bishop Auckland College to replace Steve Broomhead who had moved to Warrington College. It was quite a lively meeting, particularly surrounding the issue of East Durham's successful bid to merge with the Agricultural College.

Later in the month there was an appointments meeting for the new post of head of the Catterick Centre as it had been agreed that it would be beneficial to have a designated manager working with the planning team. I was delighted when Mike Cox was offered the job. I had appointed Mike some years earlier to an engineering post and his enthusiasm and obvious talent had been recognised internally and externally by our customers. Later in the day I participated in an RSA visit to Teesside University that I had organised to view the Virtual Realty Centre. It was a well attended event with several Fellows bringing their children along to get a glimpse of the future.

The government had been considering the impact of new technology on learning and decided to launch the 'University for Industry' (Ufi) in 1998 to develop people's skills and work with employers to increase employees' capabilities. The aims of Ufi were to work with partners to boost individuals' employability and employees' productivity by:

1. ispiring existing learners to develop their skills further;
2. winning over new and reluctant learners;
3. transforming people's access to learning in everyday life and work.

There was considerable discussion within the FE sector about the impact of Ufi and whether it would be a threat or an opportunity. Its first chief executive was Dr Anne Wright, who had been the vice-chancellor of Sunderland University and seemed a strange choice to many people. Within the regions there were many discussions taking place and I attended meetings relating to Ufi hosted by North Yorkshire TEC and two days later another meeting by Durham TEC. So little was known that the meetings probably created more questions than answers and some TEC officers may have seen it as a threat. Ufi established 'learndirect' as its business arm and fortunately for the colleges it focused mainly on publicly funded provision and delivering services directly to individual learners through learndirect centres and its website. Colleges had the opportunity to become centres and many did take the decision to participate, including Darlington College. I saw the move as particularly important to my plans for Catterick, as learndirect would have the funding to generate on-line materials on a national basis, whereas I had set up a team with Angus Byrne to develop our own materials that was a costly exercise and less efficient than a national scheme would expect to be. In June 1999, in an interview with the *Times Higher Education Supplement*, Ufi's Anne Wright and chairman Lord Dearing said the government 'is content' with the Ufi's huge student expansion projections and they called on ministers to back up their commitment to the flagship lifelong learning project with major increases in further education funding.

Another government initiative was the introduction of Centres of Excellence and I attended two meetings, one at Tyneside TEC and the other at Teesside University. Between the meetings, North Yorkshire TEC organised a Life-long Learning Conference at Harrogate. This replaced the County Council's World Class North Yorkshire Conference but it was just as enjoyable and informative. Two days later I did a presentation to the Darlington Townswomen's Guild on 'Education in the 21st Century'. I travelled to London for Project Connect Conference in Westminster. Project Connect was a commercial organisation dealing in various computing resources and it had been a good supporter of NILTA conferences.

During Ernie Haidon's time as chief executive of NILTA there had been little international involvement but the Council had supported the proposal for a visit to the Annual Convention of the Association of Canadian Community Colleges (ACCC) in 1998 and Ernie had commissioned Sue Parker, former principal of Harlow College and Gwent College, to organise the visit in May. I had a great respect for Sue having known her for several years and I had persuaded her to become vice-chairman of NILTA when she was at Gwent. Unfortunately, things did not work out for her at that college and she had to resign and take up a job in the private sector. This also meant she had to step down from the NILTA post and Fred McCrindle took on the NILTA vice-chairman's role.

We had attracted quite a good response to the visit and I had decided to go and Sarah Farley had also expressed interest and I supported her application. Mary Barker also joined the group along with a number of senior and middle managers. On Friday 22 May we spent the day flying from Gatwick to Winnepeg via Minneapolis and booked into the Crowne Plaza Hotel which was also the convention hotel. After breakfast we were welcomed and introduced to the ACCC officials and then set off on a conducted tour of the city. Winnipeg, the capital city of Manitoba, lies at the bottom of a low lying flood plain in the Red River Valley that has an extremely flat topography, as there are no substantial hills in the city or its vicinity. This meant that there were few spectacular views and we had to concentrate mainly on the man-made structures. In the evening we were the dinner guests of the ACCC.

The conference started on Sunday morning and ran for two and a half days of key note addresses, optional tutorials and discussions, as well as a large exhibition of educational suppliers. The group seemed to enjoy their experiences and on Monday evening we had a meal in a revolving restaurant at the top of one of the tallest hotels in the city. After the conference closed, we had a visit to Red River College to observe Canadian community college education at first hand. In the evening we joined the other conference members for the closing dinner. Ideally, we would have preferred to have stayed in Canada to see several other colleges but that was not possible so Sue had arranged for the group to fly to Minneapolis so that we could visit USA colleges. Consequently, on Wednesday we took an early flight from Winnipeg to Minneapolis. We were booked at the Days Inn Hotel but soon after we arrived it became apparent that the facilities fell far short of expectations. To her credit Sue tackled the hotel management and they agreed to our transfer to the Ramada Hotel and this was very superior in comparison.

Sue had organised a full session of visits and we immediately set off for St Paul's Technical College, located in the heart of Saint Paul's Cathedral Hill and it had been educating people for employment since 1910. Saint Paul's College is the oldest of the metro area's public two-year colleges. St Paul is the other half of the twin city and although I had been to the AACC Convention here in 1995, I had not seen anything of the St Paul half. I was not surprised to see a well-equipped college in well-appointed buildings containing smart courteous students. Later in the day many of us travelled to the Mall of America to visit the largest shopping complex in the world.

During my visit in 1995, a tour of Normandale College had been included and I was quite pleased that Sue had booked a full day visit to Normandale on the Thursday. We had an excellent day and joined the staff and students on the college lawns for a barbeque lunch that was served by the college president and some of his senior staff. Apparently, this was an annual event towards the end of the academic year. I was again impressed by the excellence of the student services provided by the college that reflected the importance given to student welfare and well-being. With the temperature hitting 86°F we were quite pleased to be outside in the shade. In the early evening Sue had booked dinner on a Paddle Boat that sailed leisurely along the Mississippi River. This was a real treat and all the members of the group enjoyed the experience.

On our last day we visited Metropolitan University that gave us an opportunity to witness a higher education institution. Metropolitan was not a typical university as its average student age was thirty-two and with slightly more female students than males. It offered a very wide range of study programmes. The university also had a centre for community-based learning, providing support for students across the university, to integrate community-based learning and civic engage-ment with academic reflection. Through internships and courses they provided a meaningful experience for the participating community, organisation or business and the student. After the visit we had lunch in the museum attached to the university before boarding a coach for the twin city tour of Minneapolis and St Paul. This had proved to be a very good visit although there was one instance that quite shocked me. Shortly after arriving in Minneapolis, Sue had approached me and explained that one of the men in our party had been making improper advances to some of the women, including herself. Upon further questioning I discovered that Sarah and Mary had also been approached, the common factor being that the three women were attractive blondes. When I prized out the name of the culprit I was astounded, having known the individual for many years. There was a confrontation and apologies were given and accepted. I learned later that the man had a reputation within the sector for similar activities!

It was back to basics on Monday morning with a new staff induction session before attending an AoC regional committee meeting. The rest of the week was devoted to internal meetings and catching up with correspondence, including a mountain of emails. I was soon on my travels again with a NILTA Council meeting at the

AoC offices, two days at the Annual APC Conference in Solihull and a three-day international conference in Bath. Then followed the fiftieth Huddersfield Former Students' Reunion where it was proposed to wind up the organisation because of dwindling numbers.

The bulk of the students had commenced their summer vacation and staff members were completing returns that had to be submitted to FEFC to secure the element of funding for students completing their studies. There was still the plethora of local and internal meetings to progress the many projects as well as routine corporate requirements. It was during this period that I was approached by Barry Keel, who was aware of my interest in technology, as he was considering the need for a web site for the borough Council. Apparently, he did not have any in-house expertise and asked me if I could give a presentation to his management team. Angus Byrne had established the college website several years earlier and he managed the regular updates that were necessary for our own credibility. Barry and his team arrived on Tuesday morning and I took them into the relatively new videoconferencing suite on the first floor. With some assistance from Angus I had put together a PowerPoint presentation that included several examples of other web sites that had been set up by councils in other parts of the country. We had found plenty of examples of poor websites but at that time we had identified one authority that, in our opinion, was a good model to consider. It was soon apparent that most of Barry's team were in new territory and may have been hoping that Barry would not follow up the presentation with the borough Council. But I think the message was clear that there really was no alternative and it had to be in the best interests of the community for the Council to be taking a lead in this area.

Two days later I travelled to London with Veronica and Helen to attend another Royal Garden Party at Buckingham Palace. Helen, being over sixteen, was allowed to join us but Edward was still too young and had to stay at home. It was another lovely sunny day and we all enjoyed the atmosphere of the bands, the afternoon tea and the appearance of the Queen and members of the Royal Family.

I had one day left before going on holiday and the morning was spent interviewing companies for the Catterick IT contract. It had been decided to outsource the whole IT service, including all hardware and technician support and RM was the successful bidder. There was the end of term lunch for all of the staff followed by a meeting of the Corporation Projects Committee before I cleared my desk and briefed Alan and Heather, ready for a much-needed family vacation.

Summer vacation

Our round the world trip in 1996 had generated an expectation of another family trip of similar proportions so I had spent some time on the internet rather than using an agent such as Trailfinders that I used in 1996. We were keen to spend more time in Australia and to visit a different part of the USA on the return journey.

The outward flight took us to Singapore arriving in torrential rain with a lot of local flooding. We had two and a half days in Singapore and thoroughly enjoyed the experience; a visit to the famous Raffles Hotel, a day trip to Sentosa and a half-day coach tour of Singapore were the highlights. Darwin was the next stop for four days and as expected the temperature was high and humid. We enjoyed an afternoon city tour of the town and a day trip to the Kakadu National Park before flying to Alice Springs to take a tour to Ayres Rock and King's Canyon.

We moved onto Cairns for four nights and spent a full day in the town exploring the coast. We had a coach tour of the Atherton Tableland and a second visit to the Great Barrier Reef on a catamaran. Sydney was the next stop, staying at Manly. We met our Australian friends, Lyn and Theodore, and they took us to see the spectacular views of coast, rivers and mountains. We took a harbour cruise that included stop-offs to see The Rocks, Opera House and Darling Harbour.

Saturday was Edward's sixteenth birthday and at 1 p.m. we left Sydney to fly to San Francisco, crossing the date line so that when we arrived at 10 p.m. it was still 1 August, so making his birthday last for two days! We participated in a city tour followed by a ferry trip to Alcatraz. It was a fascinating visit and Helen and Edward tried out the prison cells to have a brief experience or the life of a prisoner.

The last leg was in Vancouver. We took a city tour of Vancouver and in the evening watched a spectacular fireworks display. There was a day tour to Vancouver Island, by ferry to Victoria. We had a conducted tour of Victoria with an opportunity to visit Buchart Gardens. For our last day we purchased a bus pass that allowed us to hop on and off a circular bus route. This enabled us to reach North Vancouver and to walk along the Capilano Bridge, a simple suspension bridge over the Capilano River. The overnight return flight included a five-hour stop at Chicago.

CHAPTER 18

Darlington College at Catterick

THERE WAS A LARGE NEW staff intake and I had a lively staff induction session with an expectant audience. As work pressure had restricted my involvement with interviewing candidates to senior post holders, I did not recognise many of the new starters. The increasing number of women recruited reflected the changing curriculum with the continuing reduction in engineering being offset by an expansion in service industry courses. It was my mother's ninetieth birthday on 7th September and there was a family gathering on the Sunday to celebrate the occasion although at that time we had no idea that she would not survive to the next birthday.

Target setting had been creeping into educational practice and I had agreed a number of targets for the College with the corporation. In September there was an FEFC gathering in London entirely on target setting for colleges that sought to support FEFC's targets for the sector. Much of this was based on the original work of the Statistics Group and my PIMS sub-group, so I could not be critical of this development. Inevitably, targets were going to be linked to funding with an emphasis on student completion and success. There was the usual flurry of local and regional meetings at the beginning of the Academic Year and I seemed to be spending a lot of time driving to various parts of the Northern and North Yorkshire areas. One of the major events was the launch of the Tees Valley Informatics Strategy that took place at Teesside University. Chris Drew of NiAA led this initiative and all of the FE colleges were represented. One of the outcomes was to be another committee on which I was expected to serve.

Mary Barker came to see me accompanied by John Bushnell to discuss NILTA business. John had been a keen supporter of NILTA and had attended almost every Council meeting and some of the sub-committee meetings as well as the national conferences. This was particularly useful to Mary as John was able to provide her with national contacts.

6 October was a milestone in the evolution of the Catterick Centre. The building contractor had moved onto the site and there was the official 'cutting the first sod' with Alasdair MacConachie and I performing the ceremony accompanied by a large JCB digger. Alasdair was deputy chairman and Denis was quite happy for him to perform that duty. There was good support for the event from the Richmondshire Partnership members and the College of the Dales Group.

Two days later I had another unique experience when I attended a two-day conference at the Gleneagles Hotel in Scotland. This was an ICT event jointly organised by BT and the Scottish Further Education Unit (SFEU) and the quality of the accommodation and the meals complemented an excellent conference. I had hardly had time to get the train home and unpack before heading south for the three-day Annual NILTA Conference at Hinckley. The following week I was able to bring the executive up to date during our three-day residential at Walworth Castle Hotel.

The Northern Colleges Network was now well established and other groups of colleges had looked at its progress to consider if it could be applied within their areas. I had been invited by a group of Yorkshire colleges to share our experiences and from this the Trojan Project had been developed. The Trojan Project represented collaboration amongst all nineteen West Yorkshire colleges that sought to maximise the impact of Information and Communications Technologies on Small and Medium-sized Enterprises (SME) in the sub-region. This was to facilitate the potential for collaborative work on a sub-regional and regional basis and to enhance the development of new technology skills among staff and learners. Achieving a high level of collaboration among the colleges was the most difficult aspect of the project. The project director was Margaret Coleman who had worked initially with a group of eleven colleges in 1995/96 on the potential for electronic networking and developing and sharing learning materials. This had resulted in a bid to the Competitiveness Fund in 1996, which was unsuccessful. The bid had scored high on collaboration but the judging panel had felt that the link between the development of learning materials and the increased competitiveness of SMEs was not sufficiently established. The informal feedback suggested that it was clear that the colleges would have benefited from collaboration and connectivity, but the benefit to SMEs was not as concrete and immediate. Ironically, the failure of the bid led the colleges to become more determined to succeed in a project that they felt would have great benefit for both the business and learning communities. The project development group that comprised almost entirely second-tier college managers had been working together for about a year and clearly showed the value of colleges collaborating and communicating electronically throughout the sub-region.

The growing support for a sub-regional strategy for information and communication technology among colleges arose from a number of key factors. Firstly, the development group had easy and regular access to college principals and were in a position to influence or even lead individual college ICT strategies meant that they acted as opinion-leaders across their area. Secondly, six colleges in the sub-region were working together on a technology project as sub-contractors of a Training and Enterprise Council. They found that while they could successfully collaborate in development and delivery of training, they could not easily persuade employers of the value of attending training sessions, which were by the nature of the programme, too general. Lastly, while a number of colleges were developing good practice through specific projects, it was becoming clearer to the development group that unless the colleges worked together they would run the risk of developing along technologically incompatible lines for ease of future, low-cost connectivity, should post-Higginson connectivity ever be implemented. In addition, there was a rapidly developing view among college senior managers that unless the college sector worked together in the sub-region they would be regarded as relatively minor players in social and economic regeneration. Also, many colleges were becoming increasingly concerned about achieving value for money in developing their access to networked technology. Bearing this in mind the development group, through the principal of the lead college in the bid, convened a meeting of West Yorkshire principals to discuss and agree a way forward. By the autumn of 1996 there was support from all West Yorkshire colleges for a further bid to the Competitiveness Fund and the willingness by spring 1997 to pledge substantial matched funds to the venture. The gestation of the Trojan project was lengthy. However, once colleges were convinced of the simple, central idea of reaching SMEs through existing college students and becoming increasingly aware that new technology was no respecter of geographical boundaries, the collaboration was born.

I was heavily involved with various groups in Durham and in North Yorkshire, but with the development of Tees Valley, another set of partnerships had evolved so that my busy diary had become even more congested. Darlington was the only college that was working across all three sub-regions, which was an advantage in terms of developing the business but a challenge to maintain good links with all the partners. In October I attended meetings of five North Yorkshire groups, four Tees Valley groups and four County Durham groups. I was also a guest at NCFE's 150th Anniversary Lunch at the New Grange Hotel in Darlington.

The Adult and Community Learning Fund (ACLF) was announced in DfEE's consultation paper The Learning Age, published in February 1998. Provision for the Fund was £20 million between 1998 and 2002. A total of £2.86 million of this funding for the fifth round had been allocated to 118 new projects for 2000–2001 and 2001–2002.

The ACLF Advisory Panel had seven members: Professor Bob Fryer CBE, University of Southampton; Marge Ben Tovim, Assistant Principal, Liverpool Community College; Maureen Banbury, HMI; Jane Cowell, Vice-Principal, Warrington Collegiate Institute; Peter Shuker, Principal, Darlington College of Technology; Margaret Lally, Deputy Chief Executive, Refugee Council; Marcus Bell, Department for Education and Employment (Chair). The ACLF was managed for the DfEE by two organisations, the National Institute of Adult Continuing Education (NIACE) and the Basic Skills Agency (BSA). I suspected that Alan Wells of the BSA had nominated me and I was pleased to see that Bob Fryer was also on the panel. From the outset it was obvious that the sum available was modest when spread over four years.

The first meeting of the panel was over two days in early November in London when the members were briefed by the officials and set up procedures to invite organisations to tender projects suitable to meet the objectives of the Fund. The next meeting was just before Christmas and each member of the panel received a bumper bundle of papers from a wide variety of organisations whose total bids for the first year far exceeded the funds available for the four years. I spent a lot of time analysing each bid and drew up an order of priorities. When the members gathered together it was apparent that very few of the members had given the task the time it deserved. The officials had anticipated this and had prepared their own priority list that differed in many respects from mine. In the lengthy debates over the bids we quickly arrived at a short list although the total bids included on the short list were still well in excess of the available funds. Bob Fryer had also given the exercise a fair amount of time and in the debate he tended to support my proposals and at the end of the day compromises were reached that satisfied most of the members. For future meetings it was agreed that the officials would consider all bids and produce a first short list before the panel met thereby streamlining the task for the members.

My attempts to develop good relationships with the North Yorkshire high schools that had originally been suspicious of Darlington College had born fruit when I was invited to present awards to students at Bedale School. It was a pleasant evening and many of the parents talked to me of their children who were keen to study at the College. One parent turned out to be the RSM at Catterick Garrison. He pointed out that his daughter, who was already at the College, had to travel by public transport that took two hours to get to Darlington and a similarly long journey home in the evening. This was news to me as buses commissioned by the County Council transported many North Yorkshire students to the College but I had not realised that the journeys were so long. It gave me the idea that when the Catterick Centre opened we should consider allowing North Yorkshire full-time students to have up to two days at Catterick to reduce their travelling times.

I had been a strong advocate for both teleconferencing and videoconferencing and the former was becoming regularly used to save long journeys. Sadly, there seemed to be little enthusiasm for videoconferencing although it was widely used in other Common-wealth countries. NILTA had been involved in the European Unions 5th Framework and we used teleconferencing to crystallise our views on the final submission that Mary Barker had coordinated. The College's dedicated video-conferencing suites were being used for presentations to small groups and for staff meetings.

The FEFC had urged college corporations to have an annual public meeting so that local people could have an opportunity to hear the progress and plans of the college and to ask any questions of the Board members, including the principal. New College Durham was the first college to hold such a meeting in the Northern Region and I had accepted John Widdowson's invitation to attend as the Darlington Board had also decided to hold such a meeting. The Durham meeting was quite successful and provided a good opportunity for the college to promote itself within its catchment area. There was involvement of students in the proceedings that I thought was a particularly good idea and worth including in the Darlington event.

The following day was the first meeting of the Darlington Learning Partnership Portfolio group and I had decided to attend the meeting to observe its function before leaving the regular meetings to Sarah. The next two days were spent at Headlam Hall for the residential conference of the corporation and the next week was dominated by the three-day annual AoC Conference at Harrogate followed by a seminar for regional partnerships at the Sunderland AFC Stadium of Light.

The Higher Awards evening in December was honoured by the presence of Harold Evans, formerly editor of *The Northern Echo*, *Sunday Times* and a leading editor and director of various newspapers and magazines in the USA. I collected Harold from Teesside Airport and he spent some time at *The Northern Echo* offices before coming to the College to meet the staff and students of the journalism school. I was delighted that he was very complimentary of all the facilities that the journalism students enjoyed, as I had had several battles with some of the staff about moving from Trinity Road into the main building. The Awards Ceremony was a great success and this was followed by a dinner in the College restaurant where Harold was our principal guest.

Mid-December was quite interesting with a Darlington Partnership meeting at Northumbria Water offices at Broken Scar, a North Yorkshire Learning Network meeting at Grantley Hall, near Ripon, and the opening of Phase II of the Durham University Campus at the Stockton Riverside site. We also had the first Corporation Public Meeting where the chairman and I gave short presentations and then fielded quite a lot of questions from the audience. The general opinion was that it had been a successful evening.

There was another interesting evening at Catterick Garrison. Earlier in the year the College had been approached by the Prince's Trust to invite us to consider running one of their schemes for the young unemployed in Richmondshire. After some discussion with colleagues, I had raised this with the garrison commander and he had arrived at an arrangement for seconding a young officer of captain rank to act as the leader for one Prince's Trust team. This was a twelve-week personal development course, offering work experience, qualifications, practical skills, community projects and a residential week. Recruitment for the programme was targeted at unemployed people in the age range sixteen to twenty-four who were living in the Richmondshire area. Pat Gale had agreed to coordinate the college learning support for the course members and Gary Groom assisted in the arrangements for the presentations at the end of the programme. The first programme was deemed a great success for the course members, the young officer and the College. I was delighted to attend the presentation in December accompanied by the garrison commander and other senior officers. Also during that week there was a regional RSA visit to the new Virtual Reality Centre at Teesside University that I had organised with Janice Webster, who was leading the development within the university. It was a very well attended event and the demonstrations led to a lot of discussions later in the evening.

1999

My first engagement in the new year was to participate in an FEFC event on the EU Fifth Framework. The Fifth Framework was conceived to help solve problems and respond to major socio-economic challenges that the EU was facing. It focused on a number of objectives and areas combining technological, industrial, economic, social and cultural aspects. This approach was reinforced by the Key Actions concept. Key Actions dealt with concrete problems through multi-disciplinary approaches involving all interested parties. The FE sector bids under the Framework were obviously linked to training. I was particularly interested in the document 'Creating a user-friendly information society (IST)' that stated:

To realise the benefits of the information society for Europe both by accelerating its emergence and by ensuring that the needs of individuals and enterprises are met. The programme's inter-related research objectives focused on the technology developments of the information society and enabled the close articulation between research and policy needed for a coherent and inclusive information society.

There was another large intake of new staff to the College and I welcomed them and gave my presentation to the group. Part of the expansion was the need for more support staff to cover the increasing demands associated with the expanding new technologies, including a team that was producing on-line materials. I had set targets for each of the schools to produce materials for the programmers to place on the College intranet and in several areas the response was very encouraging. I had in mind the opening of the Catterick Centre later in the year and on-line learning was at the core of my plans for the new Centre. Angus Byrne was managing the programming team and he was fortunate that there was a team leader of outstanding ability to ensure good progress was made. I hosted a meeting of the Tees Valley principals at the College and attended an NCN Board meeting. I had handed over the chairmanship in 1998 to David Haulpt, having served for three years and had agreed to support him as deputy chairman. The following day I attended an NCFE Focus Group, which was held at York as NCFE was seeking to expand its remit as its Yorkshire equivalent, YHAFHE, had ceased to exist. After the meeting I caught a train to London and booked into the Kensington Palace Hotel, prior to a day at the BETT Exhibition. During the day I held a meeting with Owen Lynch, who I had met when we were members of NCET. Owen had been appointed as chief executive on the newly former BECTA (British Educational Communications and Technology Agency), after the departure of Margaret Bell.

I returned to a spate of local meetings, firstly with RM, that had drawn up a specification for the telematics requirements for the Catterick Centre that varied from my original list. I had been keen to include an 'iris recognition' security system but RM was not convinced that the technology was sufficiently robust at that time. I was disappointed, as I had seen the system demonstrated several years earlier at a visit to BT laboratories. However, RM had agreed that every workstation would have a videoconferencing capability as well as Internet access. Two sub-committees of the corporation and a meeting of the Darlington Partnership quickly followed this meeting.

I had a personal meeting with David Heaton, principal of the sixth form college, to try to find common ground in the competitive situation that had caused some friction in the past and we agreed to hold a joint meeting of senior managers at Walworth Castle in February. There was a farewell party for Geoff Crispin, deputy vice-chancellor at Teesside University and a member of the College Board. Geoff was taking up a similar post at Thames University and in time would become its vice-chancellor. I then had to return to the College to participate in a teleconference involving FEFC and NILTA regarding the EU Fifth Framework proposals. The following morning I attended the heads of schools' residential conference at Scotch Corner Hotel and gave them a PowerPoint presentation to summarise the national and regional developments and how they should be influencing the developments within the College. Later that week I had a meeting at the Royal County Hotel in Durham for a regional event to discuss 'Internet Strategy'. There had been much debate about regulating the content available to pupils and students on the Internet with strong support from a minority. I had taken the view that a college should determine its own rules and then monitor the use by students. I drove to York for a North Yorkshire Education Forum that was followed by a reception in Harrogate to celebrate the retirement of the North Yorkshire TEC chief executive, Roger Grasby.

It was back to the national scene for a meeting at FEFC's headquarters in Coventry to discuss the Higginson Report and to consider how the sector should take forward its recommendations. After the meeting I took a train to London and booked into the Grosvenor Hotel prior to the Charter Mark presentations the following day. Pat Gale had again done an excellent job to put the College submission together to ensure that we retained the Charter Mark accreditation. On my return I spent a full day in Middlesbrough, initially at a Tees Valley TEC meeting and then a meeting of the Tees Valley principals to discuss, amongst other issues, the Collaborative Fund.

The following day was spent in Newcastle with the morning at an industrial tribunal followed by a meeting of the regional AoC Committee. The morning was a new experience for me as one of the College staff had taken his grievance to an industrial tribunal and I attended the hearing with Simon Cassidy and the College solicitor. The claim had been ongoing since before my time at the College and the claimant was seeking compensation for industrial injuries sustained from working in poor health and safety conditions in the wood working workshops. As he had been employed in the construction industry for many years prior to teaching, Durham County Council had turned down his previous claims and, fortunately for the College, the tribunal also took the view that the College could not be held responsible. I had a full day in York commencing with a meeting of the NY Learning Network at Askham Bryan College followed by a NY Learning Partnership meeting at NY TEC where I met the new chief executive, David Harbourne.

During February there were two new initiatives. I set up a Project 21 Group to look at potential developments in the next century and the corporation decided to establish a regular development evening. I gave an open invitation to the staff to join the Project 21 Group and I was quite pleased with the turn out for the first meeting. The corporation development took the form of looking at specific issues that could be identified by Board members or by the executive team and the evening session would end with dinner in the College restaurant. The month ended with a regional AoC meeting at the College and a NiAA Board meeting in the Newcastle Guildhall, on the quayside.

After a fairly quiet February, March more than compensated with a rash of national, regional and local events. I hosting a meeting of the Tees Valley Informatics Partnership before a day in London for NILTA meetings and then the Basic Skills Agency Advisory two-day residential at the Cheltenham Park Hotel. The next week I had a meeting with Colonel Nick Gaskell from the garrison, who was also a member of the Corporation Board. The College was due for an FEFC inspection and Tony Shirley, a former engineering HMI, who was likely to lead the inspection team, came to discuss some of the issues and to advise how we should prepare for the inspection. Alan Dixon had organised the response at the last inspection but I decided to entrust Sarah Farley with the responsibility for the forthcoming event.

12 March was a special day with the College Awards Ceremony followed by the College Annual Lecture. I was pleased to have obtained the support of Brigadier Peter Pearson as our principal guest at the Awards Ceremony and Alan Wells delivered an excellent lecture to a well-filled hall in the evening.

Gary Groom's responsibilities included international activities and general promotion of the College. He was always looking for an activity that could generate good publicity for the College and in mid-March he launched the Christmas Card competition in the Dolphin Centre College Shop, another of his innovations, and I had agreed to be present to support the venture. It did raise quite a lot of interest amongst the general public and resulted in many ideas. Gary had also taken on the responsibility for the public areas of the Catterick Centre and had invited bids for furnishings in the reception and restaurant areas. I was very pleased when a local company, Curtis Office Furniture Ltd, submitted the successful bid for furniture. Owner Roger Curtis had given a professional presentation to the Corporation Sub-committee and the decision to select his bid was unanimous. Roger had produced prototypes of the items of furniture he was proposing and the style and elegance captured the imagination of the members. It was about this time that the Catterick catering, caretaking and cleaning contracts were also secured even though there was still a lot of building work to complete and I spent some time in photographing the structure as it developed.

After a short three-day Easter break in Harrogate with the family it was a trip to London to participate in an AoC/TEC review meeting as there was increasing criticism of the roll of TECs within the regions and the ongoing overlap of responsibilities with FEFC was not considered helpful to the sector. Some of the debate continued later in the week at a regional NILTA conference in Gateshead.

There was another pleasant evening to celebrate the end of the second Prince's Trust course at Catterick in the Dalesman Families' Club. The following week there was a NILTA/ FEILT event in London and after the meeting I had the pleasure of being invited to visit the BBC White City Television Centre in Wood Lane.

In December 1998, Secretary of State for Education and Employment, David Blunkett, announced that £74 million would be made available, over a three-year period, to fund improvements in information and learning technology within English further education and this initiative became known as the National Learning Network (NLN). The levels of funding for the first three years of the NLN initiative were £12 million, £20 million and £42 million, which was divided between colleges, JISC and BECTA, as managing agents of NLN. Initially, the FEILT (Further Education Information and Learning Technology) committee oversaw and approved expenditure before it became the responsibility of the National Learning Network Programme Board. NILTA worked in partnership with NLN that brought together ILT communities in both Further and Higher Education.

The Further Educational National Training Organisation (FENTO) was the NTO responsible for workforce development across the UK in the further education sector. As such, it was responsible for the collation of skills foresight information and for workforce development planning in the sector and to act as the national lead body for the development, quality assurance and promotion of national standards within further education that had been published in 1999. These standards reflected the targets set in the 1998 Green Paper *The Learning Age*, that all those teaching full-time or substantial part-time hours in colleges of further education should undertake a professional teaching qualification, as a means of improving standards of provision and student attainment in the sector. From 2001 all teacher training programmes and awards for the sector, provided by universities, colleges, and national awarding bodies, were required to be endorsed by FENTO as conforming to the standards. I was very pleased to see the move to a fully trained workforce in FE as this had been debated for many years and was long overdue.

There had been a long established link between the College and Siemens in Mulheim and I had declined on several previous occasions to make a visit to the town. However, I decided to fit in a visit to coincide with the College students return visit to Germany in late April. The departure day coincided with an AoC Fifth Framework meeting in London and after the meeting I flew into Dusseldorf airport and was met by two of my colleagues and one of the German team. They booked me into a local hotel and in the morning, at 0745, I visited Mulheim Vocational College and then the Siemens

Vocational School, which was part of Siemens Factory and operated within the German 'dual system'. I was then taken around the factory and at 2 p.m. joined the students and staff for lunch. I was particularly pleased to see how the Darlington students were working enthusiastically with their German counterparts on joint projects. There was time for a little local sightseeing before dinner with Arnil and Marget Jackel at their home. The following day was Saturday and the German staff had arranged excursions to Cologne and Dusseldorf and we had a most convivial day together. I had a little time on the Sunday morning to walk along the Ruhr River before departing for home via Cologne and Dusseldorf.

I had to complete all of the appraisals for the executive members as part of the College-wide scheme that Simon had introduced in the early days of incorporation. The original target was to have quarterly appraisals but the burden on the heads of schools with the most staff members had proved too great so that it was reduced to twice a year. The chairman was responsible for my appraisal and my salary was linked to a formula that Denis Gatfield had designed and I felt it had not sufficiently recognised my contribution to the development of the College, and despite pointing out that most of the principals in the region were on higher salaries he had remained conservative. When Alasdair took over as chairman he took a more liberal approach in interpreting the formula and my salary began to increase to more readily reflect my perceived value.

Through NILTA I had maintained good personal links with officers in the department and the FEFC, particularly those with an interest in the developing technologies. John Bushnell from the DfEE (Department for Education and Employment) had been on the NILTA Council as an observer for several years and I had persuaded his team leader to second him for part of his time to NILTA as a consultant. Keith Duckett from FEFC had responsibilities for supporting the infrastructure of colleges that included hardware, software and buildings. He also had been an active observer on the NILTA Council. I was therefore very pleased when the two of them asked to visit the Catterick site and I had the pleasure of showing them the buildings in early May. I had to get permission from the contractors to take visitors onto the site and into the buildings that were nearing completion. There was no doubt that John and Keith were as excited about the project as I was and expressed the hope that I would invite them to the opening of the Centre.

By this time we had settled on a name for the new facility. There had been a lot of discussion but eventually there was a consensus on the title 'Darlington College at Catterick'. It was a happy coincidence that the concept of a 'University for Industry' led to the creation by the Department of Ufi in 1998 to develop people's skills and work with employers to increase employees' capabilities. The organisation then set-up learndirect, which was to become a nationally recognised brand for learning. The availability of nationally developed and accredited on-line learning materials would therefore supplement the in-house materials that the College had developed to ensure more flexible learning opportunities at Catterick.

Whilst most of the FE Sector had tackled incorporation profes- sionally and had maintained the high standards of propriety set down in the Articles of Governance, some colleges had been abusing their powers and indulging in practices that many of us perceived to be bordering on the illegal. It appeared in most cases that the principal, often in association with senior colleagues, had been using the college resources for personal gain, with or without the knowledge of their corporation boards. There had been hints in the *Times Educational Supplement* of malpractice and the magazine *Private Eye* had targeted one or two high-profile senior FE people. The bubble really did burst on 21 May 1999 under a newspaper headline 'MP calls for inquiry into FEFC'. It was reported that Frank Field, Labour MP for Birkenhead and former social security minister for the current government, had written to Sir John Bourne, comptroller and auditor general at the National Audit Office (NAO), calling for an inquiry to investigate the Further Education Funding Council, amid concerns that it has been too slow to act on failing colleges. He wanted the NAO to investigate in particular the 'role of the FEFC in allowing Wirral Metropolitan College to accumulate 12 million pounds of debt'. The lecturers' union, NATFHE, had criticised the FEFC for sanctioning some of the disastrous management decisions through its North West regional committee. It also stated: 'Frank Field is demanding that the inquiry looks closely at what advice was given by the FEFC to the college when problems started to occur'. In response the FEFC defended its action over Wirral by stating:

In January 1999, the Council made a decision to ask the secretary of state to remove the then board of governors of the college from office and appoint a new board. It took this decision on the basis that the affairs of the college had been and were being mismanaged. Despite being given extensive support and advice, the then college board was unable to satisfy the Council that it could redeem the inadequacies of its financial control and planning, student number data and quality standards.

Whilst most college principals were already well aware of the Wirral problems, many of us felt that the problems at Halton College and Barnsley College were at least as bad, if not much worse.

The rest of May was as hectic as ever with more North Yorkshire meetings in York, a teleconference with Bath College, a meeting in London of the Adult & Community Learning Advisory Group, a Fifth Framework meeting and a Raising Standards in FE Conference, also in London. There were numerous local meetings and social activities linked to my position that I was expected to attend. It was therefore not surprising that the news of my mother's stroke at the end of the month and her death a week later came as quite a shock. The next two weeks were a blur with only vague memories of a visit from Tony Barren from British Columbia College in Vancouver and Monica Petermandl from WIFI in Vienna, a large private training company that Gary had identified as a partner in some of our EU bids.

Another important development came to fruition in June with the opening of the Advanced Manufacturing Centre. This was situated in the engineering workshops and replaced the Enterprise Centre, which had failed to achieve its objectives of job creation but had provided a useful base for some of our full-time students for various activities. The new Centre contained a range of state-of-the-art computer-aided machinery, thanks to grants received from the FEFC and the support of some of the manufacturers. Malcolm Price, who was head of school for all of the engineering programmes, had led the developments with his usual enthusiasm and his team of teaching staff and technicians had responded very well to his leadership. I had invited local MP Alan Milburn to perform the official Opening Ceremony on 11 June and the event was well supported by representatives from the local engineering companies as well as several members of the Corporation Board. A few days later, Alan Milburn was back in College for a regional conference entitled 'IT in 2000 and Beyond' and he was also supported by the Darlington Borough Council leader, John Williams.

At the weekend, Veronica and I attended the Catterick Garrison Open Day at Marne Barracks which included displays from all arms of the Army with a lot of military hardware on display. Unfortunately, the rain poured for most of the day and I recall chatting to the garrison commander and Richmondshire MP William Hague and his wife with our umbrellas dripping. The month ended with a group of College staff making a visit to Telford College following a visit from Telford staff to Darlington earlier in the year.

The Darlington Learning Network

My involvement nationally and regionally had assisted in the rapid development of the Darlington Learning Network. In the UK there has been a long tradition of segregating economic policy from educational policy. However, the 'information age' had already led to many developed countries placing learning at the heart of their economic strategies and there were signs that UK government thinking was moving in that direction. Prime Minister Tony Blair's assertion that 'education, education, education' were his three priorities and that participation in lifelong learning must rapidly increase, gave a strong lead to local partnerships to consider integrating learning developments into economic planning. National initiatives had included the National Grid for Learning, University for Industry (UfI) – 'learndirect' and the Information Society Initiative (ISI). In the northern region, the Prime Minister launched REEP, the Regional Electronic Economy Project in Newton Aycliffe in 1999. This initiative was developed by Northern Informatics as part of the Regional Information Society Initiative (RISI) and placed the region in a strong position in Europe to attract funding for further developments.

Within the Tees Valley, the JSU had supported the development of the Tees Valley Informatics Partnership (TVIP) that included membership on its Board from industry, local authorities, the Training & Enterprise Council, further and higher education and the media. Sector working groups provided an opportunity for organisations in the sub-region to participate in influencing developments. The activities of the cable company, NTL (formerly COMCAST), had ensured that most areas of Tees Valley would be able to take advantage of an infrastructure that would give fast access to the World Wide Web. In 1999 there were a number of sector-specific networks within the region. Discussions took place to create a regional infrastructure within a national and international framework. The six universities in the region were connected to JANET, which provided high bandwidth for research and development as well as local learning and administration. Twenty-five of the region's colleges had established the NCN in 1994. There were fifteen colleges in NCN that subscribed to the EU ADAPT project that developed sixteen modules of on-line learning materials for SMEs. There were seventy SMEs in the pilot phase and many more expressed an interest in joining when the product would generally available in June 2000. The National Grid for Learning (NGfL) was taken up by every local authority and many schools had good local networks. A regional initiative to create a Northern Grid for Learning had the support of all LEAs and the local library services benefited from national funding to establish their own network. Large companies, particularly the public utilities had their own private networks and some local authorities were developing similar structures.

In Darlington, all of the schools were part of NGfL and provided pupils with access to PCs and the Internet and training provision had been established for all teachers. Darlington College of Technology through NCN had a 2 Mb/s connection. Queen Elizabeth Sixth Form College was a member of the Northern Sixth Form Colleges Network and had a 0.125 Mb/s connection. Both institutions eventually became part of the enlarged post-sixteen infrastructure, funded by FEFC, later in the year that guaranteed a minimum connection of 2 Mb/s to all colleges. Darlington College of Technology provided a 2 Mb/s leased-line connection to its centres in Larchfield Street and Catterick Garrison and to Firthmoor Community Centre and Morton Park Business Centre.

Another initiative had been Ufi's decision to develop learning 'hubs' that would consist of a group of learndirect providers collaborating for a single Ufi contract. Tees Valley Ufi Hub was contracted to the University of Teesside Partnership (UTP) and the first development centre in Darlington would be at Firthmoor Community Centre from April 2000. Darlington College of Technology was a member of UTP and I was invited to chair the Ufi sub-group. The College was also involved in negotiations to manage two other Ufi sector hubs: the York & North Yorkshire Hub and the national 'Torch' Hub with the Army. The rapid development worldwide suggested that local communities needed to respond radically to ensure their citizens were not disadvantaged in the information society. The danger of 'an information elite' and 'an information poor' should not be acceptable, but that was already beginning to happen.

Lynn Howe called to see me in early July. Lynn had been an FEFC regional officer before being appointed principal of Redcar and Cleveland College. Unfortunately, she had a disagreement with the board of the college and she had resigned to take up a regional appointment with Ufi. Lynn knew of my involvement nationally with Ufi and my views of learndirect and its potential to enhance the 'ownership of learning' to the student. This briefing proved useful to me on the following day when there was a meeting of UTP in the morning and a meeting of the North Yorkshire Further Education Forum in the afternoon when consideration was being given to their respective bids for Ufi hubs. The following day I participated in an RSA visit to RAF Leeming that I had organised and we had a splendid day with good support from the Fellows in North Yorkshire and the NE Region. In July the Executive Committee, under the guidance of Sarah, carried out a self-assessment in preparation for the FEFC inspection.

NILTA published its Annual Report for 1998–99 that coincided with Mary Barker's first year as chief executive. Although I had handed over the chairmanship of NILTA to Fred McCrindle during the year I was expected to provide a chairman's statement to introduce the report. I was able to state that the Association had been successful in expanding its membership to embrace the majority of colleges in England plus additional associate members from the IT industries that had assisted in improved financial viability. Most of the NILTA eleven regions, including Scotland and Wales, had been active and the five national sub-committees had worked hard to raise the profile of ILT by providing exemplars of good practice across the sector. From its foundation ten years ago, the association had become a model of good practice involving practitioners from many colleges. The Annual Conference in October had been honoured by the presence of David Melville and I had been presented with a special award for 'excellence in IT' together with 'lifelong' membership.

Summer family holiday 1999

The family enjoyed a holiday in Canada. We flew to Toronto, booking in at the Royal York Hotel. We enjoyed a half-day city tour followed by a trip to the top of the CN Tower. Next day there was a coach trip to the Niagara Falls including visit to the Minolta Tower prior to boarding *The Maid of the Mist*. We travelled by train to Quebec with a short stop in Montreal. We booked into the Chateau Frontenac Hotel. We took a half-day city tour and Veronica and I had a stroll around the city area while Helen and Edward relaxed in the hotel. After two nights in Quebec we boarded a train to Montreal, booking into the Queen Elizabeth Hotel. Montreal was only a short stop with a half-day tour before our next VIA train journey to Ottawa. We did a coach tour in the afternoon. The next morning it was a cruise on the Ottawa River and visited the Eton Centre.

The following day we flew from Eastern Canada to the West, arriving in Vancouver to stay in the Stanley Suites in Stanley Park. We took the Skytrain into the Metro Shopping Centre and a walk around English Bay. The next day we had a trip to Whistler, travelling by boat to Squamish, a spectacular seaside mountain community located at the tip of Howe Sound. We enjoyed a short stay with a gentle walk before boarding a coach to Whistler. The trip allowed three hours in the town and we were left to organise our own programme. We returned to Vancouver by rail with good views of the British Columbia Coast Mountains and the ocean.

1999–2000

On our return, I spent most of that time in the College catching up with the accumulated correspondence and emails. With most staff on holiday I had few interruptions and managed to clear the backlog relatively quickly, leaving time to do some planning for the next year. In August I had a visit from the FEILT consultants who wished to get my views on networking. In the afternoon the Corporation Sub-committee for Catterick received presentations from the facility management contractors for the new Centre. The following week I met several new members of staff and carried out Mary Barker's appraisal as CEO of NILTA.

All of the executive team were back in College for the last week in August and I held a management meeting in Catterick at Howe Road where we had some temporary teaching accommodation. The meeting was followed by a visit to the Catterick Centre that was nearing completion so that it could be opened for business in September. All the team members were impressed with the high quality facilities. As we left the Catterick Project group, whose members were also delighted with the new Centre, arrived for their visit.

I travelled to Middlesbrough for an afternoon meeting of the Tees Valley principals at the College of Art and Design to catch up with their developments. The government was actively promoting the issue of lifelong learning partnerships and the next day was filled with regional meetings regarding that issue. A network of learning partnerships was set up across the country in early 1999 to promote a new culture of provider collaboration across sectors (schools, FE, work-based learning and adult and community learning) and to rationalise the plethora of existing local partnership arrangements covering post-sixteen learning. They were non-statutory, voluntary groupings of local learning providers (ranging from voluntary sector to FE/HEIs) and others such as local government, Connexions/ Careers Service, trade unions, employers and faith groups. I could claim that such partnerships were well established in Darlington and Richmondshire and the College was an active participant in all of them. In the morning I attended a meeting of the Regional Development Agency, One North East (ONE) in Washington and after lunch travelled to Newcastle for a similar meeting at Government Office North East (GONE).

As enrolment sessions commenced, I took the executive team to Walworth Castle for an away day to establish priorities for the next term and to ensure all internal and external targets would be achieved. Courtesy of the garrison commander, I had lunch with

William Hague, MP for Richmondshire, to bring him up to date with the College buildings and to consult him about a suitable person to officially open the new Centre. I was keen to get a member of the Royal Family and William and the Commander both supported the idea and advised me to contact the Lord Lieutenant of North Yorkshire, Lord Crathorne. I had a short telephone conversation with Lord Crathorne and arranged to meet him at Catterick at the garrison headquarters. This was a most cordial meeting with some friendly jockeying for which member of the Royal Family would be most appropriate. I had decided to try to get the Prince of Wales as he had several honorary colonel appointments and knew the garrison quite well. Lord Crathorne hedged his bets offering more junior royals but, with the backing of the commander, he agreed to try to secure the services of Prince Charles. In due time he informed me that Charles was willing to officiate but his diary was full until early summer of 2000. We were delighted to accept the offer.

The September meeting of the Basic Skills Agency Advisory Committee was significantly enhanced with the ceremony of receiving the UNESCO Literacy Prize '*International Reading Association Literacy Award*' for 'an initiative established in October 1993 to raise the standards of literacy among poor or less wealthy parents and their children and to extend the awareness of the importance of literacy and the role of family education.' Although this award was not directly related to the adult section of BSA, we were all delighted that the hard work of Alan Wells and his team had been properly recognised.

On 13th September the Catterick Centre opened for business and there was a gathering of the partners to celebrate the occasion with a glass of champagne. Mike Cox and his team had ensured that all of the facilities were fully functional and that by active recruitment over the last few weeks they had attracted a steady stream of customers. This confirmed that my dream of establishing a learning centre, where the learners were fully in control of their own learning, had at last been realised. All of the learning materials were available on-line and the Centre was open throughout the week to allow students to drop in whenever it suited them. There was no formal teaching and we had appointed staff to act as learner supporters, guiding the student to the most appropriate materials to help them achieve their learning objectives and to assist with the technology. All of the two hundred workstations were equipped with a facility to videoconference so that it was possible for a student at the Centre to book a v-c appointment with a specialist tutor in Darlington.

In addition, there were two large videoconferencing suites that could be used to enable staff to v-c with Darlington. One of the spin-offs was that two or three local entrepreneurs used the facilities to develop markets for products that they had developed. On the ground floor there was a Business Centre that was designed for small enterprises to use the range of state-of-the-art facilities to support their business. William Hague was one of the first people to take advantage of the facilities. So many people and organisations had supported the Catterick venture at national, regional and local level and I ensured them that they would all be invited to the official opening. Although the main object had been to establish a learning centre at Catterick, it had been decided early in the planning phase to include a child care centre aimed at supporting the young children of students and staff. The facilities were superb and it could support up to seventy pre-school children aged from six weeks and an after-school service for youngsters up to fourteen years. The facility proved very popular and the children were delightful, probably due to the excellent staff. I often popped into the Centre to raise my spirits when I was feeling pressurised!

The targets for the Catterick Centre had been established at the time of the initial submissions and we had aimed at attracting one thousand students in the first year of operation. With the planned long opening hours the staffing had to reflect the extended week with a core team of full-time staff and a larger contingent of part-time learner-support staff. This was based upon information received from the Catterick community that there would be a pool of well educated people who could be quickly trained to fill the posts. Parking space was planned for three hundred vehicles. We had sub-contracted the technical support to RM, who was also providing the computing equipment on a three-year renewal basis. There were three large open access areas, one on the ground floor and two occupying the entire top floor, contained over two hundred computers with videoconferencing and Internet access together with printers and scanners. There were also a number of laptop computers that could be made available to students who could not afford their own facilities and wished to work from home. The large reception area and restaurant were combined to provide a welcoming appearance to students and visitors and the Childcare Centre entrance was directly opposite the entrance to the Learning Centre.

The day following the Catterick opening I had a meeting to discuss Ufi and the Army. The Catterick Centre had already been designated a learndirect centre and a few students had taken an interest in following some of the programmes. The various garrison commanders had broadcast the Catterick initiative to the rest of the Army. They were very proud of the development and perhaps they had some reflected glory from being associated with it. It had not escaped the notice of the Army Education Centre that the Catterick model could be a prototype for other military centres. Our meeting looked at a variety of potential developments and one possibility that gained most support was to establish an Army Ufi Hub that would be in line with Ufi thinking. As the College was already working with the UTP to establish a Tees Valley Hub and similarly with the North Yorkshire colleges, this would be a logical development. However, military decisions of this sort were not taken lightly or quickly and it was agreed that the DETS (A) – Directorate of Educational and Training Services (Army) – would select a suitable person or persons to evaluate the proposal with a view to arriving at a decision by spring 2000.

In the previous year, I had been approached by the Army to write an article for its *Quest* magazine, which I submitted in February, and the following article appeared in the September edition:

Education is on the threshold of a revolution. Traditionally it was associated with childhood, and many people felt that there was no further need for formal study at the age of 16, after eleven years of compulsory education. Qualifications gained at school could carry you through life, because many jobs required little additional knowledge. But technology is changing all that.

Today's knowledge-based economy means that yesterday's qualifications are obsolete tomorrow. Most people now expect to have several occupations throughout their working lives and the consequences of multiple careers means that learning must be for life. Hence the government's enthusiasm for lifelong learning and the planned significant increase in spending on post-school education.

Distance learning is not new, however. Correspondence colleges have been in business for many years and the Open University has more enrolled students than any other university. However, most of the five million students in post-school education choose to attend formal classes at a local school, college or university.

The government has set demanding targets to expand the number of people who are studying for qualifications so that national learning targets can be achieved, and so that the knowledge gap between the UK and its main economic competitors is reduced. This challenge means that distance learning will become a major form of delivery, as learning providers try to overcome the barriers that prevent so many people from getting involved in study.

The big cultural change means that the student rather than the teacher will become the centre of the learning process. Learning must be available on demand at a time and place to suit the student. The technology that is making this vision a reality is the Internet. Again, the government has realised the importance of this innovation; it has created the National Grid for Learning in schools and has promised to establish the University for Industry (Ufi) next year. Most libraries, colleges and universities are already connected to the information highway and are busily developing materials for on-line learning.

Darlington College of Technology has been preparing for this revolution over the past five years and is due to open an innovative 'Telematics Centre' at Catterick Garrison this month. There will be no classrooms or formal teaching in this Centre but it will support learning for over 200 people on the premises by giving them direct access to the very latest in learning technologies. However, it is anticipated that a far larger group of people will wish to use the on-line learning materials from home, from work or from wherever they can access the necessary equipment.

The new distance learning will not be dependant on the postal service. Learning materials will be available 24 hours a day in electronic format and tutor support will be by email and by videoconferencing. Similarly, the new distance learning will not be restricted to specific printed materials but will encourage the learner to explore the Internet to discover the huge amount of high quality information available at the desktop.

The Ufi is a national initiative, which aims to provide training opportunities for those who have to balance their learning with work, caring and other domestic responsibilities. Initially people will be able to access training in Key Skills and Basic Skills, computer training, management and administration. However, it is envisaged that in the near future all vocational areas will be available, so that people can gain training in the skills they need to get the most out of their personal and working lives. The intention is to provide a range of locally based computer facilities that are easily accessible to a wide range of people, and Individual Learning Accounts (ILAs) will become available for people to start planning and saving for valuable training opportunities.

As an example, the new Telematic campus could ideally provide such a facility – easily accessible by car, bus and foot to the growing population of Catterick Garrison and it will be available for up to seven days per week. If you live locally you can just drop-in, surf the net, study for a civilian qualification or enjoy a coffee with friends while the children play and learn in the new purpose-built childcare centre. For those who live at a distance or have moved away and wish to continue to study on-line, the Centre will be open electronically 24 hours per day, 52 weeks of the year, regardless of where you live or serve.

A wide range of training and general interest modules will be available and you will to able to determine how long it will take you to achieve your learning goal. You will be assigned to a guidance advisor who will help you to plan your best training route. They will also provide you with career advice for future job opportunities, job search support and help in finding out how best to fund your training. Once you have established exactly what you want to do, you will meet your personal learning advisor who will offer you guidance on how to learn on-line.

They will show you how to use the Net, access search engines and get the most out of the wealth of information you will be able to access from the largest library in the world! If necessary you will also be able to book direct contact time with a specialist tutor who can also provide you with extra help or assist your understanding of the information and knowledge that you will acquire.

The biggest difference with this approach to learning is it takes account of what you already know and what you have already gained in a military context that can easily be converted into civilian qualifications. Families can also benefit by picking up new skills and updating previous skills and knowledge, so they too can rethink their lives in terms of new opportunities. The Telematics Centre is committed to the concept of lifelong learning and the value of family learning. The adjacent Childcare Centre can prepare all-day or weekend care for children and a range of childcare solutions will be available for anyone aged a few weeks to 14 years.

Who Pays? This will depend on your personal circumstances. In some cases learning programmes may be free or subsidised by the state, the military or other organisations. A local guidance advisor should be able to provide a wealth of useful information on how to get help if you need it. In many cases, local employers will subsidise or pay for training if they know it will improve the quality of business or competitiveness. Similarly the government recognises the value in training to helping people to get back into work and there are a number of schemes that can subsidise training for people who are out of work, lone parents or carers.

The increasing number of households that now have a PC almost as a part of the domestic furniture means that there is already widespread access to and use of on-line learning. Access to the Internet is now widely promoted for those who have a PC modem and telephone line. Experienced on-line learners will also have invested in a printer and scanner. There are several Internet Service Providers (ISPs) that will provide free access to he Internet. The only running costs, in most cases, are those of a local telephone call and the helpline subscription.

The web browser used to find all forms of information, is rapidly becoming a universal tool for the late 20th-century citizen. The realisation of this fact has led many educational organisations across the world to make their services and products available to anyone with a suitable browser. It is quite easy for a British student to sign up for courses offered by, say, Australian or American universities and colleges. The World Wide Web can provide interactive communication as well as audio, video and graphical information, so the education market is quickly becoming a global one.

Study and tutorial support are available at times that suit the student rather than those dictated by the provider. It is important to the future of education and training users and providers in the UK that our colleges are able to provide equal, if not better, IT-supported learning for regional, national and international markets. The traditional barriers to learning of distance, cost, location and time are being removed. Imaginative new technologies are ensuring that learning becomes more exciting and more easily accessible to those who have found traditional education unresponsive to their personal requirements.

CHAPTER 19

Into the 21st Century

WITH REGIONAL DEVELOPMENTS IN IT infrastructure gaining pace it was interesting to visit Monkseaton School at Whitley Bay for a meeting of the NiAA Board. The school had established itself as a leader in the secondary sector and the committee was given a conducted tour to view its developments. This was quickly followed by NCN Board, ADAPT Board and the TV Principals' IT Group reflecting the need to get all activities moving after the summer break. The UTP Board held an afternoon meeting in the elegant 'Judges' hotel, near Yarm, a venue that was too expensive for colleges but not for the university! The week ended with NILTA meetings in London and the AoC Annual Conference in the Connaught Rooms in Covent Garden. All the information stemming from these meetings had to be shared with the executive team and we held a three-day residential conference at the Cedar Court Hotel in Harrogate to get the team up to speed. I also held a meeting of all the staff to inform them of developments and the implications for the College.

There were two new initiatives in which I was invited to participate. The Foresight Programme aimed to improve the relative performance of UK science and engineering and its use by government and society. To achieve this, the Foresight Programme identified potential opportunities for the economy or society from new science and technologies, or considered how future science and technologies could address key future challenges for society. Foresight's method was to bring together key people, knowledge and ideas to look beyond normal planning horizons to identify potential opportunities from new science and technologies and actions to help realise those opportunities. The North East meeting was held in the Regional Technology Centre and there was an opportunity to listen to the programme team and to raise questions and provide local views on potential ideas. The other initiative was Curriculum 2000, which was a reform of the A-level examinations in the United Kingdom. It was introduced in September 2000 (with the first AS-level examinations held in summer 2001 and A2 examinations the following year). The focus was on moving towards a modular structure so that the units could be examined twice a year. I did not attend many of the local meetings as the College had only a modest interest in A-level subjects.

The NILTA Annual Conference was held at the Hanover International Hotel at Hinckley and it was to be my last conference as chairman, having held the office since its inception in 1989. At the NILTA AGM in December, Fred McCrindle had moved from vice chairman to take over as chairman and I was pleased to be able to relinquish the responsibilities. I was presented with a plaque showing that I had been honoured with lifelong membership of the Association. I was also flattered to be informed that there would be an annual 'Peter Shuker Award for a lifetime contribution to information and learning technology'.

David Melville, chief executive of FEFC, made a visit to the North East as part of his tour of the regions. Derwentside College hosted the well-attended meeting as David was quite popular with the principals and the event was regarded as a three-line whip by FEFC officers. With rumours that TECs and the FEFC were under threat by the labour government we had hoped to receive some inside information but, if David knew, he was not ready to reveal the likely outcome. Principals generally would not have been too sorry to see the end of TECs but FEFC was perceived as a highly professional organisation that worked hard for the sector. The prospect of a single body to replace the TECs and FEFC was not generally welcomed, as it seemed likely that it would result in a large unwieldy organisation. The cynical view was that such a body would be replaced within ten years. It is interesting to note that FEFC and HEFC had both stemmed from the 1992 Education Act but the government made no attempts to remove HEFC as, in my view, the HE sector had far more political influence through its national organisations than the FE sector had through its weaker institutional organisations.

Higher education had started to take a much greater interest in learndirect by 1999. Although Ufi stood for 'University for Industry' it had been the colleges and private sector providers that had been quick off the mark to explore the possibilities. HEFCE decided to make funds available to universities and colleges for part-time adult students who were University for Industry (Ufi) learners. Sir Brian Fender, Chief Executive of the HEFCE, said:

> We are delighted to be working with the Ufi to increase learning opportunities in higher education for individual learners and business-es. Through working in partnership, we will ensure that the Ufi's vision for promoting lifelong learning and widening access gets off to a good start within higher education. We are making funds available to support the equivalent of 2,500 full-time student places in 2000–01, but will be prepared to double that number should the demand from Ufi students wishing to study in the higher education sector next year justify it.

November was mainly taken up with local and regional meetings, including the corporation residential at the Redworth Hall Hotel and the AoC Annual Conference in Harrogate. I had two meetings with the North Yorkshire principals; the first one I hosted at the new Catterick Centre, as they were also keen to see the facilities. The Higher Awards Ceremony was again very successful with Chris-topher Payne, former Chief Constable of Cleveland, as our principal guest.

2000

The computer world held its breath on the last day of 1999 as warnings had been given that those IBM compatible computers that used the two-digit date stamp would crash as we moved into the new millennium. Angus Byrne had spent a lot of time over recent months having all of the college computers and equipment that had computers installed checked to try to anticipate any potential disasters for the college. Governments across the world had spent large sums of money in trying to do a similar job on national computers. Happily, the world did not stop at a minute past midnight on 1 January 2000 and the scaremongering proved to have been greatly exaggerated.

The year did not start too well for me as I was struck down with a bout of influenza, one of the rare occasions that I had been away from work in many years. I did recover in time to prepare for two new experiences, one challenging, the other quite pleasant. The first was a serious disciplinary hearing concerning the conduct of work placement officers. The hearing lasted two days with regional trade union officials representing the staff involved. The outcome was the dismissal of the team leader who had previously been regarded as a good member of the college staff. This was the first and only occasion I had to dismiss a member of staff in nineteen years as a principal and I felt very sad that it had been necessary. I had anticipated an appeal to the Corporation Board but it did not happen. The second College Public Meeting was on 25 January. Alasdair chaired the meeting, which attracted only a modest turnout of the general public despite a lot of effort by Gary in publicising the event. I gave a short presentation and responded to several questions from the audience. Most of comments were complimentary and Alasdair handled the odd awkward customer with his usual diplomatic skill.

A meeting of the Darlington Employers' Forum in February led to my appointment to a sub-committee to review the allowances and expenses of the Darlington councillors. The new responsibility involved setting the annual allowances for the leader of the Council together with those for the chairmen of committees and the opposition shadow chairmen. The first meeting of the sub-committee was the following week when we were presented with several proposals linked to allowances and expenses that were paid by other unitary authorities. I had anticipated that there would be some debate but most of the recommendations were simply endorsed.

A long meeting at Teesside University had preceded an evening meeting with the Tees Valley partnership trying to resolve the Ufi Hub responsibilities. The university was keen to take on the role but I had the support from the college principals for Darlington College to take the lead and this was agreed. This had the agreement of the vice-chancellor but some of his senior colleagues were not pleased.

I enjoyed the two-day Basic Skills Agency residential conference at Cheltenham with Princess Anne joining us in the evening. On Saturday, the Guild of Bricklayers held its National Council meeting at the College and I was pleased to welcome them as I had been granted honorary membership of the Guild several years earlier.

I hosted a Durham Principals' Group meeting and then dashed off to Eaglescliffe to give a presentation to the National Council of Women, a lively afternoon with quite a range of interesting questions. The following morning I was in Consett for the NCN Strategy Group before catching a train to Birmingham for the Annual FEFC

Conference where the principals were expecting news on the future funding of colleges with The Learning and Skills Act 2000 expected to be approved in July. This would see the demise of the FEFC and the TECs and herald the Learning and Skills Council (LSC) as the body for funding the sector. The next day I participated in a Governance Training Seminar at the Newbus Arms and I was pleased that several of the Darlington Board members made the effort to attend. To finish off a busy week there was a Northern Informatics Board at Doxford Park in the morning and the Annual College Lecture, in association with the RSA Northern Region in the evening. Bob Fryer was our guest speaker and his well-attended presentation was followed by a pleasant meal in the College restaurant. Later in the month I attended a DES/GONE conference at Ramside Hall Hotel when plans for the forthcoming changes in funding were debated.

In March I joined a One North East working party that was expected to produce a report on innovation in the region. It was the first of many meetings, usually held in Sunderland. The membership consisted of representatives of ONE, education, industry, local authority councils and business organisations. I was the token representative from FE whilst there were several people from universities on the apparent basis that universities were at the heart of innovation. However, the group soon established a good working relationship and there was broad agreement on virtually all of the negative factors that should be addressed in the region. That was a useful starting point for identifying innovations that could make a difference and help to rebuild an economy that had seen all its main industries collapse in a relatively short period of time. When the report was published the following year, there was a regional presentation at Sanyo in the Wynyard Business Park. Many organisations were present demonstrating new technologies and applications. The various speakers gave a very upbeat message that this initiative would create new industries and quality employment prospects for the region and I really felt that this report had been a good use of my time. Sadly, there was little progress in delivering the targets set in the report and within a year the initiative was overtaken by another ONE Report entitled 'Unlocking Our Potential – a regional economic strategy for the North East'.

With an FEFC inspection looming, I had agreed with Sarah that I would carry out a series of principal's inspections covering most areas of the College. This involved spot checks without previous notification, when I would spend up to half a day looking at facilities and talking to staff and students. As the demise of FEFC was imminent we had not been certain if we would be one of the last colleges to receive an FEFC inspection or whether our inspection would be handed over to Ofsted and ALI (Adult Learning Inspectorate) that would take over all inspections in 2001. I had attended an inspection briefing at Hartlepool College in March that had clarified the situation for the College inspection whilst giving the participants an insight into the new arrangements.

I had managed to fit in a regular commitment to the RSA regional committee and continued to organise at least one event each year. In March I worked with Peter Allatt to organise an educational videoconference with New Zealand. He had made contact with some RSA Fellows in Wellington and I had contacted Chris Tipple, the director of education for Northumberland and formerly the deputy director during my time in Leeds. I provided the VC suite at the College and about twenty Fellows and guests turned out to participate in the event that commenced with presentations from Chris and a New Zealand educationalist followed by an amiable discussion.

I had travelled to London to discuss the proposed Army Hub and to consider contractual arrangements between the Army and the College. The Army team was very keen to progress but warned me that their decision-making systems were rather slow and so we made plans for further meetings.

I had two meetings in London the following week, the first was a new group convened by JISC covering globalisation. I was the only FE person present with heavy representation from the 'elite' universities. It was an interesting meeting, with some of the dons having flights of fancy and afterwards I felt that it had been worthwhile and looked forward to a future meeting. However, it did not materialise as JISC decided that the outcome of the first meeting was sufficient for its needs. The AoC Seminar was much more down to earth and allowed the participants an opportunity to debate the pending changes to funding and inspection. As soon as I left the train at Darlington, I drove to Helmsley for a two-day residential of the North Yorkshire Learning Network at the Black Swan Hotel. Many of the issues that had been discussed in London were revisited with a local slant and some of the colleges were concerned at the potential impact the funding changes would have on them.

I started the following week with an executive strategy group meeting at the business centre at Morton Park. This was mainly to review progress against targets but also to ensure that the team was well prepared for the evening meeting with the corporation members who were having a benchmarking seminar. This entailed comparing the progress and performance of the college against national and regional averages so that any weaknesses could be identified and tackled. Happily, we convinced the members that the college was doing well in all key areas and they ended the meeting with a dinner in the College restaurant.

The 'skills agenda' was one of those cyclical statements that all governments trot out from time to time. Some fixed amount of money is made available and that is supposed to solve the problem. In a similar vein governments think that employers should invest more in training and updating their workforce but whenever there is a downturn it is usually the training budget that is first to be cut. My experience suggested that employers expected the government to cover the bulk of the cost of training and what they do themselves was usually very narrow and limited to their employees' immediate jobs with no thought for preparation for the future. It was therefore not surprising to me to be invited to attend a Skills Agenda conference in York with all the old arguments being rehearsed and the vested interests scrambling to make bids for extra resources. Coincidentally, on the same day the College was hosting the regional brickwork competitions and I was delighted when Darlington students won both the senior and junior competitions, which confirmed my opinion that the staff team led by Malcolm Jones was maintaining the high standards of previous years.

The following week was packed with appointments starting with an NCN Board meeting at Doxford Park. I had to leave the meeting to dash to Newcastle for a meeting of the ONE Innovation Steering Group before returning to Doxford Park to complete the NCN business. It was then by train to London, staying overnight at the

Great Northern Hotel so that I could have an early start for the two-day CGLI 6000 series Moderating Committee. I had been chairman of this committee since 1980 and I had expressed my reservations about the relevance of the dated curriculum that had not been seriously reviewed for over ten years. Entries had dropped steadily year by year and CGLI seemed reluctant to invest in a more appropriate syllabus to reflect the changes in building practices. The CGLI officers were sympathetic and agreed to raise the issue once again but they were not optimistic of a positive reaction.

I hosted a dinner for John Bushnell and Adrian Hall from the Department (DfEE), with Mary Barker and Sarah Farley joining us. John and Adrian had come to visit the Catterick Centre the following morning and I had pleasure in showing them how the facilities were being well used by the local residents. There was a large group of women, mainly wives of soldiers and officers, who were attending regularly and enjoying the freedom of being able to learn when it suited them. Some were taking advantage of the laptop loan scheme so that they could work from home and access their tutorials on-line. Additionally, the Army had identified a learning problem with some of their young recruits who were failing to attain the necessary minimum standards of numeracy and literacy. There was an agreement that the trainees could attend the Catterick Centre for two weeks, during which time our tutors had to get them up to the necessary standards. The staff used some on-line programmes that the students seemed to enjoy, together with personal guidance. The results were impressive with virtually every trainee reaching the required standards.

I had been pushing Gary to maintain our international links as it seemed to me that Catterick and his other responsibilities had been taking priority. He had responded by setting up three visits to our partner establishments in Slovakia, Poland and Austria. Gary and I departed from Teesside Airport, travelling to Kosice via Amsterdam and Prague. The Technical University of Kosice was our partner and the last time I had been to visit the second largest city in the country was with Graham Best several years earlier. The rector and senior staff gave us a warm welcome and I was impressed by the rapid progress that had been made in bringing the university up to western standards in a relatively short period. Our time was spent mainly between the Lifelong Learning team and the Informatics team.

We spent two days in Slovakia before flying to Vienna and we booked into the Konig von Ungarn Hotel in the centre of the city adjacent to St Stephen's Cathedral. Our Viennese partner was Wifi Wien, a large private training company servicing several industries and I was amazed at the range and quality of the resources that they controlled. We met the director and then travelled to a training facility that included a substantial 'model' hotel and restaurant where we were entertained to lunch. The catering students seemed to be experiencing the highest standards in food preparation and restaurant service. In the evening the staff took us into the countryside to a vineyard with an excellent restaurant and again we enjoyed a splendid dinner.

Our visit to Vienna was far too brief and next day we flew to Poznan via Warsaw. We were conveyed to the Poznan Hotel before meeting the rector of Poznan University of Technology. I had not been previously involved with the developments in Poland as Pat Gale had taken that responsibility. We agreed our programme for the following day before we were taken to a pleasant restaurant for dinner. We spent the following day in the university visiting the laboratories and workshops and meeting students and staff who all seemed very pleased to see us. This may have been due to the fact that I had offered a special prize for the most outstanding student to spend a week in Darlington and it had been quite a motivator for many of the students. In the evening we were taken to a classical concert in the university hall. The university staff members, who had been working with Gary and had visited Darlington on several occasions, took us on a tour of the city, including the war cemetery with thousands of graves from the Second World War. In the afternoon there was the prizegiving ceremony and I was invited to make a short presentation on the 'Darlington Prize'. The winner was a smart young man who was overwhelmed when his name was announced and he received warm congratulations from his colleagues. That was a fitting end to our European trip and we departed from Poznan the next morning (Sunday) flying into Teesside via Heathrow. This visit brought to an end my direct involvement with international partnerships that had commenced with the 'velvet revolution' in Eastern Europe around 1990. Although there was still some scepticism amongst Corporation Board members, I believed that the overall advantages of developing partnerships had brought benefits to many students as well as promoting the College through-out Europe. All of my travel costs and those of my colleagues had been covered by EU grants. The potential to develop full cost business with international partners who were interested in adopting some of our business practices never really materialised, despite the role that I gave to Les Baker. Les would regularly knock on my door with stories of deals in the offing but the contracts were never forthcoming and I could not be too surprised when international links was not a priority for my successor.

For the majority of my time at Darlington I had enjoyed a harmonious relationship with the Corporation Board but one issue had caused me some difficulty. It started at the end of Geoff Nichol's chairmanship and continued more vigorously under Denis Gatfield's three years in the chair. It concerned the role of vice-principal. Alan Dixon had been appointed in 1988 after Doug Boynton had departed to become principal of Telford College. Although Alan had not been my preferred choice for the job, he had been a conscientious and loyal member of my senior team. There had been long and, at times heated, debates about the issue during out of college meetings. It became apparent that they were not going to back down and that it could become an embarrassing debate at a full Board meeting. I had had private conversations with Alan, assuring him that I would not give in easily but that sooner or later the chairman would have his way. I urged Alan to become more vigorous in applying for principal's posts and he did respond and was short-listed on several occasions but he either withdrew or was not successful with his applications. My old friend Mike McAllister had been a guest on one of the interview panels and he had contacted Alan after the interview to make some positive suggestions on how he could overcome the reasons for his rejection. Sadly, this did not lead to a successful application. Eventually, I had to compromise and Alan was stripped of his title of vice-principal and reverted to an assistant principal on a salary that was protected but would remain static until the other members of the team caught up. Alan coped bravely with this indignity and in mid-April he came to see me with his resignation as he had been appointed as the North East regional director of the Association of Colleges. In the lead-up to Easter I completed all the staff appraisals of the executive and directors and gave a PowerPoint presentation to the full staff on the Friday morning. In the evening we had the Annual College Awards ceremony with David Kelly making the presentations.

The first week of the Easter break was a mixture of a family outing in London and a two-day working conference with the Army regarding the Army Ufi Hub. On the Monday, the family outings included a visit to the controversial Millennium Dome via a ferry ride and then a trip on the London Eye. Unfortunately, black clouds limited the visibility as we reached the highest point on the Eye but we still enjoyed the experience. Tuesday and Wednesday required my presence at the conference to support the other members of the executive team and by concentrating our minds we overcame the potential pitfalls that had been raised by the Army's representatives. If all of the proposals that we had agreed were to be implemented it would provide the College with a very useful income stream for many years and would help to offset some of the investment in the Catterick Centre.

Immediately after the Easter break I was pleased to host a visit from our partners from Vienna, only a month after visiting them. I also hosted a day at the Catterick Centre for the Tees Valley colleges that had expressed a wish to look at the innovations that were operating there.

In addition to the usual local and regional meetings there were two new commitments. The first was the Richmondshire Learning Partnership that had its initial meeting at Leyburn and secondly, I was invited to join the panel to select the 'Citizen of the Year' in the Town Hall. This was an interesting initiative by the Council and I was flattered to be invited to join the small panel that had to select a person from a shortlist.

I had hosted several business breakfast meetings over the years to promote the college and when Business Link approached me with a request to host one of their breakfast meetings I was pleased to oblige.

The government had introduced an 'Adult Learning Week' and Darlington Council, through the Learning Partnership, had sponsored the event in the town. The College always had candidates for the event and we had won various categories several times in recent years. The prize evening in 2000 was in the Arts Centre and again the College performed well in both the team and individual awards.

June was a special month for the College with the official opening of Darlington College at Catterick by HRH The Prince of Wales on 8 June. The weather was excellent and Prince Charles arrived with Lord Crathorne who introduced Alasdair, who in turn introduced the members of the corporation. I then took HRH to the Child Care Centre where he was really in his element, getting down on his knees to the level of the youngsters and talking to each one of them. We then proceeded to the Learning Centre where we had arranged some demonstrations of the learning being achieved by local people in an innovative setting. At the end of the visit I made a short presentation and HRH made some very complimentary remarks about the facilities. Two weeks later the new Centre was honoured by a visit from Rear Admiral Bland who was then at the Ministry of Defence and was interested in this new development. It was also in June that I made two visits to Chelsea Barracks to finalise the arrangement for the Army Ufi Hub. Chelsea had been selected as one of the first stations in the network that planned to embrace all British Army establishments worldwide.

Veronica and I were invited to the Open University Degree Ceremony in Newcastle. It was a pleasant day with Betty Boothroyd, the former Speaker of the House of Commons and the Chancellor of the OU presiding and entertaining the award winners and their families.

Since incorporation the College had installed software to support the administration of the institution. The lack of any national direction or even local agreement had meant that each college had to make its own decisions on which of the several available systems they should purchase. Initially, we had selected FEMIS that had been developed by the former FE Staff College in Blagdon. The initial demands on the colleges for statistical information came from FEFC and as a member of the Statistics Group I was in a privileged situation to influence the outcomes. As colleges became more sophisticated corporations, the demands on the MIS systems increased and Angus Byrne had a key responsibility to liaise with other members of the executive team and software providers to ensure that our systems did keep pace with the changes. The financial systems were probably the most complex and critical and Debbie took the lead in the purchase of a system from another supplier. By 2000 Simon Cassidy was demanding a better system for personnel management and it was agreed to put the new specification out to tender and eventually a suitable product was selected. Another area that was under review was estates management and the corporation had agreed that this should be put out to tender to add to the cleaning contract that had been outsourced for several years.

At the end of June there was a dining out for Alan Dixon; I entertained the Darlington heads to dinner in the College restaurant and Veronica and I were pleased to attend another Beating Retreat at the Garrison. Alan was not the only senior person leaving the College. Les Baker, who had held several senior posts including managing Quadrant and leading on some of the international projects, took early retirement. Similarly, Adrian Dent, Kevin Frame, Brian Hopkins and Libby Selman, who had all had senior curriculum roles, decided to retire. Mike Cox, who had been appointed to be responsible for the Catterick Centre was moving to a senior post with Chris Hughes' Further Education Development Agency. The retirees were taking advantage of an early retirement package that Simon had negotiated with a view to reducing the salary bill for the coming year. All of these senior staff members had made valuable contributions to the College, especially since the introduction of incorporation.

The first two weeks in July saw more interest in the Catterick Centre with the Richmondshire Partnership holding its meeting there and a North Yorkshire governors' training day took advantage of the resources. I decided to have an away day for the executive team to ensure appropriate coverage throughout the summer break period and to tidy up any outstanding issues.

The Remuneration Committee of the corporation met and I again found myself having to make the case for executive salaries. Alasdair was more sympathetic than the previous chairman and, with the departure of Alan Dixon without replacement it allowed the committee to be a bit more generous.

The Tees Valley FE principals had established a formal grouping, named FE Plus (FE+) with a full-time officer, Shaun Place. This initiative followed a similar move by the Tyneside colleges. The object was to raise the collective profile of the group with local authorities, local businesses and funding bodies. In 2000, the seven colleges had a combined budget of £62 million, employed almost

3,000 teaching and support staff and provided educational support for over 50,000 students, 13,000 from outside of the sub-region. We hoped that these statistics would raise the general ignorance of the press, public and the sub-regions key decision makers. Initially, there was a positive response to the grouping with some good publicity in the local newspapers and radio stations and this seemed to be sufficiently positive for the group to continue.

Summer holiday 17 July–8 August

Veronica and I were pleased to have Helen and Edward joining us again for a trip abroad, this time to the USA. We flew to Chicago and had time after arrival to walk along Michigan Drive and visit the History Museum and the Broadcast Museum, the latter mainly for Helen's interest. We also visited the Seares Building and Navy Pier.

We boarded the California Zephyr to Denver, arriving 150 minutes late, which at least meant breakfast was not too early. Denver is reputed to have three hundred days of sunshine in a year; the downside of the long, dry period is the risk of forest fires and there were fires raging in the state of Colorado during our stay. We visited the city to explore 16th Avenue Mall and the Cherry Creek Centre.

I picked up the pre-booked Buick Park Lane hire car and drove past Boulder and Estes Park before arriving at Laramie, Wyoming. We visited the Laramie's Wyoming Territorial Prison and explored the Snowy Mountains before travelling to Casper where we visited Fort Caspar Museum. We departed Casper and travelled to Shoshone and Thermopolis where the temperature reached 100°F. We stopped at the latter to visit the museum and thermal springs before continuing the journey through spectacular mountain countryside to arrive at Buffalo, having covered 260 miles in the day.

We headed north to Sheridan, then east through Bighorn Park, stopping at the visitor information points and the Shell Falls and Canyon in northeast Wyoming. We arrived at Cody, Wyoming, where Veronica and I were allocated one of the 'historic bedrooms' that seemed to us to be almost as primitive as in historic times with only air conditioning being added! Helen and Edward had been allocated a twin room that was comfortably modern and they were certainly not willing to do a swap. The hotel hosted a regular 'gun

378

fight'. All re-enactors created their own authentic costumes. We joined a large crowd of spectators and thoroughly enjoyed the gun fight that lasted some time and involved many of the spectators.

Next stop was Yellowstone Park, a fifty mile drive due east of Cody. We stopped regularly to view sulphur springs, waterfalls, canyons and geysers, including Old Faithful, which erupted on schedule and onto Teton National Park and eventually arriving at Idaho Falls. There were further stops at Pocatello to visit the Fort Museum, Ogden and Salt Lake City Airport where we were due to return the car and fly to Seattle for the last stage of our holiday.

We stayed at Seattle for the next seven nights. Our first three days were spent in exploring various parts of the city. On 5 August we had a pre-arranged meeting with Emil Sarkissian who had been working in the city since completing his studies at Darlington College and Teesside University. He took us in his car to Bellview on the outskirts of the city where we enjoyed a pleasant dinner together.

CHAPTER 20

Final Year

AT THE END OF AUGUST I attended the first meeting of the Review of UK Occupational Standards Committee in London. This was a government committee to which I had been appointed to represent the further education sector. There were representatives of the private training providers, examining bodies, TUC, LSC, QCA, together with members drawn from the various occupational standards groups. There were also a variety of observers and assessors from government departments. The committee chairman was John Hillier, head of personnel of Weetabix Limited. I attended many meetings over the next year with some interesting differences of views causing lengthy and at times heated debate. The report was eventually published at the end of 2001 and it seemed to be well received by John Healy, Minister for Adult Skills. Also at the end of the month I was pleased to host a visit from Prof. Rodica Tuduce and her daughter Rodicuta from Bucharest University in Romania.

With enrolments underway in September, I had a meeting with the Prince's Trust followed by a visit to Catterick by the regional directors of the Open University for Yorkshire and the North East. This meeting with the Open University directors led to proposals for Foundation Degrees for Army personnel.

In the evening there was a special meeting of the Corporation Board to consider the issues raised by the pending changes in the sector. As usual there was the flurry of meetings of the various committees that I attended. Derek Fraser invited me to the Riverside Stadium as his guest for the Middlesbrough v Macclesfield match whilst later in the month I entertained visitors from Hungary.

With so many new initiatives springing up and our FEFC inspection due in early 2001, I had plenty to report to the staff with my start of term briefing. I was able to report new business of £360,000 stemming from four Ufi contracts, an Army contract and a non-Schedule 2 grant. With regard to the inspection, I was able to report on the seven programmes that would be inspected together with the eight 'focussed items'. There was also a three-day executive residential at Walworth Castle to address the challenges and to try to identify potential problems and anticipate the considerable changes that would result from the introduction of the Learning and Skills Council.

Later in the week we had a visit from Lord Bryan Davies, the chairman of FEFC, who was touring the country to thank colleges for their support and to assure us that the new arrangements would be in the best interests of the FE sector. However, not many of us were convinced and I had my first thoughts about the timing of my retirement. I had enjoyed being a principal and being involved with so many local, regional and national bodies, but I was aware that the College would have to make several changes to accommodate the new funding and operational environment. I had promised Alasdair that I would remain as principal during his three years of office and that would have taken me to sixty-five when I would have had to retire under the current arrangements. I did not make my feelings known at the time but I continued to ponder my future and eventually presented Alasdair with my resignation letter to take effect from summer 2001. The timing was to allow the corporation ample time to advertise and appoint my successor and to provide time for a proper hand over of responsibilities. The post was advertised before the end of the year, with a view to shortlist applicants after the Christmas vacation and to interview candidates in February. News of my intentions spread quickly and I received a call from *The Northern Echo* for an interview.

On the Sunday I drove to Hinkley for the NILTA Annual Conference, my first after resigning as chairman and the first time that the Peter Shuker Award was made. It was presented to Keith Duckett of the FEFC for his major contribution to the sector to ensure that all colleges had access to the latest technologies. I returned to Darlington on Monday evening for a meeting of the executive team followed by a visit from the FEFC inspection team at mid-day. The highlights for the rest of a fairly quiet month were the Higher Award Ceremony, the TEC Annual Awards Ceremony at the Tall Trees at Yarm and the Darlington Partnership meeting with Graham Whitehead, the BT futurist, as our speaker.

November started with the last FEFC Annual Conference in Birmingham. Although FEFC had only been in existence for eight years, in my opinion it had been successful in enabling colleges to move from a heavy reliance on LEAs to successfully managing their own resources. Certainly some of the colleges had abused the trust that had been given to them but most corporation boards and their principals had acted in the best interests of their local populations and provided an improved educational service. Both Sir Bill Stubbs and David Melville had made positive contributions to the service and many of the FEFC officers had given good support to the colleges. I had taken the train to Birmingham and David Haulpt had offered to give me a lift back to the North East after the conference because trains were not travelling beyond York due to heavy rain. However, we ran into torrential rain as we approached Catterick where signs indicated that the road was closed because of flooding. There was a diversion through Catterick Village and we eventually arrived rather late at the Scotch Corner Hotel where Veronica had arranged to pick me up. Veronica had already been to the hotel where she had been informed that the road was closed so she had returned home. I rang her on the mobile and, after some gentle persuasion she drove out in the pouring rain to take me home. The following morning news headlines stated that North Yorkshire had experienced the worst flooding for four hundred years.

Later that day I had a meeting at Archer Street Sports Centre with Alan Dodd and Ian Stephenson to consider the Centre's future. I had been obliged to accept the Centre as a package with Larchfield Street at incorporation but it had not been commercially or educationally viable and I was keen to part with it. Alan was aware that developers were interested in constructing a retail centre in that general area and that there could be an opportunity to dispose of the Centre. David Melville followed up the FEFC Conference with a visit to the regions and I attended the North East morning event with the other principals in Sunderland. After the meeting I travelled up to Newcastle to attend the One North East Strategy Board meeting.

I attended an away-day event for the Darlington College managers. This event did not happen as often as I would have wished but this gathering, held at the new Catterick Centre, provided an opportunity to direct the attention of the team to my views on the way that FE had to develop and to ensure that each member was geared up to the FEFC inspection. For most of the managers this was their first experience of the new centre and they all seemed to be very impressed with the environment and the facilities. One of the spin-offs from the day was the action taken by the school of management to support on-line learning management programmes with the option for students to book a videoconference meeting with a specialist tutor in Darlington and I was pleased to see that this offer was taken up by several students. The Corporation Board also decided to hold its two-day residential at Catterick, although we had to use Blackwell Grange for the overnight arrangements. Even though many of the Board members had attended the official opening of the Centre, they had not seen it operating normally and this again was useful in being able to visually demonstrate the different learning environment.

Other activities in November included the first AGM of the Richmondshire Partnership and the three-day AoC Conference in Harrogate. That was to be my last AoC Conference but I did enjoy the gathering and I was pleased to see my old friend from Huddersfield, Paul Grundy, representing his principal from Aylesbury College. It was during that week that we welcomed the director and some of his senior staff from the Austrian training college in Vienna and I spent some time with them, including a pleasant dinner in Richmond. That evening coincided with the national Children in Need campaign by the BBC and the BBC North East coverage included presenter Wendy Gibson reporting from Richmond Castle. So our visitors had the unexpected pleasure of seeing some spectacular activities by local people and Darlington College students who were raising money for the good cause.

The Adult Community and Learning Fund group met at Sheffield to review earlier decisions and to finalise grants for the following year. Several of the original approved projects had not started or had been delayed so that we needed to decide whether the under-spent money could be reallocated to those projects or to exclude them. As with previous meetings there were some heated discussions as vested interests sometimes became apparent but Bob Fryer usually managed to persuade members to arrive at sensible decisions.

I joined the Tees Valley principals at a dining-out dinner at the Tontine Hotel for Alan Clifford who had been a principal in Middlesbrough for many years and a person for whom I had the greatest respect. The following week I met with Geoff Pennington and four of his LEA colleagues to discuss the forthcoming changes within the sector and some of those issues were also discussed the following evening at the Corporation Board meeting. There was a Tees Valley Principals' away day at the Newbus Arms Hotel with the development of FE being a key item on the agenda. There had been changes within the group with John Hogg at Middlesbrough to replace Alan Clifford. With the pending merger between Middlesbrough College and Longlands College, Stewart Ingleson at Longlands had simplified the situation by successfully applying for the principal's post at Preston, leaving John Hogg as the front-runner for the new college. Margaret Armstrong at Stockton and Billingham had survived a lot of criticism about her plans to close the Billingham campus and to build a new college on the riverside close to the Durham University campus. Tony Sutcliffe at Hartlepool still had a leading local councillor as his chairman of governors when most of us had brought in people from industry and commerce. Dave Wilshaw at Cleveland College of Art and Design always seemed far more relaxed than the rest of us and cherished his healthy quantity of higher education work to bolster his budget. He had fought off a take-over bid by the university at the time of incorporation and had very little competition for his specialist areas.

My presentation to the staff contained a lot of statistics about the progress of the College and the FE sector since incorporation. The national information had been gathered from FEFC conferences and TEC sources and I hoped that by sharing this information with all of the staff that they would appreciate how well the college had performed in comparison to the sector as a whole and the improvements in performance that were a credit to all of them. The key points were as follows:

> Promise of new funds to pilot Educational Maintenance Allowances (EMA); Increase in Access Funds, Learner Support funds, Childcare, Standards fund and Individual Learning Accounts (ILA); new provision for fourteen to sixteen year olds.

I was able to demonstrate that the Average Level of Funding (ALF) for the College had returned to £17 per unit after three years at well below that level and that the convergence of funding would be achieved in the following year. This had taken much longer than

FEFC had stated in 1993 and as Darlington had started at the lowest end of the spectrum I felt that we had been seriously disadvantaged for eight years. For example, in 1994/5 Darlington was receiving £6 million less than a similar sized college at the higher end of the spectrum and our FEFC budget had remained at just over £8 million throughout those years whilst increasing our units by over thirty per cent. It was only thanks to the hard work of many of the staff members to attract funding from a variety of other sources that we had managed to balance the books and avoid the problems experienced by some colleges that had fallen into debt.

Thanks to improvements in our MIS software, Angus had produced statistics to show the home base of our students. Fifty-two per cent came from Darlington and Tees Valley and forty-eight per cent came from North Yorkshire and County Durham. We also knew that of the 5,390 Darlington-based FE students, 4,147 attended Darlington College, with 935 attending QE Sixth Form College.

2001

Sarah and I met the FEFC inspectors on their arrival on the first Monday and showed them the rooms that we had set aside for the team members. The room contained all of the substantial body of statistical evidence that had been requested in advance together with copies of timetables for all of the vocational areas to be inspected. We had agreed the days that the inspectors needed to see the chairman and other members of the corporation as well as a visit to the Catterick Centre. When all of the inspectors had assembled, I gave them a PowerPoint presentation of my perceptions of the College, including our self-assessment of the strengths and weaknesses, and then withdrew to my office to await any requests. Sarah had masterminded all of the details we had identified to meet the inspectors requirements over the week.

Pat Gale had initiated the Student Council that met on a monthly basis and members had shown a clear commitment and enthusiasm for the College, both during inspection and at the Annual Public Meeting when fourteen students acted as ambassadors for the College.

The inspection was expected to end on Friday with confidential verbal feedback to the chairman and me. My formal meeting with the lead inspector was on Tuesday when I was grilled over management structures and operational methods. I had a healthy respect for the inspectors but few, if any, had personal experience of being a principal and chief executive so that their views had to be based on comparisons between colleges. On the Wednesday I met with the inspection auditors who were looking at the financial management of the College. Fortunately, Debbie had been handling our finances expertly since incorporation and, although I was very much involved in the initial allocation of resources for each financial year, I knew that Debbie would maintain overall control of expenditure. The College had never been in deficit since the transfer from the LEA despite the very tight budget allocation from the FEFC.

On Thursday morning I had the misfortune to encounter black ice on leaving home and collided with a lamppost that caused damage amounting to repair costs of £2,700. Although I was shaken up by the experience, I managed to get into College to be available to the inspectors. On Friday afternoon the inspection ended and two inspectors, Sue Middlehurst and Dave Pattison, came to see me. I had known Dave for many years as he had been a student of mine at Huddersfield and had hosted a NILTA meeting in Edinburgh when he was head of construction there. Most of the comments were very favourable and I was told that the team inspection leader would meet the chairman and me the following week to see the draft report. The speed of the process was unusual but with the demise of the FEFC inspection team the system had to be speedy. I received a copy of the draft report on the following Friday morning and Alasdair and I had time to peruse it before the meeting with the inspector in the afternoon. The draft report was quite pleasing but, although we had not achieved any Grade 1's (scale 1 to 5), we had avoided any 4 and 5s that would have required a re-inspection. The management and corporate areas were both awarded Grade 2, and I know that Alasdair was disappointed not to receive a Grade 1. There was fulsome praise for Sarah as the College coordinator and the excellence of many of the sessions that had been observed. There was also a complimentary reference to Catterick.

The appointment procedure for college principal moved forward with the short-listing on 18 January and I had seen the list of eighteen applicants, which included five principals, eight deputies or vice principals, together with Sarah Farley and Simon Casssidy as internal candidates. I knew five of the external candidates who were from colleges within the region. Sarah and Simon had asked me if I would provide a supporting reference and I was able to agree but I did warn Simon that I thought he had little chance. I passed my comments on the applicants to Alasdair but that was my only involvement in the process. In due time the corporation appointments panel short-listed five or six of the candidates that included Sarah and only one of the principals.

Professor David Melville, Chief Executive of the FEFC, presented the Annual Lecture in February. The event was held in collaboration with the Northern Regional committee of the RSA. This was followed by the Annual Awards ceremony with Olivia Grant, former chairman of the Durham TEC, as our guest and speaker. I was pleased that Edward had been selected for a prize in the computing section and Veronica and I beamed with delight when he went onto the stage to receive his award.

The following week there was a three-day inspection of our Ufi provision and the verbal feedback at the end of the period was very complimentary. However, I felt that the knowledge of the application of information technology to support learning of the inspection team was not strong. I had also noted this lack of first hand experience was evident in the FEFC team doing the full inspection.

Another week on and the short-listed candidates assembled for the three-day interview process. In the morning I gave a presentation that clearly spelt out the strengths of the College and made some observations on areas for improvement. This was followed by lunch and an afternoon escorted tour of the College buildings in Darlington and Catterick. In the evening the candidates were joined by members of the corporation for dinner. The following day was devoted to interviewing the candidates, which resulted in three candidates, including Sarah, being selected for the final interviews on day three. I joined the three candidates for dinner when they had a final opportunity to raise any questions. After the interviews the following morning, the corporation formally appointed Sarah as my successor. I was very pleased for Sarah but I did wonder if the Board members had imitated the practice in several colleges in playing it safe with an internal appointment, particularly when one considered the experience of most of the other candidates. The other members of the executive team were quick to congratulate Sarah but I felt sure that several of them had reservations about working for a former colleague who had at times been quite critical of them.

I gave a PowerPoint presentation to the staff meeting in which I showed that enrolments in the last academic year had reached 20,469 with an income of almost £20 million. Retention rates for the year were similar to the previous year at eighty-seven per cent against the national benchmark of seventy-nine per cent, whilst achievement rates had risen to sixty-nine per cent against the national benchmark of sixty-seven per cent. The College had gained the RoSPA Gold Award for safety to add to our Charter Mark and Investor in People awards.

During the following weekend there was a tragedy for one of our teaching staff. Ray Lea was an experienced and enthusiastic caver and he regularly led teams down potholes in the surrounding area. That weekend he was in the Yorkshire Dales when he was trapped below ground by flash floods and he lost his life. There was a lot of press coverage and it was revealed that Ray had developed an excellent website all about local potholes. Ray Lea's funeral was at Holy Trinity Church and his wife had asked me to say a few words about his contribution to the College and I was pleased to speak briefly about a good colleague who had been popular with his students.

On the Tuesday I had an interesting meeting with Neil Mason from Marconi regarding a proposed project in South Africa that they intended to sponsor. Ruth Gee, who was now employed by the British Council, had suggested to Marconi that I might be interested in being involved, especially as I would be retiring later in the year. Of course, I expressed an interest and Neil agreed to send me information of the outline project.

The following morning there was a meeting of the NY Lifelong Learning Partnership at Boroughbridge and one of the members was the principal who had been unsuccessful in his application for my job. He seemed to have recovered from the interview ordeal but I felt sure that he was unhappy about the outcome. It was back to College for a meeting of the Corporation Search Committee that was charged with the task of identifying potential board members for vacancies or potential vacancies. A meeting of the Corporation Board immediately followed this meeting and Sarah had been invited to attend to receive the congratulations of the members.

The next two days were out of College with a trip to London for the Basic Skills Agency Advisory Committee, an AoC regional meeting in Newcastle College and a Durham IT meeting in Spennymoor. I also had a visit from David Melville who was visiting some of the colleges. David's contract with FEFC would soon be ending and he had secured the post of vice chancellor of Middlesex University.

At the beginning of March there was another meeting of the Occupational Standards group in London. At short notice I was informed the trains were not running north of Doncaster, so I had the dilemma of not attending the meeting or driving fast to Doncaster to catch a train. I chose the latter and arrived at Doncaster station to find that the car parks were already full and I eventually parked about half a mile from the station. With time running out, I dashed to the station and just caught the train as it was about to leave the platform. It took me quite a while to recover and I have little memory of what happened at the meeting! This was just one example of train delays or cancellations over the many years I travelled from the north to London, but to be fair the bulk of the trains did run and mainly on time. My regular train was the 0730 from Darlington that had only one stop at York and was scheduled to arrive at Kings Cross at 0945, a big improvement on the sleeper that I had to take when living in Skelton.

The construction of the Catterick College did not slow down the accommodation developments in Darlington. There was a rolling programme for the upgrading of the building and acoustic doors had been fitted for the performing arts programmes. The project would cater for all forms of music performance and recording and included a main performance area, control room, vocal booth, plus two rehearsal rooms. This project was significant because it had involved full collaboration between the school of construction and the estates section that had rarely worked together. FEFC had responded positively to the College's request for funding to construct an Early Years Learning Centre at the rear of the Cleveland Avenue site to replace the modest resources in the former caretaker's house and to bring it into line with the Catterick facilities. The Centre opened later in the year.

The College opened its new Travel Agency that was located within the main entrance of the Cleveland Avenue site. It had the professional support of Mr Derek Wills of Derek Wills Travel Limited of Stokesley. The agency served two purposes: firstly, to provide valuable work placement for students attending leisure and tourism programmes and secondly, to offer travel advice and bookings to the College and its customers. Adjacent to the Travel Agency was a new Student Advice Centre staffed by Diane Muckle, my former secretary who had become a key member of the student services team. The overall effect of these two initiatives was to enhance the appearance of the main entrance and create a lot of interest from students and visitors.

About this time I had a visit from Richard Auty and one of his colleagues from Darlington Borough Council to discuss some of the issues that had arisen at the Darlington Partnership meeting and to get my views on the plans that were being developed for the future of the town. The following week I had a visit from a newly appointed officer of the Council, Paul Wildsmith, Director of Corporate Services, who visited me for a useful discussion.

Between appointments I was conducting the appraisals of my senior colleagues that enabled frank discussion to take place on both sides. Several of the team were clearly worried by Sarah's appointment and expressed concerns about their ability to work with her. I tried to give reassurance, but I was privately aware that Sarah did not have the highest regard for at least two of the team.

I visited the Open Day at Morton Park where our management and business studies programmes had expanded under the direction of Kevin Frame and his team. There was a meeting of the NCN executive group where I started to hand over my responsibilities to other members. In the evening, with the TEC structure coming to an end, there was a final Tees Valley TEC dinner at the Thistle Hotel in Middlesbrough. Some of the TEC officers had been offered jobs within the local LSC structure whilst others had decided to look for alternative employment. Two weeks later North Yorkshire TEC held its final event at the National Railway Museum in York, a rather more exciting venue than the Middlesbrough hotel.

NILTA had enjoyed a long and friendly relationship with BT and Mary Barker had arranged for the March meeting of the NILTA Council to be at Martlesham in Essex, where BT's Adastral Park was the location of its main research facilities. Because of this remote location for most of the Council members, it was agreed that we would stay in a hotel near Ipswich and this gave us some time to relax and catch up with developments within the sector. In the morning we travelled the short distance into Adastral Park where BT colleagues met us. They had arranged for us to visit some of the demonstration areas where we could see the latest application of the various technologies that would probably be on the market in the near future. The following Council meeting was a bit of an anticlimax after the excitement of the visit.

There were two North Yorkshire meetings during the month, one at Catterick for the principals and one at York College for the FE Forum. The annual trip to London for the CGLI Moderating Committee was in early April and I stayed two nights at the Grosvenor Thistle Hotel in Victoria as the Occupational Standards Committee was held the day after the CGLI meetings. After a busy post new year period, it was a relief to have a break for Easter where we had a family lunch at the Rosedene Hotel in Sunderland with all the Shuker family together. We then travelled to Warwick for a short three-day break, staying at the Honley Court Hotel at Kenilworth.

On the first Monday after the break, it was the annual Tate Vin evening, always one of the highlights of the year when head of school Peter Bell and his team provided an opportunity for their students to display their skills before a critical audience of judges and guests. The meal was excellent and the service impeccable but I felt a little sadness, as this was to be the last Tate Vin for me. The following evening the Corporation Board had a meeting at Morton Park so that they could have an opportunity of observing the work that we were doing there.

On 1 May I gave a presentation in the garrison headquarters to a group of Army officers who had been urged to attend by the garrison commander. The College already had in place an expanding portfolio of courses that were on offer at Catterick and the 6,000 enrolments in the first two years of operation had exceeded all expectations. The contract to support young recruits who had literacy and numeracy problems had seen a considerable number of trainees attending the two weeks of intensive learning and almost all had reached the required standard to allow them to continue with their military training. We had also been working with the Army Education Corps centres to avoid any confrontation and to ensure that they referred people to the College. I believed that the garrison commander felt that many of the officers on the garrison were ignorant of the facilities that were available for military personnel through the Army Ufi Hub that would enable them to continue their studies to wherever they were posted. The session seemed to go well and I hoped it would become a regular briefing as the turnover of officers was considerable. It was back to Catterick the following day to welcome the adjutant general to the Centre as the commander was keen to ensure that high ranking visitors were aware of all developments that would enhance the facilities in the garrison.

In addition to bodies such as NILTA, AoC and FEDA that organised conferences, there were also private training companies that offered programmes targeted at the FE sector. Network Training was one such company and they had approached me to give a presentation in London in May. I had made some discreet enquiries to see if I would be causing some upset but it appeared that other colleagues had been involved in earlier events. I therefore accepted the invitation and found that there was quite a large group of people and I did know several of them. It was a pleasant event and the novelty to me was getting paid for a presentation that I would normally have given without charge.

The following week Ruth Gee and Peter McKitterick-Smith of Marconi came to visit me and to observe the developments at Catterick. I was due to fly with them to South Africa the following week and they wished to discuss strategies to impress the South African government that the UK could help them to upgrade their FE service. We were aware that the UK was not the only country that had been invited to give a presentation and Ruth was keen that I led the UK presentation and Peter had agreed after seeing the impressive set-up at Catterick. I had been sent a copy of a large document that analysed the current FE situation in South Africa and it was clear that the only colleges offering a quality educational experience were those that had been solely for the white population.

The vast majority of the colleges were for the black community and they were of a poor standard.

I flew from Teesside to Heathrow to meet the other members of the UK team and we were shown to our business class seats for the flight to Johannesburg. It was a ten and a half hour flight and we arrived early on Tuesday morning and transferred to our hotel at Sandford. The rest of the morning was spent in meetings with British Council and Marconi staff who were based in South Africa and they were most helpful in alerting us to the political and educational system in the country. In the afternoon we visited Troy College and that confirmed my fears that the colleges were poorly equipped in terms of the buildings and resources for learning. The following morning, I went with Peter to the Marconi offices to set up my PowerPoint presentation so that all the team were aware of the agreed approach. The South African team knew that a team from India would be making the first presentation and that I would be expected to follow. They were not sure if any other country had turned up. Marconi's involvement, as well as supporting the project in principal, was to fund a pilot project of up to £2 million if the bid was successful. British Council was covering transport and accommodation costs.

The conference commenced with lunch where I met with the full team from British Council and Marconi. Eight presentations were scheduled for the afternoon and I was on last. This caused me a little concern, but at least I would be able to see all of the other presentations and, hopefully, identify any serious competition. The Indian presentation was well received but it seemed to me to offer only learning software on CDs without any overall strategy. My presentation seemed to go down well and I received more questions than any of the other presentations and that was followed up by a group of local teachers and educationalists that wanted to discuss my proposals after the presentation. We had dinner in the Conference Centre and I met the South African deputy president who was representing the government. The following day was made up of seminars and four discussion groups and I attended one of the discussion groups. The conference ended at lunch and the Marconi South African staff took me for a trip to Pretoria for a bit of relaxation before our night flight to the UK. There was much

393

optimism in the group and Ruth Gee was convinced that the UK bid was now the favourite.

I returned to the College to find that NATFHE had called a national strike and that the local branch was picketing the College. I felt a bit disappointed, as the College had implemented all of the national agreements on pay and conditions of service recommended by the AoC. The picket line was in place on Tuesday morning, the day that I was expecting a visit from South African educationalists from the Free State. Fortunately, they arrived ten minutes after the pickets had withdrawn at mid-day. I took the visitors to Catterick after they had looked around the main site and they then travelled to the Walworth Castle Hotel for the night.

I attended a meeting of the TV Lifelong Learning Partnership in Middlesbrough before returning to College to catch up with all the outstanding matters of the last week and to leave instructions with colleagues as I was taking a family holiday the next day. Helen had just successfully completed her journalism degree at Central Lancashire University and Veronica and I had given her a choice of a short holiday venue and she had chosen New York. We flew from Teesside to Heathrow and then to Newark airport in New York. We spent a full day exploring the city on foot before attending the Broadway musical *Beauty and the Beast*. There was a day trip to Ellis Island taking in the Statue of Liberty and on our return we went to Wall Street and Harlem. 28 May was Memorial Day and we visited the Empire State Building and the World Trade Centre, both buildings offering spectacular views across the city. There was time to have a stroll in Central Park and a bit of shopping before returning back to the UK.

With my time rapidly running out I had to ensure that Sarah was as well briefed as possible so that when the Army invited me to Tidworth Camp in Salisbury, I asked Sarah to accompany me. In early June we travelled to Salisbury by train via London and booked into a local hotel. In the morning we visited Salisbury College, meeting the principal and vice-principal and assuring them that our contract with the Army would have little effect on their business locally. We then travelled to Uphaven to meet Colonel Tim Moore and Brigadier Purves, the Army education key people, and we formally signed the Ufi Hub contract that would allow all UK Army centres around the world to log into the Catterick on-line facilities.

I was convinced that this would guarantee a regular income to the College for the foreseeable future.

The next week I was invited to the Catterick College crèche for a farewell party for the centre manager, Helen. I attended my final meetings of the Higher Education Business Partnership at Teesside University, the Richmondshire Partnership Executive at Catterick and the FE plus group at the College of Art and Design. The following week Alasdair and I had lunch with two new Corporation members, Gerry Osbourne and Kevin Richards and gave them a quick visit to the new nursery at the rear of the College.

I attended a conference at the St Peter's Campus of Sunderland University followed by dinner at the Stadium of Light football ground. In mid-month I had my last meeting of the AoC regional committee at Derwentside College before returning to Darlington to see the College Performing Arts students giving their interpretation of *Odysseus* at the Arts Centre. The following day Veronica and I attended the Open University Degree Awards ceremony at Newcastle Civic Centre.

In June there was the final meeting of the Occupational Standards Committee in London and the following evening Veronica and I attended a Beating Retreat followed by a splendid dinner in the Officers' Mess. The next Monday I attended my last NCN executive meeting, followed by three days' leave for family business that included a trip to Ealing Cathedral with Veronica and her mother to participate in the celebration for Father Tutto who had officiated at our wedding.

I was not the only member of staff retiring. Malcolm Price, head of school of engineering, had also decided to leave after spending his entire teaching career at the College. I joined in the celebrations for his retirement at a party held in his honour. On the Friday evening we had a senior staff dinner that gave me the opportunity of thanking my colleagues for their support and to wish them all ongoing success. By the beginning of July, most of the students had left but there was still a steady stream of regional, local and internal meetings to keep me occupied. An afternoon and evening at Catterick for the NY Learning Network and the Richmondshire Partnership gave me the opportunity to thank the members for their support in the developments at Catterick. The art and design students put on an excellent fashion show and on the Thursday I was pleased and surprised to receive a visit from Mary Barker and John Bushnell. John had previously been seconded from the department to NILTA and since he had retired he was working part-time for the Association.

In the evening Veronica persuaded me to go to the College for a meal. When we walked into the restaurant I was overwhelmed to see a vast sea of familiar faces from my past and present. Jack Place and David Anderson had travelled from Leeds and Eric Tuxworth, Mike Guggenheim, Jim Pratt and Eric Twigg, former Huddersfield colleagues, had travelled from West Yorkshire. Robin Bullough had travelled from Cumbria and Alan Wells and his female colleague Jaz had travelled from London. Canon Bob Spence, former priest at St Augustine's Church and a founder member of the chaplaincy that I set up in my early days was also present. One person who I certainly did not expect to see was John Ransford, former chief executive of North Yorkshire County Council and now holding a very senior post in London. He had given me considerable support in establishing the College in North Yorkshire as well as the Catterick Centre. NILTA was well represented with Malcolm Himsworth, Ernie Haidon and John Bushnell. Mary Barker had not been able to stay as she had a family commitment. I was pleased to see a number of my principal colleagues. The executive team was there, together with Alasdair and local contacts such as Derek Wills. It was a wonderful evening and when I thought things were drawing to a close, we were ushered into the quadrangle to be entertained by The Newcastle Pipe and Drums Band. Bryan Robinson, a promising younger member of staff, was the conductor and after the marching stopped the band played several pieces before Bryan announced that he had written a special piece for me. The band played the piece and I very moved when Bryan presented me with a plaque with the music on it. It was a great end to a memorable evening and I had no doubt that Gary Groom had been responsible for all of the considerable effort to pull the whole event together.

On Friday there was the traditional end of year staff lunch when I usually presented awards to staff that had been chosen for their good contributions to the college and for me to wish retiring staff good health and happiness for their future. I did my usual presentations but things were a little different with colleagues making presentations to me for a change. The engineering staff had designed and manufactured a chess set and the carpentry and joinery staff had constructed the chessboard. As I had admired similar gifts that had been made for distinguished visitors to the College, my colleagues rightly assumed that I would be pleased to receive a similar gift. I was also flattered to receive a large framed photograph of the Angel of the North that now hangs in the lounge in my home.

On the Monday there were still meetings to attend as well as completing my appraisal of senior colleagues. Helen's graduation was on Tuesday and Veronica and I were delighted to attend the ceremony in Preston. I had to dash back after the ceremony for my final Corporation Board meeting. On Wednesday I held my final executive committee meeting that gave me an opportunity of thanking the team again for their support and commitment, particularly since incorporation. I felt they had all been very loyal to me even though I was aware of certain frictions between some of them. Debbie had been a stalwart throughout, ensuring that our finances were in a sound state and gaining the respect of all of the college staff. Simon had the difficult task of introducing new conditions of service and balancing the needs of the institution and the expectations of the staff. Angus had led the introduction of new technology with a great deal of flair and could claim much credit for the set up at Catterick and the expansion within the main building. Pat had maintained a lower profile than the others but had established excellent student services and had led on several initiatives that had brought credit to the College. Gary had raised the profile of the College in the local community by inspirational promotional campaigns and materials as well as taking a key role in the Catterick environment and supporting my international aspirations. Sarah had been pivotal in the successes of the main function of the College, the curriculum development and leading the various teaching teams tirelessly to achieve higher standards. Although Alan Dixon had moved on, he had been with me since my arrival at the College in 1988 and he had always been a loyal, hard-working colleague. I hosted a meeting of the Darlington Partnership to round off the week.

Veronica and I travelled to Huddersfield on 13 July to participate in a 'Farewell to Holly Bank' event in the old teaching block. The university had decided that it no longer needed the Holly Bank site and had sold it to a housing developer. We booked into the Cedar Court Hotel before going to Holly Bank to meet many old friends. It was a nostalgic affair and it marked the end of fifty-four special years of FE teacher training, even though there would be facilities at Queensgate. The evening finished with a spectacular fireworks display.

The Corporation Board organised a Retirement Dinner for me at Headlam Hall Hotel on 18 July and every member of the Board was present, together with Veronica and my executive team. It was a delightful evening with all three of the chairman that I have worked with during the period of incorporation from 1992.

I concluded my final address to my friends and colleagues as follows:

> Friends, I am coming to the end of forty-eight years of continuous employment, thirty-eight in FE, twenty-eight years in senior management including nineteen as a principal. For the last twenty-nine years I have had the support of Veronica who has had to sacrifice her career to enable me to fulfil mine. It is time to go gracefully and find some quality time together.
>
> Thank you for a wonderful evening. To my old friends thank you so much for joining me today. To my local colleagues and friends, it has been a pleasure and privilege to work in Darlington – thank you for you support. I wish you continuing success and will view progress from the sidelines with interest.

With most of the college staff on leave, the College was quiet and I started the task of sorting out the accumulated documents in my office. There were still a few meetings to attend including my last NCN Board and the Durham ICT Group. Dela Smith invited me to present awards at Beaumont Hill School on 20 July and this was perhaps symbolic as Dela had been the first head teacher to contact me on my arrival at the College. By the end of the month I was just about ready to depart but an unexpected invitation to Veronica and me to visit the nursery to join their 'Teddy Bears Picnic' was a happy way to finally retire after thirty-eight memorable years in further education.

CHAPTER 21

Post Retirement

M Y FORMER PA, Gaynor Dobie, had invited Veronica and I to attend her wedding on 5 August with an opportunity to meet her husband-to-be at a small event at Bishop Auckland Golf Club on 3 August. David Fries was a Canadian who Gaynor had met during her time in Bermuda and it was a pleasure to meet him and some of his Canadian family, as well as Gaynor's family.

The Darlington head teachers had presented me with a Garmin eTrek personal navigator as a retirement gift and this was a good excuse to embark on several walks in North Yorkshire and the Durham to test it out.

Helen had successfully graduated from Central Lancashire University and had been applying for radio journalism jobs. She had been invited for interview at a radio station in Wrexham, so Veronica and I accompanied her, staying overnight at the Cheshire Cat Hotel. Helen was offered the job and that resulted in several more trips to the Wrexham area to assist in finding suitable accommodation and it was eventually decided to purchase a new Barratt two-bedroomed property in Wrexham. Helen went off to Preston for a weekend with some of her university friends and Veronica and I booked into the Maenan Abbey Hotel at Llanrwst where we had our special dinner during our HF duties at Colwyn Bay in 1971. The hotel was not as grand as we remembered but it was a pleasant apart from the arrival of an extremely noisy rugby team on Saturday evening.

In October, I performed my last official duty by presenting the awards at Wensleydale School in Leyburn where Veronica accompanied me and we had a very pleasant evening with the staff, pupils and parents of the school. I was still active in NILTA and travelled down to London for a Council meeting. There were two additional NILTA commitments during the month; firstly, a meeting of the International Committee and then the Annual Conference that was held in Blackpool for the second time. As on the previous occasion the attendance was very good, despite the poor rail service to Blackpool on a Sunday.

Veronica and I enjoyed a week in Belgium, travelling by Eurostar to Brussels for three nights before travelling on to Bruges for four nights. It was an enjoyable break and the first holiday we had taken together without the family for many years.

Retirement had given me an opportunity to consider my involvement with the RSA. During my earlier years on the North East Regional Committee I had attended most of the committee meetings and had organised at least one event or lecture most years. However, I had not attended many of the other events or had aspired to take a major role on the committee. Marshal Meek had been chairman of the Regional Committee for most of my early years but RSA HQ had determined that regional chairmen should not serve indefinitely and had decided on a structure where a Fellow would serve one year as deputy chairman, followed by two years as chairman and then a further year as deputy chairman. At the regional AGM in September, I had agreed to be elected deputy chairman for 2001–2002, with a commitment to be the chairman from 2002 to 2004. This would be a critical period, as the RSA would celebrate its 250th anniversary in 2004. I had persuaded Sarah to become a Fellow several years earlier and she had agreed to join the regional committee in 2001. However, she did not appear to enjoy the meetings and resigned from the committee at the end of the year.

With my chairmanship starting the following year I was keen to introduce some innovations. The primary one was to issue a programme card to all Fellows in the region so that they had ample warning of forthcoming events. The existing system depended on letters from RSA HQ being sent directly to Fellows about three to four weeks before the event. Some Fellows had opted to receive the information by email but at least half of the North East Fellows did not have the technology at that time. I was surprised when there was opposition to my proposal until I agreed to do all the work.

Regional chairmen and officers were occasionally invited to RSA HQ in John Adam Street, London to discuss issues with the national chairman and officers. Chairman Peter Allatt asked me to go with him to John Adam Street as a substitute for the regional treasurer. It was my first visit to John Adam Street even though I had been a

Fellow for about nineteen years. It is a splendid building with excellent facilities for lectures, meetings and research. Although the relationship between the regions and head office was often cool, the meeting with officers was cordial and we seemed to make some progress with the suggestions from the regions. The national plans for the 250th anniversary were being discussed and regions were urged to organise their own celebrations in addition to the national programme.

Northern Informatics was coming to an end because of a lack of national and local funding. Chris Drew organised a farewell dinner in Jesmond for the Council members, officers and partners. Veronica and I booked into the Jesmond Hotel so that we could enjoy an evening and reflect on the valuable contribution that NiAA had made in raising the profile of information technology in the region.

2002

Just before Christmas I had received a confidential communication from 10 Downing Street informing me that the Prime Minister was minded to recommend to the Queen that I receive the honour of Officer of the Order of the British Empire (OBE) in the New Year's Honours List. I was expected to reply confirming or not my willingness to accept the honour, which I duly did. This meant that I had to keep the news confidential until 1 January 2002 when a full list of the awards would be published. As Veronica had seen the envelope with 10 Downing Street on it, I could hardly avoid letting her into the secret, but that was the extent of my little indiscretion.

The South African project was still active and the British Council had asked me to organise a programme for a group of South African educationalists that would be visiting the UK in mid-January. I travelled to Coventry to meet with the Marconi team to get an update on the progress of the project and to brief them on my plans for the visit. The South Africans arrived the following day and I gave a presentation on further education in the UK and shared the programme for the next five days.

We had been allocated a comfortable coach to travel to the various centres and on 29 January we travelled to the North East to visit Darlington College and the Catterick Centre. As my presentation in Johannesburg had used Catterick as a model for the South African proposed solution, I was able to demonstrate the practicalities of the proposed project. We spent the night at the Walworth Castle Hotel and I felt confident that the visit had started well.

On the next day we travelled to Nottinghamshire to visit Newark and Sherwood College where my NILTA colleague, John Gray, was principal. John had also incorporated many of the innovations by using the information technology that was then available. He spent the entire visit with the South Africans and gave an excellent presentation on his views on how further education should develop. The following day took us to Shropshire for a visit to Telford College where my former vice-principal, Doug Boynton, was principal. Like John, Doug devoted his time to the visit and also gave a lively presentation. The coach then took us to London for an overnight stay before a day at Marconi's offices for meetings with various people with e-learning experiences. I bade farewell to the visitors the following morning and felt pleased with their enthusiasm and appreciation of their experiences in the UK.

At that time the South African project seemed to be progressing quite well but Marconi was experiencing financial problems and its support for the project was significantly reduced. Also, the British Council had appointed Ruth Gee to their Hong Kong office and that meant my main link with the Council was lost. Therefore it soon became clear that there was little prospect of my direct involvement in the project in South Africa. I had been appointed to the steering committee for the project but the meetings took place in Johannesburg without any of the UK-based members. I continued to maintain contact with Sindy Mafanga, who had been appointed as the Project Manager and with Don Henning, who was Marconi's (South Africa) nominee to the project. I received a progress report from Don in March 2003 setting out the positive outcomes as follows:

Curriculum – The Curriculum Design has been completed for the first phase.

Learning Programmers – Various learning programmers have been evaluated, selections have been made, some materials obtained and these are currently being incorporated in the learning platform. (See LMS.)

Learning Management System (LMS) – Contracts have been signed with Potchefstroom University and their locally developed LMS, 'Varsite', is being used and modified for the requirements of the project.

Training and Transfer of Skills – A number of training sessions for about 25 people have been held with regard to the use of the LMS and the learning programmes. (These have been funded from Marconi funds as well as from the ISETT SETA funding. The latter has made R1mil (about £100,000) available to the project.)

The Project Manager, together with a number of other relevant players had recently completed a further study tour to the UK funded by the British Council. (R200 000.00 (about £200,000) had been made available by them.)

Dedicated Center – Approvals for modifications to the Troyeville buildings are still being awaited but internal refurbishment has already begun. A room to house the present available equipment and staff is expected to be ready by the end of this week. All costs for this are borne by the Gauteng Education Department.

Satellite Centers – Development at these (except for some staff training) is on hold until such time as the Dedicated Center is operational

Staffing – A Center Manager has been appointed and funded by the Joint Education Trust Fund – this is in line with the Gauteng Department of Education's intention to use the Dedicated Center as one of their Schools of Focused Learning. (This is an initiative that will be launched in February and involves six 'Schools of Focused Learning' in different fields – one of them being ICT Education.)

Equipment and Communication Links – Servers and five workstations have been set up temporarily at the MCSA building and these have been used for training purposes and initial development of the LMS. (This equipment was purchased from the ISETT SETA funding because of the request to curtail the Marconi spend for a period – the SETA funding is intended strictly for manpower development and not really for equipment but this move enabled us to continue with our programme.) This equipment had been moved to Troyeville since January

Recruitment of Learners – A recruitment and selection framework has been conceptualised and will be set in motion as soon as the Dedicated Centre is able to operate.

Marketing and Publicity – The project was exhibited at an FET Convention in October and another exhibition is planned as part of the launch of the 'Schools for Focused Learning' in February. The launch will be funded by the Gauteng Department of Education and will provide another opportunity to profile Marconi.

Sindy's contract as the project director came to an end in 2005 after three years. She sent me a copy of her final report that reflected her disappointment that all of the objectives had not been achieved but it seemed to me that significant progress had been made in establishing the 'Hub' at Troyeville and one centre at Ellis Park.

Sindy's lengthy report included the following statement that I thought summed up the key outcomes:

> Phase 1 of the Troyeville structural refurbishment had been completed and officially handed over to the Gauteng Department of Education (GDE). Phase 2 for Troyeville would involve the sourcing, installation and commissioning of IT hardware and peripherals and GDE has recently made a further allocation of R1 million available.
>
> The Ellis Park campus of the Central Johannesburg College (CJC), which was an approved satellite centre for the project, was specially modified, refurbished and equipped for the deployment of technology. It was set up for initial trials and concept proving in parallel with Phase 1. The Centre had forty networked computers running off a single server which hold all the course programs, internet simulation, student registration details and administrative packages. Enrolment of learners began in September 2003.

As well as my involvement with the South African project, I was approached by the Department for Education and Skills (DES) to act as an advisor to an E-learning Task Force set up by Secretary of State, Estelle Morris. The chairman was Steve Morrison, chief executive of Granada plc, and the other members of the Task Force included Lorna Cocking, Bob Fryer, Steve Molyneux, Maggie Semple, Janice Shiner, Ruth Silver, John Taylor, Ed Morgan, Beejal Patel and Sonia Damle. I had known Bob Fryer, Ruth Silver and John Taylor for many years and although I recognised their abilities it did make me wonder why they had been selected and by whom. Gary McKenzie was the DES officer who acted as secretary to the Task Force and he was my contact with the project and would provide any information that I may require. The DES framework contained some of the following information:

POST 16 e-LEARNING STRATEGY TASK FORCE:
FRAMEWORK

The Post 16 e-Learning Strategy Task Force, announced by Estelle Morris on 31st January, will explore how e-learning can enhance and improve learning opportunities for young people in colleges and for lifelong learners.

Specific topics for consideration by the Task Force will include:
  (i) ways of increasing participation through use of e-learning;
  (ii) the potential for a personalised e-learning curriculum;
  (iii) flexible access and delivery to reflect individual choices and diverse patterns of learning;
  (iv) progression routes to further study and lifelong learning;
  (v) skills and attainment;
  (vi) the potential for work-based learning;
  (vii) training and development for tutors.

The Task Force will explore the impact that e-learning can have on participation rates in FE/lifelong learning and how it can support the raising of educational standards.

The framework for this investment is the e-learning strategic aims, which will:
  (i) create an accessible infrastructure which makes ICT universally available to learners;
  (ii) make ICT integral to all our learning processes and stimulate the development and acceptance of new ways of learning;
  (iii) create, implement and support a dynamic framework for ICT skills and a corresponding framework for teachers.

In this context, what we want the Task Force to look at:
  – What e-learning is already available?
  – Where is it making a difference and is there potential for future development in these areas?
  – What are the opportunities for further e-learning initiatives?
  – What are the barriers?
  – How can the profile of e-learning be raised?

The first meeting of the Task Group took place on 6 March at Granada Headquarters, the London Television Centre, where the chairman had his office. After the introductions, Ann Limb (now chief executive of Ufi) gave a useful presentation that included workforce development, online assessment, diagnostics and social inclusion. After lunch, Ed Morgan, a senior researcher, gave a presentation on 'A Critical e-Learner' and this was followed by the initial views of the members of the Task Force.

The chairman wrote to several organisations, including NILTA, to seek views and ideas of what is good about the current e-learning provision and where there may be shortfalls and how they resolved them; as well as to ask for the organisation's agreement to request recent material from the organisation that could help shape the Group's thinking.

Estelle Morris had requested a rapid response from the Task Group and meetings of the group had been set out with a view to report to her by mid-May. However, when you select a group of people with key responsibilities within their own organisations, there will inevitably be times when some members will not be able to attend. This problem was immediately felt when the next meeting at the end of March had to be postponed because of the chairman's absence. Over the period allocated the Group was never complete with some key figures only appearing once or twice. I produced a weekly report for the chairman and DFES that included different aspects. There was a request to research work-based learning and I spent a good deal of my time in that area. I also looked at e-assessment and was advised by Gary to contact Ann Wright (formerly of Sunderland University and Ufi, who was now leading a small team in the DFES) to identify any on-going work in the department. I had a meeting with Ann that revealed that there were many similar ongoing studies (possibly fifty!) already in existence that had been established by different interests within DFES. I found this quite incredible and a dreadful waste of public money but I was assured from other DFES offices that this was not unusual. However, I carried out my own research within the sector and its examination boards and personally benefited from the evidence that I collected.

The Task Group met with the Secretary of State on 13 May at the Belfry Hotel near Sutton Coldfield. This was the famous golf course and our meeting coincided with a major tournament. I was quite annoyed to be left out of the direct meeting with Estelle Morris, as only Task Group members were included in the briefing and dinner.

The final recommendation of the Task Group were:

1. By 2010 everyone should have access to ICT as a basic skill as an entitlement. The ICT entitlement should include an e-learning skills component.

2. Expand the concept of Curriculum On-line for Schools into Post-sixteen learning. College On-line should be supported by an implementation programme. The first step should be a feasibility study, completed by March 2003. Government should explore ways to stimulate the development of appropriate course material as part of the study. The Feasibility Study must include a mapping of content to identify gaps in provision. The phased introduction of College Online should begin in September 2003, with the initial focus placed upon the access available to the fourteen to nineteen age group, whatever their learning environment, and the linkage between Curriculum Online and College Online. The early implementation should ensure that the systems are compatible.

3. Undertake a fundamental review of the funding of adult learning to consider the central role that e-learning can have in increasing work based learning. Working with partners to identify existing models using e-learning to increase in the workplace. We recommend that the new funding initiatives are specifically targeted to boost the use of College Online as a workplace tool. SMEs should be supported and offered incentives to engage in relevant, appropriate occupational online learners. Investors in People UK should explore embedding access to e-learning opportunities in the standard as part of their new strategy to engage SMEs.

4. Funding to be provided, in the first instance, to enable an additional 5000 mentors to be available by April 2003 to support tutors on and off line in the areas of greatest need. Existing ICT tutor mentor programmes and support networks should be brought together into a single National Tutor Mentoring Programme, centred around a database and forum of resources at mentornet.org.uk which may be accessed on demand by tutors and ICT champions.

5. Government supports a single return to work support and guidance route map, 'Which Way?'

The anticipated strategy that was expected to emerge from the Task Group report did not appear. Whilst I was disappointed, I was not surprised, as the Secretary of State had not impressed me, as she seemed to have little genuine enthusiasm for this area of education.

Nor was I surprised when she resigned a few months later, stating that 'she did not feel up to the job'.

On 1 May Veronica and I, accompanied by Edward, took the train to London to book into the Victoria Thistle Hotel prior to my investiture at Buckingham Palace on the following day. Helen joined us, having travelled from Wrexham. I had booked a limousine to transport us in the morning to the Palace and to remain with us all day until we had to be back at the railway station. The weather was fine and we arrived at the entrance to the palace to be quickly ushered through the gates and into a courtyard where we were escorted into the Palace. I was taken to one of the staterooms where all of the people to be invested were gathering. Usually about 120 people are invited to each investiture and each one can invite up to three guests. The families and friends were taken off to another location whilst we were eventually briefed on how to approach and address the monarch. As 2002 was the Golden Jubilee Year, the Queen did not do many investitures and the Prince of Wales was to act at my investiture. At the appointed time we were lined up in order of seniority of appointment with knights going first and OBEs somewhere in the middle.

At the start of the ceremony, Prince Charles, escorted by the Lord Steward, entered the Ballroom of Buckingham Palace attended by two Gurkha orderly officers. On duty on the dais were five members of The Queen's Body Guard of the Yeomen of the Guard. After the National Anthem had been played, The Lord Steward stood to the right of HRH and announced the names of each recipient and the achievement for which he or she was being decorated. In the queue, I was next to another educationalist from Northern Ireland and we chatted to pass the time. Eventually, I reached the front of the queue where my name was checked by one of the Gentlemen Ushers to ensure that I was in the correct sequence. I had to wait until my name was read out and started to move as the reason for the award was announced. On reaching HRH, you turn and give a court bow before stepping forward to receive the medal and shake the hand of the Prince. He was well briefed and asked me if I was coping with retirement and then enquired about the Catterick Centre. Two steps backwards, another bow and turn to the right to walk across the front of the Ballroom and out of the opposite door to which I had entered.

Through the door I met an official who took the medal and placed it in a leather wallet and then I was allowed to join the guests at the back of the Ballroom. After HRH had retired, I joined all the other recipients and met up with the family. We slowly shuffled with the crowd along corridors and down the magnificent staircase and into the courtyard where photographs were being taken. The limo was waiting for us and we were taken to Simpson's on the Strand for lunch. Here we met up with my brother Richard and his wife Jill who had travelled from Horsham to join in the celebration lunch. We had a fine meal with plenty to drink before departing in the limo for our respective stations.

In September 2002 I became chairman of the RSA North East Committee for the next two years. I automatically became a member of the RSA Council along with the other ten chairmen from the other regions. At my first meeting of the Council Penny Egan, the director, gave an introductory talk to all new members and we were issued with a substantial introduction pack that clearly articulated our duties and responsibilities. HRH Prince Philip, Duke of Edinburgh was the president of RSA. The Council chairman was Dr Neil Cross and Sir Paul Judge was the deputy chairman. The RSA AGM was held in October and there were three further meetings of Council planned for the year.

The first regional programme card was issued for 2002–03. It created much interest amongst the other regional chairman when we met at the next Council meeting and in due time, several of them adopted the printed programme.

During my time at Darlington College I had hosted an RSA event each year. Since retirement I had arranged events at various locations. During my two years as chairman I organised three events, two in Darlington and one in Newcastle. The first was a visit to Sherwood's of Darlington managed by my friend and former chairman at the College. The second event was a visit to the A1 Locomotive in Darlington where the Trust was in the process of constructing the first main-line steam locomotive to be built in this country for more than forty years. The event was concluded with a visit to the adjacent Darlington Railway Museum. The third event was a lecture given by Chris Hughes, Chief Executive of the Learning & Skills Development Agency and a former colleague in County Durham.

Whilst the normal programme was progressing, I had established a small group of committee members to assist me to plan the region's celebrations for the 150th anniversary of the Society. The main event was to be a banquet dinner at Durham Castle followed by a lecture. I approached several high profile national figures before deciding to invite the Duchess of Northumberland to talk about the Alnwick Gardens developments. I was delighted that the dinner was well supported by Fellows and friends. The setting in the magnificent thirteenth century Great Hall was very appropriate for the occasion and for a presentation by the Duchess and my vote of thanks.

At a national level the Queen had granted the RSA a Garden Party for up to 7,000 Fellows and friends. A group from the North East Committee travelled down to London and Marshall Meek, a past regional chairman invited the group to be his guests at the Caladonian Club that was quite close to Buckingham Palace. The weather was appalling with constant rain, unlike my three previous Garden parties when the weather had been ideal. The Duke of Edinburgh had been the President of RSA for more than fifty years and the plan was that the the Queen or the Duke would be introduced to all of the regional committees. It had been decided that the North East Committee would meet the Queen and I was instructed that I would be introduced to the Queen by the national chairman Sir Pauil Judge and then I would introduce the members of my committee to Her Majesty. With the rain still pouring down we were assembled in the appointed rows and I was peering through the gloom waiting for Sir Paul to appear after introducing the Scottish members. However, there was no sign of Sir Paul and the Queen appeared looking through her transparent umbella. I hesitated for a moment before moving towards Her Majesty and decided to take the initiative to introduce myself. The Queen took it in her stride and spoke to all the member of the committee before we moved to the tents for refreshments.

The completion of the Task Group's work and the South African project brought an end to my paid consultancies and my only professional involvement was with NILTA. I was still a member of the NILTA Council but I was becoming more interested in the International Group that was chaired by Sue Lovell. We met with representatives of the British Council who were keen for our involvement in CEDEFOP, the European operation that encouraged educational exchanges between individuals from member countries. Sue had organised one event and I was considering putting forward a submission to run an event in 2004. Ann Osler, the only other active member of the Group, had agreed to organise a visit to the AACC Conference in California.

Under Fred McCrindle's chairmanship the Council was being coerced into giving up NILTA's independence and to merge with AoC. Although I had initiated discussions with AoC several years earlier it was apparent that NILTA's role would be less significant than I had hoped. I was therefore far from happy with the direction that was being taken but I found myself heavily outvoted. At that stage, Mary Barker had supported Fred as she had established a new home in the London area and it was obviously more convenient for her to be London-based than having the NILTA office based in Leeds. Many NILTA members shared my view that losing the expertise and experience of the Leeds-based team would not be desirable but AoC was not interested in maintaining the Leeds office and the people working there were not prepared to move to London. However, the legal document, completing arrangements for the AoC/NILTA merger, was signed by both Fred McCrindle and Chris West, and passed to the AoC on the 7 August 2003, bringing to an end fourteen years of independence. In July 2004 the Leeds office closed and business was transferred to AoC in London. A group of founders joined the Leeds team for a farewell lunch in Leeds at the end of July.

I continued to attend the AoC/NILTA Strategic Advisory Committee (SAG) and there were some positive signs of progress despite my reservations. The International Group was most active with an organised visit to the World Skills in Helsinki in May 2005 when Ann Osler and I led a group of senior and middle managers on a one week visit that also included a visit to an IT training centre and meetings with local educationalists. It was a successful visit and I produced a DVD of the UK competitors in action for each of the participants and the NILTA team. In June Mary Barker left AoC NILTA for a similar post in supporting the secondary sector institutions. Rather belatedly she had become disillusioned with the AoC treatment and her demotion within that organisation. Sally Ann Saul was appointed to replace Mary. I had known Sally Ann when she worked for RM and it seemed a good appointment although she had no recent experience of working in FE. Jean McAllister, principal of Shipley College, had become chairman of AoC NILTA after Fred McCrindle lost his job following a merger between Reading College and Thames University. Jean had been a good friend for many years and I had a great respect for her. I had been pushing for a residential weekend to bring key people together for a brainstorming to try to renew visions and identify targets for the future. After various attempts had failed, instead of the residential, we had a special meeting of SAG in December 2006. Not surprisingly, little was achieved.

My last major involvement with NILTA was organising a CEDEFOP visit in October 2006. The planning had started the previous year when I met with a lady from the British Council who was to be my guide for the project. In accordance with the original submission, I assembled a small team comprising Alan Dixon (AoC Regional Director for the NE), John Peacock (Sunderland College) and Alan Race (New College). They gave me splendid support in compiling a one-week programme that was approved by CEDEFOP. In addition to visits to Sunderland and New College, I had planned for visits to Newcastle College and Stockton Riverside College. The Regional Development Agency had to be involved and I eventually managed to make the necessary arrangements for the CEO of One North East to welcome the visitors at the start of their programme. Other visits were planned for Teesside and Sunderland Universities, but trying to find a private training provider proved extremely difficult. Eventually, I was directed to the North East Industry Cluster (NEPIC) based at Wilton and they agreed to host the final visit. Accommodation was an issue and by good fortune I was able to secure sufficient accommodation at Ushaw College on the outskirts of Durham city. CEDEFOP was responsible for recruiting participants to its various programmes and I was given access to part of its website to monitor recruitment. Eventually, there were fourteen participants from twelve countries. As fifteen delegates were the permitted maximum, I felt quite pleased to have attracted so many people.

My initial submission to CEDEFOP was prepared in March 2005 and when I received approval in September, the details had to be amended to meet its observations. That gave me a year to organise all of the details, as AoC/NILTA was not able to offer any secretarial support. Even so, I thought that I could accomplish the task comfortably but in practice it took considerably more time than I had anticipated and it was mid-June before I secured an agreement with NEPIC to participate. I also had difficulty getting involvement from the Learning and Skills Council but eventually one of its regional officers agreed to give a short talk to the group on the last morning of the course. My old friend Gareth Davies had moved on from his post at Northern College Network to take charge of the Regional Support Centre Northern (RSC). Following the integration of further education as a full-funding partner of the Joint Information Systems Committee (JISC), thirteen JISC RSCs were established across the UK in 2000. Gareth was the manager for RSC North East that provided support to colleges of further education and a designated number of higher education institutions. Gareth had also agreed to talk to the group at Ushaw College. The last link in the chain was Ufi learndirect and I expected that to be straight forward. However, the regional manager was moving to a new post and her successor had not been appointed. I requested a contact in the private sector that was a learndirect centre but she did not feel that there was such a centre that was of the right standard to impress the vistors. Therefore, I made contact with Sarah at Darlington College and she agreed to host a short visit to the learning centre that was located in the main entrance of the new college. As the visits covered most of the region, it was necessary to provide suitable transport for the party and I decided to hire Lee's Coaches Ltd from Langley Moor. The proprietor of the company was Mr Lee who was very accommodating and the driver who was allocated for most days was excellent.

CEDEFOP preferred a programme that assembled on a Sunday and ended on a Thursday. Travelling to County Durham by public transport on a Sunday was not going to be easy for people travelling as far as from Portugal in the west to Bulgaria in the east. I had sent out detailed instruction by email for the participants travelling by air and rail. Some had found it impossible to travel the full journey on one day and had broken their journey for a short stay in London or Scotland. I arrived at Ushaw College in the early afternoon to ensure that I would meet all of the participants as they arrived and to assist the duty staff with the administration. The bedrooms were rather simply furnished but adequate for our purposes and the rooms for lectures and recreational activities were quite pleasant. The programme assumed that all of the participants would arrive in time for the evening meal and I had planned to give a formal welcome and introduction to the programme. All but two of the party arrived on time, the last two arriving just before midnight. English was the language for the visit and all participants were expected to have a good command of the language. Three of the party had modest skills and this proved a challenge for them, as the presenters did not always observe my advice to speak slowly and clearly. I gave a short introduction to the programme and it was agreed that the delegates would begin their presentations and as many as possible would be completed before the meal at 1945. The presentations were well received and short discussions followed each presentation. The average time for each presentation plus questions was twelve minutes so that twelve were completed during the evening, leaving two for the morning.

On the Monday morning, the two late arrivals were welcomed and gave their presentations. Alan Dixon joined the group and gave an overview of vocational education and training in the UK and I followed with a short presentation on the English further education sector. The minibus departed at 1030 and travelled to the offices of One North East in Newcastle. We received a warm welcome from Gillian Collinson and Pat Richie, Director of Strategy and Development. Dorothy Smith, Regional Director, Learning Planning & Performance, LSC gave a presentation on vocational education and training in the region and then we were joined by Chief Executive Alan Clarke who added his greetings. Pat Richie then gave a presentation on the socio-economics of the region and referred to the revised Regional Economic Strategy, which had just been launched. The RDA provided lunch and there was an opportunity to discuss issues with the RDA officers.

The minibus then travelled the short distance to Newcastle College, the largest FE institution in the region with 45,000 students. We were met by Sandra Peacock, the FE curriculum & ILT manager, who took us to the recently opened Lifestyle Academy for a presentation covering an overview of e-learning at the college. The group was divided into two and taken to see several classes of students. We left that building and walked to the Centre for Trade Union Studies that ran programmes for trade union officers and members. Unfortunately, there were no students in the Centre during our visit so that the group only met staff and were given examples of learning materials. The Centre used learndirect materials as well as material produced in the college. We returned to the Lifestyle Academy and observed a sports therapy lesson using an electronic white board and a lesson involving the VLE (virtual learning environment) blackboard, which was used throughout the college. At the end of the visit, there was an opportunity to discuss issues raised with Sandra and her colleagues whilst enjoying some refreshments. On leaving the College, the minibus took the group to the Sage Music Centre in Gateshead where we were able to admire the architecture and the facilities. The group then walked the short distance to the adjacent Baltic Centre for Contemporary Arts to view the building and its exhibitions. The minibus took the group back to the Ushaw Conference Centre for a review of the day. A leader was appointed by the group to guide discussions and identify issues to be included in the visit report. A useful discussion followed and numerous issues were identified. On conclusion of the discussion, all but one of the group members accompanied me on the minibus into Durham City to a local restaurant for dinner.

Tuesday was a full day of visits commencing with New College, Durham. However, very thick fog caused traffic delays in the Durham area so that the minibus arrived thirty minutes late at Ushaw and eventually arrived at New College forty minutes late. Inevitably, this had a major impact on the prepared programme of two hours that was reduced to ninety minutes, and some of the activities were either curtailed or eliminated. Principal John Widdowson and Alan Race welcomed the participants and we were split into two groups for a tour of the relevant parts of the campus. The college had enjoyed a very good enrolment and this was apparent from the numbers of students in many of the areas visited. Alan explained that the campus had been completely rebuilt and had only recently become fully operational. He outlined the Cisco installed infrastructure that supported the latest learning technologies. E-portfolios and podcasting had to be covered quickly before leaving the college for the next stop at the Shiny Row campus of City of Sunderland College. The knock-on effect of the earlier delays also meant a late arrival by about twenty minutes at the Shiney Row campus of the College. John Peacock welcomed the participants and Merv Stapleton outlined the e-learning strategy of the College. A copy of the strategy was included in the pack of materials presented to the group. We were split into two groups for a tour of selected areas. Again, the delayed arrival upset the planned programme as students were on their lunch break and therefore not available for questioning in the classroom. However, staff members were available in most areas and were willing to respond to questions and share their ideas. The debate continued over lunch where several college staff joined the participants.

The final visit of the day was to the University of Sunderland and we departed from Shiney Row almost on time. The weather had improved significantly and the minibus driver made a short stop at Penshaw Monument, a local place of interest. Owing to a misunderstanding, half of the group started to take the long walk to the top of the hill on which the monument was located and only urgent shouts caused them to return. This unintended diversion meant a slight delay in arriving at the university where we were greeted by Professor Peter Smith and four of his colleagues. We then had four presentations on strategy and e-learning practice but, despite the fact that I had agreed with Peter to include students, none were present and so a major opportunity to get a user view was lost. We headed back to Durham where there was sufficient time to pay a visit to Durham Cathedral and some stayed to listed to Evensong. The delegates made their own arrangement for an evening meal and I dashed home for a meal with Veronica.

Wednesday was also busy with four planned visits. The minibus took the group to Darlington College which had opened its new campus five weeks earlier. Linda Norman welcomed the participants and introduced the regional manager of learndirect, Liz Kitson. She gave a brief overview of activities in the region and then we had an opportunity to talk to staff and two mature students who were in the centre at that time. Principal Sarah Robinson joined us briefly to add her welcome.

The next stop was to Stockton Riverside College where we were greeted by Principal Sujinder Sangha and Paul Wren. Surinder outlined the college strategy before Paul conducted an online demonstration of 'Elluminate' linking with a colleague at another college site. Two further presentations were given, one on the Retail Academy and one on the E4 Net Project. All three initiatives were found to be of interest to the participants. We did not see any learners as all three projects were serving off-site customers. The college entertained the group to lunch before the minibus travelled to the University of Teesside for the next visit. I had planned this visit with Professor Philip Barker, a highly respected e-learning champion in the HE sector. Unfortunately for the group, Philip had been invited to speak at a conference in Hawaii at the same time as our visit, so he had made arrangements for three of his colleagues to meet us. We received three presentations on e-learning at the university but again did not meet any students that had been requested at the planning visit.

The last visit involved travelling eastwards to the Wilton Centre, formally ICI but now split into several different companies. We were hosted by NEPIC (North East Process Industry Cluster) where we were greeted by Chief Executive Stan Higgins, who gave a strategic overview of training within the partnership of companies. Mike Deeming, who had been the main driver for the e-learning initiative outlined the progress to date and this was followed by a presentation by Huntsman Polyurethanes, the company that was piloting the project on behalf of NEPIC. One of the trainers then gave a short talk on his involvement and the progress of the middle-aged staff that had been following the course. It was explained that for safety reasons we could not go into the Huntsman site where the training took place. The presentations took much longer than planned and we left the site thirty-five minutes late. The minibus returned to Ushaw College and we had little time to prepare ourselves for the reception and Conference Dinner. Seven guests, who had supported the visit, and Andrea Duenschhede of the British Council, joined the participants for a pleasant evening.

Thursday morning was an opportunity to fill a couple of gaps and to provide some expertise to cover any issues that the participants would wish to receive. John Widdowson and Dorothy Smith willingly gave up thirty minutes each of their time to respond to college and LSC issues respectively. Sally Coady from learndirect's head office and a former regional manager gave a presentation on the current developments and ambitions of the service. Gareth Davies gave a lively overview of the role and responsibilities of the Regional Support Centre. This left the remainder of the morning and the afternoon for the participants to work on their joint report to CEDEFOP.

The planning was at times challenging but the North East humour and willingness to participate made it very enjoyable. The actual visit made all the planning worthwhile and I am sure that most of the participants would have gained professionally and personally from the experience.

My involvement with AoC/NILTA had steadily declined and I offered to stand down completely but Jean was keen to have my support during her chairmanship. I did attend the annual conferences but mainly to be present at the awarding of the Peter Shuker Award. For example, in 2007 my old friend and fellow founder, John Gray, received the award and the following item appeared in the educational press:

> On behalf of AQA, Andrew Bird, AQA's Deputy Director General, recently presented the prestigious Peter Shuker Award at the annual conference of the National Information and Learning Technologies Association (NILTA). AoC NILTA is one of the longest established e-learning organisations in the UK and the Peter Shuker Award, named after distinguished educationalist and NILTA founder Peter Shuker, recognises outstanding contribution and commitment to development and delivery within the post-16 sector.

Reflections

I have very few regrets about my many years in further education. It has provided me with a mainly enjoyable working environment and I have had the good fortune to work with many excellent colleagues at all levels in the five establishments in which I have been employed. My 'dream' or long-term ambition to see the student at the centre of the learning process with the opportunities to learn at their own pace in their own time was just beginning to emerge when I retired in 2001. Sadly, it would appear that English FE has not taken the full advantages offered by the new and emerging technologies to move collectively to a student-centred model of learning. Since retirement I have witnessed other countries taking that initiative and I fear that unless there is a radical change in attitude, English FE will be seen as dated and second rate within the developed countries.

I have tried to analyse the reasons for the failure to progress during the last ten years or so. I believe that incorporation in 1993 provided a major step forward in releasing colleges from local authority control that in many cases had stifled innovation. Most colleges responded enthusiastically to the challenges and opportunities of incorporation and with good support from the FEFC progress was made on many fronts to allow colleges to collaborate in exploring new methods of delivery, and innovations were made in numerous colleges. Funding was made available to raise the quality of educational buildings so that they were more flexible to respond to the learning needs of future generations of students. Also, colleges were able to purchase large quantities of computing equipment to increase the opportunities for students to learn more flexibly and to take full advantage of the vast store of knowledge that became available through the Internet.

However, there was a downside to incorporation at both national and local level. Nationally, a central bureaucracy replaced the influence of individual colleges in representing the strengths of the FE sector. ACFHE and APC, which were traditionally managed by serving principals and colleges, were initially replaced with the CEF and AoC that later merged to become the AoC. Whilst principals and chairs of corporation boards served on AoC committees, officers of the AoC became the main route to advising and influencing MPs and central government. At the college level Corporation Board members tended to lack the experience of senior local authority officers, particularly in the appointment of senior staff and many boards took the safe option of appointing internal candidates instead of bringing in 'new blood'.

The government's decision to replace FEFC and the TECs with the Learning and Skills Council failed to take forward the sector and the Ofsted inspection system was little improvement on its predecessor. The top down approach adopted by central government has been a mixed blessing with every change in legislation leading to major issues for the colleges. These problems often stem from the fact that there is very little personal experience of further education amongst politicians and civil servants, David Blunkett being a special exception. Education ministers do not tend to stay in post for very long and I have witnessed education ministers who have tried to introduce innovations to enhance their own careers rather than improve the service to students. Another development that has occurred since 1993 is the merging of colleges and in some cases leading to very large institutions spread over several towns. In my view this is only viable if the objective is to provide a coherent educational experience for students with learning available on demand rather than in traditional settings. In some of these extremely large institutions Corporation Board members and chief executives have become too remote from the primary object of learning and management becomes the overriding issue with the staff and students becoming pawns in a big chess game. It is an exciting time, but sometimes we appear to be so buried in the trees that we cannot see the size and shape of the wood. Owing to the emphasis on efficiency and good management, there is a danger of developing a generation of principals and Corporation Board members who have to be more interested in applied accountancy than they are in education.

Another worrying aspect is the trend to believe that all good ideas are developed locally and that there is no need to visit other countries to observe how post-school education is developing. My interest in international further education started with visits to Germany and France organised by the Department of Education and Science and by the HMI. Since then, my many visits to North America, Europe and Australia have all resulted in expanding my vision of how education should be evolving for the benefit of the learner rather than the institution. I believe there is an urgent need for today's education leaders to broaden their experiences by examining practices in other countries.

My views were reinforced by comments made by a very distinguished former permanent secretary to the Department of Education and Employment in a newspaper article regarding further education:

> ... the framework for local agencies makes it difficult for them to work effectively. It is more about process than outcomes, with ring fenced funding and cash channelled down silos and narrow targets.

This makes no sense to the learners, who desperately need services that coalesce around their needs. The system doesn't encourage agencies to collaborate in helping the most disadvantaged.

Costly auditing procedures, targets and inspections discourage institutions from sharing resources and responsibilities. Instead, it makes them introspective because they constantly have to think about the outcomes for their own institution. Also, inspection regimes judge institutional performance on paper results without necessarily looking at its impact on the wider outcomes led by other organisations.

The way the government works makes people cautious and uninventive. The whole system makes leaders risk-averse because they have to concentrate on making sure their institution comes out as well as possible.

If we are going to have organisations sharing resources to the benefit of their learners, there needs to be more space for the education professionals to use their initiative.

I would not wish to conclude my narrative on a negative note as I have continued to see young people who are enjoying their experiences in FE colleges. There has been recent funding available to allow corporation boards to either replace old buildings with completely new premises or to make substantial improvements to existing buildings. Most of these buildings now provide excellent learning environments and students appear to be taking full advantage of the facilities.

Having enjoyed a very fulfilling and mainly enjoyable working life it was not easy to detach myself from the environment that had engulfed me for fifty years. Since joining Durham County Cricket Club in 2003, it has provided good entertainment and new friendships during the summer season. There was also more time to devote to Veronica and the family and to adopt a more sedate lifestyle.

Index

Aberystwyth 59, 60
Acklam Park 28
Adult and Community Learning Fund
  (ACLF) 342
Adult Literacy and Basic Skills Unit
  (ALBSU) 166
Allatt, Peter 370, 400
Alloway, Bernard 43, 55
Almond, Brigadier John 222
American Association of Community
  Colleges (AACC) 270
Anderson shelter 1
Anderson, David 101, 245, 396
Anne, Princess Royal 235, 242, 368
Armstrong, Hilary 181, 185
Armstrong, Margaret 159, 325, 384
Armstrong, Richard (Dick) 160
Army Emergency Reserve 22, 52
Army School of Civil Defence 17
Association for Colleges (AfC) 219, 271,
  294
Association of Colleges (AoC) 219, 305,
  374
Association of Colleges of Further and
  Higher Education 169
Association of Principals of Colleges (APC)
  125
Atlanta, USA 292, 293, 295
Auckland Harbour Bridge 22, 298
Aviss, Llew 177
Ayresome Street Junior School 6

Baker, Les 190–377
Barker, Mary 257–411
Barnes, Philip 44, 48, 62, 72,
Barr, Frank 25, 41, 42, 51, 61, 113
Basic Skills Agency (BSA) 286–389
Basis for Choice 116
Beating Retreat 198–395
Beeton, Jeremy 237

Bell, Margaret 192, 220, 327, 262, 295,
  297, 346
Bell, Peter 391
Bell, Sid 77, 78
Bell, Stan 193, 236
Bernstein, Ruth 246
Best, Graham 170–289, 372
BETT Exhibition 188, 246, 288, 304, 346
Bewell, Peter 128
Beynon, Cyril 53
Bhopal TTTI 82
Bielefeld 48, 49
Billyard, Ian 185
Binks, Graham 101, 130
Blackdown Barracks 48
Blackshaw, John 51
Blair, Tony 170, 312, 324, 354
Blenheim Palace 5, 6
Blunkett, David 349, 420
Blythin, Arthur 22, 33
Boffey, Brian 130
Boland, Jim 77
Bowles, Mary 167, 244
Boynton, Doug 145–159, 374, 402
Bradford University 61, 67, 72
Brain, Clive 169, 216
Bramley Grange 102–142
Bridge, John 267, 305
Britannia Works 9
British Association of Construction Heads
  (BACH) 250
British Council 82–93, 133, 231, 321–417
British Educational Communications and
  Technology Agency (BECTA) 346
Brittan, Lady Diana 180
Brittan, Lord Leon
Brno Technical University 189, 196, 228,
  318
Brooks, Austin 167, 181, 224
Broomhead, Steve 247, 312, 331

422

Brown, Carol 186, 237, 262, 272
Brown, Jack 55
Brown, Ken 81
Brown, Sheila 151, 214
Browning, Colin 82
Bucharest Technical University 228, 234, 238
Bullough, Robin 65, 136, 205, 396
Bunting, Arthur 41
Burnham Further Education Report 76
Burnill, John 102
Bush, Derek 41, 63, 74
Bushnell, John 320–396
Business Education Council (BEC) 93
Business and Technician Education Council (BTEC) 134
Business Link 198, 375
Byfield, Keith 139, 147, 172
Byrne, Angus 169–376

Campbell, Sue 231
Capey, Dr John 212
Carnell, Bob 184, 236
Carroll, Denis 22
Cassidy, Simon 218–376
Catterick Garrison 149–363
CEDEFOP 411–418
Certificate in Pre-Vocational Education 116
Chadbourne, Paula 134
Chambers, George 56, 75
Charles Trevelyan College 34, 35
Charter Mark 259, 288, 347, 388
Chell, Harry 101, 121
Circular 7/70 149
City and Guilds of London Institute xviii
Clark, Howard 325
Clarke, Mike 325
Cleveland Technical College 52, 73, 75, 79, 93, 111, 325
Clifford, Alan 325, 383, 384
Clinton, President Bill 271
Coleman, Margaret 340
Colleges Employers Forum (CEF) 219, 230
Competitiveness Fund 267–341
Computer Aided Administration 63, 111, 126
Computer Aided Learning 63
Computer Based Learning in FE 118

Constantine College 9, 21
Construction Industry Training Board 81, 111
Construction Technicians Certificate 65, 70
Cook, Anita 177
Coombs, Brian 52, 74
Cooper, Jack 100
Corns, Walter 26, 28, 42
Coultas, Alan 224
Coulthard, Oliver 193, 214, 248
Council for National Academic Awards 39
Cox, Mike 251, 332, 359, 377
Cracknell, David 102
Craddock, Peter 206, 265
Crecsi, Louis 147
Crispen, Geoff 248, 331, 347
Croll, Don 124, 140
Crosby, John 38–55, 74
Crowe, Fred 184, 217
Crowther Report 10, 151
Curtis, Roger 349

Daniels, John 107, 124
Darlington and Stockton Times 180
Darlington Business Forum 220
Darlington Business Venture 187, 198, 205, 220, 223, 241, 274
Darlington College at Catterick 177, 307, 339, 352, 376
Darlington College of Technology 53, 138–362
Darlington Construction Centre 236
Darlington Employers Forum 246, 298, 368
Darlington Learning Network 354
Darlington Learning Town 307
Darlington Lecture Association 155, 180, 205, 226
Darlington Partnership 317–397
Darlington Rotary Club 181, 204, 213, 224, 313
Daubney, Mike 161, 165, 195
Davies, Gareth 208, 331, 413, 418
Davies, John (Huddersfield) 41–43, 55, 74
Davies, John (Darlington) 145, 159, 191, 209, 231, 251, 306
Davies, Lord Bryan 381
Deavin, Stanley 97, 103, 114
Decciaco, Ken 140

Deepcut 13, 15, 22, 33, 67, 70, 95, 109, 113, 115
Dent, Adrian 140, 193, 231, 300, 377
Dent, Colonel Mike 264
Department of Education and Science (DES) 65, 102, 119, 122, 149, 420
Dixon, Alan 146–414
Dixon, Bob 41
Dobie, Gaynor 175, 232, 321, 399
Dodd, Alan 214, 269, 273, 382
Doghouse Cricket Club 34
Donnely, Alan 305
Dorman Cup 9
Dorman Long 9, 10, 12, 22, 197, 298
Downing, David 64
Dr Barnardo's 1, 2, 5
Drew, Chris 267, 290, 305, 339, 401
Duckett, Keith 236, 320, 351, 381
Duke of Edinburgh 109, 205, 409, 410
Duke of Edinburgh Award 109
Dunaujvaros Polytechnic 194, 208
Durrans, Ken 106, 134, 140
Duthie, Ian 55

e-learning 402–418
Eade, David 131, 141
ECCTIS 2000 188
Edexcel 313
Edgerton hostels 42
Education Act 1944 xviii
Education Act 1988 172
Education Assets Board 223
Education Support Grant (ESG) 169
Eindhoven University 227, 228
Eppleton 33, 38
Esteve-Coll, Dame Elizabeth 205
European Social Fund (ESF) 221
Evans, Fred 176
Evans, Harold 152, 344
Evans, Keith 106
Evans, Ron 27, 51
Evening Gazette 11, 34, 78
Exelby, (Dick) Richard 146, 151, 167

Fallon, Michael 192, 193, 202
Farley (Robinson), Sarah 291–387
Fartown 28, 47
FEFC Statistics Group 238, 242, 297

FEMIS 134, 254, 376
FE Plus 377, 395
Fifth Framework 345–353
Fisher' Education Act of 1918 xvii
Flinn, John 42
Flowers, Ron 151
Foresight Programme 365
Forth Road Bridge 22
Foster, Derek 202
Fothergill, Richard 19
Fox, Roger 65
Frame, Kevin 259, 377, 390
France, David 187, 220
Franchising 222–319
Franklin, Peter 64
Fraser, Derek 234, 309, 327, 380
Friends Provident 12
Fryer, Bob 342, 343, 369, 383, 404
Full Technological Certificate 25, 65
Further and Higher Education Act 1992 172, 185, 209, 212, 366
Further Education Corporations 211
Further Education Development Agency (FEDA) 299–392
Further Education Funding Council (FEFC) 209–419
Further Education Information and Learning Technology (FEILT) 350
Further Educational National Training Organisation (FENTO) 350
Further Education Unit 104, 117, 131, 340

Gale, Pat 176, 232–385
Gale, Wesley 73, 77
Gannon, Brian 106
Gaskell, Colonel Nick 348
Gatfield, Denis 214–374
Gee, Ruth 192–402
Gent, Bernard 34
George, Max 102, 116
Gibbens, Barney 173, 196
Gill, Walter 12
Goldsmith, George 55
Gordon, Lewis 149–180
Gosling, Kate 52, 74
Gossage, Mick 307
Grant, Brian 51

Grant, Olivia 387
Grasby, Roger 269, 347
Gray, John 164–418
Green, William Herbert (Bill) 25, 42, 44, 51, 61
Greenwood, Norman 73, 75, 77, 83, 93
Greenwood, John 75, 78
Grimshaw, Keith 144, 157
Groom, Gary 290–396
Grundy, Paul 44–62, 383
Gupta, Rabi Das 89

Hague, William 354, 359, 360
Haiden, Ernie 132, 207–229, 301–396
Hall, David 238, 315
Hall, Jack 26–55, 120–250
Hamilton, Jack 33
Harbourne, David 348
Harker, Tom 162, 231, 232
Harman, Harriet 329
Harris, Angela 199, 231, 232, 266
Harris, Rod 241, 259, 319
Haselgrave Committee Report 93
Hassell, David 242
Haulpt, David 312, 346, 382
Heaton, David 244, 248, 347
Heaton, Jim 102
Henderson, Bill 22, 31
Henderson, David 167
Henderson, Graham 330
Her Majesty's Inspectors (HMI) 48–420
Hetherington, Alan 147, 330, 331
Higginson Report 290, 299, 347
Higher National Certificate 9, 22, 25, 35, 203
Hillier, John 380
Himsworth, Malcolm 132, 163, 164, 172, 185, 208, 228, 233, 245, 254, 256, 257, 283, 292, 301, 396
Hogg, John 325, 384
Holiday Fellowship 6, 20–70, 116
Hollis, George 225, 314
Holly Bank 24–74, 101–115, 397, 398
Holmes, Guy 287, 324
Hopkins, Gordon 241
Horne, Chris 143, 147, 156, 161
Howe, Lynn 237, 325, 356

Huddersfield College of Education (Technical) 37, 41, 81, 86
Huddersfield College of Technology 45
Huddersfield Cricket Club 28
Huddersfield Polytechnic 45, 74, 114
Huddersfield Technical Teacher Training College 22
Hugh Bell School 7, 8, 10
Hughes, Chris 147, 179, 303, 377, 409
Hughes, Stephen 170, 251, 320
Hume, George 100, 130, 131
Hutchinson, Les 41

Industry Training Organisations (ITOs) 203
Innes, Jack 29, 31, 32, 38
Institute of Building 55, 114
Investor in People 316, 388
Ingleson, Stuart 325

Jacques, Les 101, 121, 123
JANET 263–355
Jarvis, Colonel Chris 190
Jenkins, Bishop David 264
Johnson, Hugh 100, 130
Johnson, Stuart 97, 102, 110, 120, 131
Johnson Hill Ben, 328
Jones, Malcolm 371
Jordan, Jim 41, 44, 55
Joseph, Sir Keith 129

Keel, Barry 309, 336
Kelly, David 214, 375
Kennedy, Dame Helena 319, 320
Kitchen, Trevor 77
Kosice Technical University 255
Kostroma Technical University 319, 321

Langstone, Harry 173
Lawson, Fred 231
Lea, Ray 388
Learning and Skills Act 2000 369
Learning and Skills Council (LSC) 369, 380, 390, 414, 417
Learning Works – Widening Participation in Further Education 319
Leeds College of Building 48, 96, 99, 118,

119, 127, 128, 132, 137, 142, 143, 144, 161, 174, 233, 250, 291
Leigh, Debbie 204, 214, 218, 226, 232, 266, 307
Les, Carl 214, 330
Libby, Don 173, 195
Lister, Eleanor 331
Local Taxation (Customs and Excise) xvii
Longlands College 52, 94, 325, 330, 384
Lord Crathorne 359, 376
Lorraine, Peter 28, 47, 57, 68
Lowcock, Bert 144, 146, 162
Lyddon, Brigadier Peter
Lynch, Owen 192, 298, 346
Lyonette, David 187

MacConachie, Alasdair 163–213, 323–340
MacLennan, Alex 64
McAllister, Jean 412
McCrindle, Fred 325–366, 411, 412
Major, John 288
Managed Information Protocol Presentational Service (MIPPS) 285, 286
Manders, Colonel Bob 39, 106, 190
Manpower Services Commission 96–184
Mansell, Jack 104–131
Martin, Slovakia 199–315
Mason, Neil 388
Maxwell, Estelle 274
McAllister, Mike 41–89, 182, 374
McKiterick-Smith, Peter 392
Meadows, Dorothy 247
Meek, Marshall 400, 410
Melling, Geoffrey 104
Melville, David 300–389
Merry, Gordon 145, 162, 182
Middlesbrough CC 9
Middlesbrough Midweek League 11
Midgley, Hilary 154
Milburn, Alan 181–202, 300–354
Mills, David 31
Mitchell, Keith 157, 195
Modern Apprenticeship Scheme 184
Mons Barracks 15
Morgan, Selwyn 145, 147, 159, 162, 163
Morris, Charles 13
Morris, Estelle 404, 405, 406
Morrison shelter 2

Muckle, Diane 160, 196, 390
National Association for Information and Learning Technologies in FE (NAITFE) 173–254
National Association of Teachers in Further and Higher Education (NATFHE) 79, 226–304
National Council for Education Technology (NCET) 192
National Council for the Training of Journalist (NCJT) 167
National Grid for Learning (NGfL) 326, 354, 355, 362
National Information and Learning Technologies Association (NILTA) 173, 254, 418
National Learning Network (NLN) 350
National Service 12–22, 177
National Vocational Qualifications xviii, 142
New Brunswick, Canada 280, 281, 292
New College, Durham 64, 79, 139–415
New Technical and Vocational Initiative 119
New Training Initiative 119
Newcastle College 29, 31, 79, 148, 162, 208, 329, 389, 412, 414
Nichol, Geoff 181–218, 264–374
Northern Colleges Network (NCN) 284, 292, 299, 310, 340
Northern Consortium for Child Care and Education 247
Northern Council for Further Education (NCFE) 79, 148, 155, 187
Northern Echo 152, 187, 197, 206, 214, 225, 231, 291, 344, 381
Northern Informatics Applications Agency (NiAA) 267–401
Northern Intermediate League 36, 42, 47, 53, 57

O'Brien, Bob 130, 137, 138
Old, Alan 325
O'Neil, John 244
Ordinary National Certificate 10
Ottilini, Carl 167
Owen, Clive 170, 198, 224, 277, 323

Parker, Norman 29, 32, 37, 38
Parker, Sue 301, 333
Peacock, John 412, 416
Pearson, Brigadier Peter 349
Pearson, Peter 145, 159, 191, 209, 251
Pennington, Geoff 300, 309, 326, 383
Philips, Norman 65
PICKUP (Professional, Industrial and
    Commercial Updating) 144, 145, 231
Place, Jack 48, 96, 99, 105, 119, 127, 134,
    135, 233, 245, 396
Portugal 242, 315, 413
Powell, Dylis 23, 30, 60
Poznan University of Technology 373
Pratt, Jim 42–67, 96, 106, 168, 396
Price, Malcolm 270, 353, 395
Priestley, Tom 101, 121
Prince's Trust 277, 288, 345, 349, 380
Prince Andrew, HRH The Duke of Kent
    323
Prince Charles, HRH The Prince of Wales
    359, 376, 408
Princess Anne, HRH The Princess Royal
    325, 242, 368
Private Finance Initiative (PFI) 268–328

Race, Alan 412, 415
Ramsey, Charles 280
Ransford, John 303, 396
Rawlinson, Sue 231
Read, Malcolm 313
Referees Association 11, 21
Regional Development Agency, ONE
    North East 322–414
Regional Information Society Initiative
    (RISI) 310, 354
Research Machines (RM) 111, 177, 237,
    312
Review of UK Occupational Standards 380
Richardson, Reg 75
Richie, Jane 236
Ridley, Peter 180
Ripley Castle 2
Robbins Report 31, 39
Robb-Webb, John 100, 130
Roberts, David 121, 124, 126, 142, 233
Roberts, Brigadier Martin 190
Robinson, Laurie 52, 62, 97, 108

Robinson, Stella 151
Robson, Don 185, 208
Rockett, John 253
Rooker, Margaret 26–61
Rose, Reg 124
ROSLA (Raising of the School Leaving
    Age) 78, 79
Rosser, John 231, 298
Rowarth, Mike 162
Rowley, Peter 196, 262, 323
Royal Army Ordnance Corps 13
Royal Garden Party 135, 182, 336
Royal Society of Arts (RSA) xviii, 163–410

Sarkissian, Agop 215, 225
Saunders, Peter 41, 42
Scar Fell Pike 20
Sewell, Derek 140, 175
Shephard, Gillian 288
Shipley College 26, 151, 412
Siddons, Mary 101, 124, 134
Simpson, Myra 44, 70
Single Regeneration Budget (SRB) 252,
    253
Skinner, Jim 151, 181
Smith, Dame Dela 166, 214, 225, 398
Smith, Jon 202, 238, 311
Smith, Kingsley 157
South Africa 388–410
South West Durham Training 152
Sparrow, Geoff 48
Spence, Fr Bob 166, 181, 396
Squires, Bill 55, 127
Staff College at Coombe Lodge 77, 157
Stainsby Old Boys 21, 28, 80, 197
Stanford, Brian 271
Stanford-Bewley, Philip 26
Stanway, David 123
Stephenson, Mavis and Guy 80
Stevenson, Frank 35
Stevenson, Ian 187
Stockwell, Malcolm 196
Stones, Joe 100, 130
Stubbs, Sir William (Bill) 207, 212, 248,
    300, 382
Students Union 26, 42–71
SuperJANET 283
Sutcliffe, Isabelle 205

Sutcliffe, Tony 325, 384
Svistov Economic University 301

Tabinor, Harry 269
Taj Mahal 90, 91, 92
Tate, Joanna 331
Taubman, Dan 304
Taylor, Arthur 75
Taylor, Barbara 26
Taylor, John 63, 404
Taymouth Castle 18
Teaching and Learning Technology
    Programme (TLTP) 310
Technician Education Council (TEC) 93,
    111, 134
Technical Instruction Act of 1889 xvii
Teesside Partnership 233, 324, 356
TETOC 82, 259
Thatcher, Margaret 203
The Crowther Report 10, 151
The Maastricht Treaty 170
Tickner, Peter 231
Times Educational Supplement 37, 274,
    304, 327, 352
Tipple, Chris 105–131, 370
Topping, Fred 25, 42, 51
Townsend, Dr Christina 288
Training and Enterprise Council 184, 285,
    341
Trojan Project 340, 341
Tull, John 104, 112
Tunstall Preparatory School 2
Turner, Laurie 147, 172, 191, 217, 237,
    293
Tuxworth, Eric 67, 96, 396
Twitty, Bob 146, 159, 179

Unified Vocational Preparation (UVP) 104,
    126
UNISON 275
University for Industry (Ufi) 332–367
University of Teesside Partnership (UTP)
    324, 356

Vallance, Joe 29, 31

Wadsworth, David 102
Wainwright, Howard 48, 105
Walker, Roy 114, 118, 132, 133
Wallace, Alison 317
Walsh, Norman 55
Walworth Castle Hotel 155, 165, 191, 206,
    248, 340, 381, 394, 402
War Office Selection Board (WOSB) 15
Ward, Roger 219, 236, 263, 264, 305
Watson, Chris 180, 193, 216, 232, 255,
    264, 266, 288, 290
Webster, Janice 345
Wellbourne, Cynthia 302
Wells, Alan 166, 178, 207, 279–396
West, Chris 137, 170–188, 208, 411
Whisky Money xvii
White, Andy 75, 82
White, Sue 192, 214
Widdowson, John 311, 316, 344, 415, 417
Williams, John 202, 214, 324, 331, 354
Wills, Derek 390, 396
Wilmore, Peter 105
Wilshaw, David 325
Wilson, Harold 36, 72
Wilson, Tom 244, 312
Wood, Michael 162, 232, 290, 307
Work related non-advance further
    education (WRNAFE) 140
Wright, Anne 208, 332, 333

York College of Arts and Technology 27,
    138
Yorkshire and Humberside Council for
    Further Education 79
Young IT Technician of the Year (YITTY)
    257, 296
Young, Lord David 165
Youth Training Scheme 119,128, 166, 183,
    184